H50 016 203 9

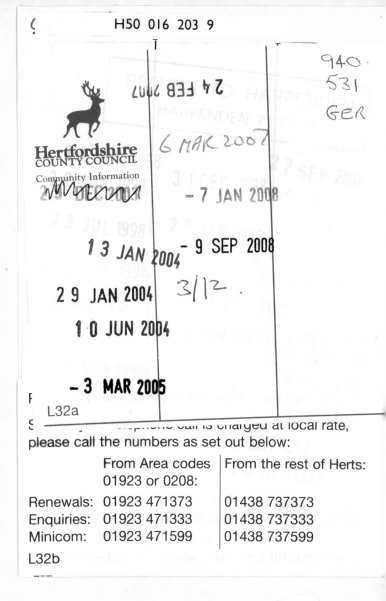

940·
531
GER

Hertfordshire
COUNTY COUNCIL
Community Information

L32a

S...............................phone call is charged at local rate,
please call the numbers as set out below:

	From Area codes 01923 or 0208:	From the rest of Herts:
Renewals:	01923 471373	01438 737373
Enquiries:	01923 471333	01438 737333
Minicom:	01923 471599	01438 737599

L32b

D1471000

MB

Helga
The Continuing Story

By popular demand Helga continues her story. It gives a condensed version of her first book with added happenings and describes her life under Hitler, her flight from the Russians and how cruelly the population who were left behind in Königsberg were treated by the Red Army.

The family returned to their homeland, Switzerland, with great hopes which were soon shattered. Neutral Switzerland had not much compassion for the poor returning emigrants. Helga had to forget her medical studies, there was no money. She took a course in commerce, worked as secretary in an hotel, met her future husband under very romantic circumstances, and left Switzerland.

More struggles followed when she discovered that the eldest of her two sons was handicapped. This was a new challenge. Alone, without parents or friends and coping with a new language, she succeeded in finding qualified people to advise and help her with her son. She persevered against all odds, ensured him a good education and helped him through the several stages of treatment. Encouraged by a caring husband, Helga studied again at the age of forty and became a teacher, although dogged by serious back trouble, which was eventually corrected by an operation.

Helga Gerhardi

Helga

The Continuing Story

After escaping from the advancing Russian Army, experiencing extreme hardship and danger, Helga, a Swiss emigrant, found her new life a further test of her incredible will and courage.

VIRONA
PUBLISHING

First published 1995 by Virona Publishing
24 Putnams Drive, Aston Clinton, AYLESBURY, Bucks. HP22 5HH

The right of Helga Gerhardi to be identified as author
of this work has been asserted by her in accordance with
the Copyright, Designs and Patents Act 1988

British Library Cataloguing-in-Publication Data.
A catalogue record for this book is
available from the British Library

ISBN 0 9521933 1 0

Typeset by Virona Publishing, Aston Clinton
Printed by Staples Printers Rochester Limited

Author's Note

This book has been written by popular demand and is divided into three sections.

Part One gives a short synopsis of my first book HELGA, where I described my life under Hitler and being a refugee from the Russians, including a few happenings in my life, not mentioned before. Although east and west Germany are now united, Königsberg (now Kaliningrad), the surrounding area and the access to the Baltic has remained Russian.

Part Two is the story of my family's return to our homeland, Switzerland, and the difficulties we had to start a new beginning.

Part Three shows how eventually I settled down in England, got married and had two sons.

Even that was not easy. A good husband had to compensate for the lack of family and friends, the learning of a new language and the death of my parents. There was the struggle to get my handicapped son accepted in the community, the fight to get him a good education, the worry about his operations, the hard work and concern to keep the home together in sickness and in health.

But there was also love, happiness and kindness from strangers. My time as a refugee had taught me courage, I never lost it.

I learnt a new profession and was successful in my chosen subject. I always worked and the extra income helped to lay the foundation for a good future. I am content now and feel happy and secure in the country of my choice.

Helga Gerhardi

Acknowledgements

I would like to thank the following:

Victor, my son, who assisted in getting the book ready for print

Brett, my grandson, who drew the map onto the computer

My husband, for all his help, understanding and patience

Dr Hilary Johnson, who did the final editing of the book

Martin Haydon for designing the cover

To Bob who helped me through every crisis.

Thank you.

CONTENTS

PART ONE

HITLER'S GERMANY

PART TWO

A SWISS EMIGRANT

PART THREE

A NEW CHALLENGE

ILLUSTRATIONS

PART ONE

HITLER'S GERMANY

CHAPTER ONE

Tilsit - Move to Königsberg

My grandfather emigrated from Switzerland and started a dairy business in a small town called Tilsit, in East Prussia, on the river Memel, next to the Lithuanian border.

He was a frugal and hardworking man. His new cheese, called "Tilsiter," became very popular and can still be bought today in several European countries, including England.

My father George Hans was born in Tilsit. He took over the dairy business, got married and had three daughters and one son.

I was the second daughter, born in 1924. At first I was a great disappointment to my father who wanted a son. Astra, my eldest sister was my mother's favourite, and little Christel, the third girl, blond, delicate and shy was adored by my father. Hans, the boy, being the youngest, and also a small premature baby, was loved by all. I was the girl in the middle reminding my parents of my presence through naughtiness, obstinacy, and when I was older, going my own way.

The house we lived in had no garden. There was only the dairy yard, which was cobbled, but we had a park close by, where we were often taken by the nurse. Hans, being such a small baby, was left at home. I didn't take much notice of him in the earlier days, but played more with Christel. I always felt I had to protect her. Astra, we called her Sternchen when she was young, never wanted to have anything much to do with us. She was only one year older, but she was different. She was dissatisfied with everything, and always complained.

We had a very big pram, one of those lovely old-fashioned big-wheeled ones. In the centre of the pram was a hole, covered by a wooden lid, and under the hole was a big box hanging down. The idea was that when the child was big enough to sit up, the feet could be put into the box for a

1

more natural sitting position. You could have one child each end, with both of them putting their feet into the centre box.

It was a joy to go out in the pram. The only thing was, it was I who had to sit in the middle; with my legs dangling over the side of the pram. Christel sat on one side, and Sternchen on the other. They had their feet in the box. My position was an uncomfortable one, so I mostly walked instead. I remember some lovely trips to the other side of the River Memel, where there was a good sandy beach. This of course was in Lithuania, as the border went through the middle of the river. On the return trip the nurse would fill up our foot box with fruit, which was cheaper in Lithuania. The customs officers never suspected this type of smuggling.

One year, my mother decided to have a rented garden. It had a little summer house, a few flowers and some vegetable beds, even strawberries. My parents did not come with us very often. It was left to the nurse to take us. We were pushed along in the big pram. We had picnics there, sometimes spending all day in the garden and summer house. Before we left again, the paths had to be raked. In this way, one could see if anybody had come in. We all had a little rake and were allowed to help. I preferred the big one with the long handle. Although I was told not to use it, I still got it from time to time, until the day when I hurt myself.

Whilst raking with the long rake, I pulled it hard, and one of the prongs got between my toes. I screamed, nurse came running and picked me up trying to stem the blood, and wondering whether I would lose one toe. It looked quite frightening, particularly as I had been barefoot, and dirt, earth and blood were now mingled together. Anyway, I had the best place in the pram on the return journey.

My two sisters felt very sorry for me. The nurse kept on telling me that I might lose the toe, and maybe even the foot, but I told her that our doctor was very clever, and I was sure he would make my foot better.

The doctor was called to the house, and my foot cleaned and bandaged. We didn't have injections against Tetanus in those days, and iodine was used to clean wounds, or *Wasserstoffsuperoxyd* (hydrogen peroxide). This was a lovely big word for a small child to say, and I made sure that everybody was told what was poured onto my foot. When it was poured on, it used to foam up, and it was fascinating to watch, but painful. My mother always had it in the medicine cupboard, to clean cuts and wounds and, as I was rather wild, it was used on my grazed knees more often than on anybody else's. The chemist used to supply my mother with an exceptionally large bottle of this penetrating antiseptic.

In order to help the healing process of the foot, I was not allowed to walk. So the big pram was used again. I was taken to the nursery school in it and once there, somebody pushed it into the garden, where all the other children were playing. I was quite in demand, because occasionally I would permit a friend to join me on the other side of the pram. They all spoilt me, giving me the best toys, and I was sorry that after the summer holiday my foot had healed, and I could walk again.

The big pram was forgotten for a time, until we found it again after we had moved to our house in Königsberg. I must have been eight years old by then when we discovered it in the attic. This room was very big. On wet days the washing was dried there. At other times it was empty, except for a big box where my mother kept the spare feather beds in the summer, and the racks with the shelves for the storage of the apples. My mother would permit us to play there on rainy days.

One day we discovered the big pram, covered up with some dust sheets. What a find! And what fun one could have with it! Hans was soon sitting in it, and Christel and I chased round the attic with it, or pushed it from one person to the other. When Hans got fed up, we filled the pram with teddy bears and dolls and sometimes when chasing around a corner, the whole thing would fall over, and dolls, teddies and cushions would fly out of it.

We always put the pram back, and covered it again with the dust sheets, and a casual observer wouldn't notice that it had been disturbed. And then one day it happened:

'Yippee!' I shouted, chasing with the pram along the attic and pulling hard to get it round, so that it wouldn't hit the sloping roof at the end. One wheel came off, and it tumbled over.

Dead silence! Then Christel cried, whilst Hans and I tried to push the wheel back on again. Of course it wouldn't stay on. We pushed and dragged the pram to its resting place, leaned the wheel on to it in the right position, covered it up and left the attic. Christel was told to be quiet, and not to tell. We didn't seem to like the attic after that, which surprised my mother, but I don't think she thought much about it because the weather was fine, and we could play in the garden.

One day, a lady arrived, and I heard my mother talking to her about this lovely pram she had, which was in excellent condition. They made their way up to the attic. I followed, keeping a good distance away. My mother lifted the dust sheet, and the lady agreed it still looked in good condition. Then my mother released the brake, and started to push the pram.

The wheel, with a gentle bang, dropped to the side on to the wooden attic floor, vibrating a little before resting, and then of course the pram carriage dropped down to one side.

'Oh dear', sighed my mother, whilst I very gently shut the door.

Listening at the key hole, I heard a few exclamations from both ladies and some talking, but when footsteps came nearer to the door, I flew downstairs into the garden. I warned Christel and Hans, and told them not to say anything.

At supper time my mother told my father that it was disgusting of the removal people to break something and then not to tell her, but now it was too late to complain, because the pram had been there quite a time.

My father was looking at us, but by then I was in deep conversation with Christel, telling her about something that had happened at school in the morning. I kicked her leg, in case she wanted to say something. At the same time I watched Hans, in case he had forgotten that he was not allowed to say anything either. Sometimes I found it quite hard to cover up happenings! - The "pram situation" ended peacefully. - It was sometime later, when we went into the attic, that we noticed that the pram had gone.

There are other things I remember about our life in Tilsit:

I was the only one who went to nursery school, probably because I was so unruly. This was only in the mornings. In the afternoons I sometimes wandered into the dairy, where everybody knew me, or went into the shop, through the back entrance, coming in from the yard. I was not allowed on to the road. In the shop I usually asked for some cheese, which I loved. My father sometimes took me into the dairy, and I was fascinated to see the milk and cream running down the cooling pipes. They looked like a big old-fashioned washing board, and were full of cold water. Refrigeration had only just started then, and my father did not install it until later. Once or twice, he gave me a little cup, and I was allowed to hold it under the cream which rippled over the pipes, and then I could drink it. There were big piles of butter on the wooden tables and when passing through my father would scrape the back of his right thumbnail over the pile, and then taste it. Sometimes he would just nod, at other times he would tell the dairy man to add more salt, or put one heap of butter with another one.

My father only ate very fresh butter, he never touched margarine, and all our cooking had to be done with pure butter. He always said he would lose his taste for the right butter if he didn't take care. Nobody could fool him about the freshness of the product. Our butter on the table was always unsalted, because my father said that with salt you can hide the age of the butter. I wonder what he would think of today, with the European butter mountain?

His speciality was the Tilsiter cheese. I was always astonished to watch how he tested the cheese for ripeness. I would follow him into the cellar. It smelt mouldy, damp and of course, of cheese. The cellar seemed enormous to me. There were rows and rows of shelves by the wall, with a small passageway in the middle, covered with wooden slats to walk on, as the floor was kept damp. On the posts holding the shelves were instructions about the cheese. When to turn it, when it was put down, when it was tested, and the probable finishing date. To test the centre of the *Laib* of cheese, my father produced a kind of corkscrew, with which he drilled into the cheese. He then pulled it out producing a stick of cheese. He tasted the end, which came from the centre, then pushed the rest of the cheese back into the hole, smoothing the outside over with his thumb. He then added to the instructions the date of the testing, and some remarks. The cheese sampler was always in his white overall pocket.

Often I could do what I liked because the nurse thought that I was with my father. One of my favourite places was to hide behind the big settee in the living room.

Sometimes my mother had a coffee afternoon with some lady friends, and I would listen in to their conversation unobserved. Some of the talk I didn't understand, but some of it was most interesting. I discovered that my brother was a "premature" baby.

I had never heard of that word. He was already famous, I thought. My father was "very fond of the ladies." I knew that, because I had seen that he was fond of my mother, and at nursery school he would kiss the hand of the teacher. My grandfather, according to a lady, "had been a very frugal man," keeping his money in gold coins. So I discovered that he was a very rich man.

One day they started talking about me:

'Oh yes,' my mother said, 'Helga is a very bright little girl. She sometimes accompanies her elder sister to school. She never gets lost. She could find the way there and back even if she had her eyes closed.'

Sternchen had started to go to school when she was six years old. At first my mother took her and fetched her. After a while my sister went alone as there were no roads to cross. My mother said I could go with her, because then I would know the way when I started to go to school. Having heard now that I could find the way, even if I had my eyes closed, I decided to try this out. So, after depositing my sister at school, I suddenly, on my way home, closed my eyes. Things went quite well at first. I imagined where I was, and slowly walked on. Gradually I got more confident. I cheated a little, looking just a tiny bit, and I was right where I thought I would be. So I went a bit faster, and then - bang! I saw stars before my eyes, and my head hurt. I opened my eyes, but could hardly see anything, and then I heard a kind female voice saying:

'Are you alright? You have just walked into the lamp post and hit your head. Why don't you look where you are going?'

Why should I, I thought. I had been told I could find the way with closed eyes! Grown-ups are funny, making such untrue remarks.

Nurse was quite shocked when she saw me. I had a big bruise on my forehead, but I wasn't going to tell her what had happened. In the afternoon I confronted the ladies at their coffee meeting, and told my mother that it wasn't true that I could find the way to school if I closed my eyes. There was a lot of giggling and laughing going on, most unkind in view of my large bruise.

Our nursery was on the third floor and on rainy days we played there. We had some big cupboards for our toys and an old settee with a high back rest where nurse often sat supervising us. We had one nurse who always locked us in. She let us play alone while she was in her room, which was next door. When we got too noisy, she would open the door and come in and tell us off.

One day when she had locked us in we discovered a new game. Hans would climb on to the windowsill and from there on to my back. I would then run across the room and throw him on to the settee with lots of giggles and laughter. Sternchen was playing with her doll, and Christel watched us, laughing with us. She also wanted to have a go and climbed on to the windowsill. I turned my back to the window so that she could climb on to it, but she didn't do it.

'Come on then, I am waiting,' I said, and turned round. Christel had gone, and the window was wide open. I guessed what had happened and got frightened. I banged on to the locked door, calling the nurse. She didn't believe me that Christel had fallen out of the window. She thought

I was making it up to draw attention to us, and because I wanted the door opened. Eventually she opened the door, and when she realised Christel was missing and saw the window open, she ran downstairs.

I had got down the stairs before her. I met the foreman's wife, who had Christel in her arms, wrapped in a bath towel. Christel looked very white, and blood was running down the side of her head and face.

Nurse ran and phoned the doctor, and called the dairy men to find my parents. I just sat on the settee hugging my knees and thinking: I couldn't help it, I was only having fun with her, I wanted her to laugh like Hans when I threw her from my back on to the settee.

There was a tremendous row with the nurse. Apparently she had a boyfriend in her bedroom, that was why she had locked us in. My father gave her notice straight away.

Everybody seemed to have forgotten about us, except the foreman's wife. She was a very kind, motherly woman, and she stayed with us reading us some stories. I don't think we listened very much.

When things quietened down, my parents fetched me and brought me to my father's *Herrenzimmer* (study). This was quite a big room. A beautiful large oil painting hung on the wall opposite the door. Underneath stood a large leather settee with some comfortable armchairs to match, forming a half circle. A little low table was in the centre. Christel was lying on the settee covered with a blanket. She looked very pale and tiny, with a bandage around her head. My parents took me inside the room. Because Christel didn't move I got frightened and thought:

She is dead!

I had been told dead people don't move any more.

'That's what you have done', said my father, and pointed to Christel. I just looked at him and said:

'I always loved her'. Then I ran away.

I have never forgotten that picture of my sister, and it haunted me for years. I was only five years old, and it was not my fault that this had happened.

Christel had to have some stitches in her head. The worst thing was that with the shock she also lost her speech. She understood everything, she even smiled sometimes, but she wouldn't talk. The doctor said it would come back through another shock, or in time. This is exactly what happened.

We all went for a walk one day in the park. My mother was pushing the little pushchair with Hans. Christel and Sternchen were holding the pram on each side. I had run off, skipping along with my skipping rope. I was suddenly confronted by a large St. Bernard dog. He just stood there, looking very friendly. He was big, as big as I was. He didn't growl. I put my hand out and touched him, and he came closer. He liked me and wanted to be stroked. I put my arms around his neck, and he felt warm and soft and furry. I thought I must show him to Christel. I often shared things with her and always told her everything. I pulled him on his collar, and he very obediently came with me. When I reached my mother and the other three, they stared at me. Sternchen, Hans and Christel looked frightened, but I knew the dog was alright. I pulled him towards Christel and said:

'This is a lovely kind dog, come and stroke him.'

At that moment, the dog jumped up, and put his front paws on Christel's shoulders. She screamed:

'No, no, no!'

My mother pulled the dog away, comforting Christel and scolding me for touching a strange dog. Suddenly a lady and a bigger boy appeared taking charge of the dog. The lady assured my mother that the dog was very friendly. I don't think my mother listened to her very much, because by now even Sternchen cried. She had enough to do to console two children, look after another one in the pram, and scold me for running away. She gathered us all together and made her way home. Suddenly I said:

'Christel said "No, no, no!"' My mother didn't say anything, so I repeated it. And then I said to Christel:

'Say no!' She looked at me. My mother stopped pushing the pram and stared. Sternchen, who didn't like me being in the right said:

'She never said anything, she cannot talk.'

'Please say it again,' I begged Christel, 'say no, I know you can talk. Please say no.'

It was important to me, because my mother wouldn't be so cross if Christel had got her speech back. She opened her mouth and tried to say something, and then suddenly she said:

'No.' Then she looked at me and smiled and said again: 'No'. After that, she looked at everybody, and said 'no' each time.

My mother took a deep breath, and then she kissed Christel. She looked at me, and suddenly she kissed me too.

Christel started off with a few words, then small sentences, and gradually fluent speech. She had lost her speech for nine months, and was four years old by then. She had a lot of catching up to do.

In 1931 we moved to Königsberg, the capital of East Prussia. My parents had a house built on the outskirts of the town. Königsberg had good schools and a university and my parents felt this was important for us four children. From then on my father had to travel to Tilsit and Ragnit where his dairies were, and often came only home for the weekend.

We had to move out of our new house for a short time because it had not dried out properly.

In Tilsit I went to a small private school and had learnt printing. In my new school I was expected to write in the old German writing, called *Sütterlinschrift*.

The teacher wrote the alphabet down for me in capital and small letters, and told me to write a row of each. It does not necessarily follow that if you know how to write your alphabet in *Sütterlinschrift*, you can join the letters into words to be perfect in spelling.

We had dictation every day, usually small sentences. This was done on our slate boards. When it was finished, the teacher went round and corrected the work. All the children who had made no mistakes would get a one. They would then hold hands, stretching from one desk to the next, sometimes missing one out, because the person had made mistakes. I never seemed to get it right, going back every so often into print with a few letters. The spelling was correct, but sometimes I just couldn't remember how to write a certain letter, and I had to be quick so as not to miss the next words in the dictation. I did try hard, not so much because I wanted to learn it, but I wanted to hold hands like the others, be one of them.

There was only one other person who never had her words right. This was Alice, a girl from the gypsy camp. We became friends. We consoled one another.

Alice was a beautiful girl, with dark long hair, and flashing black eyes. Her father wanted her to go to school so that she would learn to read and write, because most gypsies couldn't do that. The other children didn't like Alice, they said she smelt and told lies and was stupid. I think she was a bright girl. She had difficulties at school, because she was never long enough in one town. Her parents travelled the country in their caravan. Alice loved gay coloured things, particularly ribbons, so I gave her mine from my plaits, and told my mother I had lost them. Actually I, too, started to fancy gay coloured ribbons, and my mother got very cross because I kept on losing them and then wanted new ones again. Alice in return gave me coloured beads, and a beautiful black and white striped large glass marble, which had a spell on it. Her grandmother had given it to her to give to me, because I was always kind to her grand-daughter. She gave me the marble a week after I had had a big argument with the teacher, and I must say, the charm worked. What happened was this:

One day I thought I had everything right. I knew all the words and how to spell them. The teacher found one letter wrong. She scratched two lines across the slate, and wrote a big five on it, the worst number one could get.

'You don't try,' she said, 'you will never learn!'

The letter which I had written wrongly had appeared in other words where I had written it the correct way.

I told the teacher this, and showed it to her, and explained, or tried to explain that the dictation was rather fast, and it was really only one letter.

'Don't argue,' I was told. But I kept on, and was nearly in tears.

I looked at Alice. - Don't cry, - she mouthed.

Alice never cried, or at least I never saw her cry. Oh, I wouldn't cry either, no, I wouldn't. I closed my lips and banged the table with my fist.

'Hold out your hand,' said the teacher, and with that I received two strokes with a special ruler she kept.

After school Alice tried to console me, saying that she never got all the words right either, and it didn't matter. I agreed, and said that from now on, I would make mistakes on purpose. As we were the only two who had never held hands in class we would hold hands in the playground and after school. Our friendship was sealed!

I made mistakes on purpose. The teacher just looked at me, but said nothing. I am sure she knew what was going on. After a week Alice gave me the striped glass marble and said:

'You try today, and you will spell everything right, you see, the marble will help you. My granny put a spell on it.'

When we had dictation I touched the marble in my pocket and everything seemed so much easier. When the teacher did the corrections, I had got everything right and got a one. I couldn't believe it. I was allowed to hold hands stretching out over two desks, as a lot of the other children had made mistakes. Poor Alice wasn't holding hands, but she smiled at me, being happy for me. At playtime I wanted to give the marble back to her so that the spell would also work for her, but she said that was no good, as her grandmother had put on the spell only for me.

I wanted Alice to come home to us, because she said her mother never baked cakes, and she didn't know what home-made cakes tasted like. Her mother was always busy with all the children she had. I think there were seven or eight brothers and sisters in Alice's family, but she was the only one who went to school.

I asked my mother whether I could bring my friend Alice home for coffee and cake, and she said that would be alright. She also promised to bake an apple cake, my favourite. Alice couldn't believe it when I gave her the invitation. Nobody had ever asked her to come home with them.

The bombshell was dropped by Sternchen. She told my mother that Alice was a gypsy, smelt, and was dirty.

'She is a very clean gypsy,' I said.

My mother was concerned, she didn't like the idea at all.

'I don't like you making friends with gypsies,' she said, 'but as you have already asked her, she will have to come, but don't ask her again.'

I was glad she could come, I didn't want to let Alice down, and I promised my mother that Alice would be clean. I told Alice to be very clean and nicely dressed, and also that I would pick her up at the entrance of the camp where she lived. The camp was fenced in, with a large gate at the entrance, which was never locked or closed. Some gypsies had no caravans and lived in huts or shacks. The whole place was most untidy.

I picked up Alice at the gate. She looked lovely, a real gypsy, with a longish skirt, a gay blouse, boots, a bright red ribbon in her hair, which I had given her, and beautiful long golden earrings. I hoped my mother wouldn't recognise the ribbon. My mother had baked the promised apple cake, and the table looked lovely with the plates and cups and saucers, and the sandwiches and the cake. Sternchen refused to be with us, but Christel and Hans joined us. Alice was very good with Hans, looking after him, and helping him with the sandwiches and the cake. I had told Christel about Alice, and she kept on looking at her. The two looked so different, Alice dark and Christel fair. Alice didn't say a word, but she did eat, and she liked our coffee. It looked like real coffee, but was made from roasted oats. My mother didn't think it was good for children to have real coffee, because of the caffeine in it, so we always had this type of coffee.

Afterwards we played snakes and ladders, which Alice had never played. She said they never played in the caravan, as it was always her job to help to look after the children. I thought it was a lovely afternoon, so did Christel, and Hans liked Alice too. I told Alice not to forget to say thank you to my mother. I knew that that was very important. Alice didn't forget. My mother was very kind, and packed the rest of the sandwiches and the cake for Alice to take home. I knew my friend had enjoyed herself, because she whispered to me:

'Thank you ever so much. I have never had such a beautiful afternoon, and I will never forget it, or forget you.'

The next day Alice informed me that I could come and see her granny's caravan one afternoon. I was very excited, but when I told my mother, she wouldn't let me go.

'These people are different,' she said. 'I prefer you to find another friend.'

When I told Alice I wasn't allowed to come, she was very upset. So I said I would come one day straight after school, without telling my mother. I just would come home late. I had done it before, when I found something interesting on the way home from school.

One day, when Alice said it was alright, we ran all the way to the camp in order to save time. We walked through the big gate. I was quite shocked when I looked around. There were lots of dirty children playing with bicycle and pram frames, shouting and running about. There were heaps of old twisted metal and boxes, and on the occasional grass patch was a horse tied to a post. The children stopped running and stared at us. Alice pulled me along.

'Come and see my granny,' she said.

Granny lived in a gypsy caravan, a real old-fashioned one. When Alice opened the door she said:

'Come in, come in, Alice has told me all about you. You were very kind to give her all the sandwiches and the cake, I had some too.'

The old woman was very old, she was big, not tall, just big, with lots of skirts and a head scarf. She, too, wore lovely long golden earrings. The caravan was quite small, but she had a bed, and a kettle was hanging in the corner. She was sitting at the table, with cards laid out in front of her.

'Shall I tell you your fortune?' she said and smiled, and I noticed she had no teeth. I didn't like that. Suddenly I felt frightened.

'No,' I said, 'I have only come to have a look. I must go home, my mother will be cross if I am late.'

Alice looked at me, but she didn't say anything. I had another look around, then opened the door, got down the steps, and ran back to the gate. Alice followed and said:

'You didn't like her, did you?'

'Oh, I did, but she is so old, she must be 100 years old, and all those wrinkles, and no teeth.'

'This is what happens when you are very old, but granny is very clever, and people come and have their fortunes told. She wanted to do this for you, and all for nothing.'

I felt very uneasy, and all I wanted was to get home. So I said goodbye to Alice, and ran off.

I never told my mother where I had been. Alice and I stayed friends for a little longer, but then we moved into our house again, and that was the end of the friendship. I had promised to write, but there was so much to do after the move, that I never got round to it. Alice never wrote either, and now she is only a memory.

Although Swiss is a dialect of German, we never spoke it at home because my father was already born in Germany. We children therefore never realised that we were foreigners until Hitler came to power. It was the 30th of January 1933. My father did not vote and I was involved in a snowball fight with children from the neighbourhood because they thought we were Communists.

The second school I went to in Königsberg was called "Friedrich Ebert Schule," after the famous socialist leader. The name was changed to "Adolf Hitler Schule" after 1933 and the school became a showpiece for the new regime.

I was very keen on sport, and the new facilities supplied at this school were excellent. The thing I didn't like was the shower room. In those days a lot of houses still had no bathrooms. The school governors made the decision, as they now had the new shower facilities, they would make use of them, and give all children at the school the opportunity to have a shower once a week. This was not a voluntary thing but an order, and the only way to get out of it was to miss school, or bring a note from the parents that one was ill with a cold.

Every Wednesday was shower day for the whole school. There were two large shower rooms - one for the boys and one for the girls - with a large basin, and a row of twelve pairs of showers in the centre, which squirted the water simultaneously at an angle away from the centre. Twenty four girls got washed at the same time. We had to bring our soap and towel on Wednesdays and have them ready in class, so that when we got called, we could take them and march off in line to have our wash. Everything was done quite methodically, like being in the army.

We had two great big women helpers in bathing suits who supervised us, making sure we had a good wash, even our hair. First we had to strip completely, then we got wet, and the water was turned off. After that one had to soap the body and hair, and then the water was turned on again for a rinse. If you didn't use enough soap, one of the women would come and give a helping hand with soap and a brush, which was quite hurtful. If we made too much noise, they would turn the water to cold. After the first protesting screams, it got very quiet, because everybody wanted the warm water back. There was not much time permitted for drying, and it was often quite difficult for me to put on my clothes, particularly in the winter when we had long woollen socks because of the frost outside. We were not allowed any powder, and the hair had to be dried thoroughly with a towel and combed through. We all looked like licked cats afterwards. I only stayed at this school for two years and then moved to the Grammar School.

At the age of ten all boys and girls had to join the Hitler Youth. My parents did not allow me to do this. Living on the outskirts of the town a tram ride away from the school, my classmates did not take much notice of the fact that I didn't belong to the "Party." I joined the local BDM (Hitler Youth) for some of their meetings and even a weekend trip, and enjoyed it. But my father was adamant in his refusal. We were Swiss and had to live quietly because of his business.

Gradually I, too, saw the changes under Hitler. All public positions were only to be filled by Aryans (a new and very important word for us). The National Socialist Party was the only legal party in Germany. The churches were nationalised. Strikes and lockouts in industry were forbidden. Racial laws were passed against the Jews, and their persecution begun. All synagogues were demolished.

It was terrible to see how homes and businesses of Jewish people were broken into. The Jews were supposed to be the cause of all Germany's misfortunes! Even one of my Jewish classmates disappeared.

Hitler and Goebbels made speeches and it was obligatory to listen to them. At school we assembled in the hall for this and the radio and loudspeakers were supplied by the party. Every home had to have a radio and people who could not afford one were supplied with a free *Volksradio*. Seeds of hate were planted and grew and anti-Semitic thinking was encouraged.

CHAPTER TWO

School - Summer Holidays

Certain days of the year at school were allocated to communal outings. Each class could choose where to go. If an outdoor trip was chosen, an alternative was discussed in case of rain.

A very popular trip was to go and visit the big castle in the centre of the town. This was established in 1255 and was originally also a fortress. The *Schlosskirche* (castle church), with its tower and spire, 82m high, was added in 1584. In the cellar were the famous *Weinstuben* (wine rooms) called *Blutgericht* (blood court). This was the prison at one time. Many people died there or were beheaded. The *Weinstuben* were visited by all the officers of the different Königsberger regiments, and by business people, like the owners of the big shipping companies. The rooms were not big, but high and arched, with walls which were black with age. They smelt of red wine, because this was stored there in great barrels. The rooms were dimly lit and no lady was allowed in the *Blutgericht Kneipe*. My father used to go with friends to have a drink there, and tell us gruesome stories from the olden days, when people got tortured and beheaded.

The royal apartments were in the east wing. This was where our visit usually started. Because the floors were made of beautifully inlaid wood and highly polished, nobody was allowed to enter without putting on the big felt slippers, which were supplied to everybody. They were popular with us in any case, because one could get some speed up and slide beautifully through the big rooms. We certainly polished the floors! The guide kept in front with the main group and, as long as I didn't bump into any furniture, which might make a noise and draw his attention to me, I could have some good slides.

Although I didn't seem to have paid much attention to the guide, being busy sliding along the floor, I still remember a few things, like the empty iron suit of armour in the entrance hall, which belonged to *Herzog*

Albrecht, who changed from a Catholic knight, on the advice of Luther, to a worldly *Herzog* (duke). There was the beautiful throne, on which Frederic I sat when he was crowned, and which nobody was allowed to touch. There were the rooms which the sad Queen Luise occupied when Napoleon was conquering Europe. She wrote a small verse on the window glass with her diamond ring about the tearful nights she spent there. The guide made a point of showing it to everybody. There was also the room where the first Prussian King was born.

We always visited the *Schlosskirche*, with the big black eagle, built in the baroque style. Here, King Frederic I and Wilhelm I were crowned. Around the altar were the death plaques, to honour the dead of the East Prussian regiments. Every night at sundown, trumpeters played the hymn from the tower:

Nun ruhen alle Wälder ... (Now rest all woods...), as a finale to the closing day. I have heard it a few times, when I was in town in the evening.

The castle has disappeared. It was bombed during the last war, but could have been repaired. The Russians who live in the town now, made sure that no stone was left. Everything has been cleared away, and an ugly tall building put in its place.

The castle trip could be done on a wet day, but to travel on one of the boats along the River Pregel one had to have a good day. There were two different trips offered to us, either through the town and harbour, or a longer one going along the river to the Frische Haff.

Going to the Haff was a quiet and leisurely trip. The river Pregel is narrow and winding, and flows along wide meadows. If one looked over the flat land, one had the impression that there were many rivers which came from the east, the south, and the west, but it was the same winding Pregel. The river flowed slowly, and the grass on its shore was thick and soft, and well liked by the black and white cows. Occasionally one passed a lonely farmhouse. There was quite a lot of traffic on the river, large sailing boats, steamships, and fishing boats bringing their ware from the Haff and the Baltic, and occasionally a motorboat. Heavy black freighters, full of wood, travelled from Memel to Königsberg, to the cellulose factories. Once we reached the Haff, at a place called Gross Holstein, we were allowed to leave the boat for a short time. After that we had the same trip back.

I enjoyed the boat outings into the town better. There was much more to see and hear. The river water was not so clear there, and some of the girls objected to the different smells of tar, oil and coal, mixed with the smell of fish, vegetables, and bad fruit. But everything was so colourful, busy and noisy. There were seven bridges in the town, and we passed through some whilst they were open, folded back from the middle.

The river divided in the middle of Königsberg, forming an island, the Kneiphof, with the beautiful cathedral, called the Dom, and the *Rathaus* (town hall) on it. Five bridges lead to the island, and we went under all of them on our round trip. Fish and vegetables were sold straight from the boats by fishermen and women, who had come early in the morning to the town. The women were shouting, encouraging their customers to buy potatoes, celery, onions, carrots, swedes and fish, like eel, herring, Flundern, sprats, etc. The river everywhere was full of boats loading and unloading. Everything was noisy, with people talking, shouting, sounds of horses hooves on the wooden planks of the bridges and cobble stones on the quay, the rattling of the trams and carts, and the occasional sound of the horn from a big steamship. We passed the great silos, where wheat and corn were stored - 'They are among the biggest in Europe,' said our teacher - and the large tall warehouses by the side of the cobbled quay, which had more wooden shutters and wooden doors than walls. Tired, patient horses stood in front of their carts full of sacks, waiting for the men to unload and fill the warehouses.

After an exciting day like this, I took a long time to go to sleep at night, because I kept on hearing the different noises from the busy town in my head.

Sometimes we had half a day at the Zoo. This was not very far from our school, and was an interesting place. I took my pocket money with me, and paid for a ride on the donkey and the elephant, and the extra ticket for the reptile house. Our favourites were of course the monkeys and their tea parties. We made the visit as part of our biology studies, because the Zoo also had specimens of stuffed birds and bones and replicas of extinct animals.

The school visit to Palmnicken, to see the *Bernstein* (amber), made a great impression on me. Palmnicken was situated on the Baltic where, right on the beach, the open cast mines were working to look for the *Bernstein*. Millions of years ago, the Baltic and part of the Samland were covered by thick untouched woods, consisting of palms, oak trees, conifers and firs. Any wounds inflicted on the trees by the weather or animals would be covered by resin. The sea eventually covered the woods, which became the sea bed. Waves then loosened the hardened resin from the trees, and the water threw it on to the sandy beach. That's how the

Bernstein was formed, and for the last 6,000 years it has been known as an *Edelstein* (precious stone).

In and around Palmnicken, about 50 to 60m deep, was a 6 to 7 m thick seam of "blue earth." This seam had been exposed and was removed with large diggers, and the *Bernstein* then taken from it. From every cubic metre of blue earth, one could sieve and wash out 1Kg of amber, and about 5,000,000 Kg were produced annually. Only the best resin pieces, in colours from red to gold to yellow and blue were used for jewellery, approximately 20%. The greatest part went to industry, which used it to make oil, lacquer and similar things.

Already *Herzog* Albrecht had artists working on these precious stones. There were several workshops in Königsberg which specialised in the artistic work on the *Bernstein*. The only stones that remained untouched by artists were those which contained little insects or fauna from the original wood, as they were witnesses of the origin of the stone. These were polished, and often had a very unusual shape.

We had a tour of the mine and after that also visited the artistic workshops in Königsberg. All this of course is finished now. Palmnicken is Russian, and the German workshops have gone. The Russians have started to mine the amber again, calling it the gold from the east.

The summers in East Prussia were beautiful. I am sure it rained quite often, because this was needed by the farmers for their crops, and they were usually good, but I remember more sunny days than wet ones. We often went out at the weekend for a day if my father was at home and we could use the car. On dull days it was the woods and on bright sunny days the beach and the sea. There was the fast train to Cranz, where there was hardly a space left on the beach, as nearly all of Königsberg seemed to have had the same idea. Whoever had a car chose other places, like Rauschen or Georgenswalde, where one could also go for walks in the woods.

Rauschen was situated above the beach, and for people who found the walk up and down from the beach too steep, there was a cable car. One could branch off from the coast road on to so-called cart tracks, and find unoccupied places on the beach. My father often did this, and once or twice we got stuck in the mud when he tried to turn round. There was nothing for it, we all had to push, rocking the car forwards and backwards first, then a tremendous push, and my father, being the driver, would put his foot down and shoot off, not stopping until he was on really firm ground, or back on the road. We had to follow, sometimes having to walk quite a long way. Still, it was fun.

Before coming home from the beach, we would buy freshly smoked Flundern, a fish that is only caught in the Baltic. The fishermen smoked them on the beach, and it was fascinating to see the fish hanging up like on a washing line in the smoke. They were still warm when we bought them.

Halfway back home, my father would pull off on to a field or meadow, and we would sit down on the grass and eat our Flundern. This had to be done very carefully, so that the spine didn't break. The head and tail also had to be left attached, because once the fish was eaten the bones served a second purpose. We used to lay them in rows across the road, and then wait for cars to go over them. They usually slowed down when they saw something in the road and us four children sitting by the side of it. Once they went over the bones they made quite a cracking noise, which was greeted by us with a hilarious shout! I sometimes had an extra fish only for the bones. By the time we came home we never wanted anything more to eat.

Whenever we went out in the car my mother always insisted on all of us going to the toilet first. My father didn't like to stop for us. He would only stop if he himself had to go. When that was the case, he would get out of the car and say:

'Everybody out! Boys on one side and girls on the other side!' With that he would disappear with my brother, and my mother would take Christel, Sternchen and me to the other side of the road. In order to avoid any arguments about stopping, my mother would insist on us all going to the toilet before the journey. Often one or the other of us didn't need to go, but she would just say:

'*Geh anbieten.*' (Go and make an offering).

Over the years this has become a saying known by all my family, even being taught to the next generation.

The summer holidays were quite long, anything between six and eight weeks. We always went to Zoppot. The reason for this was my mother. She had been born near Danzig (Gdansk) and of course knew Zoppot very well, as this was the seaside beach for Danzig. It was also very well-known all over Germany because of its casino, its spa facilities and particularly for the *Waldoper*, the opera in the woods. We had a summer house there, right by the beach.

My mother's mother and her brother owned an apartment block in Danzig. Grandmother looked after the house. She had single people or couples renting the apartments. Uncle Erich worked for an insurance company.

I knew all about the apartments, because we once went to stay with my grandmother and Uncle Erich. We travelled all alone from Königsberg to Danzig. The boat left Königsberg harbour at eight o'clock in the morning, arriving at eight o'clock in the evening in Danzig. My mother packed a big overseas trunk which was locked, and Sternchen had the key on a string around her neck. Under no circumstances should she open the trunk. The only person who could tell her to do it was the captain, who was a friend of my father's, and had promised to keep an eye on us.

The boat carried freight for Danzig, and there was only a handful of passengers on it. As soon as the boat set off the captain announced over the loudspeaker that he had four unattended children on board and asked all passengers to help to look after them. We got thoroughly spoilt on the trip, as we were the only children, and everybody wanted to give us fruit or sweets or cakes.

We never touched the sea, but went along rivers, canals and locks and eventually came to the Nougat, a branch of the River Weichsel (Vistula) and to Danzig. It was a leisurely trip, the water calm, except when we came to the Nougat, and it was a lot of fun. I cannot remember much about the journey, but I do remember what happened when we came to the border.

Sternchen, having been told not to open the trunk, decided to lock herself into the toilet. She told me she wouldn't come out until the customs people had left the boat, and I was supposed to come and tell her when they had gone. The customs people looked very severe in their black suits with gold braid, so I decided to be very good, and seated myself on the big trunk, watching them questioning the other passengers, looking at passports, and opening some suitcases. Eventually, two of them came to me, accompanied by the captain.

'That's a big trunk,' one of them said, looking at me kindly.

'It's ours,' I replied. 'We are going to stay with my grandmother in Danzig.'

'These are the children I told you about,' said the captain to the official. 'I know the family. They are travelling alone to Danzig. I have their passports and papers.' Before anybody could say anything about opening the trunk, I said quickly:

'It's locked and you can't look at it, because my sister has got the key and has locked herself in the toilet. She won't come out until the boat is travelling again, because she is frightened. I know, because I have to tell her when everybody has gone, and the boat is going again.'

The two officials looked at one another, and then at the captain, who shrugged his shoulders.

'You had better fetch your sister here,' one of them said.

I ran to the toilet. Sure enough, the door was closed and when I knocked and called, Sternchen replied. I told her what had happened.

'You should not have told them about the key,' she said. 'Just go back and tell them you cannot find me. I am not coming out until they have left and the boat moves.'

I took my time to return to the trunk, and when I got there everybody had left. The passengers were crowded at the top of the gangway, and the customs people stood amongst them, talking to the captain. I hid behind some of the grown-ups, watching what would happen next. Suddenly the officials shook hands with the captain and left, the gangway was pulled up, whistles were blown, and then the big horn blew and the boat started to move. I skipped back to Sternchen and knocked on the door shouting:

'It's alright! It's alright! They have left, and the boat is moving again.'

Sternchen opened the door carefully and looked out, making sure it was true what I had said. She then marched off disregarding me and, not saying a word, going up on deck to see whether the trunk was still there. She climbed up and sat on it, biting her fingernails. She always did this when she was worried, uneasy, or not sure what to do. I watched her and thought, she will probably tell my mother what I had said, and wondered whether I would be in trouble again. Still, they had not opened the trunk, so Sternchen had been quite clever in disappearing at the right moment. When I saw the captain coming towards us, I disappeared, but sneaked back to hear what he had to say to Sternchen.

'You shouldn't have gone away,' he said. 'There are only clothes in your trunk. The customs officers wouldn't have taken anything away, or harmed anything. That was very naughty of you.'

Sternchen was a very pretty girl with her blue eyes and dark hair, and when she looked up to people they usually felt sorry for her and protective. The captain put his hand reassuringly on her shoulder.

There was great excitement when we arrived. The boat had to get close to the quay before we could disembark, and when I saw Uncle Erich standing there. I waved and shouted:

'Uncle Erich, Uncle Erich!'

He waved back when he saw me. I suddenly really looked forward to the holiday in Danzig. I liked Uncle Erich. He was tall and very fair and although he limped, because of his wooden foot, he was such a strong man, and always kind to me. The captain made sure we had all our little bags and of course the big trunk, and the sailors helped us off the boat, shaking hands, and waving to us. We had a taxi, and the big trunk was tied onto the back of it. I had never been in a taxi before, so that was also something very new to me. I enjoyed the stay in Danzig, because I was allowed to do what I liked, and could read as much as I wanted to.

Uncle Erich had kept all his boy's books, and I read as many as I could. He had a whole series of books by Karl May, about the Indians and their fights against the white man. As soon as I had finished one book I got the next one.

Sometimes grandmother would take us all for a walk and meet Uncle Erich after the office was closed. Once or twice, we went to grandfather's grave on the way back. Grandmother said it had to be tidied up. It always looked alright to me, but she pulled a few weeds out, raked the earth and picked up some stones. She made us all stand by the grave and say a prayer. I said mine out loud, but she didn't like that. She said one whispers prayers. I couldn't understand that because how could grandfather hear a whispered prayer under the earth where he was asleep? Still, I had promised my mother to be good, so I quickly whispered another short prayer.

My parents arrived by car to fetch us. We were told that we would spend the rest of our summer holiday in our new chalet in Zoppot.

As soon as we got there, I had to go and inspect everything. Our bungalow was built from wood, with a veranda running around three sides of it. One side was built on to the dirt path, later a road, and the opposite side stuck out a little over the beach and sand, with posts supporting it. There was a space left underneath which, we discovered later, was a lovely spot to sit when it was raining.

Zoppot itself was very elegant. There was the *Kurhaus* (spa pavilion) and *Kurgarten* (spa gardens). There was the 1km long pier, where the boats arrived from Pillau with holidaymakers. Next to the private beach came the open beach, used by everybody. The lovely fine yellow sand was the same everywhere.

As soon as I had inspected the chalet, I realised that this was paradise. It wasn't an elegant place. It had wooden floors, covered with a few rugs. We three girls had to sleep together, Christel and I in bunk beds, Sternchen on a single bed. Hans had a tiny room, my parents a bigger bedroom, with a small bathroom. There was another bathroom for all of us to share, a kitchen and a sun room, which took the whole width of the chalet and looked out to the sea. It had big sliding windows, which we often kept open.

One entered the bungalow from the road, but there were steps from the kitchen, leading down on to the beach. There were also steps next to the chalet to reach the beach. We had all our meals in the sun room by the windows, and used to sit there in the evenings also.

That first summer in Zoppot was only a short stay, because we had already been with my grandmother for part of the holiday. The return journey was by boat from Zoppot pier to Pillau, through the Gulf of Danzig, (we called it the Ostsee), and then by train to Königsberg. I never liked the boat trip, because I always had to have a tablet for seasickness and once or twice I was sick.

After that, we spent every summer holiday in Zoppot. My father could not spare long spells from work and would come for a week or two. My mother would make jam and bottle fruit in Zoppot, and that had to be brought back. My father would take this in the car. The journey by car took longer than our boat and train trip. The reason for it was the Polish Corridor.

Danzig was a free port so, once my father left the town, he had to go through the border into Poland. Often there were long queues, because the cars were searched. My father had a German car, so it was assumed that he was German and he had to queue up like everybody else, to be searched. Once he showed his Swiss passport, he often was passed through without any further stopping.

Only once did I travel through the Polish Corridor and that was when I was very young. My mother took me with her to stay a few days in Danzig. My grandmother was ill and my mother felt she had to go and see her.

My mother arranged for a friend to come and stay in the house and look after Christel, Sternchen and Hans, but she took me with her, as I was always the unruly one. We went by train, and my mother had one suitcase, a rug and cushion, and she decided to take a Tilsiter cheese with her, a whole one, packed in the usual cardboard box, as if being posted.

The journey at first was not very interesting. There was another elderly couple in our compartment, who smiled at me and asked the usual questions:

'How old are you? - What is your name? - Are you going to school?

- Where are you travelling to?' etc.

I replied politely to all questions, having promised my mother to be good. I decided to get away from them and tried to open the sliding door into the corridor. My mother was reading a magazine and didn't notice what I was doing, so the elderly gentleman thought he had better stop me:

'You must not go outside, you might not find your way back,' he said.

'Rubbish,' I replied, 'I only have to look through the window in the door and see where my mother is,' and with that I opened the door.

I did not get outside, because he put a heavy hand on my shoulder, preventing me from slipping through the half opened door. At this moment my mother looked up and realised that there might be trouble, so she quickly said to me:

'I will take you for a little walk along the corridor,' and she got hold of my hand, pressing it firmly, which meant don't fuss or make trouble.

My mother and I walked to the end of the corridor and there she had a little talk with me. Whenever she did this, she made me feel very grown-up, and when she even asked me to help her, and in such a kind way, I was always determined to do what she wanted. She explained that grandmother and Uncle Erich were very fond of Tilsiter cheese, which was difficult to get and expensive in Danzig. Because of this, she was bringing them a whole cheese, packed in a box.

'When we come to the border,' she said, 'I will sit you on top of the box, and wrap you up with the rug. Just curl your legs up, and you can have the cushion for your head. You must go to sleep, and if you can't do it just shut your eyes and pretend. You are quite good at pretending. When the customs men come, I will talk to them, even open my suitcase for them to look at and show them my passport. But all the time this is going on you have to be asleep.'

'What about the lady and gentleman in the compartment?'

'Well, that's just the point. If you upset them, they might say something about the box you are sitting on, so you must be nice to them. You are such a sensible and big girl now, I am sure I can rely on you to help me.'

'Oh, of course, and I will only peep once, I promise.'

'You must not open your eyes, the customs men might see it,' warned my mother.

'Don't worry, I will close them quickly.'

My mother looked at me with a frown. I think she was not quite sure whether it had been such a good idea to get me involved in this. We returned to the compartment, and I smiled at the gentleman.

'She had her little walk,' my mother said. 'I think she feels better now, and will sit still. I might put her to sleep in a little while. Children are always impatient on long journeys.'

She gave me a picture book to look at, and I smiled again at the couple, and then looked at the book. All seemed forgiven, because they both smiled back. After a little while they, too, felt like a walk and left the compartment. This was the moment when my mother felt it was time to settle me for my sleep. She put the box with the big round *Laib* of cheese into the corner of the seat by the window and I climbed on top of it. It was not all that high, and by the time I curled up my legs and she wrapped the rug around me, it looked as if I was sitting on a cushion. My head rested on a small pillow, and I thought I might be quite comfortable like that for a long time. I was mistaken, because the box was hard. Before I could say anything, the elderly couple returned, and sat down opposite.

We got to the border, the train stopped, and then there was silence.

Suddenly there were voices and opening of doors and somebody saying:

'Passports, please.'

I had closed my eyes for ages when at last our door opened, and somebody came in.

'Passports,' said a deep voice.

'Anything to declare?' said another voice, and then added: 'Open your suitcases.'

'This lady is Swiss,' said the deep voice.

I couldn't bear it any longer, I had to have a look. I did not look through my fingers, that is much too obvious, but I just opened my eyes ever such a little bit. I saw that everybody was standing. My mother was in front of me, so the two customs officials couldn't really see me.

I could open my eyes completely without being seen. The elderly couple were struggling to get their suitcase down from the rack. One customs official was looking at the passports, and the other one was helping my mother to get her suitcase down!

Fancy that, I thought, he is even helping her to get the suitcase down.

My mother glanced at me, and was shocked to see my eyes open. I quickly closed them, and then I heard her say:

'I have got one of my children with me, she is the second one.'

The names of all four of us were in both my parents' passports until we had our own and she was pointing out which one I was.

'She is rather tired,' continued my mother, 'so I put her to sleep.'

As I could not see what was going on, I can only say what I think happened, and add to it what I know from hindsight.

The Poles disliked the Germans and as my mother was Swiss she only had to open her suitcase for a glance by the customs men, and then close it, with one of them even helping her with the case up and down from the luggage rack. The elderly couple, being German, were not treated so helpfully. They had to open their cases and were thoroughly searched. I don't know what the Polish officials were looking for. It is also possible that my mother got better treatment because she went to Danzig and was only travelling through the Polish Corridor, whilst the couple lived just across the border.

A lot of German people lived in the Polish Corridor, as it had been German before the First World War. The old lady had some bars of German chocolate in her suitcase, for her grandchildren, she said. They had to pay duty on them. German chocolate was apparently taxed in Poland, according to the customs officials.

I gradually got more and more uncomfortable on the hard box, and as my mother had sat down in the meantime, I could feel her at my feet, I pushed my legs several times against her, as a sign of impatience. She got up and wrapped me up a little more with the blanket. I sighed and turned over, trying with a sign to tell her how uncomfortable I was. There was another thing that was troubling me, and that was the smell of the cheese. I had noticed it before, the faint cheese smell, but now when I turned over, lifting the rug a little, the smell became quite strong. Even the others in the compartment had noticed it by now. Everybody of course thought it was me who had done it. So my mother said:

'I think I will open the window a little.'

'No!' shouted the deep voice belonging to one of the officials, 'No window opening allowed!!'

His voice was very commanding and he continued:

'You close curtains also. No looking out of windows in Poland. You not see anything! You told when allowed to look out again!'

With that he closed the windows and curtains firmly and switched on the light. It was very bright in the compartment now, even I knew this with my eyes closed. The two officials then left, probably not liking the smell either, because they left the door open.

At last I could open my eyes. The elderly couple were busy packing their cases again, as everything was scattered on the seat. My mother was sitting down at the door of the compartment, to give me plenty of space for my feet. She looked at me and put her finger over her lips. As the door was wide open, I could see along the corridor for a little. All curtains were drawn and there was nobody standing there. It was as if we were in a cage, with all windows shut and curtains drawn. The train started suddenly. There had been no whistle, so it was unexpected, and the old lady and gentleman still standing up and packing nearly fell over. They sat down quickly, never saying anything. I think they were hurt by the treatment they had received at the border, particularly as my mother had been dealt with in a different way. When the train was again rolling along quite fast, my mother said:

'Let me help you to close your cases.'

She felt sorry for them, I could see that.

'No, thank you,' they said, 'we can manage.' They finished the packing, and closed the cases. The train soon stopped, and that's where the couple left us. At last I was able to get up. I was sure I was crippled for life from my hard seat, but I soon recovered. I was told by my mother that I would have to do the same thing again when we came to the next border into Danzig. This next border crossing actually went very quickly and I didn't have to sit too long on the box. It was also lovely to have the curtains drawn back and the window open. I asked my mother about the closing of the curtains and the shut windows. I wanted to know what would happen if one disobeyed this order.

'Don't try it,' she said 'They will shoot at you. The Poles only permit certain trains through the Corridor, and then only if nobody can see what they are doing. I don't like travelling by train, that's why we usually go by boat. Papa doesn't like travelling through the Corridor by car either, there is always such a long wait at the border. At least it is not so bad for us, because we have Swiss passports, but it can be most unpleasant for the Germans, as you have seen with that elderly couple.'

The return journey was uneventful. Again we had to close the windows and curtains whilst we were on Polish territory and there was quite a delay at the border. After that, I always thought of the Polish Corridor as a strange, secret, forbidden land.

Zoppot to me was happiness, freedom, playtime, sunshine, and relaxing of rules and people. Even my father was more relaxed when he stayed with us and would join in the fun at the beach. I got the occasional smacked bottom, not as hard as at home, and it was soon forgotten.

Sternchen and I could soon swim, so we were allowed a lot of freedom. We were already on the beach before breakfast, digging holes, building castles with rivers to the water, swimming or rolling in the sand.

The baker brought fresh poppy seed and soft rolls in the mornings. We left a cloth bag hanging on the front door, with a note for the order and except for Sundays, we had fresh bread every day. My parents got up late sometimes and then we didn't have breakfast until ten o'clock. It didn't matter. Time was not important. The same thing happened about lunch or supper.

We were quite a crowd, about ten of us, and we would venture as far as the private beach by the *Kurgarten*. Along the free beach, and at the *Kurgarten* beach, people had the so-called *Strandkörbe* (beach baskets). A *Strandkorb* was a tall open box made from cane, and lined with padded cloth. At knee height was a solid seat, the top of which lifted up, so that one could put clothes and bath towels into it. People sat inside, protected from the wind, and even the occasional short shower. If turned against the sun, it was for sunbathing. One could hang the bath towel in front, and change into swimsuits behind it. People were very proper in those days, and there were no bikinis either. Some *Strandkörbe* folded back, like a deck chair. The young people usually lay on the sand, only using the seat of the *Strandkorb* for their clothes. It was mostly granny or grandfather who sat in the basket. The *Strandkörbe* had huge numbers painted on the back for recognition, because they all looked the same and one hired them for a day or a week. In the evenings, when everybody had gone, or when it started to rain, the caretaker would tip them over, so that the open side was facing the sand, and in this way keep the inside dry.

Hired-out baskets would lie all over the beach, but the unoccupied ones were at the top end of the beach, next to the guard's little shed. We often helped the guard to push the *Strandkörbe* over in the evenings, or to lift them up in the mornings, and that's why he never told us off when we played hide-and-seek with them when the beach was empty. This was a lovely game with the baskets. One could hide behind them, or crawl underneath, dig a little hole, and look out. Trying to find somebody, one had to watch the baskets, and if they moved, one knew that somebody was underneath.

One day we made a great discovery. I think it was one of the boys, called Fritz, who had seen it first, and he would only take a few of us with him to see it. Christel and Hans were not allowed to come, and Sternchen wasn't even told about it. Fritz said we might have to run fast, so he only wanted good runners with him. I promised Christel that I would tell her all about it afterwards, so she in her turn promised to look after Hans.

We always made promises to one another, when we were really serious, and meant them. A promise never gets broken, that's what my father told us. If in doubt, one doesn't promise it, but rather says 'I will try.' Anyway, we were off, only four of us, along the beach, the free beach, and on to the private beach. After that we got to the pier.

'We can get to the other side under the pier,' said Fritz, 'the water is not deep, you won't even get your bottoms wet, but you have to bend down, as it is low in parts. Anybody not wanting to do it can go back, but once you come with me, you have to come back the same way.'

Nobody backed out, and Fritz guided us under the pier between the big posts. It was pretty eerie and quite painful bending low all the time. There was only one good thing about it, I thought, nobody would follow us under the pier if we had to run back. Also, the Baltic has no tide and the water wouldn't get any higher. We came to the other side, and another beach. More people, more baskets but, towards the back of the beach, a wooden enclosure.

'That's it,' said Fritz, 'that's what I wanted to show you. There is a door on the other side, and sometimes a woman comes out of it. That made me think, why only women, not men or children? And, why does it look like a big wooden house without a roof? Anyway, there is a hole in the wood and you can look through it. We can't go all together, so let's play here for a bit, and after a while I will go and have a look. After that you can go, but only one at a time.'

We chose in which order we would go. When Fritz came back, the next one went and then the next, and after that came my turn. I really had no idea what I would see. Now I realise what an innocent silly girl I was in those days.

I was terribly shocked when I looked through the hole. What I saw was a women's nudist camp, or a sun-worshipping corner for women on the beach. What shocked me so much was the size of the naked women. They all looked old and fat to me, lying on padded benches, sweating, and shiny with sun oil. Some were wiping the sweat off with a towel. I had seen my mother naked and although she had had four children, she had a beautiful body compared to these women. Thinking back today, I wonder whether this was like a sauna, with people sweating to lose some weight, and then going for a swim in the cold sea.

After having a good look, I ran back to let the next person go, but never said a word. I couldn't very well show Fritz or the others what I felt, because I suddenly realised that I was the only girl amongst them.

Actually, the way they were making remarks about what they had seen, I don't think it struck them that I was a girl. I told Christel about it and she, too, was shocked. She couldn't believe that people would lie in the sun without a swimsuit. How innocent we were then!

One of the highlights of the summer was the flower festival. Cars, horses and carts, motorbikes, cycles, prams, anything on wheels was decorated with flowers and entered for the big parade. The final of this big event was the prize-giving by the fountain in the *Kurgarten*. The front of the *Kurhaus* was towards the street, and the rear of the building was in the *Kurgarten*, with its large restaurant, and the three open terraces, one above the other. Opposite the terraces was the beautiful big fountain, with lovely coloured lights, which changed from red to blue to green to yellow to white, and back to red again at night. All vehicles decorated with flowers were numbered and would finish up parading around the fountain. This was the only day when the big gates of the garden were opened to allow the vehicles to enter, because at no other times were vehicles, not even bicycles, allowed in the garden.

The best seats for the flower festival were on the terraces of the *Kurhaus*. My mother liked the middle terrace and the middle table, from where we got the best view. On the festival day, at ten o'clock in the morning, Sternchen and I had to go and sit at this table. I was allowed to order an ice cream and eat it slowly. At eleven o'clock, Sternchen was allowed to order an ice cream. Just before twelve o'clock Christel would arrive, sometimes with Hans, sometimes without him, and order an ice cream. Between quarter and half past twelve o'clock, my parents arrived. Lunch was ordered, and at about half past two, the first flower vehicles would arrive. My mother had this well organised, but sometimes it didn't go smoothly. The waiters didn't like us to sit there for hours and only have two or three ice creams. They didn't earn anything and therefore tried to get rid of us. Of course they guessed the reason for our sitting there, and once we nearly did get pushed out.

I had finished my ice cream, and whilst I wasn't looking the waiter took the empty plate away. Because there was nothing on the table the waiter told us either to leave, or to order something else. It was only 10.30 by then, and Sternchen was told not to have her ice cream until 11 o'clock. She wouldn't budge.

'No,' she said to the waiter, 'I don't want anything at the moment and neither does my sister.'

The head waiter came, and it was most embarrassing, with people watching from the other tables, to carry on with the argument. Eventually I said:

'I will have another ice cream, please.'

The head waiter stopped talking and looked at me, then he passed the order on to the waiter, and walked off.

'You haven't got any money,' hissed Sternchen.

'I ordered it for you,' I said. 'It is your ice cream which you are supposed to have at eleven o'clock. You will just have to have it a bit earlier.'

'I won't eat it,' she said, 'and I won't pay for it either.'

'Then it will just have to melt,' I said.

When I saw the waiter coming, I said to Sternchen:

'I must go to the toilet,' and ran away, leaving her there sitting alone. Of course she had to pay for the ice cream, because the waiter always took the money from us straight away. Children could disappear without paying, he had told us that before. When I returned, Sternchen was furious, and later, when my parents came, she made a big story out of it, how naughty I had been, etc. But this time she didn't get away with it, because my parents realised what a battle we had had to keep the table, and that it wasn't easy for us to sit there for hours with nothing to do. The waiter was charming to us when my parents turned up and ordered a meal for six people!

My mother was quite right. It really was the best table to sit at and see one vehicle after another driving around the fountain and then away. The flowers were beautiful, and so were the girls sitting amongst them. An awful lot of work had gone into the design and decoration of some of the open lorries and cars. There were six prizes, and the winners drove a special round around the fountain. After that, it was a free-for-all, with the flowers pulled off the vehicles and thrown into the crowds.

We had coffee and cakes late in the afternoon, and sometimes my parents stayed on for the evening to see the dancing in the fountains. This usually happened if they met friends, and had invited them to share our table. We children would never sit long at the table, but run off, only to return from time to time for some food, or to enquire when we would go home.

The dance in the fountain was something special and unusual. The ballerina, or main dancer, would be in the centre of the fountain, dressed in the usual little stiff, white short skirt. Some other dancers would be in the water on the outside of the big basin, below the raised centre fountain. Everything was dark, the dancers got into position, the music started (records through loudspeakers), and then the water and the lights were turned on. The ballerina had only a small space in which to move, but her movements were beautiful, illuminated by the different colours of the lights, and the water, which shot up into the air, and then to the outside. The girls in the bottom basin danced very gently, so as not to splash the water, but by the end of the dance they were all quite wet. The ballerina did not get too wet, because the water sprayed to the outside. One year, they had a performance of "Puss in Boots" in the theatre, and it was Puss, with her red boots, who performed the dance in the centre.

The other big occasion which took place in the *Kurgarten* was the *Kinderfest* (Children's Festival). An extra entrance fee was charged at the gate for the children, and they received a card, which entitled them to free entry of competitions and entertainment. There was a small roundabout, swing-boats and chairs and sometimes a ghost train. At the competitions one could win different prizes, like a painting and drawing book, coloured pencils, balloons, streamers, whistles, etc. I was usually quite good at the more sporty competitions. At one of them, both legs were tied together. Eight to ten girls of similar height and age were chosen, and we had to hop a certain distance. At another competition we had to compete by hopping along, tied in a sack, called *Sackhüpfen*. There was also the "egg and spoon" race. From these races, I brought back quite a number of prizes.

The climbing of the greasy pole was really more for the older boys, but I did attempt it once. The pole was quite high, and got thinner and thinner the higher one went. A ring swayed above, with sausages hanging underneath, to which a rope was attached. The general idea was to climb up and take a bite of sausage and bring it back and receive a prize. The only trouble was that when the boy was just about to bite it, the man pulled the rope a little and the ring with the sausages went up. I had practised climbing the pole at school and was quite good at twisting my legs around it, and pulling myself up with strong arms. So one year I decided to have a go at it. One reason was also that the prizes were so much better than at the other competitions. I could even win a torch, very useful for reading at night under the bedclothes.

At first, the climbing went quite well, but every time I thought I could take a bite, the sausages disappeared. After a time I got tired, and my arms started aching. I was not giving up. I could hear people below shouting encouragements, and then somebody shouted:

'It's a girl, look at her, she is already quite high.'

With that I glanced down and saw hundreds of faces looking up at me, at least it looked like hundreds of faces. It made me feel funny, and I realised it was not a good idea to look down. Slowly I did one or two more pulls with my arms, but again the sausages disappeared. The pole had become thinner by now, and when I moved again it started to sway. For the first time I got afraid. Suddenly I didn't care whether I got a prize or not. I knew I had to get down slowly, not sliding, because then I would burn my hands and legs. I looked up at the sausages once more, they were so close, and then I heard my father's loud voice:

'What do you think you are doing with my daughter. She is only a child, and a girl at that. That height on the pole is dangerous, and only for older boys. Give me that rope at once, and let her have a bite, so that she can come down before she falls.'

And suddenly the sausages were in front of me, and I took a bite. The crowd cheered and called out:

'Well done, well done! She has got a bite, she has got a bite!'

I climbed down slowly. When I reached the ground I was shaking. My father took my hand, and the man gave me the torch and a bag of sweets, and the people were clapping.

'That was well done,' said my father, 'but don't ever climb that pole again. This is a competition for older boys, not girls. Whenever will you become a lady, and stop competing with boys?'

'Don't worry, Papa, I won't do it again,' and I continued under my breath, 'I was much too frightened to repeat this adventure.'

In the evening we had fireworks, and the children's lantern procession. Every child had a paper lantern attached to a stick with a candle inside.

The lanterns were in different shapes, round, square, oblong, like a fish, duck or the moon, in stripes of different colours. We all lined up, the candles were lit, and then we marched in a long column through the *Kurgarten*, which was a very pretty sight. The finale was a barbecue, where everybody got a "hot dog," and there was plenty of beer for the grown-ups.

On dull or rainy days, we all went into the wood to collect blueberries, wild strawberries, or mushrooms. My mother would bottle the blueberries, and make jam from the strawberries. One could go mushroom picking even if it was raining, because the wood was so thick that one hardly got wet. Actually, one picked the best mushrooms in the rain. That was the moment when they came out. There were a number of different types of edible mushrooms, and my mother knew them all. There were the little brown ones, like trumpets, called Pfifferlinge, a delicacy in the restaurants. There were the white champignons, and there was the big Steinpilz (translated stone mushroom), which could weigh up to one pound. We ate a number of them, but the rest were cut up into pieces, strung up, and put to dry under the roof, on the veranda. We used to sit for hours threading pieces of mushrooms, with a thick needle, and thin, strong linen thread. When dry, the mushrooms were packed into old biscuit tins, and in the winter they were used for soups, stews, and gravy. Afterwards, we used to smell of mushrooms, and our fingers were black from the pollen. My parents had their own entertainment, and would often go out in the evenings with friends, or alone. Whilst we were very young, we had our cleaning woman coming in to watch us in the evenings. When we were older, Sternchen was made responsible for looking after us. She was only one year older than myself, but my mother said she was a responsible adult, and we were the little children. She always had been different from us, and this separated us even more from her. Still, I do remember that once or twice she did join in some of the fun we had after our parents had left us alone.

Sternchen had become rather friendly with a girl from one of the other bungalows, and one moonlit night we all decided to have a hide-and-seek on the beach behind or under the *Strandkörbe*. Sternchen's friend came along too, and we all met under our bungalow. We had a fantastic time on that moonlit beach that night, and even Sternchen enjoyed it, keeping together with her new friend. We got to bed before my parents returned, and they were very surprised that in the morning nobody was up early. My parents would go to a dance or the casino in evening dress. We all used to think how smart and beautiful my mother looked. My father, too, was a very handsome man, and I know for a fact that he, being away such a lot from home, had had a number of lady friends. I heard my parents arguing over it many times when I was older.

A big occasion was the *Waldoper*. Performances like the Nibelungenring by Wagner, Parcival and Lohengrin took place in the open-air theatre in the woods. Only singers with very powerful voices could participate in an open-air opera, as no microphones could be or were used. Tickets had to be ordered well in advance, as performances were always sold out. People came from all over Germany, often only staying two nights, to go to the *Waldoper*. My parents always had tickets for two or three performances.

Once my mother took me with her, because she had two tickets and my father had not arrived. We had to dress warmly, and put some cream on, to keep the midges away. As it was a dull day, and there was the possibility of rain, we took our bathing caps and bathing wraps, plus a cushion each with us. We sat out in the open, and were not allowed to open an umbrella, as this could disturb the view for the people behind. I cannot remember much about the evening, except that it was absolutely fascinating and beautiful. The opera was Siegfried, and the hero arrived on a real horse, tied it to a tree, and walked over to the little stream to drink. Whilst bending over to scoop up the water in his horn, Hagen, his so-called protector, pushed the spear into his back, where Kriemhilde, Siegfried's wife, had sewn a little cross. I have never forgotten this scene, it was so real. The only thing that disturbed me was that all the men, and particularly the women, were such big people, with tremendous chests. Some of the parts were rather sad, and it is easier to feel sorry for a pathetic, thin little woman, than a big one. But I suppose, to have a powerful voice, one had also to develop a powerful chest, and in those days one didn't go on diets like now.

We sat quite comfortably on our cushions, and because the man in front of me was rather tall, I also sat on my bathing wrap. It didn't rain, and I only had a few gnat bites where I had missed putting on the cream. The next day I had to tell Christel all about it, and of course all my friends, as they, too, had never been to the *Waldoper*. I gave quite a good performance of Siegfried drinking and dying!

I never liked Sundays when my father was with us. This was the day when we were shown off in the *Kurgarten*. My mother was very clever and artistic, and she always made our clothes. She would buy material and make us three girls the same dresses, and sometimes a shirt for my brother from the same material. We also had to have the same ribbons in our hair, and white socks on. Only the shoes were different, particularly mine, as already then I had very large feet for my age. On Sundays we all got dressed the same, in lovely light-coloured starched dresses. Everybody could see that we were three sisters and one brother.

My parents marched proudly around the *Kurgarten*, nodding to people they knew, stopping sometimes to talk to somebody, and enjoying the admiring glances from people who thought us such a lovely united family. In between, my father would hiss:

'Helga, shoulders back, walk straight,' and my mother would add softly, but loud enough for me to hear:

'Don't walk like an elephant, Helga, lift your feet up, don't turn your toes inside,' etc.

It was so boring to walk along with nothing to do. If I walked with Christel, I would tell her all sorts of things to pass the time, but if I had to walk with Sternchen I would pinch her bottom just for fun. After that there was trouble. We had to change over and I had to walk with Hans. He was not too bad, only he would not walk fast enough. My father, who always walked with a stick on Sundays for elegance, would push me with it to hurry up. He thought it was I who walked slowly. Sometimes we sat down in an outside café - there were several of them - and had ice cream or cake, but nearly every time I seemed to get my dress dirty and got told off. As soon as we got back, I took my dress off, and put my old clothes on, or if the weather was still warm enough my swimsuit, and was off into the water.

Holiday for me in Zoppot was casual wear, sun, beach, and swimming in the sea.

Our garden yielded a lot of fruit, vegetables and flowers, and nothing was wasted. My father didn't do a lot of gardening, but he took a great fancy to a special pair of garden secateurs, which my mother had given him one Christmas. On Sundays he used to go around the garden and cut off branches from trees, bushes and hedges. We had a beautiful lilac hedge running along one side of the garden. It seemed to like my father's cutting, because it produced no end of purple blooms.

One day, my mother came back from the market, where she used to go to buy fresh fish and chickens, and told us that they were selling the lilac there for 15 Pfennig a branch, and it didn't even look as nice as ours.

'Why can't we sell ours?' I said.

'We are not really market people,' said my mother, 'and, in any case, we haven't got a stall.'

I thought about it, and the beautiful lilac we had in the garden, and how much pocket money we could make, and then I said:

'We don't need a stall. We could cut two large bunches of lilac, and tie them to the front and the back of my bicycle. I can cycle to the market, and sell them for 10 Pfennig a stem. In the meantime, Hans and Christel can bring me another lot of branches on their bikes. If anybody complains, or I have to pay stall fees, I would just cycle away, but if I am allowed to sell the lilac there, I don't mind paying the stall fees. I earn money from selling, so I can afford to pay for it.'

My mother did agree that I had thought this out quite well, and so did Hans and Christel. On the next market day, we got up early in preparation for the selling of the lilac. My mother cut the lilac, and I tied it to my bike. We did the same to Christel's bike, and then set off to the market. Once there, I found a spot, partly in the shade, and told Christel to go back for another lot of lilac, as now she knew where I would be. I laid my bicycle down, and the flowers on the wheels, and started to call out to people:

'Fresh lilac, fresh lilac! 15 Pfennig a branch, or two for 25 Pfennig!'

It didn't take long before I had sold nearly all the lilac. Everybody bought two branches. I had one of my mother's old handbags tied to a string around my neck, and I was kept quite busy, what with calling, selling, and changing money, that I didn't notice the market supervisor approaching me, until he stood before me.

'Have you paid your *Standgebühr*? (standing charge), he said.

I was so surprised, that I forgot all about the statement I had made before, that I would cycle off if I met the supervisor. All I could say was:

'No, nobody has asked me for it. How much is it then?'

I looked round, there were stalls everywhere, but some people were selling their goods from baskets. Next to me was an old woman selling onions and carrots from big baskets. She was watching me and the supervisor, and said:

'Just pay him, it isn't much if you are only here for two hours.'

That's it, I thought, I am only here for a short time. So I said again:

'How much is it, I am only here for an hour or two.'

The supervisor looked at the lilac which was left, and then at me, and mumbled:

'If it is only an hour, one Mark will do.'

Well, that was not very much, I had earned more by now. So I paid my *Standgebühr*, got a ticket as a receipt, and carried on selling my lilac, smiling at the old lady next to me. Soon Christel and Hans arrived with more lilac, and as I wanted to sell them quicker, I dropped the price to 10 Pfennig a branch. It took me more than an hour to sell them all, but as the supervisor didn't return, I got away without paying any more.

We were rich! We had plenty of pocket money! I bought the old lady a cup of coffee from one of the stalls, and thanked her for helping me out with her advice. She gave me a toothless smile, and told me to come again.

On the way back, we bought an ice cream each. My mother divided the money, gave us each a small amount, and told us that the rest would be there when we wanted it. She didn't like us to have too much money in our pockets. The following Saturday we went again. We found the old woman, who this time suggested to bring a bucket. She showed us where we could get some water, so that we could keep the lilac wet. We went for three or four weeks, until the lilac was finished. Each time I bought the old woman a drink, because I was grateful to her for her help and advice.

We did the lilac-selling for a few years, but I never met the old woman again. I don't know what the others did with their money, but I bought books with mine. My mother would sometimes take me with her when she went shopping in the town, or I would meet her in the bookshop Gräfe und Unzer, the biggest bookshop in Europe, so we were told, which was already founded in 1722. I would go to the shop by tram after school, and choose some books and, if my mother approved, she would pay for them out of my "lilac money." My favourite authors at that time were Agnes Miegel, an authoress from East Prussia, and Selma Lagerlöf, a Swedish writer. I was also very interested in Greek mythology, stories and novels about the Vikings, and historical novels, dealing with kings and queens. My passion for reading was satisfied through the lilac money.

CHAPTER THREE

Treatment of Jews - Outbreak of War

In 1938 Hitler annexed Austria and the Sudetenland returned to the Homeland. His popularity sky-rocketed. The same year he visited Königsberg and by accident it was I who had the chance to shake his hand. I was the envy of my classmates and scared of what my father would say, who did not like him. I was glad that it never got into the local paper.

I had my first kiss that year - most unromantic - and suddenly I was not a child anymore.

My father went through a business crisis at the beginning of 1939 because Germany put a tax on any food and milk imported from Lithuania. Nearly all the milk for my father's Tilsiter cheese came from that country. In March Hitler annexed the town of Memel and the Memelland in the eastern part of Prussia, and the import tax for food and milk was scrapped. My father's business was safe again.

On September first 1939 the German attack against Poland began and a new type of war had started - the Blitzkrieg. Poland was overrun with a speed that astonished everybody, even the German people. At school the war was made part of our history lesson. Everybody was for the war. A number of fathers were called up, but none of them got killed yet, and except for a generous food rationing which soon followed, life carried on as normal. Helma, my first boyfriend, joined the marines as a cadet at the age of sixteen.

Not everybody received the same treatment in Poland. The Germans who, because of the different peace treaties in the past, had been living in Poland, were welcomed back to the Reich, and so were part-German Poles. The same happened to other Germans, like in Yugoslavia and Czechoslovakia. A lot of these people could only speak a little German, whilst some of them could not speak German at all. They were called

Auslandsdeutsche, and had a special identity card. In order to encourage them to come back to the homeland, they were often even given special treatment. Hitler felt that in this way he could prove to the world that the land that he took was really the German Reich's entitlement.

The Poles were inferior in the eyes of the Germans, and were treated so. Pure Poles could not own real estate. They did not receive any higher education. The Poles brought to Germany to work were paid a very low wage, and received fewer rations than the Germans. They were not allowed in museums, libraries, theatres, cinemas, or to go on trams or railways. In other words they were not allowed to travel. Even to use a bicycle they had to have permission in writing from the German authorities. The upper classes, like the business owners, teachers, and even priests disappeared, or finished up in labour camps. After the occupation, anything of value was looted or requisitioned. The museums were closed, and no more newspapers were allowed to be printed. There was the death sentence for any anti-German gesture. The Poles suffered more in the war than any other occupied country. Even the Russians, who took part of Poland, eliminated them.

The Jewish people received the same treatment, and gradually seemed to disappear. Before 1939 they were robbed. Their businesses and valuables were taken away, and they were often deported. After the outbreak of war, they were put into ghettos.

The German people in the main did not know what was going on. There was only one party, the Nazis, and they had no opposition. It was only those who had experienced the SS who were afraid if there was a knock on the door, and we were some of them.

To make it obvious that Poles and Jews were inferior, they had to wear an identification. All Jews had to sew a yellow Star of David, the size of a small coffee cup saucer, on to their clothing. The Poles' identification was a black "P" on a white background. Later on, there were the workers from the east, from Russia, who had to wear the identification *Ost* (east). As all these marks were on the outdoor clothes, everybody in the street could recognise them.

At school we had two new girls joining our class who came from Poland, Isabella and Alexandra. They were half-German. Their German mother had married a Pole. After his death she married a German homeopath and they came to Königsberg to live. Isa, as she was called for short, was sixteen years old when she joined us in the autumn term of 1940. She spoke quite good German and, of course, fluent Polish. Ola, a shortened version of her second name, Olga, was two years older, but because her German was not very good our headmaster had suggested that they should both enter the same class. They told us about the school they had been to in Poland, which was very strict, but excellent. We soon realised that the sisters knew more than we did in all the science subjects. Both of them had difficulties with German, particularly Ola who, thanks to her sister, didn't fall too much behind. If Ola didn't understand something, Isa was permitted to explain it to her in whispers. Gradually this became less and less.

The two sisters were accepted by everybody in our class, but amongst the teachers there was one who didn't seem to like them, particularly Ola. Isa could be quite forceful, and was able to answer back, but Ola was quiet, introvert, a little shy, and would never reply to any accusation even when she was wrongly accused. Isa would sometimes stand up for her. Mrs Lemke, who taught us English and German, often picked on Ola. She didn't like her because she was half-Polish. Sometimes I felt very sorry for Ola, and would do something silly to draw Mrs Lemke's attention away from her, because Ola never defended herself.

Once, when she told Ola off again, I made a little paper plane, and just threw it into the air. I had given it a good push and it sailed along from the back bench where I was sitting, as far as the teacher's desk.

'Who did that?' snapped Mrs Lemke.

'I did it!' I said and stood up. We always had to stand up when we addressed the teacher.

Mrs Lemke looked at me surprised, because she never expected anybody to own up to it. Her attention was taken away from Ola, and from the corner of my eye I could see Isa, pulling her dress, telling her with that gesture to sit down.

'And why, may I ask, did you throw that paper?' said Mrs Lemke, with a very quiet, but commanding voice.

'It is not a piece of paper. It is an aeroplane. I wanted to see whether it could fly.'

'In the middle of the lesson!'

'I had just finished folding the paper into that shape. In any case, this wasn't exactly a lesson that we had just now.' I said this very quietly. The girls started to giggle. Mrs Lemke got red in her face and exploded:

'You impertinent girl, you will get a *Tadel* for this!'

She was shaking with fury and grabbed the class book to write the *Tadel* remark into it.

It is Friday, I thought, and if I behave alright for the rest of the day and get no other *Tadel* there would be no blue letter arriving at home on Monday. One *Tadel* a week was not notified.

There was absolute silence whilst Mrs Lemke wrote, and some girls looked at me, smiling a little. They knew why I had done it.

'May I sit down, please.' My voice broke the silence, and all heads turned.

'Certainly not!' shouted Mrs Lemke, 'I have not finished with you.'

But there was really not much to be said after that. Mrs Lemke looked through the class book and probably noticed that this was my first bad remark for the week, which was unusual. She felt that she wanted to punish me more, and so she ordered me to write an essay about impertinence and give it to her on Monday. She then decided to let me stand for a while, which was a mistake.

I started to tread noisily from one foot to the other, rocked about, which made the desk squeak, coughed a little, blew my nose and of course nobody in the class could concentrate any more. I was very good in German, having read a lot, and Mrs Lemke often relied on me for the right reply to her questions. Having to stand like this, I refused to lift up my hand for a reply, and the girls wanting to help me, pretended not to know the answers to any of the questions Mrs Lemke put to them. Eventually she allowed me to sit down, and when the bell went, and the lesson was finished, the whole class gathered round me to chatter, and give their remarks to what had happened, even before Mrs Lemke had left the room.

'Why did you do it?' somebody said.

'You know she gets into a temper straight away,' said somebody else.

'You did it for Ola, didn't you?' said Isa.

'She always tells Ola off for making mistakes in German, and we all know she works very hard and looks up words in the dictionary,' I said. 'Ola told me she spent three hours on the last essay. I only spent one hour.'

'Never mind,' Ola replied. 'I've got used to her always finding faults in my work. It was good of you, Helga, to help me.'

'I didn't help you, I wanted to see my aeroplane fly,' I said laughingly.

This was not the end of the story. Our next lesson was Latin, which was taught by our headmaster. Whilst we were doing some written translation, he looked at the class book. He often did this on a Friday, as this was the day when the books were collected and brought into his study for the weekend. It had been a good week, nobody had been late for school, and my *Tadel* by Mrs Lemke was the only one. When we finished our translations, Mr Walsdorf looked at the class, and then at me.

'Miss Zirkel, I see Mrs Lemke had to give you a *Tadel* for impertinence. This is a very serious offence, and I am surprised to hear about it. I would like to know what happened.'

I told him exactly what had happened, starting off by telling him that Mrs Lemke had criticised Ola's homework again, although she had spent such a long time on it, and that Ola never said anything. He had difficulties in hiding a smile when I told him about the plane which Mrs Lemke called paper, and the remark I made that we hadn't exactly had a lesson. I think he thought I had been really rude to Mrs Lemke, and looked a bit surprised when he realised I had finished talking.

'Is that all?' he said.

'Yes, Mrs Lemke said I was impertinent, and gave me a *Tadel*. She also told me to write an essay about impertinence by Monday.'

'I would like to read your essay. You can bring it to my study. And now let's get on with our lesson,' he said.

Over the weekend I wrote my essay. I gave several examples of impertinence, looked up the meaning of it, and contradicted Mrs Lemke by saying that to speak the truth was not impertinence. I had only spoken the truth when I said that I wanted to see whether my plane could fly, and when she said it was the middle of the lesson, I had to contradict her, because when I threw my plane into the air she did not give a lesson, but criticised a pupil who had worked hard. I handed my essay in and got it back two days later with the following remark:

'You have not sufficiently covered the subject, and I do not agree with your remarks.'

She also marked my work with a five, which was a very bad mark, a no pass mark in an examination. I took the essay to the headmaster's study. My work was returned to me via Mrs Lemke. She gave it to me without saying a word, just laying it on my desk. At the bottom of my essay was written:

"A most interesting piece of work which I enjoyed reading." It was signed: Walsdorf, headmaster.

I knew that Mr Walsdorf and Mrs Lemke had talked about me and Ola, but neither of them said anything. Mrs Lemke was a little more patient with Ola, and a bit more careful with remarks to the class for the next few weeks, but then she gradually became her old self again, and whatever she did she never was a popular teacher.

The treatment of the two sisters from Poland by Mrs Lemke showed that not everybody accepted the *Auslandsdeutschen*, or the half Polish people, particularly in the eastern part of Germany. Isa and Ola, having a Polish father, had to apply for German nationality which they eventually received.

More and more men were called up, particularly when Hitler occupied Denmark, part of Norway and marched into France. We had less and less male teachers.

In the autumn of 1940 we older school children had to help on the farms with the harvest. Suddenly we had to practice air raid defence, fire fighting and had lessons in First Aid. Things had become serious. This was the preparation for the Russian war, which started on June 22nd 1941 and was right on our doorstep.

The first bombs were dropped near our school the next day. The mother of one of my classmates got killed and later on her father at the Russian front. The pain and destruction of the war had reached us too. Winter arrived earlier than expected, was the hardest for half a century, and hit the German troops unprepared. They were still in summer uniforms. At school we had to knit balaclavas, mittens, scarves, and collected illustrated papers, which then were posted for Christmas as little gifts to the armed forces in the east.

The cinema was the only amusement we had. I took every opportunity of going to the pictures. My mother came with me sometimes. I was not allowed to neglect my homework, so when my mother curtailed my cinema visits I had to think of a way out. I did a lot of sport, and decided to miss out some attendances at the sports club and go to the pictures instead. Some films were only for adults. We had divisions, and these were sometimes strictly observed, it depended on the management and the size of the cinema. The division was at fourteen and eighteen, in other words, some films were not allowed to be seen by children under fourteen, and others not by young people under eighteen. The woman at the ticket office would sometimes refuse to sell a ticket to young people she thought to be "under age," or ask for proof of age. This was not too bad, when one had not paid, but there were some places which dealt with young people in a different way. They did not query the age of the person when they bought the ticket, but at the interval, which we had between the long *Wochenschau* (news) and the main film, all the lights were put on, and the manager walked along the gangways, looking at the rows, and picking out the people whom he thought were "under age," and told them to leave the cinema. There was no age limit to see the news! One had paid, and couldn't see the main film!

I was only sixteen years old, but I often saw films for the over eighteen's. I usually picked a small cinema in the town for this, arriving a little late, pulling my collar up, and when buying the ticket making sure my hair fell a little over my face to hide how young I really was. I was never sent out, once I sat down at the pictures, but once I was refused entry. The picture was shown in our local big cinema, and when I went to buy the ticket, slightly disguised, with the collar up and my hair in my face as usual, the woman at the office asked me:

'Are you over eighteen years old?'

'Of course I am,' I said indignantly.

'Can you prove it?'

'No.'

'Unless you can prove your age, I cannot sell you a ticket.'

I walked off feeling very cross and embarrassed, especially as I had queued up for some time, and people behind me could hear what was said. I was determined to get into the cinema to see this film. When I got home I looked for Christel to discuss things with her. I often did this, and she sometimes had a good idea, or helped me, even covered for me, as long as she didn't have to lie. She couldn't do this successfully. We decided that the only way I could get into the cinema was to make myself look older. I had a very nice coat with a small fur collar, which looked grown up and elegant. I found one of my mother's hats which fitted quite nicely. It had a small brim and a feather on the side, but was a little tall. The main thing was, it had a veil attached to it, which covered half the face. It looked absolutely super on me, and I fell in love with it.

The trouble was the shoes. I had rather big feet, and as my feet had grown a lot lately, I had to have several pairs of shoes and hadn't had much choice. The last pair my mother was able to get for me were men's shoes, flat, comfortable, practical, but not elegant lady's shoes for somebody with a hat and veil. They were only alright to go to school with, and for everyday use. My mother had several pairs of high-heeled shoes, but they were a little tight on my feet. Still, they had to do. I put them on and started to practice walking with them. Christel laughed her head off. There I was, with an elegant coat and hat, a little lipstick on my lips, stumbling along in these high-heeled shoes. Gradually I got better, but my feet were aching, so we decided I'd better leave the visit to the pictures until the next day. In any case, I had to find a handbag, if possible big enough to hide the shoes and the hat in, because my mother would never let me leave the house dressed up like that! Christel promised to come with me to the back of the cinema, and help me to put on the hat. In return I promised to tell her the contents of the film.

The next day things really went well. My mother was going to be out for the afternoon and evening. She even permitted me to go to the pictures, without asking which film I wanted to see. I left the house with my hat pinned on, and an old handbag from my mother.

Christel and I made our way to the picture house. I must have looked a sight, with my tall little hat and veil, elegant coat, and flat beige shoes. Christel carried the high heeled ones in a paper bag under her arm. We had decided that I would change my shoes at the cinema, and she would take my flat shoes back, so that I only had to walk one way with the tight, high-heeled shoes. I changed my shoes and walked up to the box office for my ticket. There was another woman selling the tickets now who hardly looked at me. I walked, no, I stumbled to the door of the big hall, which was already in darkness. The usherette guided me to a seat with her torch, helping me once or twice when I was stumbling, thinking I could not see in the dark. I was glad to sit down and take my shoes off. They certainly were tight. I saw the news, and then the big lights came on. I was busy fiddling with my handbag, as I didn't want to look up. Some people were leaving, others were coming in. I could hear somebody sitting down behind me. Suddenly, a female voice said:

'Excuse me, but could you take your hat off, it is rather tall, and I cannot see.'

The bright lights were on. The manager would probably go along the aisle in a minute to look at the rows. I couldn't possibly take my hat off until it was dark. I also knew that there was a rule that if people could not see because of a hat, one had to take it off. Then it came to me what to say, and imitating my mother's voice, who spoke a very refined German, I replied:

'Certainly, if it disturbs you. But would you mind if I wait until it is dark again, because I really need to have my hair done, it is so unmanageable, and that's why I have covered it up. I am going to the hairdressers tomorrow.'

I turned my head slightly, hoping she would not look too closely at my young face.

'That's quite alright, don't worry, as long as I can see the film,' came the reply.

The manager had already passed my row, and I had not even noticed it. When the lights were out, I took my hat off, and kept it on my lap, and as

I was afraid that I might lose my shoes which I had taken off, I put these on my lap also. I enjoyed the film, called: *Der Blaufuchs* (The blue fox). It was the story of a young man falling in love with a call girl, who always wore a silver-blue fox. I was able to put my hat on before it was too bright in the cinema and also my shoes. I made my way outside mingling with the crowd.

It was dark outside and had started to rain. I had about a fifteen minute walk home. I wondered whether Christel had come to pick me up after all, bringing my comfortable shoes and my umbrella, but there was no sign of her. I could not risk the hat getting wet, so I quickly took it off and stuck it under the coat. I wobbled off. My feet were soon wet and painful. The shoes were not only too tight, the heels were most uncomfortable too, and I kept on tripping over. There was nothing else for it, I just had to go home barefoot. I took the shoes off and my stockings, because these were in very short supply during the war. I pushed the stockings into my handbag, and the shoes into my coat pocket and ran home. I arrived wet, tired, out of breath and with sore feet.

From time to time my father had big new ideas which had to be put into action straight away. One of his ideas was to have chickens, so that we would always have eggs. Everything was rationed, including eggs. Often, by the time we received them, they were bad, having been stored too long. My mother used to get very upset about this. We were always short of eggs. Sometimes we only got one egg a week per person, and when they were not even fresh and we had to throw them away, my mother got cross. She always felt that the owner of the local dairy did not like us, because we only bought eggs from him, and sometimes the skimmed milk, to which we were entitled. He knew very well that my father supplied us with butter, cheese and milk.

One day, when my mother had a bad egg again, I had to take it back in a cup. Mr Kurz told me he could not replace a broken egg. I told him that the egg was bad, and asked him how we could find out whether it was good or bad without cracking it. All he said again was that he could not replace a broken egg. After that, my father decided to have the chickens. We had a Polish girl, Olga, working for us at the time, and my father said she could help to look after them. We were entitled to one chicken each in the family so, with Olga included, we got seven chickens, and coupons for corn for the seven chickens. Until the chickens started laying we still got our egg allocation.

Christel and I decided to punish Mr Kurz for always giving us the old eggs. Every time my mother used an egg for cooking and baking, we would first make a small hole in the egg and smell it to see whether it was bad. For a while the eggs were alright, and then we had some bad ones again. The smell from the little hole was quite strong. Christel and I went off to the dairy. People usually came early in the morning to get their milk, and we waited until the shop had quite a number of people in it, before we entered it.

'Next please,' said Mr Kurz.

I produced the paper bag with the two eggs, and asked him to replace them, as they were bad.

'How do you know they are bad?' he said. 'I only sell fresh eggs. As soon as I get them, people buy them.'

'Would you like me to show you that they are bad, or will you replace them now whilst they are whole,' I replied.

'There is nothing wrong with these eggs,' he said again, looking at them lying there on the counter. He could not see the little hole on the top. He looked at the woman behind me, and added:

'Everybody knows all my food is fresh.' And then he mumbled: 'These foreigners, complaining all the time.'

With that he had finished with Christel and me, and ignoring us asked:

'Who is next in the line to be served?'

'Mr Kurz, these eggs are bad!' Whilst saying this, I took one of the eggs and threw it on to the counter so that it broke. A terrible smell came out of the egg, and before anybody could say anything I crashed down the second egg. After that Christel and I quickly left the shop and so did a number of customers. Everybody knows that bad eggs have a pungent smell!

The story of the eggs ran like wild fire through the district, and we suddenly discovered that Mr Kurz had been unpopular with several families. People stopped me in the street to tell me that it was good that somebody had at last taught him a lesson. We never entered his shop again. We had the chickens for the eggs, and we got our skimmed milk from another dairy further away.

The chickens started to lay quite well, but when they were not laying we had no eggs at all. My father announced that he would get more chickens. If one had more chickens than one was entitled to, one had to give up extra eggs. This had to be on a regular basis whether the chickens laid a lot of eggs or not. Our neighbour had quite a number of chickens, and told us that sometimes he only had enough eggs for the collection, and hardly any for himself. My father was not deterred. He arrived very late one evening, when it was already dark, and brought in a box of chickens, which he had covered with a blanket to hide them from prying neighbours' eyes.

'Oh no,' my mother said, 'we cannot have these chickens. If the neighbours see more than seven chickens in the garden, they will soon query it.'

'But they won't,' said my father, 'I have worked it all out.'

'Tomorrow morning I will ring the chickens, and let out seven red ringed ones into the garden. By dinner-time, they will have to be changed over with the other seven chickens which have been kept inside.'

'And who is going to do it when you leave again after the weekend?' enquired my mother. 'Where are the chickens going to lay their eggs? And how are we going to feed them, as we only get corn for seven chickens on our coupons?'

There was silence whilst we all looked at my father.

I think I will have to explain now where our chickens lived. My father had a good sized chicken pen built into a corner of the cellar, making use of two walls and the ceiling. The pen was built on posts, to bring it higher up, because the cellar was half below and half above the level of the garden. This allowed the chickens to climb up a small ladder-shaped board, and then get outside through a hole in the wall, which could be closed with a sliding board from outside the pen. The floor of the pen was made from tightly fitting boards. The front was divided into three pieces made from strong wire mesh, surrounded by a wooden frame, of which two were hinged doors. Inside the pen were two perches for the chickens to sit on. At the opposite end from the wall opening were the two egg-laying boxes. The entrance to the chicken pen, the hole in the wall, was under the back stairs, quite a sheltered area, which was enclosed with wire mesh.

This was not big enough for seven chickens to run and scratch around. So my father built a chicken runway along the wall of the house, which continued behind some bushes. It finished in the garden where a certain area was fenced in, to allow the chickens to run and scratch. The top of the chicken run along the wall was made of wood, and as this corner at the back stairs was rather sheltered, we often sat on the chicken run reading, or doing our homework. It was just like a low bench, with half the cellar window still exposed.

My father said the food for the chickens was no problem. He hoped to get some extra corn from some farmers he knew. In any case, he could get potatoes, and chickens liked cooked potatoes and meal. When he was not there, Olga would have to change over the seven chickens in the middle of the day. If Olga was busy, there was always Helga who could do it. I only had to get up a little earlier in the morning to let one lot of chickens out, and when I came back from school I could change them over again.

'Why always me?' I said. 'Why not Sternchen or Christel or Hans?'

'Christel and Hans are too young, but Sternchen could also do it sometimes,' was my father's reply.

Olga, coming from the country, was quite good with the chickens. She showed me how to catch them and hold them, so that they could not flap their wings. The change-over at dinner time was not all that easy, because the chickens didn't want to get back into the cellar. Gradually Olga managed it, and I often helped her.

My mother felt that two lots of chickens were enough, and told my father so. She also could not see how we could move three lots of chickens around. I think even my father had realised what a lot of work the chickens were, because apart from the change-over, there was the cooking of the potatoes to be done. Sometimes we were short of corn and potatoes, and the chickens had to have short rations. They made an awful row when this happened, and we often thought the neighbours must wonder what was the matter with our seven chickens!

Eventually we had a broody hen. She kept on sitting on the eggs, and sometimes it was difficult to get her off them. My mother decided we might as well have some chicks, and we could probably kill them for food. We exchanged some eggs with our neighbour, who had a cock. My mother was at a loss as to where the hen could sit. She couldn't be in the chicken run or the cellar. Eventually my mother got her a space in the attic. She was told that that was quite a good spot, as a broody hen hardly ever went away from her eggs. My mother made the hen a comfortable straw nest, laid paper in front of it and a bowl of water and some corn. She put twelve eggs into the nest. The hen seemed to like her lonely place. Olga or I would go every day to change the water, and the paper when necessary, and see to the food. The hen was quite content, turned her eggs occasionally, but never strayed too far away from the nest when stretching her legs. Eventually we had twelve lovely little chicks, which the whole family enjoyed having. We even fought for the privilege of looking after them and feeding them. Some of them finished up in the cooking pot, and some replaced the badly-laying chickens.

My mother lent a broody hen to our neighbour once or twice, who let her have some honey in return. Honey was impossible to buy, but our neighbour had bees. He was only allowed to keep a proportion of honey and, in return for passing some to the food ministry, he got extra sugar for feeding his bees in the winter.

I always wondered what happened to the honey that was given to the authorities, because we never saw any in the shops.

In May, Olga had to leave, and the responsibility for the chickens was passed on to the only capable person in the family, to me!

My father straight away boosted me up about my capabilities, and my skill in a number of things, and ended by saying:

'You are the only one whom I could trust to be in charge of the chickens. The others will help you, you only have to ask.'

Sternchen and I did not get on very well with one another. We both hated the job. I was in charge, and was responsible for getting it done. I would call Sternchen in the morning to come into the cellar and help me to get seven chickens outside. She was always late and sometimes didn't turn up at all. Her help was a little better at dinner time, because my mother reminded her, and sent her outside to help me.

The chickens had soon scratched all the grass away from the area allocated to them in the garden, and it was not exactly a nice sight so close to the house, but it was war and we had a supply of eggs. The cellar, too, soon started to smell of chickens and chicken droppings. My mother replaced the straw in the nests from time to time, but gradually the perches and the floor in the pen got really thick with the chicken droppings. My father decided to organise the cleaning of the chicken house in the cellar. I knew what that meant! It would probably be me again who had to do the dirty part of the job, and the crawling into the small places! I was able to put it off for two weekends, organising handball games and invitations (in writing!) to some of my school friends, but then my father gave us all two weeks notice, saying that we all had to be prepared to help him to clean the chicken house.

As feared, it was I who had to crawl into the pen, and with a shovel fill a bucket up with the chicken dirt. I handed it to my brother, who climbed up on a box and handed the bucket to Sternchen and Christel through the cellar window. They carried it to the compost heap, emptied it and returned the bucket. In the meantime I had filled up another bucket and handed it to my brother, who then took the empty bucket from my sisters, and gave them the full one.

A human conveyor belt was formed, supervised by my father, who gave my brother a hand from time to time, as it was quite heavy for him to push the bucket through the high cellar window. Every bit of dirt had to be cleaned off in the pen. I felt quite sick when I had finished, because the work was done in a confined space, and the smell, even with the window open, was very penetrating. It hung on my clothes and my hair, and even after I had had a bath I could still smell it.

My father said he felt very proud of me, and for once I received a very generous amount of pocket money. Although I was praised I promised myself that I would never marry a farmer or have my own chickens when I was grown up, and I have kept that promise.

There are two more things I have to tell about our "chicken period." My mother suddenly discovered that the chickens ate the eggs! She found a broken half-eaten egg in the nest. At first my brother was blamed for not crushing the eggshells small enough, therefore giving the chickens a taste of eggs. The chickens got the extra calcium from the egg shells. He assured us that he always made sure the eggshells were finely crushed. Maybe it had not been eaten, but only broken in the nest? To find this out one had to know how many eggs to expect during the day, and compare them with the number collected. My father knew how to find this out, and nobody had to guess who would be allocated that job!

It was me again, and it was no good rebelling, because I had brought home a bad school report, and this was my punishment. I knew very well that even if I had had a better school report I would still have got the job, another excuse would have been found to allocate it to me.

'You have to feel whether the chicken has an egg or not,' said my father.

'How?'

'Lift up the tail and put your finger in it!'

I looked at his laughing face, then walked out of the room.

'If you want to be a doctor, you should not object to it!' he called after me.

My father ringed the chickens with numbers. Then he produced a book, already lined into columns, into which I had to mark every day which chicken number would have an egg. At the bottom I had to add up how many eggs we could expect, and Christel, the egg collector, would write underneath how many were collected.

'This egg testing will also show us which chickens are laying, and which ones only eat the food,' said my father.

'I will be late for school if I have to do all this in the morning. Now I will have to catch fourteen chickens, up till now I only had seven chickens to separate. Sternchen hardly ever helps me, she always comes late into the cellar.'

'This time she will have to help you, I will see to it.' And with that he walked off to find Sternchen.

As a rule I didn't complain to my parents about my sisters or Hans, but Sternchen took advantage of this and hadn't turned up at all in the mornings lately.

My father came back with Sternchen, who looked sheepishly at me.

'She has been told to help you with the chickens.' Then, taking the book where I had to mark in the eggs, he added:

'I am making another column in which you have to mark in Sternchen's attendance every morning and dinner time. How often has she been late?'

'Sternchen hasn't come at all in the mornings for a week. First she was late, then she turned up only occasionally, and now she doesn't come at all in the mornings.'

I looked at my father and could see he was getting cross. I knew what his temper was like, and I suddenly felt sorry for Sternchen so I added:

'She does help me at dinner times.' Even that was only partly true.

My father was furious by now, and Sternchen looked frightened. He really told her off, and praised me at the same time. I think from time to time he realised that although he had four children, it was usually only I who contributed any help to the family. Because of this, the more difficult and heavy jobs were piled on to me, which was unfair. His voice was quite loud, and my mother came quickly from the kitchen. She saw my father in a temper and Sternchen looking frightened at him.

'Now, Hans, calm down,' she said. 'Whatever is the matter?'

He soon told my mother and asked her whether she knew about this.

'Sternchen hasn't been too well lately,' she said, 'and Helga has not complained. She can manage, can't you Helga?'

She looked at me imploringly, knowing that she had to calm my father. She always protected Sternchen. I knew there was nothing wrong with her.

'From now on I have to do extra jobs with the chickens in the mornings,' I replied, 'and Sternchen must help me, otherwise I will be late for school.'

My father did calm down eventually, and reminded me to mark in Sternchen's attendance. He told her that she would be punished if she didn't help. Sternchen was frightened so she turned up every morning. Even so, it took us quite a time, and I often had to skip breakfast so that I wouldn't be late for school.

We found out which chickens were laying eggs, which ones were good layers, and which ones were bad layers, and also that the chickens did not eat eggs. The bad egg layers became boiling fowls, and were replaced, and I was allowed to discontinue the feeling of the chickens after that.

The second and last thing to mention about our chicken period concerns the food, which became more and more difficult to get. The food allocation for the chickens was very low, and even my father couldn't help much. As we had too many chickens, we were in an even worse position than our neighbour, although I always thought that they, too, were cheating a little.

We didn't live far from the River Pregel, where boats arrived from Lithuania and the main ports of Germany. My mother had the idea that I could cycle to the river, and see whether there were some boats which had brought corn, or any other dried food.

'When they unload, they sometimes break a bag,' she said to me, 'and you can pick or sweep it up. The chickens won't object to a little bit of dirt.'

I cycled to the river along the cobbled road of the Holsteiner Damm, with a bag, dustpan and brush, looking for any signs of spillage of corn. There were some big boats moored at the side, but I didn't know what they had brought. There were no big silos here like in the centre of the town. We had one or two mills by the side of the river, where wheat and rye were ground into flour, so this arrived on the boats here first.

Suddenly I saw some maize on the cobbles. I leaned my bike on to a lamppost, got my dustpan and brush out, and swept the maize up. There was quite a bit of maize. My mother was right, somebody had carried a sack of maize with a hole, and some grains had fallen out. The hole must have been small, because my bag was only half full when I got to a closed gate, where the spillage stopped. I returned to my bike, and heard a man calling from one of the boats:

'What are you looking for? Since when do we have young girls sweeping cobble stone roads?'

'I am looking for some food for our chickens,' I replied, 'and have just found some maize. It is not much, but even a little helps.'

'You can come and sweep our boat,' he called out laughingly.

I tied my bike to the lamppost, took my bag, dustpan and brush and walked up the gangway on to the boat. It was the one which had arrived with the maize, and there was plenty of spillage. I started straight away, working with my little brush, sweeping it into the dustpan, and then putting it into the bag. I was afraid the sailor had only made a joke, so I thought if I carried on quickly he would realise that I was serious and desperately wanting the maize. He never said a word, and when I looked up I saw that he was watching me with a little smile. I stood up to straighten my back, and he said:

'It is a big boat, if you keep on sweeping with your little brush you will have to work for days, and will also have a bad back. I'd better find you a big broom.'

'That's alright, don't worry,' I replied, 'I only have a little bag.'

He hardly listened to me but went off. When he returned my bag was already full, and I couldn't see how I could carry any more. But he had thought of everything. He brought me a broom, and a big paper sack.

'There you are,' he said, 'now you can sweep properly. We don't pick up spillage, we usually hose down the deck. It will be done tomorrow morning. So if you want to sweep it today, you are not taking anything away from anybody. Tomorrow morning it all goes into the river.'

I thanked him, but he only laughed. I swept the whole deck, and filled up the paper sack. After that he let me sweep the deck below also, and I filled up another bag. He spliced some ropes whilst I was working, and some of the other sailors returned from their afternoon off in the town. They all laughed, joked, and teased me, but they were good humoured. I was covered in dust from sweeping, my back and arms ached, but I felt happy, because it had been a successful afternoon. I had plenty of maize and dirt.

The trouble now was how to get all this on to my bike. I had difficulties in lifting the paper sack. With so many strong hands around me, it didn't take long to load up the bike. My bag was hung on to the handlebars, and so were the dustpan and brush. The paper sack was tied on to the back luggage carrier, but there was no room for the second bag.

'You will have to come again,' said one of them. 'How far away do you live?'

'I could be back in half an hour if I cycle fast,' I replied.

'Alright then, we will still be here, the boat doesn't leave until the day after tomorrow.'

Once I came back, the sailors tied the sack on to the luggage carrier, and then the nice sailor who had told me to come on to the boat appeared, grinning all over his face, and carrying two small bags filled with maize.

'These have no dust in them. Mix a bit of maize with the corn so that it is not too rich for the chickens, and next time you see us you can bring us an egg.'

He tied the bags on to the handlebars of the bike.

'When are you coming again? I will come and see you.'

'We never know, but it won't be for another three or four weeks.'

I never saw the boat or any of the sailors again, although I cycled there a few times, and I was never lucky again in finding any corn or maize for our chickens from any of the other boats.

My mother, was very pleased indeed, and to reward me she cooked an egg that evening, although I said I didn't want it. She couldn't understand that I was not very keen on eggs ever since I had all that work with the chickens. Even today I rarely eat an egg. I had been forced, although out of necessity, to look after the chickens, and lost a lot of my spare time, which I would have liked to spend on sport, or with a good book, and eating an egg always reminds me of the smell of the chicken house when I had to clean it out.

Again more soldiers were needed, and in the summer of 1942 Königsberg was used as a collecting and assembling point for the new armed forces. We had soldiers from the different satellite countries, Rumania, Hungary, Slovakia and Italy, and there was also a volunteer Spanish division stationed in Königsberg for a time. Most of the soldiers and officers didn't speak German, or had only a limited knowledge of the language. Even so, we young girls had some boyfriends amongst them.

The bombing of west Germany started in May 1942 and children from the bigger cities like Köln, Düsseldorf, Essen etc. were evacuated to East Prussia. We had no bombing in Königsberg because of the limited range of the aircraft in those days.

The battle for Stalingrad was lost on January 30th 1943 when Field Marshal Friedrich von Paulus surrendered the rest of the 6th army to the Russians after five months of the greatest military blood-bath in recorded history. Hitler raged and called von Paulus and his soldiers cowards because his pride was hurt that German troops had surrendered. They should have shot themselves instead. Most of them never returned to their homeland because of the terrible treatment they received as prisoners-of-war.

More and more returned letters with the stamp *Gefallen für Grossdeutschland* (killed for great Germany) across the envelopes arrived at German homes. For the first time a ripple of anxiety went through Germany that maybe the war was wrong and could be lost.

When I was seventeen years old, I fell in love with Herbert, a NCO. in the *Luftwaffe* (Air Force). We met every day for a week in Rauschen, the seaside resort by the Baltic. I had no chance to say goodbye to him before he left for the Russian front. A few weeks later one of my letters was returned with the remark *Gefallen für Grossdeutschland.* I cried, he was only twenty-four years old and full of plans for the future. His laughing face haunted me for a long time. The letter was the first one in a special box which I started then. Many more letters and photographs of dead friends were soon to follow.

In September 1941 I started to go to dancing classes, which was part of the education of well-brought-up girls and boys. We didn't only learn how to dance, but also how to behave correctly and how to dress. Here I met Wolfgang from the boys Grammar School, who became a very special friend. My mother adored him and in her thoughts had already married me off to him. She was forever worried that there would not be enough men left after the war for her three daughters.

My time was divided between school, homework, sport, dancing lessons, boyfriends to meet, letter writing to the ones who were in the army or Air Force, because I was popular and understanding. I neglected my school work, I enjoyed life, and the war and the Nazi party were far away.

At eighteen, in 1942 Wolfgang was called up as officer cadet. At the same time I met Theo, an Air Force sergeant who was shell-shocked. I saw the seriousness of life and what could happen in the war, and suddenly I felt much more mature.

At home we had visits from the SS and realised we were foreigners. My mother had to deal with these visits as my father was only home for weekends and sometimes not even that. Petrol had became very short for civilians. Cars were only allowed for party members, doctors and some very special business people, most of them in uniform. The visits by the SS were very worrying. They looked for arms, papers, anything so that they could accuse us of something, as they thought we must be spies. The house was searched from top to bottom with my mother's beautiful white linen strewn all over the floor, dirtied by black boots.

Wolfgang came home on leave and wanted to get married. The shy young boy had become a man and was afraid he would lose me. He was posted to the Russian front and didn't know when he would come back. I was not ready for marriage. I wanted to finish school and study medicine, something I intended to do since I was quite young. I promised to write to him. We hugged and we kissed. I didn't cry but I had a lump in my throat. He left and I never saw him again.

Although I seemed to be more with boys in those days, I also had one or two girl friends. Next door to us lived Christa Röscher, whose father had a wooden leg.

Christa joined up as a student nurse at the age of sixteen, and was qualified by the time she was eighteen years old. We met again when she came home on leave, and she came to see me, and we talked and talked. I couldn't hear enough about all her experiences. She had travelled all over Europe, being transferred from one hospital unit to another. She had been to France and Greece, and to several places in Germany. I envied her, her experience, her knowledge, and her maturity. She was only one year older than I, but had already seen parts of Europe, whilst I was still at school.

'You envy me my experience,' she said, 'and I envy you your innocence. Nursing during the war is no fun. It is hard work, long hours, seeing mutilated, destroyed, or dead bodies, and the horrors of what war can do. I always think that if some of the generals who send soldiers into battle would work a few days in an army hospital at the front, wars would finish quickly, with a peace treaty rather than battles.'

Christa was disillusioned with the war and with men, but she admired some of the doctors. She found it difficult at home too, because her parents were so much older, and her father, having lost a leg in the First World War, refused to talk about war. Christa was glad to come and see me, to have an excuse to get away from home. She never stayed long with her parents, always saying that she only had a short leave. She confided to me that she often spent a few days with another nurse at her home, because she didn't like to stay with her parents. There was nothing to do at home, and the parents hardly talked. As time went on, Christa's leaves became shorter and shorter, and in the end she didn't come home at all.

The other friend I had was Hilde Lange. We started to know one another because we had the same piano teacher. Hilde had two sisters, one older, Dora, and one younger, Margot. Hilde and I were born in the same year. Her father worked in an office in the town and, when the war broke out, he was called up. He came home occasionally, wearing a sergeants uniform. I didn't see much of him, because the short time he was at home he would not go out much. Hilde and her family lived in a big downstairs flat with a small back garden.

Dora got married in 1939, just after the war with Poland broke out. Her husband was an official in the SA, and had a permanent job with them. He was a devoted Nazi and adored Adolf Hitler. He always wore his SA uniform, black boots, black trousers, and brown shirt and jacket with the swastika arm band. I don't know where Dora lived when she was first married, but suddenly she moved back home. She had already two children by then and was expecting again. Her husband's job was now in the occupied territories of Poland, and Dora didn't find it easy to cope with two young children and the new pregnancy. Mrs Lange wanted to look after her, especially as this time Dora was expecting twins.

Hitler encouraged large families, and everybody in the SA and SS could expect good promotion after the birth of the fourth child. By the time Dora was married four years, she had her four children. The Lange household smelled of cooking, washing, and babies, and there was always one of the children crying or screaming.

Mother and Granny (Dora and Mrs Lange) were responsible for the feeding of the children, the washing and the nappy changing, and the two aunts (Hilde and Margot) took them for walks, and played with them, to give the others a rest. They all adored the children.

Hilde did not go to Grammar School, but eventually went into a draper's shop as an apprentice. Hilde was good at sewing and knitting, and often knitted a garment, or embroidered a tablecloth to be sold in the shop where she worked, giving her extra money. She was a pretty, tall, and very thin girl. She was terribly unhappy about her figure.

'I don't mind being tall,' she said, 'and I hope to put on weight all the time and fill out a little. But what upsets me is that I have no bosom. I try and eat a lot, but because of the food rationing the only things that are plentiful are potatoes, and all I get from eating them is a *Kartoffelbauch* (potato tummy).

She was envious of me, because I had developed early, and already wore a brassiere by the age of fourteen. Hilde used to commiserate with my sister Astra, who also didn't seem to develop a bust. The two of them used to have whispered conversations, and by eavesdropping once or twice, I discovered that Hilde recommended a cream to Astra, which would help with the development of the bust. Astra didn't make friends easily, but for a time she was very pally with Hilde, and I know it was only so that she could borrow the "Wondercream." I am afraid it did nothing for Astra. Even my parents remarked that it was most unusual for a girl to develop a bust so late. My mother tried to be kind to Astra, saying that it would grow, there was plenty of time, but my father was very cruel sometimes. I always remember what he used to say about Astra and her chest:

Sie hat ein Brett mit Wartzen. (She has a board with warts).

Hilde was different, the cream worked! I had not seen her for a time, and when I met her pushing the pram with her nephew in it, I could see straight away that Hilde had more shape. She had a tight pullover on, and her bosom was sticking out. It was not as big as mine, and seemed to be much rounder, but it certainly had grown. Hilde kept on laughing when I remarked how wonderful it was that the cream had worked. She assured me it would get even bigger. She actually could feel it growing. I thought the process had happened rather quickly. I told Astra about the "Wondercream," but she said it was silly, she would never stoop so low as to use a cream, and interfere with nature. Although she said this, I knew for a fact that she had tried it.

When I met Hilde again her bust was even bigger, just like mine, and she wore the same size brassiere as me. She was very proud of her figure now, and also started to wear high heel shoes.

There was more to the story of Hilde's bosom. I passed her house one day as she was looking out of the window. She called out:

'Come in the garden, I haven't seen you for ages.'

I went in, but said I didn't have much time. We sat on the garden bench. Dora's two little children were playing in the sand-pit, and Hilde told me about her boyfriend.

'Fritz is in the tank division. He is twenty years old and very much in love with me,' she said. 'Promise you won't tell anybody, but we are secretly engaged.'

'I am so pleased, Hilde, I hope you will be very happy. But you are only seventeen years old. Don't you think that is a bit young?'

'That's why it is a secret. I couldn't tell my parents, they would say the same. We not getting married until the war is over.'

'Let's hope this will be soon.'

The children in the sand-pit started to throw sand, and one of them got it in his face and eyes, and started to scream. Hilde jumped up and picked the little boy up, hugging and kissing him, and trying to clean his eyes. I watched her and thought:

She is like a mother to the little one, and her face is so full of love and caring.

And then I noticed it.

'Hilde, what has happened to your bosom! It has moved to the side!'

One of her busts had moved towards her armpit, getting dislodged through cuddling the little boy.

'Ah well,' she said, 'you might as well know it.'

And with that, she put her hand under her pullover, and took half the bust out and showed it to me. It was a ball of wool.

'Hilde, how could you do that! And I even told my sister Astra that the cream worked.'

'Actually, I have a bit of bosom, but not as much as you. My mother warned me that this might happen. It's a good thing it was you who saw it, and not Fritz. Maybe I had better finish with the wool imitation.'

'Don't you think Fritz will notice that your bust has shrunk?'

'I could wear a loose blouse for a time. In any case, I won't see him for a bit, as he is in training.'

Hilde stuck to Fritz, and when she was eighteen years old she got officially engaged. I, too, was introduced to him. He was a nice chap, very young, very smart in his uniform, well-spoken, but not quite the person I had expected to choose a girl like Hilde. He obviously came from a far superior home background to hers, with his father being the headmaster of a *Grundschule*. (Secondary School). Hilde was a very pretty girl, honest, clean, loving, smartly dressed and quite clever, but she still was only a shop girl. The Germans stuck to their own class as a rule, and a headmaster's son and a shop girl didn't really mix. I knew there might be trouble, especially when Hilde explained that Fritz hadn't told his parents about the engagement yet.

'We are going to wait until Fritz has proper leave, and then we are going to Berlin to see his parents,' said Hilde.

She was very excited, and the young couple looked so happy. Mrs Lange gave them a little party in November 1942, to celebrate the engagement, and Hilde asked me to come along too. I gave them a bottle of wine as a present, which was difficult to get. Mr Lange had come home, but Dora's husband could not get time off to come back to Königsberg.

After that, Fritz was posted to Russia, and Hilde waited for his letters. She wrote every two or three days, but Fritz's letters were irregular. He wrote how cold it was, and asked Hilde to post him some warm socks and scarves. Hilde started knitting straight away.

Just after Christmas, Hilde came to see me. I was very surprised, because although I knew Hilde and we were friendly and neighbourly, met in the street, and sometimes sat in the garden, we did not really invite one another, or visit one another, we were not such great friends. I took Hilde upstairs to my bedroom. I felt she wanted to tell me something. She looked cold and pale, and a little frightened. She suddenly said:

'I think I am going to have a baby.'

I looked at her aghast. To have a baby, and not to be married, was a terrible thing. In a lot of stories I had read, parents threw their daughters out of the house if they were pregnant. Families could never live down the sting. Poor Mrs Lange already had Dora and four young children in the flat, and now Hilde.

'Have you told Fritz?' I said. 'He is the father, isn't he?'

'Yes, he is the father. We are engaged, of course, but, but ...' She looked at me with unhappy eyes.

'I feel terrible in the mornings. Just like Dora did, and my mother keeps on looking at me. I think she knows, but doesn't want to know. It is my father that I am frightened of.'

After a minute or two she suddenly laughed, although tears were running down her cheeks, and added:

'The funny thing is, I always wanted a big bosom, and now I can feel it swelling up, and it is really big even without the wool.'

'Oh Hilde,' I said, 'you can still joke. You'll see, it will be alright. Fritz loves you. You will have to write to him straight away, and when he comes on leave you will have to get married.'

I remembered what I had heard on the radio recently, and said:

'Maybe you could get married by proxy. I heard that this could be done. There was a programme about it on the radio the other day, and I have also seen it on the newsreel. A certain day and time is set for the marriage. Fritz has to sign the papers at that particular moment in front of two officers, and you do it here, either at the registry, or the war ministry office. You will have to enquire and tell Fritz about it. But I think, first of all you will have to tell your mother. Why don't you talk to Dora. She had four children, she should understand.'

'Dora is married. That is a big difference. I will find out about the proxy marriage, that is an idea, and you are right, I will have to tell my mother. You will still talk to me, won't you?'

'Of course I will, you know that.'

'I am glad I have talked to you. Shall I tell you something, I am looking forward to having Fritz's baby. I always have to help with Dora's babies, now I am going to have one of my own.'

Hilde told Dora first, and then the two of them told her mother. She wrote to Fritz, who replied that they would get married on his next leave. The proxy marriage was not possible, because Fritz was on the front, fighting, and moving about.

Soon all the neighbours knew that Hilde was expecting a baby, but things were suddenly different. She was not ostracised, people were very kind to her, and enquired when Fritz would get leave, or had she heard from him. Hilde kept on going to work. She had finished her apprenticeship, and was now employed in a bigger store in the town, to where she travelled by tram. There was only one thing that bothered her, and that was that she hadn't heard anything from Fritz's parents. Fritz had written to tell her that he would write to his parents, telling them about the forthcoming wedding when he had his next leave. He also said he would ask his mother to write to Hilde.

'I don't think Fritz has told his parents about the baby,' said Hilde. 'They probably don't want him to get married, particularly to a girl they have not even met.'

'I don't think that matters,' I assured her. 'You are both of age, and can do what you like.'

The fighting in Russia was not the same any more in 1943. The war had gone on too long. By the time the rains came in early March, everything sank into the mud. The Russians now received supplies from the United States and Great Britain. They were better equipped and had more planes. The Germans needed their *Luftwaffe* for counterattacks, following the air bombardments in the main part of Germany.

There was one big battle near Kursk, which was predominantly a tank battle. The Germans had two new tanks, the Tiger and the Panther, but they were not as good as the Russian tanks. The battle was very fierce, destroying a great number of tanks. It was lost by the Germans, and called the graveyard of the great Panzer army. The Germans never recovered from it.

Fritz had been training with a new tank and when Hilde heard about the battle and did not get any letters from him, she got very worried. She kept on writing, particularly as by now she was quite big with the baby. I helped her to write a letter to Fritz's parents, as she said her spelling was not very good. She only said in it that she was worried about him, as she had heard about the battle, and hadn't had any news from him. She did get a short reply. The parents, too, had not heard from Fritz. They promised to let her know if they received news, and asked her to inform them if she got a letter first.

It must have been at the end of April or beginning of May when Hilde received the terrible news that Fritz had got killed. The parents, as next of kin, had been informed by the military command that their son had died for the honour of Grossdeutschland. They had a memorial service for Fritz in Berlin, and posted printed cards to inform their relatives and friends. One of these was posted to Hilde. She was shattered, and wouldn't leave the house for days. Margot, her sister, came to call on us, and asked me to come and see her.

'She won't eat much,' said Margot. 'She just sits there and reads his letters, and then looks at the card with the announcement of his death. My mum says it will harm the baby. Maybe you could snap her out of her grief. She won't go to work either.'

I went to see Hilde and was quite shocked when I saw her. She was very calm, too calm actually, and she had changed. She suddenly reminded me of her mother. She seemed older, her face had lost the young childish look. She was more like a woman, and when she spoke she chose her words carefully, not bubbling everything out like she used to do. She listened to what I had to say, and looked at me resigned as if she wanted to say: 'I have heard all this before.'

But I must have said something to arouse her, because she suddenly took a deep breath and said:

'It is alright, you know, I am thinking of the baby, and I am glad I am going to have it. Mum said there is no worry about money. The baby's clothes will come from Dora, she has plenty, and her husband is getting everything organised so that I get help, because I am having a "War baby." There are lots of them about, and I am going to a meeting next week, to get to know some of the other girls with babies. It is the thought of never seeing Fritz again, and that the baby has no father. I am not going to live on "hand-outs." Mum and Dora will look after him, and I can go back to work and earn my own money. I will soon be up for promotion at the store. The manageress is very pleased with me.'

'You call the baby him, are you sure it will be a boy?'

'Oh yes, and I am going to call him Friedrich, Fritz for short, like his father and grandfather.'

'Have you told Fritz's parents about the baby?'

'No, I don't think they are interested. They only sent the announcement with nothing else, not even a sympathetic note, or a sentence on the back of the card. I think that they never wanted Fritz to marry me.'

"You should tell them about the baby. They are going to be grandparents. Fritz was the only child, maybe it will make a difference in their outlook concerning you.'

'I might do it later, not just now. If I want help with the letter, I will come to you.'

This time she didn't ask, will you help me? She made decisions and informed me. That was good, she had matured, and would now get on and cope with things and life, a woman rather than a young girl.

Hilde had her baby in August 1943, and after a week Margot, her sister, came and asked me to go and see her. Hilde looked very happy, and the baby was lovely. It was a boy, just as Hilde had said. She asked me to help her to write a letter to Fritz's parents. Hilde had been to several meetings with young mothers whose husbands or fiancés had got killed. She had discovered that one could get married to a killed soldier posthumously if one had a baby and the grandparents recognised it, or proved through letters from the father of the child, that he had intended marriage.

'I have got the letters,' said Hilde, 'but, of course, it would help if Fritz's parents would speak up also.'

So we set out a letter explaining things, and asking whether Fritz had informed the parents about his forthcoming wedding, and whether he mentioned that Hilde was pregnant.

The reply to this letter was like a bombshell! Hilde could not believe what she read. She came to see me with the letter in her hand.

'Look at this,' she said. 'Read it. It is the reply to my letter to Fritz's parents.' And she gave me the letter.

The mother wrote to say that Fritz had informed them that he intended to marry Hilde, but he never mentioned anything about the baby. When he got killed they were terribly upset and thought that this, of course, would also be the end of the relationship with Hilde. They never realised that they could be grandparents one day, but had just lived from day to day with the pain of having lost their only son. They would like to welcome Hilde with open arms as their daughter-in-law, and if she could possibly travel with the baby and come to Berlin, they would make the arrangements there for a posthumous marriage. Maybe they could even have the christening in Berlin, as they missed the engagement party. They included some money for Hilde's journey, and for the baby, and hoped Hilde would not be offended.

It was a very warm-hearted letter by a mother who had suffered and suddenly saw a straw to hold on to. Her son, although dead, had a child, and she wanted that child, and would therefore also accept the mother who had borne that little boy. I don't think that I realised all that at the time. Hilde and I were two young girls who didn't really reason everything out. We were happy to hear that Hilde would be married after all, and little Fritz would carry his father's name.

Hilde travelled to Berlin but returned before Christmas. She was now a married woman, with a widow's pension, and little Fritz had had his christening. Hilde said the grandparents were very nice, but she was afraid that the grandmother wanted to keep the baby.

'I thought I had better come home,' she said. 'The grandparents are too possessive. If I hadn't been feeding the baby they might have taken him for good. In any case, I was homesick, I had nobody to talk to. There is also a lot of bombing going on, and we had to keep on going into the air raid shelter. I am better off at home. I might go and visit them again later, or when the war is over.'

Hilde told us about the bombing in Berlin. The capital was not the only town that suffered. Hamburg too was gradually devastated by Allied strategic bombers, through day and night attacks. People started to flee the cities. Stalingrad had been a disaster, and the German people mourned, but the town was on the Volga, and hundreds of miles away. Hamburg was on the river Elbe, in the heart of Germany.

In August 1943, there suddenly came the realisation that there could be a possible defeat, particularly when more and more towns which had specialised factories were bombed.

CHAPTER FOUR

Some War Facts - Radio Station

I finished school in the Spring of 1942 but was not allowed to start at university unless I did some *Kriegsdienst* (war service).

I worked for three months as a waitress and three months as a conductress on the tram. Both jobs were hard, but I enjoyed the time. I learnt something new, met a number of different people and was shown in this way what work was really like.

The Grammar Schools for boys and girls were close together, and because of this I had a number of boyfriends. They had to join up very young. Most of them started as officer cadets at the age of seventeen or eighteen. Ernst started as my pen-friend and got killed a year later. Soon after that a letter addressed to Theo, my shell-shocked Air Force friend, was returned marked *Gefallen für Grossdeutschland*.

On the day I started at university the news came that two more of my friends had got killed. By now I had lost five young friends and my box started to get filled with the letters and photos of them. The next one was Helma, a neighbour's boy with whom I had played ever since we moved to Königsberg. His destroyer was sunk. He was only eighteen. He knew he would die when we met last.

We had a very big house and garden in Königsberg and my mother found it difficult to cope with the housework and four children. The only help one could get were foreign girls from Poland or Russia. We had different Polish girls and one or two hilarious experiences as they were not used to a modern household like ours. They were frightened to see hot water coming out of taps and terrified of the noise when the toilet chain was pulled. Sascha, a Russian girl, was the last one we had. When she discovered we were Swiss, she became our friend and couldn't do enough for us. She joined us for our last Christmas in our house in 1943.

It was a very cold winter and in my Christmas Holiday I had to work again as conductress on the trams. The newsreels showed the soldiers in Russia all dressed up like mummies with ice hanging on their eyebrows, beards and the openings in their balaclavas. The temperature there was 30 to 40 below zero and it seemed impossible that people could cope in such cold weather. There was not much fighting because the fuel was frozen and the tanks had to be dug out every few days.

All medical students had to spend their free time working in a military hospital, particularly at the weekend. We learnt what the war was like in Russia through talking with the patients and seeing their wounds. There were soldiers without toes, without fingers, without ears. They had either broken off in the frost or they were amputated because of gangrene.

The Russian offensive started in June 1944 and we had a number of reconnaissance flights over Königsberg. A few bombs were dropped. My parents evacuated some of our better furniture to a small town and my mother left to stay with her brother and family in Tuchel, taking with her the family silver. My sister Christel joined the Red Cross because her school class was closed. Everybody over sixteen years of age had to do some war work or they would not receive food coupons. My other sister, Astra, after finishing her training, was put in charge of the diet kitchen in the Barmherzigkeit Hospital. So that I was not living alone, Gitta, a university friend came to live with me. Her father was killed in the Polish war, one of her twin brothers got killed in France and the other one was missing. Her mother had a nervous breakdown and was in a sanatorium. Gitta was glad of my company.

On a visit to my mother in Tuchel I met Hermann, an army officer, who was a doctor of physics and chemistry and worked on the V-1 and V-2. He was very German and thirteen years older than myself. He fell in love with me straight away. He was stationed not far from Tuchel where the V-2 had a practice range. We met every day, driving around in his open car. He proposed after two weeks, even asked my father for my hand in marriage. I was flattered, I was impressed, but I was not in love. I told him I would like to meet his family first.

Back in Königsberg the war became really serious for us. We had now to put up with several bombardments. When the anatomy building was destroyed our studies stopped, and we had to work full time in the military hospitals. Gitta, my friend, left and joined the *Luftwaffe* as air force helper. Astra, whose hospital was bombed out went to stay with my mother. She wasn't feeling very well, and complained about dizziness and shortness of breath. My mother brought her to the south of Germany to

Oberstdorf to live in the mountain air for a time. She returned for a short visit to Königsberg and tried to persuade Christel and me to join her in Tuchel so that we could get away from the bomb attacks in Königsberg. When we refused she gave me a small phial with cyanide and had a serious talk with me.

The Red Army had come closer and had already entered East Prussia. We heard from the wounded soldiers how the Russians raped the women and shot or clubbed the men to death. My mother was afraid. She made me promise that I would look after Christel, even if we had to leave the town.

I made a short trip to Greifswald to see Hermann's parents, but I did not like them. My mother begged me not to finish with Hermann who was such an eligible future son-in-law. She was trying to marry me off.

In November we had another big bombing attack on Königsberg and I was buried in the local air-raid shelter for hours. When the doors were eventually opened there were a lot of dead women, children and old men in the back of the bunker. They had died because of lack of oxygen. A mass grave was dug next to the church and many familiar faces from our neighbourhood were buried there. We had no flowers, but covered the big heap of earth with branches and greenery from the hedges. We made little crosses from twigs, putting on them messages to the loved ones. Family Lange and all the children were evacuated into the country. I received the news that Gitta my friend had got killed. Nobody told her mother. Her mind was already too confused after the loss of her husband and two sons. I informed her aunt and uncle.

In December the work in the hospital increased and medical supplies became so short that we had to use paper bandages. The wounded arrived in cattle trucks. There were hundreds of them every day. I kept my mind blank and picked out the ones who were still alive and needed attention. Some of them were no more than seventeen years old. They were children and often already maimed for life with the loss of arms or legs. Many times I stayed the night in the hospital as there was no time to travel home. I always kept in contact with my sister Christel.

My mother wrote to say that she was worried about my father. She hadn't heard from him for a long time and she was afraid. She told Christel and me that she had to travel to Oberstdorf to see my sister Astra as she had met a man who wanted to marry her. She promised to be back for Christmas. We, too, hadn't heard anything from my father or from my brother who had been evacuated with his school into the country. I realised that the Russians were nearer to Königsberg than we were told, because refugees started arriving in the town.

Christmas passed and there was no news from anybody except Hermann, who wrote a letter from Greifswald. In the New Year some of the hospitals were evacuated and the wounded brought to Pillau harbour to be shipped back to the main part of Germany. That meant that the Russians were trying to encircle Königsberg. It was time that I left too. Through a misunderstanding I lost contact with Christel and had to start my flight as a refugee alone.

In January, most of the preparations by the people to hold back the Russians were useless, because there were no soldiers to occupy the fortifications. Hitler had sent more and more divisions to fight the Allies in the west.

The Red Army was a tremendous fighting machine when they entered East Prussia, determined to repay the Germans in their own kind for their Russian policies. The result of this was the great flight of the civilian population to the west in the worst German winter on record.

All roads and paths were covered with refugees. Snakes of carts, people and animals pushed slowly forward. As soon as the snow clouds cleared Soviet fighter planes appeared, dropping their bombs on to the helpless columns. In the north everybody was on the march to Pillau, the Baltic harbour. Anybody reaching the port had some hope of getting away from the oncoming wall of the Russian might by boat. In the south the Russians made their way to the industrial complex of Schlesien (Silesia). Many people believed the propaganda given out by Hitler and Goebbels that the Russians had been stopped. Instead they surprised unprepared villages and ransacked them, raped women and young girls, and shot or hanged the men. There was plunder, devastation, violation and abduction.

There were two places our family had always talked about, which we thought would be safe from the Russians: Tuchel, where my mother was with her brother's family and Greifswald where Hermann's family lived. I decided to make my way to Elbing where the Swiss Embassy was, and after that to Tuchel. I discovered there were no more trains from Königsberg. It was bitterly cold, fifteen degrees below zero, and even with my blanket wrapped over my head and around me I couldn't get warm. I joined a trek of people who started to walk westward, because we had been told that we could cross the frozen Haff and get to the Frische Nehrung, the small landstrip dividing the Baltic and the Frische Haff.

Walking along the Nehrung one could reach Danzig (Gdansk) and a ship to the west, or I could branch off to Tuchel.

Our column consisted of horse-drawn wagons and carts, prams, bicycles, sledges, motorbikes and people, people, people. At night I slept in barns or just leaning against a cart. My food gradually ran out, nobody shared. People had become selfish. Nobody knew how long the journey would last. Most people were in groups, mothers with children and relatives or friends together. I was alone and lonely. I got my first hot drink in Brandenburg and then carried on to Heiligenbeil. The road was marked with abandoned goods and frozen bodies of people and horses. Anybody unable to walk just dropped by the side and died, joining those shot by the Russian planes.

In Heiligenbeil I joined up with two wounded soldiers, Max and Friedrich. We made our way to the Haff and realised how close the Russians were when we saw the fires from the burning villages behind us at night. For the first time I felt scared. On top of that I was shivering with cold and I was hungry. At night the three of us huddled together trying to get some warmth from one another. We crossed the frozen Haff. It was a nightmare. There were sunken carts, horses that had frozen to death after breaking through the ice, and frozen bodies lying in grotesque positions on the ice. The Russians shot at us and the ice broke. I lost my sledge with my suitcase, but Max and Friedrich saved me from falling into the water. From now on I only had my rucksack and my satchel.

We walked along the rough and sandy Nehrungsroad. The Russian artillery shot at us from the other side of the Haff. It took us three days to get to Kahlberg. Friedrich got a lift in a lorry to Gotenhafen (Gdingen) because of his wounded leg. By now it was quite black. Outside the town we were shocked to see open lorries full of wounded soldiers covered with thin blankets and snow, a number of them were dead. There was no petrol to take them any further.

I discovered that I could not go to Elbing or to Tuchel, because the Russians had cut off the route to the west. In Steegen Max and I got a lift in a lorry, which was attacked by Russian fighters. We were able to jump off the lorry before it was hit and burnt out. We warmed ourselves on the hot lorry and I cried for the soldiers and the lieutenant who had died. After that we walked again, hiding ourselves in the snow when we saw planes. We joined any trek going west. Food became very short and sometimes there were fights in the refugee trek, when somebody tried to steal some potatoes from the people with carts and wagons, who still had food. I gradually became so weak that I didn't want to walk any more. I didn't even feel any hunger pangs; I was just weak. Max peeled off the dark bark from a tree and cut some of the white wood from underneath and told me to chew it and then swallow it so that my stomach had something to work. All I remember was that it hurt my teeth.

In Schlawe there were soup kitchens and we queued up twice. Max organised some bread. Two days later we came to the village of hell. What we saw there was so inhuman, so cruel and shocking that for months afterwards I would wake up at night in a sweat, when the picture of it had intruded into my dreams. All my life I have pushed it into the background.

It was a village where the Russians had been and behaved like savages, like animals. Even today I feel sick thinking of it. For the first time I touched my little phial of cyanide which my mother had given me and which I wore around my neck. I swore that no Russian would get near me as long as I was alive. I stumbled out of that village and Max followed me.

Max had been involved in a fight when trying to get some bread. Somebody had hit him in his stomach with an iron bar. When he started to spit blood I knew he was very ill. I was able to get him on to a hospital train in Kolberg. I was pushed off the train by the SS which had taken over the town and were looking for deserters. The next morning I was shocked to see men hanging from lampposts and trees with placards around their necks calling them deserters. It was a sickening sight. German people were killing German people. Life was not sacred any more.

At Kolberg station I was able to jump on to a train which was taking party members and their luggage to Stettin. We were attacked by Russian tanks and it was touch and go whether the train would be fast enough to escape. The tanks were big and cumbersome and the soldiers bad shots. The train got away.

I slept in a refugee camp in Stettin and had my first cold shower for over six weeks. I was shocked when I took my clothes off to see how thin I was. At night I got bitten by *Wanzen* (bugs), my chest hurt and I had developed a bad cough. I did manage to struggle on to a train to Greifswald the next day. I didn't realise that I was already very ill by then. People found me on the platform in Greifswald and brought me into hospital. They had to burn my clothes and cut my hair because it was so matted.

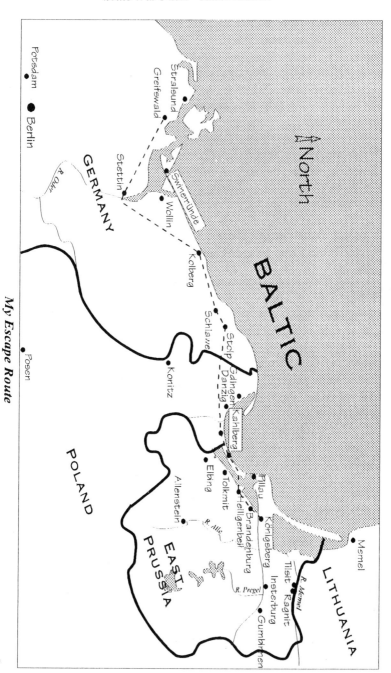

My Escape Route

I found my mother in Greifswald. We got a lift on an open lorry to Hamburg, but we never got there. Spitfires shot at us. We were able to jump off with part of our luggage, before the lorry was hit. We finished up at a nearby farm, and stayed there until the war ended in May 1945. I milked the cows and helped in the fields and my mother did the cooking and some sewing. When the British occupied the village, we moved into the hayloft.

During March and April some of the generals hoped for a special peace in the west with England and America, and then total concentration on the eastern front to halt the Russians, but Hitler was dead against it. The generals only put out feelers, because talking about it openly to Hitler would have been impossible, as they would have been called traitors.

To the south, in the Danube valley, the Soviets at last conquered Budapest, and Vienna was taken in the middle of April.

The Americans advanced into Sachsen (Saxony) and Thüringen (Thuringia), and Montgomery, with the British Army, was 60 miles from Berlin in April. Although the Russians were nowhere near the capital, Eisenhower abandoned the idea of taking Berlin, and the troops were ordered to divert to the south, in order to divide Germany.

The link up of US and Red Army forces happened on April 21st at Torgau on the river Elbe, south/east of Berlin. The British forces met the Soviets in Wismar, on the Baltic. The meeting went off happily, with toasts of vodka and wine, a lot of back slapping, and fumbled phrases in foreign languages.

On April 16th, the Russians pushed forward along and over the River Oder and Neisse. They bombarded the Germans for hours. The people in the Oderniederung (valley of the Oder), together with the refugees from the east, started to flee.

The treks, which had come from East Prussia, Schlesien, Westpreussen, Pommern and Neumark, rolled again, and the west side of the Oder was over full with people. Most of them could not find a place to stay, so they went on, often without a plan, north or south. The treks lay in woods, or on fields, either because they had no horses, which sometimes were taken away from them by the army, or because they were tired of asking for a place to stay, or because with all their worries, poverty, and wishful thinking of better days, they still believed the news in the papers and the radio, that the Soviet army was now at last broken on the River Oder and Neisse, and would never cross these. They believed it until they heard the gunfire and, although some of them started off again, it was often too late, and they were overtaken by the Russians, who treated the refugees in the same way as they did everywhere.

The Soviets reached the capital on April 22nd and three days later, Berlin was surrounded.

The war now had reached a stage where everybody who could move their limbs had to do some kind of war work. Every male, even the boys from the Hitler Youth, had to join the fighting.

The quality of the German troops varied enormously. There were hardened SS and Waffen SS men, some from the once conquered territories, who now, where the tide had turned, could not return to their countries. They fought with a great disregard for their own lives.

Then there were the *Volkssturm*, or German Home Guard, composed of tired old men, and frightened young boys, ill armed, poorly clothed, and completely without training. There were only a few troops who had been in different campaigns, and had equipment and experience. They huddled in misery and fear, manning suicidal defence positions. And behind the lines roamed the SS, carrying out executions of would be falterers and deserters.

The area where the war was actually fought now lay in ruins. It was not so bad in the countryside, as they were areas that had been bypassed by the fighting and bombing, but the cities were heaps of rubble. Railways were lines of craters and twisted rail, bridges were down, canals and rivers blocked, dams blown up, and electrical power grids destroyed. The German Homeland was utterly devastated.

Because Königsberg was my home town, I would like to tell what happened to it, and to show how lucky I was to have escaped.

All we heard at the time of the war was that the town had surrendered on April 9th, against Hitler's wishes. General Lasch, not having obeyed Hitler, was condemned to death by hanging. Over his family *verhängte* Hitler *Sippenhaft*. (This means liability of all members of a family for the crimes of one member).

It was after I left that General Lasch was put in charge of the so-called "fort" of Königsberg on January 28th 1945. He organised food for the civilians, after most of the party bosses had suddenly disappeared. He collected the animals which had come with the refugee treks, and gradually slaughtered them. Suddenly there was meat and milk for the sick and for the children. General Lasch collected all soldiers and officers and re-grouped them. Everything was done to defend Königsberg. Soldiers and tanks left from different Divisions were put together. The HJ joined in at the beginning of February. Fourteen to fifteen year old young boys got trained. They were very enthusiastic, and the old experienced soldiers took these boys under their wings. Most of them couldn't have steel helmets as they were too big for them, and fell over their eyes when they were shooting, but at least they had winter uniforms. As extra rations they didn't get cigarettes and alcohol, but chocolate and sweets!

Special commandos were empowered to punish looters and thieves. Not only the foreign workers, who had quite a bit of freedom had become thieves, but also German men and women.

The last train out of the town was on January 22nd, and a week later the sound of the sirens told the civilians of the town that this was the last notice they would get to leave Königsberg.

The Russians surrounded the city, but took their time as they did not know how strongly the town was fortified. In the town were about 130,000 civilians, Russian and French prisoners-of-war, foreign workers from the satellite countries, some soldiers, and the *Volkssturm*, most of whom didn't even have a uniform. Some of the soldiers, tired of fighting, cold, disheartened, and without ammunition, disappeared into the cellars of empty buildings.

It was the division of young soldiers who stormed Metgethen to take it back again. This was the small village in the wood where we used to pick blueberries. Here they found the bodies of plundered old men, women, and children, often frozen into lumps by the roadside. At the station were wagons in the marshalling yard full of people who had tried to get away on the last train. They were shot, and the women's clothes were slit open. There was not one house that wasn't looted. Furniture was smashed and thrown into the streets. A few people crawled from the cellars and barns, and the soldiers found girls in the wood, who had hidden themselves, and whose hands and feet were black from frost. About seventy women, having been raped again and again, were freed, also a few men. The rest had been taken on a march to Russia, which probably hardly anybody reached.

The German propaganda from the Königsberger *Rundfunk* (radio) still told people that a new weapon would come, and that a number of German divisions were on their way to help the beleaguered town. They would hit the enemy in the back.

At Easter time it was quiet and the people believed that the German offensive had stopped the Russians. They felt optimistic again. Cinemas and restaurants opened, also shops with little to buy. General Lasch knew that if the Russians attacked he would not be able to hold the town. He had hardly any ammunition, and no planes. The big Russian Air Force soon realised that the anti-aircraft guns didn't shoot.

Everybody thought that the Russians had moved back, because of the big silence - no guns, no planes, no sirens. The weather, unusual for the time of year, was mild, and the lilies of the valley and the violets were in bloom. It was the last calm before the storm.

The last battle for the town started in the early hours of April 6th. The air above Königsberg was filled with a terrible noise, which made the town tremble. Hundreds of Soviet batteries, and any amount of rocket launchers, started a fire hurricane, which lasted, on and off, for thirty hours. At the same time, Soviet planes bombed the town. Marshal Wassilewski pushed through from the north/west, through Juditten and Metgethen, and the weak German units were destroyed or gave way. Whole companies and Volkssturmeinheiten were buried in a few hours in their dugouts. Communication between the companies was broken, and most of the few ammunition depots that were left were destroyed. The Paradeplatz, in the centre of the town was in *Trümmern* (ruins). Shot up vehicles lay everywhere, and amongst them dead horses and dead people, and nobody took them away. It was impossible to bury the dead, or to extinguish the fires. The wounded bled to death, because there was nobody to care for them. The people who were left tried to find shelter in the ruins, or just waited, numb and silent, for the end.

300,000 Soviets fought against 35,000 German soldiers over Königsberg. General Lasch hoped to save more bloodshed. He sent a message to headquarters that the battle for Königsberg was at an end because the last of the ammunition was shot and the warehouses with food burnt to the ground. He asked Hitler for permission to leave the town. This was refused, because Hitler wanted a heroic finish.

On April 9th, General Lasch sent a messenger to the Russians. He realised that there was no point in prolonging the fighting. After months of being besieged, he surrendered the burnt out town to the merciless Russian soldiers. He asked them to take over the care of the wounded and the civilians.

The Russians promised in the capitulation document: respect for life, care of the wounded and civilians, enough food, good treatment for every officer and soldier as prisoner and, at the end of the war, return to the homeland or a land of their choice.

None of these promises was fulfilled. For two days the Russian soldiers were allowed the freedom of the town. Often drunk, they plundered everything, raped the women and killed everybody who didn't obey.

This was the end of 700 years of history and western culture. It was not the Russian officer, the Russian merchant, the Russian scholar, the western Russian, who eventually occupied Königsberg, but a dismal foreign power from the depth of Asia.

On the day of capitulation there were still 30,000 soldiers, 15,000 foreign workers and more than 100,000 civilians left in Königsberg. General Lasch didn't return from captivity until 1955, ten years after the end of the war. His family, by a miracle, was then still alive. He wrote a book about the fall of Königsberg: "So fiel Königsberg," which was a revelation.

Hitler was under the impression that Erich Koch, the *Gauleiter* (district leader), who was responsible for the civilian population of East Prussia, was in Königsberg. He had left, and was living in Pillau, still very affluent and comfortable. Erich Koch informed Hitler about General Lasch, the traitor, and told him that he and his party members would carry on with the fighting. As soon as Erich Koch heard about the battle of Berlin, he decided that it was time to find a place of safety. He had had his Fieseler Storch (small aeroplane) and an icebreaker ready for weeks, and he and his staff got to Hela, where they boarded the Ostpreussen. He ordered the icebreaker to land in Rügen, but was not allowed to stay there, as it was declared a fortress. Wherever he went he made his way in a very ruthless manner, ignoring the wounded and the fleeing treks, making sure that he and his colleagues got a whole ship.

Eventually he landed in Kopenhagen and disappeared, disguised in a grey major's uniform. In 1949 he was recognised near Hamburg and a British court gave him over to Poland.

It was my school friend Isa who, by telling me her story also, described what happened in Königsberg. I did not meet Isa until 1985, which was forty years after the end of the war:

By the time the Russians took over Königsberg, all historic buildings had been destroyed. Most people lived in cellars and ruins. The Russians treated the civilians and soldiers left in the town very badly. The soldiers were hit with rifle butts, and pushed along to assemble into a group. They took away their boots, watches, pullovers and sometimes even trousers. The German prisoners looked a poor lot and were herded through the town. Some of them were barefoot, and they had to walk like that, whilst the freed foreign workers and the Poles threw stones at them, and hit them with pieces of wood. The wounded remained where they were, most of them dying anyway from cruelty, no food or medicine, and from the flame-throwers which the Russians used on the buildings.

At the military hospital, the Soviets shot along the gangways to make room for themselves, then walked along throwing the dead outside through the windows. Cruelty and a disregard for the life of any German reached a height in the town.

German women who fell into Russian hands were raped, and had to remain in the town, thin, hungry, bent, always watched and guarded. It was their job to collect the dead, and to clear the fields of mines.

Germany had started the war which eventually lead to the destruction of Königsberg. The Germans killed hundreds of thousands of civilian Russian people by shooting, beating and burning them, before the victors in East Prussia revenged themselves. This is a bitter truth, which most Germans like to forget, or not recognise.

Isa, my friend, was saved, because of the fear of the Russians of catching a disease, and because she spoke Polish. She had left Königsberg whilst it was besieged, but returned, fearing her mother had been left behind. This was not the case, and when she discovered this it was too late to leave. She lived with some of the Polish women in a graveyard, which was the place where the typhoid sufferers had to remain. If the Russians discovered anybody with a disease, or even if they were ill they were shot, for fear of spreading it. Isa, too, had typhoid, but the Polish women looked after one another. Many died, because of the lack of proper nursing, hygiene and food, but Isa survived. The weather was mild, and in their makeshift shacks and hovels, they were safe from Russian atrocities.

Eventually Isa was able to get to the Polish part of the country, where she stayed with her uncle, who warned her not to mention that her mother had married a German, and that she had gone to a German school. Polish people hated the Germans, because of what they had suffered under their occupation.

Isa's mother and sister Ola, who had got married, had escaped to the west, but Isa was not allowed to leave and join them. She had no papers, and her relatives feared that she might be arrested any day. She married an old and sick Polish dentist, who offered her protection in return for her kindness and help with his illness. He was only supposed to live for a few months. Isa was married for five years before he died. Eventually she got permission to visit her mother and sister in Western Germany, and once there, she did not return to Poland. She had to leave all her possessions behind.

Hitler's last bolt-hole was the Reichskanzlei, (the Führerbunker), which was fifty feet below ground level. Here he lived, commanded and worked, together with 600 people, isolated from the world by sixteen feet of concrete and six feet of rammed earth, with ventilators whirring day and night.

The Germans continued to fight with Hitler boosting them with speeches, which were heard by everybody on the radio. He made announcements from his underground bunker in the centre of the city, and summoned vast armies that had already died in the Russian steppes. Hitler still thought that he could defeat the Russians at the Gates of Berlin.

By April 22nd it was clear that the few generals and soldiers left had no intention of attacking the Russians any more. They avoided Berlin by retreating through Brandenburg. A battle for the capital as Hitler wanted them to do, would mean to surrender in the end to the Russians, which nobody wanted. Everybody preferred to be imprisoned by the Western Allies. Hitler's birthday was on April 20th and he celebrated it in his bunker. In his last speech to the people and troops in the east, he said:

'Berlin remains German, Vienna will be German again, and Europe is never going to be Russian.'

Even as late as April 23rd the propaganda voice on the radio told everybody that it was possible to be saved and to have a kind of victory. There was an order from the *Reichsverteidigungskommissar* (Reichs-defence-commissioner), in which Dr Goebbels said:

'The town of Berlin has to fight until the last man. Fight with fanatical force for your wives, children and mothers. We will succeed!'

On April 30th Hitler shot himself and Ewa Braun took poison. Both were incinerated in a shallow trench outside the bunker entrance by Hitler's adjutant and chauffeur, as instructed in his will. The bodies were so successfully mutilated that for years there were rumours of Hitler being alive in South America.

Goebbels and his wife and children took poison, and the rest of the survivors of the bunker filtered away. Some were caught and shot by the Russians later, others disappeared into the shadows.

Until May 1st treks of refugees still rolled out of Berlin, towards the west and the River Elbe, together with columns of wounded from the military hospitals. Trains were still going the short distance to the Elbe despite air attacks. They brought 3,000 wounded from Beelitz to the river. The Swiss Embassy, together with the Swiss colony from Berlin, and the Danish Embassy, were able to leave and get to Tangermünde on the River

Elbe. On May 1st, Generalleutnant Hans Krebs arrived at the Soviet's headquarters under a white flag to surrender Berlin to Chuikov, and on May 2nd all fighting in Berlin stopped. General Weidings and his staff, the last people still to fight, surrendered. The Russians proclaimed *Pobyeda* (victory).

Grossadmiral Dönitz received a telegram from Bormann on April 30th, telling him that Hitler was dead, and that he (Dönitz) was his successor. He was at that moment in Plön in Holstein. For over a week he had heard the news about the terrible experiences that the refugees who had fled from the east had had, making their way to Schleswig Holstein. He knew that he had to finish the war, so that it was possible to save the people from the east, and the rest of Germany.

The English and American troops who had waited by the River Elbe started to move forward again. Field-Marshal Montgomery, who had stopped his troops on the river banks, started to cross the river now, together with American troops, in order to occupy Hamburg, Schleswig Holstein, and the harbours on the Lübecker Bucht. British troops reached Lübeck, thus effectively sealing off the Danish Peninsula from the Russians. Dönitz moved to Flensburg, and formed a non-party government.

On May 4th, Generaladmiral von Friedburg signed in Montgomery's headquarters on Lüneburg Heath a treaty that all troops in North Germany, Holland and Denmark would capitulate. Dönitz was in Flensburg, in Schleswig Holstein, and was asked to authorise the surrender of all troops. Alfred Jodl, General of the artillery, wanted to surrender at Eisenhower's headquarters. This was not accepted, as it didn't include the Russians. There was stalemate. In the end Eisenhower gave an ultimatum, either there was a complete German surrender to all the Allies, or they would close ranks and accept no more surrenders. This meant that the rest of the Germans would be left to the mercy of the Russians. Eventually, on May 7th, the surrender was signed in the presence of representatives of the United States of America, Britain, France and Russia.

I found my father through a miracle in Hamburg. He still had his car, but if he drove it, it would have been confiscated. He had lost his Swiss passport and none of us could prove that we were Swiss as we had no papers. We were glad to be alive.

We bought an old horse which was supposed to pull the car to the farm where we stayed, but the poor old animal never got us there. We finished up in Kisdorf on a derelict army radio station. There were two empty huts and others with broken up equipment. The *Bürgermeister* (mayor) got us some palliasses and the English occupation forces organised some pots and pans for us. There was a stove in the kitchen and my father chopped some wood for it so that we could cook. He even cut down one of the big radio masts. We had a well and the toilet was a little shed in the back with a bucket. We had a new primitive home and didn't have to go into a refugee camp. We registered with the Swiss Embassy, who were hoping to get confirmation from our home town that we were Swiss.

On Radio Station with Hitscher

There was no post and there were no passenger trains. Food was rationed, and one was lucky to get it. My father exchanged the horse for a bicycle and I started my second journey.

This time it was summer and the war was finished. The roads were full of travelling people all trying to get home or looking for relatives. The concentration camps and prisons had been opened, and not all people that had been behind bars were innocent. It was a dangerous journey for a twenty-one year old girl travelling alone.

I made my way south to Mainburg to look for my sister Astra, and travelled from the British to the American occupied zone, a journey of over 800 Km on a bicycle which broke down all the time.

I slept in barns, I slept in haystacks, I even slept in prison. Years later I went back to Gerabron where I was imprisoned by the Americans. The place is now a private house and the small village has become a town. The outside of the building looks the same, except the word *Gefängnis* (prison) is missing. Inside there is still the winding staircase where I carried my bicycle upstairs. The memories came back, particularly of Sam, the kind American sergeant with whom I fell a little in love. He had such beautiful soft brown eyes. He took me to Crailsheim to see the commandant, and had my bicycle mended for me.

Gerabron Prison

Prison Stairs   **Rathaus Crailsheim**

On my trip south I met kind people and cruel farmers. I had help from British and American soldiers and eventually found both of my sisters in Mainburg. Christel had quite a story to tell. Astra was expecting a baby. The father of her child had been taken away by the SS before the end of the war and never returned.

I brought both of my sisters back to the radio station. My brother found us through the Red Cross in Hamburg where we had filled out a card that we were looking for him. He too had a long story to tell.

The other person who arrived on the radio station was Hermann. By now it was the middle of September 1945. I was shocked when he arrived. My face must have shown it. He thought I was overwhelmed with happiness and couldn't speak.

My mother was thrilled to see him. Here she was, with three daughters and none of them had a husband, and there was Hermann an eligible bachelor. 'Don't spoil your chances,' she whispered. 'He is in love with you.'

I was not unkind to Hermann, but I was reserved. We were all extremely interested in his story, and in what had happened to him.

Hermann, having worked on the V-1 and V-2, had always been very secretive about his work. With the war now finished, and the Russians and Allies having taking over the rockets and the blueprints, he was at last able to tell us the truth.

'I was stationed in Peenemünde,' he told us, 'and belonged to Dr Wernher von Braun's designer team. I liked von Braun. He was a scientist and only interested in his research. He was in trouble because he refused to join the SS. Himmler arrested him, accusing him of putting space exploration on a higher level than military projects. It took the joint effort of the Armaments and War Production Minister, Albert Speer and General Dornberger, to get him released, because they insisted that without Braun there would be no V-2.

We had two evacuations in three months with our rocket station and blueprints from Peenemünde. The first one was when the Red Army advanced towards Peenemünde, when we were transferred to Nordhausen.

This plant, in the Harz mountains, south-west of Berlin, was the world's first underground aircraft and missile factory site. Tunnels led to the underground plant which made the V-2 rocket. The vast underground labyrinth of this factory, was the world's biggest of its kind. The Dora concentration camp was nearby, and the labour force for the underground factory was drawn from there. The building of this factory was an unbelievable achievement. There was a full-sized railroad track, that ran all the way through the tunnel. The side tunnels were filled with machinery, engines and rocket parts. There were kilometres of tunnels. Some machinery produced parts for the V-2, others for the Junker engine. We assumed that we would surrender to the US Army in Nordhausen, but we were again evacuated, this time to Oberammergau.

On April 11th, Nordhausen was captured by the Allies. It was totally intact, with hundreds of completed V-1 and V-2 rockets. On May 7th we were imprisoned by the US 7th Army in Oberammergau near Garmisch Partenkirchen.'

Hermann didn't say much about the kind of treatment he received as a prisoner-of-war, but I assume it was quite good, otherwise he would have said so. He continued:

'The US authorities in Washington wanted the rocket specialists to work in the United States. Terms and conditions were worked out quickly, and contracts signed. The Peenemünde research documents, which von Braun had buried to prevent them from falling into the hands of the Soviets, were handed over to the US Army. The crates of documents were on their way to the United States only hours before their hiding place became part of the British Zone of Germany.

The Nordhauser Works had to be handed over by the Americans to the Red Army. Before doing so the rocket assemblies and jet engines were shipped to the US together with all records.

The Allies did not destroy Nordhausen, and when they had to move out of Sachsen/ Thüringen and the Red Army arrived, they were able to resume production at the rocket factory at once.

The Soviets had made sure that they got the important rocket places, Peenemünde and Nordhausen, but they did not get the designs and the designer teams.'

'Have you signed a contract to go to America with von Braun?' I asked Hermann.

'No,' he said, and looked at me with cold eyes. 'I am not a traitor. I do not give German knowledge and experience to the enemy. If the others want to do it, then that is their business. I could not live with the thought of having betrayed my *Vaterland*.'

I was surprised by Hermann's reply, and I could see that my mother and father felt the same. My mother had probably already counted on me going to America. But I also admired Hermann for his decision. He loved Germany and was proud of his fatherland, and even in defeat he was proud of his nationality.

Hermann continued:

'You must have heard about the atom bombs dropped by the Americans on Hiroshima and Nagasaki, on August 6th and 9th. The whole world was shocked with the results. I am sure the scientists regretted that they had developed them. - With so many destructive weapons already in use, what will the next war be like? I do not want to have anything to do with that. I have seen enough of war and destruction.

I want to get married, have children, a good job, and live a peaceful life at last, before I am too old to enjoy it.'

Hermann left for Hannover, where he lived, after three days. I felt guilty that I had not told him that I couldn't marry him because I didn't love him. My mother had persuaded me to keep quiet. I saw him once more, this time in Hannover. By then he was obviously very taken with his landlady, a young war widow with two children. After that I just didn't contact him any more, and didn't write to him after we returned to Switzerland. I am sure he realised that this war romance had come to an end.

At this point I would like to add the following:

Von Braun, and the 120 Peenemünde designers, engineers and technicians who had accepted service contracts with the US Air Force, carried on with the research and rocket production at Fort Bliss. On April 15th 1950, they moved to Huntsville, Alabama, and half of the group have made their homes there. Von Braun was on the US NASA team that put the first man on to the moon.

I had to go to the village of Kisdorf every day to collect the skimmed milk, because we had no refrigerator. One day I met two women, who were running along the road. They stopped me quite excitedly and told me to come with them. They had heard that somebody had opened up a *Schuhlager* (shoe store room). They knew where it was, and if I went with them I could have as many shoes as I liked. The three of us got to Kisdorf and to a district where I had not been before. Behind a large building was a wooden hut with all the doors and windows open. It looked as if the doors had been forced open. There were a number of people there, in and outside the hut, and there were shoes and empty and full boxes everywhere. People just grabbed shoes and then ran away. When I eventually got into the hut I walked on dropped shoes and squashed boxes. However was I going to find shoes of my size? My mother and Astra had the same size but Christel had smaller feet, and Hans and my father, I was sure, had big sizes, but I didn't know which ones.

People had already pulled the shoe boxes off the shelves and everything was piled on to the floor. It was difficult to move, my feet kept on sinking in between shoes and boxes. I looked through them for my size, often only finding one shoe in the box. Some people made an effort to try them on first, but soon gave up that idea, because of all the pushing and shoving that was going on. On the top of the sea of loose shoes and boxes, I found some nice men's shoes, and hoped they would fit. I stuck them under my blouse. I also eventually found three pairs of lady's shoes which I thought might fit us, when suddenly a shout came:

'Police! Get out quickly!'

Everybody pushed towards the door, some jumped out of the windows and landed on thrown-out boxes and shoes. We all knew we were doing wrong.

When I got out I saw a jeep from the military police coming around the corner, so I ran in the opposite direction, holding desperately on to my shoes which were stuck under my blouse and arms. I heard shouting and whistling, but I was determined not to stop. I dived between houses, along one or two small streets, until suddenly I reached a tall maize field. Gently I walked into it, and hid there.

I heard jeeps chasing along the road, I heard shouts, but I did not move. I was completely hidden. I knew that if I moved the tops of the maize would move too, and might give away my hiding place. I sat there for hours, or so it seemed.

At first I was even afraid to move my arms or legs, but when I got too stiff I eventually stretched out my legs and made myself more comfortable.

I looked at the shoes. There were two pairs of sandals, quite pretty, with some gay-coloured cloth straps on the top. The sole was made from three pieces of wood and a wooden heel. All of it fastened to a strong canvas cloth. Germany was short of leather towards the end of the war, and this type of shoe had already appeared in the shops in the last year. The three pieces of wood made it possible for the foot to bend when walking. The third pair of shoes seemed to have a leather top, whilst the sole was made from *Ersatzgummi* (artificial rubber). The shoes were black, firm, excellent walking shoes. All three pairs fitted me, and I now hoped that the pair of gent's shoes would also be alright for somebody in the family.

Eventually I decided I could move, but as I did not want to go back to the road where I had come from, I walked, pushing myself gently through the maize in the opposite direction, orientating myself by the sun. It seemed to take ages before I got out of the field, but when I did, I soon realised where I was, because I had travelled around the district with my bike. I did not think I could get back to the radio station with all the shoes under my blouse and arms, so I hid them in the maize field, walking back into it after earmarking a tree.

When I got back to the radio station, I found that everybody had started to worry about me, because I had literally been away for hours. I had left early in the morning and it was now afternoon. They were all very interested in my story. I returned by bike to my marked spot, taking two bags with me to hide the shoes. I met a few people whilst cycling through Kisdorf, but nobody took any notice of me, and I returned safely with my shoes.

Unfortunately the gent's shoes did not fit my father, but they fitted Hans. I kept one pair of sandals and the shoes, and my mother took the other pair of sandals, saying that Astra couldn't wear them because of the divided wooden soles. As an expectant mother it was not safe to walk on those thick-soled sandals, she could twist her ankle walking on them.

The winter of 1945/46 on the radio station was hard. We had very little fuel and hardly any food. Wood was needed for the kitchen stove, so that my mother could cook.

My sister Astra had her baby in January. She had a small iron stove in her room so that she and the baby could keep warm. My mother made sure that Astra got enough to eat. We all had to part with some of our rations, and my mother hardly ate anything.

For Christmas we had an old boiling fowl which my father had exchanged for some cigarettes. The six of us had it for two days. At least the watery soup had some chicken taste. We mostly spent our time in the kitchen to keep warm near the stove, as it was again a very cold winter. I had to break the ice in the well every time we wanted some water

My mother nearly killed herself walking the 10 Km to the hospital to see Astra and the new baby. Christel and I took over the visits, but we too had to stop it as we were too weak for such a strenuous walk.

I found some *Mieten* (clamps) with animal fodder, a kind of turnip. I collected them at night. My mother became an expert with this food. We had them raw, grated, cut in pieces or sliced. We had them cooked in different shapes or mashed, with water and salt or a little milk. Nobody liked the food, but it filled the stomach. Astra hardly ever ate this root. She had to feed baby Monika and my mother made sure she had good food.

Animal Fodder (like Turnips)

Proof of our Swiss nationality arrived at the beginning of 1946 and we all got a Swiss passport. This also entitled us to food parcels from the embassy which were a great help. I went to Hamburg to look for a job as we were getting short of money. In any case, I got bored being on the radio station with nothing much to do, and watching Astra being spoilt by my mother.

I had to walk to the underground station and then take the train. This meant getting up at 4.30 a.m, and never getting home before 9 p.m. But once I had a job, I was entitled to accommodation in the town, particularly as I also had a Swiss passport. I got a room with a family and only went home for the weekend.

My father, too, left for Hamburg after a row with Astra and my mother. He couldn't bear to see my mother ruining her health slaving away for her daughter because of the baby.

Eventually we all moved to Hamburg and waited for a transport back to Switzerland. Life was not too bad in the last few months in Germany. We had the extra food from the embassy. My brother went to school again. My father had a paid job, clearing away the debris of the war with his bare hands, turning rubble into building material, and burying the dug out corpses.

Through my job I got contacts with the British Occupation Forces which improved my school English. Franz the *Ausläufer* (delivery man) at "Roku" where I worked, introduced me to the Black Market, where I exchanged cigarettes for clothes.

I had an emergency appendix operation performed by Professor Strauss, my old anatomy lecturer. I had worked for him in the military hospital in Königsberg. He never charged me for his services. He, too, was a refugee, and only too pleased to help me.

Even my social life improved a little and I went on a night's boat trip organised by Franz.

Franz had been a corporal in the Air Force and felt that he was lucky to have a job. He was born and bred in Hamburg, and before being called up he had worked in a tool factory. He had been married, but his wife and two children got killed in one of the bomb attacks on Hamburg. He never talked about them.

One day he arrived terribly excited, and told us all that we should join an outing which he would organise.

He wanted to hire a boat and a band, and we would all travel along the river by night. He knew of a lovely restaurant with a fantastic dance floor, which was not bombed out! There would be no food, but Franz said there would be a log fire in the restaurant garden, and he promised to organise some potatoes for us. We were allowed to bring friends, the more the merrier, because he said this would make the tickets cheaper. He had to pay a flat rate for the boat.

Everybody was very enthusiastic, and we all looked forward to the luxury of a hot, baked potato in the open air. It was the end of May, and the weather was already quite warm. I prayed for calm water. Franz kept on selling the tickets, inviting practically everybody he met. I had nobody to go with.

Franz said I shouldn't worry, he would find somebody for me, and if not, I could always dance with him. Wally, my friend in the office laughed about that, and said Franz was more her age than mine, so he said he would dance with both of us.

The trip was a great success. The weather was beautiful, warm, no wind, and the moon was shining. Franz had found me a partner, a young man, about twenty-five years old, who was a commercial artist. I have never forgotten his name because two days after our boat trip, I went to see him in his tiny studio, and he gave me a little picture which he had painted. It had his name on it. On the back he had written that this little gift was something to remind me of the "Night Boat Trip." His name was Eberhard Kupka, and the painting was of a fragile looking pink anemone. It is a lovely little picture, I still have got it.

Our boat trip started at eight o'clock in the evening, and whilst the boat was gliding along the still waters the band played. There were fairy lights everywhere, and couples soon started dancing wherever there was a space on the boat. Wally and Franz were sitting with me and Eberhard, and we kept together on the trip.

Franz had a big bag with the potatoes, and he said there was also another surprise in the bag. The trip lasted about two hours. We could see the restaurant from the boat because it was lit up with fairy lights which were also in the garden. When we got near to it we could see the bonfire. We helped Franz to put the potatoes into the hot ash. He said he would watch them with Wally, whilst we went dancing, because the band had already started to play. Franz didn't only have to watch the fire, but also the potatoes, which were very precious, with the food shortage.

We danced, we laughed, and we had fun. The potatoes - there were two of them for everybody - were delicious, and there was the surprise. A few bottles of wine, which Franz had got on the black market. Franz even organised some glasses from the restaurant, but counted them, and begged us to return them, as he would be in trouble otherwise.

The return trip early in the morning was quiet. The band didn't play any more, people were tired but happy and relaxed. Some went to sleep, others just sat there, arms entwined. Some couples were kissing and embracing, there was soft talk and whispering. Eberhard cradled me in his arms, and even Franz had put his arm around Wally's shoulders. He looked tired and drawn and sad, and he said softly:

'I will never forget my wife Ilse and the children. We were happy together. We used to go on boat trips. Ilse loved dancing. Her aunt used to come and stay with us so that we could go out together. I don't know why

I was allowed to live, not even being wounded, but Ilse and the kids had to die. I don't mind about the home, that can be started again, but they say Ilse and the children are dead. They never found them, everything was burnt, and I don't even have a grave to go to. Sometimes I think they will come back, this is only a dream.'

I looked at Wally. Tears were running down her face, and I could feel my own tears running over my cheeks. Franz didn't intend to make us all sad, he only spoke out his thoughts. For a few hours we had forgotten the war and what it had done to all of us, but the misery, the poverty, the destruction and the pain were still there.

'Don't spoil the lovely night,' said Wally, softly, to Franz. 'We were all happy until you spoke, and now look at us, Helga and I are crying.'

'Oh, I am not crying,' I replied quickly, trying to smile. 'I think we are all tired, and also not used to the wine, it loosens the tongue.'

Franz kissed Wally, and then he kissed my forehead. 'Sorry,' he said, and walked off.

Eberhard hugged me a little and whispered: 'Go to sleep.'

And that's what I did, at least for a little while. It was beautiful to see the first morning light, and the sun trying to come up. Franz joined us again before the end of the journey, and said he would take Wally home, if Eberhard took me home, which, of course, he did.

PART TWO

A SWISS EMIGRANT

CHAPTER ONE

Rückwanderer - A New Trade

At the beginning of September 1946 we returned to Switzerland.

On my last morning in Hamburg, I had a good walk before starting off for the embassy. My mother said I looked tired, and asked me whether there was anything troubling me. I just shook my head and helped with the suitcases and Monika's pram. I had asked Franz, at "Roku," whether he knew somebody with a handcart. He said he would come himself. Sure enough, he turned up with a cart, which was big enough for all our cases and Astra's box.

People stared at us walking along the pavement. First came my parents, then Astra and Christel pushing the pram with Monika, and then Hans and Franz pulling the cart, which I helped to push. At the embassy there were already a number of people waiting, and it wasn't long before the coaches and the lorries arrived. Astra had a window seat in the coach, and my mother took Monika out of the pram and gave her to Astra. She made sure Astra was alright, had the bag with the nappies, and also the bottles with milk and some rusks. Franz helped us to get the cases, the box, and the pram on to the lorry, and then he kissed me goodbye.

'Post me a card,' he said. 'I would like a picture of Switzerland, and if you have some money send me a bar of Swiss milk chocolate!'

He was joking, but he said he was glad that I was able to go to a country which had not been destroyed by war.

My mother and I discovered that the best seat was on Astra's box, which we had pushed behind the driver's cabin. We put a blanket over the top, to make it more comfortable to sit on. Christel, Hans and my father sat on the benches arranged along the sides of the lorry. There were a few more people on our lorry with their belongings.

Everything was very clean and organised. We left exactly at the time we were told we would leave, and we stopped after three hours, again exactly at the time we were told we would stop. We got a hot cup of coffee from thermos flasks, and some biscuits, and were allowed to disappear into the wood. There were two nurses and a guide on the coaches.

My mother fussed around Astra and Monika. She spread out a blanket on the grass so that Monika could crawl about. Astra kept on talking to my mother, telling her how difficult it was to hold Monika in her arms all the time because she wouldn't sit still. She had pains everywhere from holding her. I didn't want to listen to her complaints, so Christel and I walked around a little to stretch our legs, and Papa and Hans followed us.

The guide called us when it was time to climb into the lorry again. When I sat down on the box, I suddenly stared at the pram, and so did Christel, Hans and Papa. We couldn't believe it, because there, in the pram, sat Monika.

'Oh no,' I said.

Astra had an excellent seat in the coach because she had a child, and now she had passed on Monika but still kept the comfortable seat.

'Astra certainly knows how to do it,' I said to my mother. 'If she wanted to have Monika in the pram, she should have let you have her seat in the coach and sit here on the box.'

'Monika ought to go to sleep, and she is used to do this in her pram,' said my mother. Nobody else said anything, so I kept quiet.

Sure enough, Monika went to sleep and was no trouble. At dinner-time we stopped at a village hall, where we all were given sandwiches together with a mug of soup. I took this opportunity to remind Astra that Mama was much older than her, and if Monika was in the pram in the lorry, she should change places with her mother, even if it was only for part of the trip. She took no notice of me, and when we started off again she was the first one on the coach, whilst we struggled to get on to the lorry lifting Monika, so that she could be put into the pram.

I think the little girl enjoyed the rocking of the pram. We had to hold the handle, because the brake didn't seem to hold the pram firmly enough. After a time Monika got bored and tried to climb out, so my mother took her out of the pram and played with her. People like babies, and soon Monika travelled from person to person, everybody making a fuss of her. I was convinced the same would have happened in the coach, if Astra had been a little more approachable.

But the pattern was set. Astra, for the rest of the trip, sat in the coach, and Monika travelled with us in the lorry, where my mother changed her nappies, fed her and nursed her.

In the evening we stopped at a half bombed-out school, where we had a hot supper, served in the hall on trestle tables. We went to sleep on bunks, which were standing in the undamaged classrooms. In the morning we had a Swiss breakfast with rolls, butter, jam and *café au lait* (half milk and coffee). We were gradually introduced to Swiss luxury, and we all enjoyed this. After that, we all had our places again in the lorries and the coaches, with Monika travelling in the pram with us, and Astra in the coach. I felt that it was up to my mother to make Astra sit in the lorry with her child, which she didn't do.

We got quite excited when we came near the Swiss border, and of course everybody wanted to look out. Our lorry had a tarpaulin, and some of the men rolled it back a little, so that we could have a better view. At Rheinfelden we all had to get out at the border and produce our new Swiss passports. We had a special parking place, where the coaches and the lorries had stopped in a half circle, and the guide asked us to stand close to the vehicles. Three customs officials came and stamped our passports. They hardly looked at them, and they never bothered about our luggage on the lorries either. I was surprised about this, and also that we didn't seem to go near the official customs buildings. We had a special corner, which was fenced off. At the large entrance gate a big notice said: *Rückwanderer* (returning emigrants).

One could see that everything was well organised, but why were we kept away from the main buildings? My father thought that in this way the authorities could probably deal with us quicker - we were quite a crowd. I accepted his explanation, but I still didn't like the fence and gate, through which we had come in and left again. - We were all given a small parcel with sandwiches and fruit, and there was special baby food for Monika.

My first impression of Switzerland was a surprise. It was so clean and fresh-looking, and full of colours. I saw a woman in a red coat, she was laughing, whilst talking to another person. People had gay summer clothes on, and walked about leisurely. I had never thought much about colour, and only now realised that throughout the war, and even now, we dressed in dull colours, grey, brown, black, serviceable colours, which would not get dirty, and would wear better.

We had no flowers in parks and gardens and most buildings were destroyed, so that the towns and villages were full of rubble and dirt. Here, there were flowers in the gardens, and window boxes made the lovely undamaged old houses look pretty. Nobody seemed to be in a hurry. The shops were full of food and goods, and there were no queues. This was wonderland!

'The first thing I will buy when I have some money is bitter chocolate,' I said to Christel. 'I will eat it until I am sick.'

'I will help you to eat it,' she replied, 'but I would like to get a decent pair of shoes, a pretty pair, not always useful ones, and not again in black or brown, but in red - or, what about green?'

'Everything is so beautiful,' said my mother. 'I am glad we have decided to come here. It will take years before Germany is built up again, if the Allies permit it.'

We stared at the buildings, the shops, the people, and the Swiss people stared at us, sitting in a lorry with the tarpaulin half rolled up. We were the poor *Rückwanderer*, and looked like them, in our dull, cheap clothes, and dirty hands and faces. One couldn't keep clean in a half-open lorry. I didn't care, things were so different and exciting, and there was so much to see, and to absorb.

Our convoy moved out of Rheinfelden along good asphalt roads, and there were beautiful fields and meadows with fat brown cows, some of them with bells around their necks. We travelled along the River Rhein.

That's Germany on the other side, I thought. How silly to divide people by a river.

Our vehicles passed through a large open gate which was closed behind us. We had arrived at a camp. We climbed out of the lorry and I helped my mother with Monika. Astra found us, and put Monika into her pram. My mother told us that we must all keep together. We could see a large building, and a number of wooden huts with notices or names on them. Everything looked very austere and spotlessly clean, but gave me the feeling that I was in an army camp. There were fences everywhere, and behind them fields.

We are locked in, I thought. Is that what they meant when they said we had to be in quarantine first?

We had been told that this would happen, but I never realised what it meant. I had only once been imprisoned, in Gerabron, but that turned out alright. I didn't like this camp. Even when I left Königsberg in that terrible winter, with all the suffering I had, I was free, I could go where I wanted to go. Now I was behind bars, and neutral and free Switzerland which was supposed to be the beginning of my future had imprisoned me. I was shocked, but worse was to come.

We were told to leave our suitcases and our belongings next to the lorries, but to make sure they were unlocked. They all had to be *entlaust* (deloused) and disinfected. Some people objected and said their things were clean. The reply was that this was the rule. - The next thing was that men and women got separated, and mothers with young children had to be in another group. Papa and Hans left, and so did Astra with Monika. My mother, Christel and I stayed together.

More lorries and coaches had arrived, and some more women and girls joined our group. A woman guided us to a hut, and told us to get undressed. Again some people complained, but we were told that this was the rule. Everybody had to have a shower, and our clothes would be disinfected in the meantime. We had to put our clothes into a bag, and when giving it up, a label with a number was tied to it. The attendant passed a duplicate number to the owner, with an elastic to put around the wrist. There was no point in being shy, three attendants saw to it that all our clothes came off. After that a door was opened, and we were pushed into a big shower-room. Everybody was given a piece of soap, and told not to forget to wash their hair. This reminded me of the showers we had in the new Adolf Hitler *Schule* when I was a child.

Before I got to the shower-room door I heard an argument. I turned round to see what had happened. There was a woman with a head scarf, like a turban, and she refused to take it off. The attendant argued with her. The woman cried and tried to hold the turban on, but the attendant pulled it off. People gasped, because the poor woman had no hair, and a terribly scarred red head. I looked at her arms, and saw the telltale numbers tattooed there - the sign of the concentration camp. She stopped crying, just stood there, her arms were hanging limp, and her shoulders drooped forward, giving her figure a dejected and resigned position. She was painfully thin and pale, and her body trembled. One or two people started shouting at the attendant, others joined in, and there was quite a revolt. Somebody got hold of the scarf again, and tried to put it on to the poor woman's head, and a big motherly woman embraced her in sympathy.

The poor woman was so obviously a victim of some kind of torture from a concentration camp.

There we were, all naked, except for the attendants, who looked a little frightened. We were not prepared to let one of us be hurt in such a shameful way.

'Get a towel for her; if she is not allowed to have a scarf on,' said one of the women to the attendant. 'You ought to be ashamed of yourself for doing this. Why didn't you ask her why she wanted to keep the scarf on?'

'I did,' replied the attendant, 'but I couldn't understand what she said.'

It turned out that the poor woman didn't speak any of the Swiss languages, she only spoke Polish. Of course, being a *Rückwanderer* didn't necessarily mean that you came from Germany. Swiss people had emigrated to all parts of the world, and now, with the war finished in Europe, they returned from a number of countries. As long as they could prove that they were Swiss, even if it was the second or third generation, they were allowed to return, and many only spoke the language of the country where they had lived.

One of the attendants did go and fetch a towel, and the big woman wrapped it around that poor head. Everybody was very kind to her, and smiled at her, and one or two pressed her arm in an encouraging way. I think she could feel our sympathy. Once she had the towel around her head she looked up shyly, and seeing our understanding faces she whispered something, which we took as a kind of "thank you."

The shower door was opened again, and I was in the next group to go in. There were a number of showers on opposite walls, and once the water was turned on, the whole room seemed to be full of water. We had no taps, the water just kept on coming, not too hot, and not too cold. The water smelt of disinfectant, and stung my eyes. Suddenly it stopped, and a voice told us to put on the soap, again reminding us not to forget to wash our hair. I couldn't see anybody, because the room was full of steam, so I don't know whether the instructions came from an attendant, or through a loudspeaker. After that we had another lot of water to wash the soap off. The door opened at the other side of the room, and everybody who walked through it received a bath towel for drying. The Swiss were clean and organised. The conveyer belt had started, and it continued like that. Once we had dried ourselves, we were told to put the towels into a big basket and were given a clean white sheet to wrap around ourselves. We were asked to sit down on the benches by the walls and wait. Every so often a door opened, and four women were asked to go into the next room. We gradually moved up, because people came out of the shower room on one side, and disappeared through the door on the other side. Everybody was very apprehensive, wondering what was on the other side of the door.

Christel sat next to me, looking very frightened. My mother had got separated from us, and had already gone through that door. I felt that I just had to know what was going to happen to us. We were treated like cattle, pushed from one place to the next, without any explanations. Surely they could treat us like intelligent human beings? We had done nothing wrong.

'What is going to happen to us next?' I asked the attendant who stood by the door.

'You are going to be examined by a doctor,' she replied.

Switzerland was making sure that no *Rückwanderer* brought any lice, bugs, or diseases into their country. I am sure nobody blamed them for their precaution, but the way it was done was not very kind. Our turn came, and Christel and I walked through the door. The room we entered had three desks, one on either side of the door, behind which a woman was sitting with a typewriter. The third desk, a little larger, was in the corner on the right. Behind it sat an elderly man in a white coat with a stethoscope around his neck, obviously the doctor. There were also two or three nurses in uniform walking about and attending either to the doctor or to the women who had to be examined.

There was a cubicle with a curtain in the left hand corner. There was not much privacy in that room, because the doctor carried on examining (looking up and down) a naked woman when we entered. I was told to approach one of the women with the typewriter, and clasping my sheet tightly around me I walked to the desk. My particulars were typed on to a card: My name, date and place of birth, home town and canton, single, profession (medical student), etc. A nurse took my sheet away, measured my height, and weighed me. All these details went on to my card. Then the card was turned over, and I was asked what illnesses I had had, and what type of immunisations, if any. The last question was in which country or countries I had lived and travelled through. The nurse then took my card and asked me to come over to the doctor.

I had to wait for him, because he had taken somebody into the cubicle in the corner, and I could hear voices coming from there. When the doctor came back, he took his surgical gloves off and threw them away. He washed his hands. I knew he had given a woman an internal examination. He made some notes on a card, then added it to a pile of cards already on his desk. I saw, from the corner of my eye, a big woman coming out of the curtained cubicle, accompanied by a nurse.

At last the doctor's full attention came to me. He read my card, then smiled, and asked kindly:

'Where did you study medicine?'

'In Königsberg, in East Prussia.'

'A long way from here. I have heard it was an excellent university. How long did you attend lectures? Have you worked in a hospital?'

He certainly seemed interested, but at the same time he looked me over, listened to my heartbeat, knocked on my chest, and made me lift up my feet so that he could examine my soles. I did answer all his questions, but I had the feeling he was not really listening. This was routine, he had a lot to do, and with hundreds of women to examine why should he suddenly be interested in one of them. The nurse looked through my hair, but she couldn't find any lice there!

'Who took your appendix out?' he suddenly said.

I told him where it was done, and that it was my old professor who had performed the operation.

'Clever man,' he said. 'I have never seen such a small scar. Look at it, nurse, the Germans certainly have some skilled doctors.'

With that, he had finished with me, and I was glad I didn't have to go into the corner cubicle. Nurse gave me my sheet to cover myself up, and opened the door to the next room. Already a number of women wrapped in their sheets, including my mother, were waiting there. Christel came into the room soon after me. We whispered to one another what had happened to us, but we all had the same treatment. More and more women entered the room, and we all looked like ghosts with our sheets.

Suddenly another door opened and two women entered pushing along a huge basket on wheels. I could see the bags with our clothes inside.

The numbers were called out, and gradually everybody collected their clothes, and we were told that we could dress ourselves. My clothes smelt of disinfectant, and some pieces still had powder left on them. Because they were pushed about in the bag, they also got very creased.

'They sprayed everything with disinfectant powder,' said my mother.

'We will all smell of moth balls now,' I replied.

Our sheet went into the large basket. After that we were told that, if we wanted to be together in one room, we ought to stay together, because now we would be allocated our accommodation. My mother enquired about Astra and Monika, but was told, as Monika was not one year old, Astra would be in a different hut. Families could meet during the day, but otherwise slept and lived in separate huts. Each hut had several rooms, and there were four double bunk-beds in each room, accommodating eight people.

After the announcement, little groups started to form. The three of us didn't really mind who wanted to join us, we didn't know anybody, so we just kept a little apart. The two attendants kept on picking out groups of eight, and giving them instructions where to collect their luggage, and which room and hut to find, until at last it was our turn. There were only five of us left, Mama, Christel and I, and two more women.

'You are lucky,' said the attendant, 'you are only five, so you can have more space in your room. You will have to decide who takes the top bunk, as only one of you needs to climb up.'

'I don't mind being on the top bunk,' I replied.

We collected our luggage and found our hut and our room. It was very clean, with bare scrubbed floors, four double bunks, two on each wall. The beds had white sheets and dark blankets. Between the bunks were two white chairs and a curtained window on one side. Along the wall opposite the door were eight narrow wardrobes with hanging space and a shelf above. In the centre was a table with four chairs. I chose the top bunk by the window, and Christel the one below me, and of course my mother decided to have the bunk next to Christel. I unpacked my dresses and hung them into the wardrobe, but left the rest in my case, pushing this under Christel's bunk. We had been told to go to the large building as soon as we had finished, where we would meet everybody, and have our meal in the large hall.

It was evening now and we all were pretty hungry. We had only had the sandwiches and fruit for lunch at the border.

After looking around we found Papa and Hans, but couldn't see Astra anywhere, so we just queued up for our supper, and then sat together at a large table with other people, leaving a space for Astra. The meal was very good. There were also plenty of cold drinks, and even coffee, served in big mugs with some sweet biscuits.

Papa and Hans told us what had happened to them, and we told them what had happened to us. They, too, had to leave their clothes behind and got a sheet and had their showers and examinations. They said we were lucky having a room for only five people. They had eight in their room, and Hans had the bunk above Papa.

We were nearly finished with the meal when Astra turned up, without Monika. Mama fetched her, as soon as she came through the door, and got her a meal. Astra had had the same disinfectant procedure and examination as us. Monika was taken over by a nurse in the meantime, and was probably also disinfected and examined. Astra had a room with three more women with children under one year. Her room had single beds. The babies were kept together in another room for the night, which was supervised by a nurse, and Astra was told to collect Monika in the morning for breakfast. So now she had a baby-sitter for the evening.

After the meal the camp warden made some announcements and gave some explanations. We were told that we had to stay in the camp for three weeks. We all had to have jobs, to help in the running of the camp.

People were needed to help in the kitchen, to clean the shower rooms, toilets, hall, etc. Every room had to organise their own room cleaning, taking it in turns. There were even a few people needed in the office, and anybody with medical skills, or nurses, were also wanted. As soon as we had finished our food, we could go to the end table, where four attendants were sitting, who would give out the work allocations. - We were also told that we had to report at the X-ray hut the next day for a chest X-ray, and that everybody had to visit the "Jobs Allocation" office, to register for a job or training. For the young people, there was also a careers adviser in one of the offices.

Both my parents got a job in the office. My father had quite a monotonous one in the registration department, but my mother, who was very good at shorthand and typing, was soon in demand by the different permanently employed camp people. Hans, being young and sporty, was told to look after a group of young boys in the morning for an hour and a half and in the afternoon for two hours. There was a meadow where he could get them to play a ball game, or any other sport. Christel and I, having had nursing experience, were told that there would be something for us in a day or two, but in the meantime we should go and have our X-rays, and see the "Job Allocation" office.

The next day there were queues at every office, even the X-ray one. Lunch was from twelve o'clock until two o'clock, and all offices were closed then. We decided that we would all meet at 1.30 for lunch, hoping to avoid a queue, and also to fit in with Monika's afternoon sleep. Astra said the women took it in turns to look after the babies, so she had some free time on and off. She seemed quite happy with the arrangements, and the nurse in charge of the baby room was efficient and kind.

We met, as arranged, at 1.30 p.m. Only my mother had had her X-ray by then. She didn't have to queue, she was taken in by one of the staff, because she was in demand, and not allowed to waste her time queuing. Lunch, again, was very good, and there was plenty to eat. - Christel and I had our X-rays in the afternoon, but after that it was too late to go to the "Jobs Allocation" office, so we decided to leave it until the next day.

Because it was raining in the evening, most people stayed on in the dining hall, sitting together in groups, and talking about their past, their lost homes, their lost friends and relatives. It was a relaxed atmosphere, and everybody was friendly, and only too willing to talk. There was nothing else to do. We had no books, no papers, no games to play, only each other's company.

The next day we all eventually got to the "Jobs Allocation" office, and in the evening we reported to each other what had happened. I will never forget this day. It was the 24th of September, two days before Christel's twentieth birthday. It had nothing to do with Christel's birthday, but because of her birthday I have never forgotten the date. This was the day when my big dream of becoming a doctor one day was shattered, and I was told to decide to do something else, so that I could quickly get employment and earn my own living.

I was interviewed by a man of about thirty-five. He was in a hurry, because of the great number of people he had to interview. I had the feeling as if he timed himself, allocating certain minutes for each interview. He filled out a card whilst asking me questions: name, age, what type of school, and how long I went to it, any other education, what qualifications, any hobbies, etc. what certificates. Unfortunately I had no certificates, only my card that I was a medical student at the Albertus Universität in Königsberg.

He asked me whether my parents had enough money for me to carry on with my studies. I told him that everything was under Russian occupation. He told me I could not carry on with my studies in Switzerland for two reasons:

One: The school attendance in Germany had been cut by one year because of the war and, therefore, my matriculation would not be recognised in Switzerland.

Two: Because I had only just started with my studies, I didn't qualify for a grant. If I had been at the end of my studies, he would have put my name forward for a *Stipendium* (grant).

The whole thing just didn't seem to make any sense. On the one hand, my matriculation, which I had to have to enter university, was not recognised in Switzerland, so I couldn't carry on with my studies, and on the other hand, if I was nearly finished with my studies, started after a matriculation which was not recognised in Switzerland, he would recommend me for a grant so that I could finish studying medicine.

If I insisted on becoming a doctor, I would have to go back to school for a year, to get my matriculation, and then start again at university. I was twenty-two years old, I couldn't very well go back to school and mix with seventeen and eighteen year old girls, and where was the money going to come from for my living and the school fees? I knew that the interviewer was trying to put me off medicine. It would mean a tremendous grant to keep me for several years, money for the school, for the university and my books, plus living accommodation. The interviewer thought that, maybe, by the time I had finished my year at school, and got my matriculation, my father would be in a position to pay for my studies. Sometimes one could even receive part grants which would help. I think he added all this because he could see how disappointed I was. Somehow I just couldn't think of anything, except that I had been told that I could not study medicine, and that I would never become a doctor. He advised me to go and see the careers officer.

I never said anything to him. I took my student card, which I had given him to look at, and walked out of the room, out of the building, through the camp to the meadow where Hans was told to organise some sport for the boys. It was late afternoon and nobody was there. I walked right across the meadow to the furthest side, and lay down in the grass and cried.

Suddenly something inside me had broken open, and all the pain and suffering I had experienced came to the surface.

I hated our poverty, our dependence on grants and kindnesses of other people. I hated the Swiss authorities for telling us, we will help you, and then caging us in and telling us to learn something quickly so that we can earn money.

I hated God for favouring some people, and neglecting others like me. I had started with my studies. I had worked hard. I had spent time working in the hospital in preparation for my chosen profession, and now I had to give it all up. I blamed everybody and everything, even my parents for not having had the foresight to send some money to Switzerland in the early years of the war.

I cried in desperation, though I knew that crying would not alter the situation or solve anything.

Eventually I stopped crying and felt tired and exhausted. I had no more tears left, but my body still shook from the sobbing. I sat up, leaning against the fence, and gradually started to think rationally again. There was no point in relying on my parents for money for my further education. Even if my father got a good job, it would take years before he would earn enough for all the needs of his large family. Hans still had to go to school, and then to university. There was also Christel without an education, and who was going to pay for Astra and her child? She could probably get a job, but that would mean that my mother would have to look after Monika. Astra was the only one who had a finished education. So what was I going to do? I could train to become a nurse. I had already been long enough working in the hospital to know what that would be like. My parents would not have to supply any money, because the training included free accommodation and a small wage. Although being a nurse would be a profession in the medical line, I also knew that it would remind me daily that I had not been able to become a doctor, because of lack of money. I felt I could not face this. I came to the conclusion that I must find a job completely different to medicine, so that nothing could remind me of it. I still had to talk to the careers adviser, so maybe he could help me.

I walked back over the playing field to the hut with the showers and wash basins, and had a good wash. I combed my hair and looked in the mirror, and hoped it would not be too long before I could afford to go to the hairdresser. Christel and I had occasionally cut our own hair, but it needed some professional attention.

After that I went to see the careers adviser. I was in luck, there was no queue. I met a middle-aged, well-dressed, well-fed woman, who was overflowing with kindness at first. She had a pile of cards on her desk, and found one with my name on it, which had been forwarded to her by the "Jobs Allocation" office. Yes, she was very sorry that it would not be possible for me to study medicine, but there were plenty of other places where I could work, which were connected with medicine. What about if I went into a household with children, my medical knowledge would help me with that. Young girls were needed for this type of job. I would have free accommodation and a wage, and could attend classes one day a week to get my certificate as a *Kindermädchen* (nanny), after three years.

She already had one or two addresses where I could start straight away. There was also a one year full-time course, but she doubted whether I would get a grant for that, as there were only grants for six months given. I knew very well what she meant. She wanted me to go and live with a family, where I would have to help with everything, cleaning, cooking, shopping, and looking after children - another description for domestic help, for which there were plenty of vacancies. I did not need any training for that type of job. I had done enough cleaning and running around shopping on the radio station. I was not going to do this for other people, even if I got paid for it. I told the officer that I was not very keen on that type of training. She tried to persuade me, saying that she even knew some families where I would be very happy, but I said 'no.'

She then suggested that I train as a nurse in a hospital. She could arrange for an interview, if I told her into which big town I wanted to go. To gain time, I told her that I was not sure where my parents would be, and felt it might be better to wait until my father had arranged for a job. I said I would let her know as soon as I had spoken to my parents. She

115

smiled, and said she was glad I was going to train as a nurse. Her smile faded when I replied that I had not chosen the nursing profession, I had only said I would think about it and let her know once I had conferred with my parents. Up till now she had been very kind, but when she realised that I might not follow her advice, she suddenly changed.

'You will have to earn your own money,' she said. 'We are not supporting *Rückwanderer* because they don't like the jobs or training we are suggesting. We try and help, but a young girl like yourself, healthy and intelligent, should earn her keep straight away.'

'You don't have to worry about me,' I replied. 'I have looked after myself for years. I don't mind doing any jobs, even dirty ones, but I will not be pushed into any training for years, which I don't like. I have three weeks here in quarantine, and plenty of time to think about my future. You have only suggested two careers, probably because there is a demand in those, but there must be plenty of other things one can do, and I will explore every possibility. The only charity and kindness I have ever had since my parents lost everything, was the odd cup of soup and dry bread, the food parcels from the Swiss embassy in Hamburg, and my food and a bunk in this camp, where I am kept like a prisoner.'

'You are most ungrateful, and very outspoken,' she replied. 'I will make a note about this conversation and clip it to your card.'

'Please do not omit to mention that you had already some families lined up for me, where I could be a domestic help under the title of *Kindermädchen*!'

She flushed red, and looked embarrassed, and I realised that I was right with my assumption that she was looking for "maids" for families, probably even people she knew. I got up to leave, she didn't stop me, but wrote something on my card. Before I left the room I heard her say:

'Do let me know whether you want me to apply to a hospital for you to be accepted as a nursing student.'

I looked back at her, but she was still writing, or pretending to be busy with the papers on her table and didn't look up.

'I will let you know,' I said, and left.

In the evening we all met again, and everybody reported what had happened to them. My father had been told it would be difficult to find a position for him in the dairy line. There were too many people in that profession already. He could go into book-keeping and accounts but, unfortunately, he had no certificates. Switzerland insisted on proper training for every job, with a certificate at the end, and after that a written reference from every employer. My father, having had his own business, had no certificates, and of course no references. Even so, enquiries would be made, to see whether it was possible to find a job for him.

My mother was told that, with her knowledge of shorthand and typing, which she could demonstrate anywhere in a few minutes, it would not be difficult for her to find a job, but it would be best to wait until my father was fixed up, and then she could apply for one in the same town. Astra would be going at first into a home with other mothers with young children, where she could stay until my parents were fixed up. Hans, it was suggested, should finish his schooling. He had thought he might only have to go to school for another year, but was told that he probably would have to go two, or even three years more, depending on the entrance examination of the particular school he had chosen. He, too, was in trouble, because the Germans had shortened the higher education by one year. He, too, hoped my father would get a job, and the place where he lived would then be the town where he could go to school.

Christel had the same careers adviser, and the same jobs offered as myself. The officer must have known that Christel was my sister, but she never mentioned to her that she had met me already.

Christel, too, had refused to become a *Kindermädchen*, and about the suggestion of becoming a nurse, she had said she would think about it, and talk it over with her parents.

At last it was my turn. I told them that I could not carry on with my studies, and the reasons given to me. My father, who never really liked girls to go to university, because he said they never finish, but get married, looked sad and worried. I think it hurt him to realise that, if he had had the money, I might have been able to carry on with my studies. If not in Switzerland, then in Germany, where my matriculation, and the beginning of my studies would be recognised. My mother looked shocked. She had always been very proud of me, and had enjoyed saying: My daughter is studying medicine.

'What will you do now?' she said.

'I will think about it. I am not going to be a *Kindermädchen*, and I don't think I am going to be a nurse. I will find something. Don't worry, I will not be a burden to anybody.'

I didn't stay long with my parents and family that evening, but walked off to try and talk to some other people, because I wanted to find out what they were going to do. Christel joined me, and we listened to people's stories. Some of them already had a job, like the professor of biology, who was going into a laboratory in Zürich, and one or two others had relatives in Switzerland who had already fixed them up with jobs. Christel and I decided not to rush into anything, but to wait a while.

The next day a film crew arrived in the camp, who wanted some pictures for a newsreel. Christel and I went and had a look. They were fixing up their equipment by a gate, for which they had a key. Some of the equipment was inside the camp and some outside. The film crew went in and out of the camp, but made sure that the gate was closed each time they passed through, so that nobody could leave the camp. There were quite a number of people watching, and the cameraman took pictures of us as a crowd.

Suddenly one of the men approached me and said they wanted me. They also picked out two young children. The man, or director, told me to put on a head scarf which he gave me. The children had to take off their shoes to be barefoot. They then chose a man, and told me this was my husband. They wanted to film the scene of a family in a camp separated by the fence. I had to walk slowly towards the gate, holding one hand of each child on either side of me. The camera was on the other side of the gate. I had to practice several times, and when the director was satisfied the camera rolled, and the film was taken.

For the next scene, the children and I had to stand by the gate, pulling on the wire fence with sad and desperate faces. Again we had to practice first before the film was taken.

For the third scene, my so-called husband was allowed to be on the other side of the gate. The children and I had to push our hands, with outstretched fingers, and our arms through the wire, trying to reach the father, who was held back by two other men, so that he could not make contact with us.

It took all the morning and part of the afternoon to take these three scenes, and was quite a bit of fun for us. What was shown, was of course not true, and I wondered what the commentary was going to be. I asked the director, but all I got out of him was that it might be used in a newsreel, but he didn't know when. I was sorry he couldn't give me any more details, I would have liked to see the film. I never saw it, or heard anything about it.

The next day was the 26th of September, and Christel's birthday. She had no presents and no cake. When we had the evening meal, the camp warden announced her birthday, and everybody wished her many happy returns. He also asked for several people to come to his office the next morning, and my name was called out too. I wondered what the reason was, and thought, maybe, the careers officer had complained about me.

I had a very pleasant surprise the next morning in the warden's office, because I was given some money for my performance as the mother of the two children. The director of the film crew had paid for the service we gave, and the warden shared it out between the parents of the children, my so-called husband, and myself. This was my first earned Swiss money.

There was a tuck shop in the camp, and I went to it straight away and bought two bars of bitter chocolate, one for Christel as a belated birthday present, and one for me. Christel and I decided to eat it in the afternoon, as it was lunch time by then, and it could spoil our meal.

Our family were always together at mealtimes, and reported any happenings. This day, my mother told Christel and me to go to the office at two o'clock, as we could probably get a temporary job outside the camp.

She had heard something in the office about young girls with medical or nursing experience being wanted, and had put our names forward.

'It is something for approximately three weeks, but I don't know where, or what it involves,' said my mother.

We reported at the office, and the warden told us that a children's home was going to be opened in Sarnen, near Gstaad, and to get it all organised and ready they needed a few nurses or people with medical experience. The manager, treasurer and cook had already been employed, and were residing in the home. They would tell us what to do. They had been promised three girls from our camp, and the warden said:

'I have already spoken to a young nurse, who might even stay on in the home, and if you two are prepared to go and help, this would fulfil the quota. You will have to have another check-up with the doctor straight away, as you will have to leave tomorrow morning. You are being permitted to shorten your stay in quarantine, if the medical report, after your examination, is alright. I hope you will agree to go. You will get a small wage, and there will also be time off to see the mountains and the district. Gstaad is a famous ski resort, it is very beautiful, even in the summer.'

I felt that anything was better than being imprisoned in this camp, and when I looked at Christel she, too, seemed to agree, because she nodded her head slightly. So we said we would be willing to go to Sarnen. We had our examination after that and passed the health test. In the evening we packed our cases. Neither of us had many clothes, and not knowing where we would be after Sarnen, we decided to take everything we possessed with us. We ate some of our chocolate that evening.

Everything was arranged for us for our trip to Sarnen. In the morning, we met the other nurse, Helena, and were told which trains to catch, and at what time we would be in Sarnen, where we would be met. We were given the address of the home and some money for our rail tickets, also a bag with sandwiches and fruit in case we got hungry. A car took us to Rheinfelden station.

I felt extremely happy when the gates opened for us, and closed again after us. The feeling of my new freedom exhilarated me.

'We are free again, we are free again,' I whispered to Christel. She nodded and smiled. I don't think she had felt as shut in as I had, but she was happy for me.

We were dropped off at the station, bought our tickets, and caught the train, which left exactly on time. I enjoyed the journey to Gstaad through the countryside. Everything was so clean, tidy and fresh looking. I got a shock in Gstaad, when I looked up to the massive mountains.

'I wonder whether we will have time to go up in the cable car whilst we are here,' I said. 'I would like to do that, and then look down. It must look like the picture postcards they are selling, and like the pictures on the chocolate wrappings, a miniature Swiss village.'

'It is beautiful,' said Helena. 'I wouldn't mind living here for a time. They said I might be able to stay on in the children's home after it has been opened.'

In Gstaad, we had to change the train and waited half an hour for the next one. It was a very short train, and only a few people travelled on it. We found out later that it still belonged to a private company. The train stopped several times, and although there were no stations people got on and off. Once or twice the guard, who travelled on the train, deposited some boxes and parcels, just leaving them by the railway line unattended. This really was a surprise to us.

People must be very honest here, I thought.

Sarnen had a station, and we three got out there. The station master recognised us, being three girls, and told us to wait. He informed us, in guttural Swiss German, that Mr Huber was delayed, but would come and fetch us. We waited about ten minutes, when a man in his middle thirties, dressed in *Lederhosen* (leather shorts), approached us. He introduced himself as Mr Huber, the treasurer of the children's home. We had to carry our luggage, whilst he guided us along a footpath, which ran next to the railway line, then over a meadow to the home. This was a lovely place, light, airy, with large rooms. It had been a hotel once, and was bought by the "Kanton," to make it into a children's convalescence place. There were still builders busy in some of the rooms.

Christel and I shared a bedroom. We unpacked a few of our things, and then went downstairs again, where Mr Huber was waiting to take us on a tour around the home and the outside buildings, showing us what the place was like. Eventually we were told why we had been asked to come to Sarnen. It was the job of us three to clean and scrub the home from top to bottom. We would have to wash the walls and scrub the wooden floors with soap, water, and disinfectant. The Swiss certainly liked to be clean, and the use of disinfectant was given a great importance. I was very cross, and so were Christel and Helena when we heard that we had been brought here under false pretences. I spoke up:

'What has scrubbing floors and washing walls to do with the knowledge of medicine or nursing? We were informed that that was what was needed here, so that we could help to prepare this home for the opening day.'

'I do not know what you mean,' replied Mr Huber. 'I asked for some girls to come and clean the home, I never stipulated nursing or medical knowledge. I also said that I was short of two nurses, and I understand that one of you is qualified and might stay on.'

'In that case we have been lured here under false pretences,' I replied and, pointing to Helena, I continued: 'Helena is qualified, you had better talk to her about staying on.'

Helena looked uneasily at Mr Huber. I don't think she liked the idea of being a char, but what should she say and do?

'I suggest that you all have an early night, and we will talk tomorrow morning about how we are going to organise the cleaning,' said Mr Huber.

The three of us had a conference in our bedroom, airing our annoyance at the way we had been deceived, but once we had calmed down we decided that, maybe, it wasn't too bad, at least we were out of the camp.

'If we had stayed in Rheinfelden, we might have finished up with cleaning jobs there,' I said. 'Here, we are at least free, and I am sure we will have time off, and then we can go to Gstaad, or go for walks and, maybe, even up the mountains. We have a better room to sleep in than in the camp, and the food is very good too.'

Having resigned ourselves to the thought that now that we were in the home, we might as well get on with the jobs, we felt better. I had a good sleep, and was up early, as we had been told to come for breakfast at 7.30 a.m. The Swiss, we discovered, were early starters, usually getting to work at 8 a.m., because they like their lunch break from noon until 2 o'clock. After breakfast Mr Huber explained:

'I have been thinking about you three. I am sorry you were told something different about your work here, but I will try and organise things in such a way that you also have the chance to see something. I will allocate each of you a days work in the evening, and it is then up to you how you organise your day. If you get up early, and finish your work at dinner time, you can have the afternoon off or, if you want to be free in the morning, you can do your jobs in the afternoon. The only set times are the meals, because cook, too, likes his time off.'

The arrangement was excellent. Christel and I decided to work together at first, when we were given a room each to clean. I scrubbed the floors in both rooms, and she cleaned all the windows, whilst the washing of the walls was shared by us. We carried on even after the twelve o'clock meal, disregarding the two hours lunch break which everybody took, and finished early in the afternoon. We reported to Mr Huber, who inspected the rooms and was satisfied. He gave all of us some money, and told us to walk into Sarnen for a cup of coffee somewhere. Helena had done the same thing, so the three of us were off, exploring Sarnen and enjoying our freedom.

We carried on in the same way, always getting up very early, and getting the job done, in order to have time to go out. Mr Huber was very kind and helpful. He talked to us about our future. Helena said she would stay on as a nurse in the home, but Christel and I were uncertain about what to do, as we had no qualifications in anything. Mr Huber suggested to me that I ought to try and get into a commercial course, so that I could take up an office job. He made me come into the office occasionally, as part of my daily work, where I had to do some filing, accounts, and even filling out forms, using the typewriter. He wanted to show me the different types of office jobs.

The cleaning jobs were most unkind to our hands. By now they were sore and red from putting them into the hot water with the disinfectant, and from scrubbing the floors.

After the first week we got some money, and I used it to buy rubber gloves, and some hand cream. I had not bought, or even seen hand cream for years.

It gave me quite a thrill to walk into the shop and choose a suitable one. (Actually, I bought the cheapest.)

Although the work was strenuous and hard, it was a very happy time. The mountains and meadows were very beautiful.

Christel and I would walk away from the home and lie down in the grass and listen to the crickets, and feel the peace and quietness around us, which was only disturbed, in a pleasant way, by some cowbells, or the occasional whistle of the engine of the little train from Sarnen. We enjoyed and appreciated these simple things, only realising now what we had missed.

After about two weeks, Mr Huber announced one morning that, because it was such a beautiful clear day, we could all have a day off, and he would take us up the mountains in the cable car. He produced a small rucksack for everybody, into which we could pack our picnic, and a warm cardigan or jacket, and he told us to put on firm shoes. He didn't realise that we didn't have a choice of shoes but had to wear what we had got.

We had a lovely day, going up in the cable car, walking further up in the mountains to some viewpoints which Mr Huber knew, having our picnic by a little waterfall with stepping stones, meeting mountaineers, tourists, and brown and white cows, with lovely soft shiny skin, which didn't mind being stroked. They smelt of milk, and their soft, wet brown eyes looked kind and warm. The air was cool and fresh, and the sun burnt our skin. In the evening I felt very tired, and my skin prickled after I had had a shower, a sign that I had got quite sunburnt.

One day - it was during our third and last week of our stay - we all had to be at a certain time by the railway line, which went along the bottom of the meadow belonging to the home. Some more staff had arrived by now, amongst them the housekeeper, another nurse, and two more girls for the kitchen. We all had to wait for the little train, which stopped when it reached us. Mr Huber and the cook, together with the guard, climbed into one of the goods trucks and handed us the things from there, which we quickly had to lay on to the grass. There were chairs and tables, beds and mattresses and huge parcels, which we discovered later were blankets and linen. Everything had to be done quickly, so that the train was not held up for too long. I think it didn't stop for more than five minutes.

After the train left, we had to transport everything over the meadow to the home, which took us all the afternoon. We had two handcarts into which we could put the children's bed frames, whilst the mattresses could be carried by two people.

After the arrival of the furniture, bedding and linen, the house started to look more like a children's home, and when the curtains were hung up it looked very pretty indeed. The children's playrooms were full of colourful new shiny toys.

Even today, when I shut my eyes, I can see the two playrooms in my mind, with the sun shining through the pretty curtained windows, and all those colours, - red, blue, green, pink, yellow, purple, grey, brown and shiny black. I never forgot this colourful picture, my eyes had been used to looking at all the dull colours in Germany, with its destroyed and dusty towns, and its sad and disheartened people. The children coming to this home would be very lucky indeed.

My mother wrote to us. Her letter arrived the next day! What service! They had all left the camp in Rheinfelden. My parents and Hans were now living in Luzern in the Carlton Tivoli Hotel, which had been taken over by the government for the *Rückwanderer*. Astra, because she had a baby under one year, had to go to a different home outside Luzern. My mother told us that, whatever we did, we ought to insist that we come to Luzern to the Carlton Tivoli. She had already found out that there were still places in this big hotel, and she said she had also made enquiries about possible training or jobs for us. Having worked in the office of the camp, she had been able to find out a number of things.

I could see that we were coming to the end of our jobs in the home, so I talked with Mr Huber. He said we would have to travel to Bern first, to talk there to some advisers about our future, but it should be possible to visit our parents at the same time, and he would see what he could arrange. He was very pleased with us and the work we had done, and felt we deserved a treat, like a visit to Luzern.

Before leaving for Bern, we packed our things. Helena had moved into a larger room with the other nurse, and was quite happy to stay on. Christel and I only took a bag with us, because Mr Huber said he had arranged with the Tivoli, that we could have two nights there with our parents.

The trip to Bern, and the visit there to the headquarters of the *Rückwanderer*, was a waste of time. Again we met a careers adviser, who had all our particulars from the camp. She suggested that we both take up nursing training, as we already had practical experience.

I tried again to get a grant for my medical studies, but this time I was told point blank that grants were not given for any more than six months training. We both refused the training as nurses, but said we would discuss it with our parents, whom we were meeting that evening.

We arrived at Luzern railway station in the late afternoon/evening, and the view over the Vierwaldstätter See was magnificent. Again and again we were struck by the beauty of Switzerland, its cleanliness, and its colourfulness.

We had to ask our way to the Tivoli, and people stared at us, because we didn't speak Swiss German, but pure German. Their replies, although given in ordinary German, still had an accent, and sounded strange to our ears. We found the Tivoli, a magnificent, large hotel by the lake, with lovely gardens full of red, white and purple flowers. I couldn't believe that this was a *Rückwanderer Heim* (home) and I could understand my mother wanting us to come there.

My parents and Hans were very pleased to see us. They took us to the large dining room, where we had a cold supper, because everybody else had already eaten. After that we went to my parents' large bedroom to talk.

My mother told us that she already had a job working for Caritas, an international firm, who posted or delivered food parcels to the damaged European countries. People from all over the world sent money and the addresses of friends and relatives. The office where my mother worked was responsible for sending the receipts back, typing out the labels for the food parcels together with the instructions for small, medium or large ones. Replies also had to be sent to enquiries for prices and contents of the food parcels. My mother worked two hours every afternoon to get a little pocket money. In the meantime, my father had applied for jobs, and had had one or two interviews.

My brother had started to go to the Luzerner Kantonschule (local grammar school), but was not very happy there, as he had to drop two years, and was in a class with sixteen year old boys. His only hope was to prove to the teachers that he was good enough to move up a class or two. In the meantime, my parents and Hans were living free in the Tivoli, until my father had found a job, so that he could support his family. The government also gave everybody a little pocket money, with which one could buy the few necessary and personal things, like soap, toothpaste, shaving equipment, etc.

My mother had explored possibilities for Christel and myself:

'If you do not want to go into nursing, Christel, I would suggest you do something similar. I thought you might like to train in a laboratory. There is an excellent hospital here, the Kantonspital, and we could go there, and explore the possibilities, by talking to the doctors, or some of the assistants working there.'

Christel quite liked the idea. This would be a job with a future, in research maybe, which could be very interesting. In any case, it would be an easier job than nursing, for which we all thought Christel was not strong enough. Christel could probably also live at home, and attend the hospital daily.

I had already written to my mother, that Mr Huber had suggested I should take up a career in an office, and my mother had met a young girl in the Tivoli who attended a commercial college on a grant from the government. Now she told me about her research.

'I have found a school or college for you, Helga, to learn shorthand, typing and book-keeping. It is only five minutes from the Tivoli, and is called Dr Frei's Handelsschule. They give one and two year courses, or a short one for six months. You can see by the way I have so quickly found employment, that it is a good thing to learn. If you want to do something different later on, you will find it useful to know how to type, even if you forget your shorthand. I would suggest you go and see the school tomorrow morning, get all the details - type of courses, how long they take, what certificate you get at the end, how much it costs, and whether the courses are full up, or have vacancies.

I can go with Christel to the Kantonspital and make enquiries there and, maybe, even fix something up provisionally for her. In the afternoon, you can see the manager of the Tivoli, and tell him what you have done, and say that you want to stay with your parents. It is up to him then, either to make the arrangements for you to stay in the Tivoli, or suggest other training and move you to another place. He is a very nice and helpful man. I have already done some typing for him, so he knows me.'

I admired my mother for the way she had worked out everything, and I was grateful to her for already having made the first enquiries. The next day, Christel and my mother went off to the hospital, and I made my way to Dr Frei's Handelsschule. I was given leaflets about the courses, and whilst talking to a young girl about them an elderly gentleman, tall, erect, grey-haired and very good-looking, entered the office.

Everybody suddenly looked more efficient, and the whole office seemed to vibrate with his presence there. I realised that he must be an important man, so I asked the girl who he was. She looked quite shocked at me, I don't know why, surely she could not have expected me to know him.

'That is Dr Frei, the director of the college,' she whispered.

I was sure that Dr Frei had heard me talking to the girl and her whispered reply. He came over to us and asked whether he could help me. I told him that I was enquiring about courses and the price of them.

'You don't speak Swiss German,' he said. 'Are you a *Rückwanderer*?'

I told him I was, and he asked me to come into his office. He wanted to know all about my education, and why I wanted to attend one of the courses at his school. I told him that I had a German matriculation, which was not recognised in Switzerland, that I had learnt English, French and Latin, and that I had started to study medicine. He said that he was sorry to hear that I could not carry on with my studies, and then continued:

'Some of my pupils here have not learnt English at school, and have to start it now when they begin their commercial course. I don't think you will have any difficulties with our courses, considering the educational foundations you have got. We do not give an entrance examination, but accept anybody who has been to the "Middle" or "Grammar" school until the age of sixteen. I would suggest you take the six months course. You receive a certificate which is recognised everywhere. The course has already started, but I have a vacancy which you can have.'

'Thank you,' I said. 'I would like to take up your offer, but unfortunately I have not yet got a grant for the course. As a matter of fact, I have not even told our careers adviser that I am interested in a commercial course, or that I was coming to make some enquiries today. I think it is going to be a bit of a shock to the manager of the Tivoli to discover that I would like to stay in the hotel with my parents. I was only supposed to be visiting them, and now I even want a grant for a course. I will speak to him straight away, and hope that he will help me to get a grant from the government.'

Dr Frei watched me whilst I spoke. He had asked me a number of questions before, about my life in Königsberg, and about the time when I was a refugee. He smiled suddenly, and replied:

'I would like to help you. We, here in Switzerland, have not had any hardship because of the war, and should help our compatriots. I will let you have the six month course for half the price. In other words, if the college gets the course fees for three months, you can have the next three months free. Maybe that will help you to get the grant.'

I was very happy about this offer, and said so. I returned to the Tivoli, but couldn't tell anybody about my successful morning, because nobody was there. My father had gone to Zürich for an interview, my brother was at school, and my mother and Christel had not returned from the Kantonspital.

It was lunch time before I could talk to my mother. She and Christel, too, had had quite a successful morning. Christel was impressed with the layout and equipment in the laboratory, and was keen to work there. They had met the lady doctor in charge of the department, who would be willing to apprentice Christel, if she had private accommodation, as there was none available at the hospital. For the first year the wage was very small, not enough to live on, so a grant was needed to subsidise Christel's apprenticeship. Christel was also expected to take a short course of shorthand and typing, as knowledge of this was essential for the writing up of reports, and the notes which had to be taken during research. The lady doctor hoped to get a grant for Christel through the hospital, but the typing course payment was Christel's own responsibility, and she might get this through some *Rückwanderer* help. I told everybody about my successful morning, and my mother said:

'After dinner we will go and see the manager, and talk about everything. The two of you could go to the same school, you, Helga, for a full time course, and Christel, maybe a few hours a week. They might even have evening classes in Dr Frei's Handelsschule.'

We saw the manager, who was very surprised about our "go ahead" attitude, and was pleased that we wanted to get on with our education. He promised to help, made us fill out forms, and said to me that he hoped to get a quick reply, so that I could join the commercial course as soon as possible, because it had already started. He felt it was unnecessary for Christel and me to go back to Sarnen, as our suitcases could be forwarded to us here in Luzern. By saying that, we realised that he was convinced that we would get our grants, and could stay on in Luzern.

Things moved quickly after that. Christel and I were allocated a lovely big bedroom in the Tivoli, which we had to share with another young girl, Paula, who had finished a six month course at Dr Frei's Handelsschule, and had started a job in an office.

The rule was, once you start with a job, you can stay on for one month with your free accommodation, and then you have to move out, because you have received your first month's salary, with which you can pay for your food and accommodation from then on. Paula was therefore only with us for a short time.

The bedroom was large and beautiful. It was situated at the front of the hotel on the top floor, and sitting on the balcony one had a panoramic view over the lake and the mountains, particularly the Pilatus, the famous pointed mountain, with the interesting cogwheel train, which took people up to the top.

The manager phoned Mr Huber in Sarnen, and the railway delivered our suitcases the next day. Again we were impressed with the efficient service. Christel's arrangements took a week, because the doctors in the hospital had had to have a meeting, to agree to a kind of grant for her, so that she had enough money to live on. She did get it, and the *Kriegswirtschaftsamt* (war economy department) in Luzern gave us both the grant for the school, including some pocket money to buy our papers and books.

I started my lessons two or three days after I had been interviewed by the principal, on the 20th of October 1946. In my class were a mixture of boys and girls. At first I found shorthand and typing difficult, because the others had already started, and seemed to know so much more than I. Dr Frei gave me some used books free, to save me the money to buy new ones. I found no difficulties in English and German, where we had to learn how to write business letters. Most students were good at French, because exchanges between Swiss-German and Swiss-French children were encouraged at an early age, and also, many Swiss-German families had their holidays in the French-speaking part of Switzerland. I was not fluent in French, but my knowledge of the language was good enough for the commercial course.

My mother helped me with shorthand, making me practise, and Christel joined in also. She asked the manager whether we could borrow a typewriter for the evenings, when the office was closed, and we practised in our bedroom. Dr Frei also gave me permission to enter the typing room whenever I wanted to, so that I could practise there.

Book-keeping was at first a big puzzle to me. Gradually, with the help of Dr Frei and my mother, things fell into place. My German was excellent, too good actually, it showed everybody else up.

The Swiss, because they speak their *Schweizer Deutsch* (a dialect of German), often find the pure German difficult, although they read and write in the pure German form.

I had never learnt *Schweizer Deutsch*, and sometimes found it difficult to understand. Everybody around me spoke it, but tried to speak without the dialect when addressing me. At times I felt like a foreigner, the language set me apart, and I never formed any friendships at the school. There were also other reasons apart from the language. I was older than the average pupil, most of them were seventeen or eighteen years old. I gradually moved up to the top of the class in all subjects except French, and I worked harder than anybody else, spending every free minute at the college in the typing room to practice, because I knew that I had to have a job soon. I also had no real home, and could never invite anybody. Everybody was very kind to me when I approached them, but they kept mostly in little groups, often because friendships had already started at school, or they lived near one another, or did things together after college.

When we had the first snow, at the beginning of December, my classmates made plans to go skiing.

I had never skied before, at least not like they ski in Switzerland, where they have so many slopes, hills and mountains so, again, I could not join in, and felt the wall between us.

There was one girl who asked me once to come and see her in the afternoon; we finished school at 1 p.m. She was not very good in any of the subjects, except French, which she had learnt through her grandmother, who came from the French-speaking part of Switzerland. I helped her sometimes with German letter-writing and book-keeping. She wanted me to come and have coffee and cake in the afternoon. It was already very cold outside, and we had had the first snow. When I arrived at her parents' large warm flat, I was shivering with cold, and my hands were red, because I had no gloves, and only a thin coat. Her mother scolded me, in a joking sort of way, for not dressing warmer, so I just told her that I could not afford to buy gloves on my little pocket money, and I had no other coat to wear. I could see she felt sorry for me, but I didn't want pity. The girl's father, a civil servant, was there also, and by the time I left again I knew that I had only been asked because they were inquisitive, because they wanted to know all about Hitler's Germany and the war.

I was never asked again, because they got their answers on that first visit, but a day or two later, the girl gave me a beautifully wrapped present. When I opened it, I found a pair of warm gloves in it, and I was touched by the gift.

My mother was still working at Caritas in her free time, when she was not working in the office in the Tivoli, and she suggested one day that I, too, could earn a little extra money by typing addresses, etc. This would also give me practice on the typewriter. I thought this was a good idea, because Christmas was coming, and I could then, maybe, buy everybody a little gift.

My mother showed me what I had to do, and after that I did a few hours in the afternoon, and sometimes also in the evening, gradually getting a little extra money. I bought some bitter chocolate again, but shared it with Christel. We were alone in the bedroom now, Paula had left, and if I wasn't working in the evening for Caritas Christel and I practised our shorthand and typing. We used to dictate articles from the paper to one another.

My father found it very difficult to find employment. In desperation he even wrote applications for jobs he hardly knew anything about. I remember my father even applying for the job as an assistant to the director of a film company. He had no idea what it involved, but was very willing to learn, and stressed, in his application, that he had worked for a film company before, and also possessed a wonderful imagination. Both statements were true. He had once, during his student days, worked as an extra in a crowd scene, and he really imagined that he was capable of being the assistant to the director. Not only didn't he get the job, but he never even got a reply. He tried not to show his disappointment, but he was sometimes bad tempered or touchy, and we all knew how he felt.

Hans was not happy at school either. The headmaster suggested a crammer school where, through intensive teaching, his learning period could be shortened. The school was expensive, my father had no job, and a grant was not forthcoming. The *Kriegswirtschaftsamt* put forward a plan for my brother to be apprenticed in a business with leanings towards engineering, and because of the low pay for the apprenticeship years they would give him a small grant to help with his living expenses. Before doing this, he would have to absolve his military service because in Switzerland conscription exists for every young man.

Most boys joined up after school so that they could have uninterrupted further education afterwards, but some started to study and joined later, when they could make use of their acquired knowledge, like a newly qualified doctor joining the medical corps.

Hans was not keen on the apprenticeship, but neither did he want to go to school any more. So it was decided that he do his military service for a year first. After that he could think again. Our living standard might have improved by then.

He had Christmas with us, and then left, joining the *sapper* (engineering) unit. He had a hard time at first, but gradually he learnt Swiss German, and enjoyed his stay, when he was in a more authoritative position. He stayed in the army just over a year becoming a Non-Commissioned Officer. He got the rank of *Unteroffizier* in October 1947 and left the army one month later.

CHAPTER TWO

Christmas 1946 - The Flat - First Job

My parents wanted us all to be together for Christmas and, after talking to the manager of the Tivoli, it was arranged that Astra and Monika could join us for two weeks at Christmas. It was 1946/47 and was the last time that we were all together for the festive season.

I had worked hard at college, and also in the evenings at Caritas, and had got a little money saved up for a few small presents. I was determined that everybody got a gift, because none of us had had one the year before on the radio station. We had no spare money for Christmas cards or decorations, so we used the skills we had learnt at school by making our own. My mother organised some glue and paper from the Tivoli and the Caritas office, and we cut and made and stuck together snakes and garlands. We had plenty of coloured drinking straws in the dining room, and from them we made "Mobiles" in the shape of stars, triangles, squares, etc.

The manager had organised a big tree in the hall, but we all felt we wanted something in our own rooms, and that's where we used our do-it-yourself decorations. I packed the little presents I had into sheets of paper, which I had made from opened and then stuck together envelopes. They were held together by coloured elastic bands and paperclips. My father and Hans got a pair of warm socks each, very necessary clothing in the cold weather. Christel I spoilt with a lipstick, my mother got a pair of warm stockings, with strict instructions not to give them to Astra, Monika was also spoilt with a toy, and Astra was allowed to choose her present.

I didn't know whether Astra would appreciate a practical gift, or would want something different. She had earned money whilst in the home with Monika, and also received a subsidy for baby clothing and shoes. So I thought she probably had bought things for herself and Monika, and unless I knew what was needed, I might buy something she already had.

The staff in the home where Astra lived were all *Rückwanderer*. They were paid a good wage for the work they did there, the same as they would have received if they had worked somewhere else. There was a crèche where Astra could leave Monika, for which she had to pay a small fee from her wages. This money, in return, was used as wages for the nursery teachers, or helpers running the crèche. Astra cooked in the kitchen, having had training in that line. She didn't like it, but I think the reason was again that she couldn't get on with the other people. Some of the mothers had outside jobs, and then had to pay for their keep and the crèche. Astra would have liked this too, but was told that Monika was too young to be left all day in the crèche. Working in the home, she had the opportunity of going to the nursery in her break time and being with Monika. The Swiss were quite concerned about children and mothers. No child under fourteen years of age was allowed to be alone in the house. Working mothers had to organise baby-sitters or minders, even if it was only for an hour after school. There were check-ups to see whether the rule was kept and, if broken, there would be a court case.

Astra came a few days before Christmas, and we were all pleased to see her. Everybody volunteered to take Monika for a walk in her pram. She wasn't walking yet on her own, but did a few steps, guided by her mother, grandparents, aunts, or her only uncle! She was a beautiful child, with fair curls and clear blue happy eyes. She was very self-willed and everybody spoilt her, not only we as a family, but the whole of the Tivoli, as she was the youngest there for Christmas.

College, of course, closed for Christmas, so I had a few free days, which I used to make extra money by working for Caritas. I desperately needed shoes and underwear. I had stopped buying chocolates, deciding that I really couldn't afford them. Christel, although having holidays from college, had to carry on with her work at the hospital.

My mother looked after Monika one afternoon, and Astra and I went into the town of Luzern to do some shopping. Everything was beautifully decorated. There were lights everywhere, Christmas trees, tinsel, shiny bells, and balls in different colours, and some shops had soft Christmas music. People in fur coats and boots, chatting happily, choosing gifts and laughing, being happy and content, were crowding the streets and the shops. It was a picture not seen by us for years, and my eyes, so hungry for colour and happiness, took it all in with pleasure.

Astra still had her grey fur coat (goat skin), which my mother had bought her in Königsberg. It looked very worn now. I only had a thin short coat, organised for me in Hamburg. People stared at us, because we were so poorly dressed, but I didn't care. I was happy, I had started to earn some money, and soon, when I was finished with my course, I would earn more, and then I, too, would be able to buy expensive clothes.

I had told Astra that I wanted to buy her a present, and asked her to choose something in a certain price range. I said that, if it was something special, I could, maybe, spend slightly more. Astra stopped eventually at a counter with some lovely wool mohair and cashmere shawls and scarves. I tried to pull her away, as they were much too expensive.

'Come over to the other side,' I said. 'They are cheaper there. I cannot afford these.'

'I am only looking,' she said.

Eventually we moved over to the other counter. Astra picked up some scarves, but hardly looked at them before dropping them again. After that, we walked off to different departments. I urged her, from time to time, to make up her mind, because I wanted to get back to the Tivoli for my supper, as I had to work in the evening at Caritas. We came back again to the counter with the expensive scarves. Astra picked up one, and said:

'That's the one I want.'

She must have earmarked it when she inspected them the first time, because she never hesitated when we returned to these scarves.

'You know I cannot afford this,' I said. 'It is twice as much as I was prepared to spend. I said a little more, but not double.'

'I do not want anything else,' she replied. 'If you don't buy this, you do not need to buy anything else. I would rather not have a present from you then.'

She shrugged her shoulders in the usual way, turned round and walked off, without waiting for me. I followed slowly, hurt and cross and disappointed. Suddenly everything was spoilt, my happiness about Christmas, the preparations for it, the buying and wrapping of little gifts, and the pretty streets and shops.

Why, oh why, did Astra always spoil things, I thought.

I followed her out of the shop and caught up with her. She didn't say another word, and we both returned silently to the home. My mother wanted to know whether we had had a good afternoon.

Astra said the shops were crowded and full of goods, and I didn't say anything, but went to the dining room to get my buffet supper, as I had to go out again. My mother followed me, after Astra had taken over Monika, as she, too, had to go to Caritas.

'I wish that you wouldn't always quarrel with your sister,' said my mother to me.

I didn't know what to reply to that. I hadn't quarrelled with Astra, and it was unnecessary to explain what had happened, because whatever I said would be wrong. My father was right - silence is golden!

Whilst working with my mother that evening, I asked her whether she would lend me some money, as I wanted to buy something which was more expensive than I could afford at the moment. I promised to pay it back, once I got paid again by Caritas. My mother looked at me questioningly for a moment, then said:

'You are not usually extravagant for yourself, but be careful, don't get tempted by the lovely things you see in the shops, you need so many practical and useful things.'

She thought I wanted the money to buy myself something. What a joke! It was to satisfy my sister's demand, the one I shouldn't quarrel with.

My mother gave me the money, but I never told her the truth. - I told Christel about it when we went to bed, and she suddenly laughed, and said:

'I didn't ask Astra what she wanted for Christmas. She told me what I should get her, but I replied that I had already bought something for her. She was surprised about that. You should have done the same.'

'I suppose I was silly, but I thought it would be fun to go and choose something together. I will go tomorrow and get her that scarf before it is sold.'

After a little while, Christel said: 'I wonder what she is giving us for Christmas?'

'Probably nothing,' I said jokingly.

'Surely not,' said Christel. 'She is the only one who earns a good salary, more than any of us, and Mama said she hardly has to spend any money on Monika's clothes and toys, as the other mothers in the home pass things on when their children have grown out of them.'

'Well, let's wait and see.'

The next day - it was Christmas Eve - I went back early to the big store, and found the scarf still there. I bought it, and wrapped it as a present, ready for the evening. We always had our *Bescherung* (giving out of Christmas presents) on Christmas Eve.

As our bedroom was the biggest one, we decided to have our celebration there. Christel and I organised everything, pushing the beds round so that they could act as settees, and borrowing some chairs from the hall. We had a cold supper in the evening, and the manager permitted us to bring it upstairs. My father had got a real little Christmas tree, and we decorated it with some ribbons I had, and a few lametta strings which had "fallen off" the big tree in the hall. My mother produced, in the last minute, some little silver balls, which she brought from the office, saying that nobody would miss them during the holiday, as it was closed. She said she would take them back again, when she returned to the office. Hans brought some large candles, saying that a friend had given them to him. Everybody put their little presents under the tree.

We met, as we always did on Christmas Eve, with only the candles burning on the tree. Monika was fascinated with everything. It was her first real Christmas. She had a long sleep in the afternoon, so that she was able to participate in our evening celebration.

We had no piano, so my father started to sing, and we all joined in. The year before we had been on the cold radio station, now we were in a beautiful warm hotel, with a lovely view over the lake and the town of Luzern, with hundreds and hundreds of lights on. My father burnt a little piece of the tree, which made the room smell of fir, and we all felt happy, warm and comfortable in the dim light of the room. Even Monika clapped her hands, and kept quiet during our singing.

At the present time, we only used the table lamp, as we didn't want a bright light. We gave Monika her presents straight away, so that she had something to play with. There were quite a few gifts for everybody. My mother must have worked very hard for Caritas to earn so much money, because she had given everybody several little gifts, all signed from Mama and Papa. We all knew that my father had not contributed much.

He got a little pocket money, and when he went for interviews he was entitled to expenses, which were for the train and a meal. He usually skipped the meal, taking a roll with him which he took from the breakfast table, and then eating more in the evening. In this way he could put a little money by.

Everybody was happy and excited, unpacking their presents, and thanking one another. I suddenly noticed that I had no present from Astra. I glanced towards the tree, to see whether it was left behind, but there was nothing, so I whispered to Christel:

'What did Astra give you?'

'I was going to ask you the same,' she said, 'because I haven't got anything. Let's ask Hans.' With that she whispered something to Hans. There developed a whispered conversation, and then Christel turned back to me and just shook her head.

'I told you so,' I whispered, and laughed. It didn't seem to matter. I didn't really want a present from Astra. I felt sorry for her, because with her stubbornness, her demand of what people should give and do for her,

her selfishness and egoistic behaviour, she had never been able to make friends, and would not get many friends in the future. I could foresee a very lonely life for her. I was glad that I had bought her that scarf. She was surprised and happy about it, and kissed me, saying thank you with a little guilty look in her eyes.

It was Hans who suddenly touched on the subject of gifts. He only had his pocket money, even so, he had bought everybody a little gift. I had two pencils and a rubber which I needed at college for my shorthand, and I was very happy about it.

'I would like to thank everybody for their presents to me,' said Hans. 'I know that none of us is earning a wage, except for Astra but, even so, you have all given me something. I cannot find your present, Sternchen.' He used her old name, because he was cross, and wanted to annoy her. Christel, often the peacemaker, said quickly:

'I think she only gave Mama and Papa a present.'

We all looked at our parents, there was silence. My father bit his bottom lip, and looked at me. I smiled, because I thought the whole thing funny, and not at all surprising or unexpected, and I must have conveyed this to him, because he suddenly laughed out loud, and replied to my smile as if he had heard what I thought:

'You are right, it is no surprise, we should have known this before, it is so typical.'

'I don't know what you are talking about, Hans,' said my mother to my father. 'Astra has a responsibility now, she has to look after her child, and any money she earns has to last, not only for one, but for two people. It is very wise to save money, because bigger expenses will come for her when she leaves the home one day.'

My mother, as usual, protected Astra, who never said a word, but pretended to be busy with Monika and her presents.

'Let's have another Christmas carol,' said my father and with that he started one, and we all joined in. After that we had our supper, and then Hans asked my father to tell us something about his student days. My father had an exciting time whilst at university. His stories about his life were very interesting, often a little exaggerated, but always funny.

On Christmas Day all the *Rückwanderer* joined the big dinner in the dining room in the middle of the day. It was an excellent meal, goose, red cabbage and potatoes, the typical Christmas dinner. The manager had been most generous in allocating extra money for the festive season. The dining room, with the long tables, was decorated attractively. There were a number of candles on the table, serviettes with a Christmas motif, fir branches with red ribbons and silver and golden bells. Everybody had a little present from Father Christmas. This was the biggest surprise.

We had just finished our meal, and some of us had taken the plates into the kitchen, when we were told to sit down again, and be silent. We heard a lot of banging and thumping, and then the door opened, and in walked Father Christmas, with a large bag, and a small *Rute* (birch rod). We had a few children for Christmas, not only Monika, some other couples had their grandchildren in the home for the holiday. Father Christmas walked to a boy of about eight years old, and asked whether he had always been a good boy. He nodded quickly, and replied that he was never naughty. Father Christmas asked the parents, and they said that he sometimes didn't obey. So Father Christmas took the *Rute* and smacked the boy's bottom a little in jest, and then gave him a present. He did the same to one or two more children, and then came to Monika. The little girl looked at him, and when he bent over and asked her whether she had always been a good girl, she laughed and pulled his beard. He didn't smack her, but gave her a present. He then returned to the door, opened it, and brought in two more sacks filled with presents. Everybody had to come and put their hand into one, and take out their gift. One sack was for the men, and the other for the women. Even Astra was included. I had a box of beautifully embroidered Swiss handkerchiefs, and Christel had some perfume. I think my mother had a box of soap. Every *Rückwanderer* had a present that Christmas, all were very happy. We joined hands, we embraced, we sang carols, we went for a walk along the lake, and admired the snow covered mountains.

The highlight for me, thinking of that Christmas, was the warmth we had from the central heating in the Tivoli. After the terrible winters of 1944/45 and 1945/46, the only wish I had was to be warm. Presents, food and drink, Christmas trees and carols, they were happiness and excitement for the moment, but warmth, given by thick clothes and heating, was comfort, and I wanted that to last. My New Year's resolution was that whatever I did, whatever money I would earn in the future, must be directed first towards the most important comfort for me, warmth.

It is difficult to describe the feeling I had when I walked into the centrally heated Tivoli from a frosty and snowy outside, and the warmth there enveloped me. Sometimes I would just stand in the hall and think that I would like to touch it, to stroke it, to thank it for being there, but how could you do that with heat, or warmth?

All the places I went to were centrally heated, and the windows were double glazed to keep the heat in. The Swiss people were very lucky to have all this every winter, and even to have had it during the war. They would never be able to understand us *Rückwanderer*.

All of us celebrated New Year together in the big dining hall, and everybody was sure that 1947 would be a good year.

My mother returned to her job at Caritas in the New Year and was offered full time employment. It was felt that she had done so well in her part-time occupation, that she could now take over one office, and also organise the part-time work.

My father, too, was suddenly offered a part-time job at the Hotel Balance, in the centre of Luzern, as a book-keeper. It was not a very big hotel, and it was therefore not necessary to employ anybody full time. Most people didn't like part-time jobs, but my father had had so many disappointments that he felt he just had to take up this offer. He worked only late afternoons and evenings there, which left him with spare time to look for another job, and go for interviews. He soon made friends with all the staff in the hotel, particularly the cook, and before long he was supplied with free drinks, and a free evening meal.

Hans left to go into the army, and Astra returned to the home where she had been before as a cook, taking Monika with her. She cried when she left, she didn't want to go back, she said she was lonely there. I am sure this was an honest statement, and I did feel sorry for her.

Christel worked in the hospital again, and I returned to my classes in Dr Frei's Handelsschule.

My parents were told, that together they now earned enough money to leave the Tivoli and move into a flat by February 1st, when they would receive their first monthly wages. They went off flat hunting, and found a three bedroomed one in the Bürgenstrasse, on the second floor.

There was a good sized kitchen with cupboards, a bathroom, the main bedroom with a large balcony, a sitting room with balcony, and two smaller bedrooms. The thought was that my parents would occupy the large bedroom, Christel and I would share one room, and Astra or Hans could have the third bedroom, when visiting us.

Christel had been given a grant from the hospital for her food and living accommodation, so she, too, would have to move out by February 1st. It was assumed that, when I finished at the college, and had a job for one month, I, also, would join the family in the Bürgenstrasse.

The *Kriegswirtschaftsamt* gave my parents a lump sum to buy furniture and linen, and whatever was necessary for a home. My father had to sign a statement saying that if ever he got any of his money or property back, he would return this sum. He told us that he had added at the bottom of the declaration that, if he got all his belongings in property and cash, he would reimburse the *Kriegswirtschaftsamt* double.

It was left to my parents to decide how they wanted to spend the money. In other words, if the furniture was too expensive, they would have to skimp on the kitchen utensils and the linen, or the other way round. It was the manager of the Tivoli who gave us some good advice. He had heard that the Hotel Du Lac had been sold, and the new management was selling off all the contents, as they wanted to start with everything new. The manager even rang up the new director, who promised to give all *Rückwanderer* who bought anything from the hotel a special discount.

We all marched off to the Du Lac, Mama, Papa, Christel, who skipped her afternoon typing class, and I. We met a very nice man, who had been put in charge of all the selling off of the furniture, linen and kitchen equipment, and he took us round the hotel, quoting the prices for the different items.

Some of the rooms were luxurious, with wardrobes and beds made of mahogany, still looking new, and the soft chairs and settees had hardly a mark on them. We couldn't understand that this was all for sale, and that the hotel wanted to replace everything. The prices quoted to us were very reasonable, and the man said once or twice that, if we took this and that together, as it was a set belonging to one another, he would drop the price even more.

My mother wrote everything down that was possible for us to buy, so that we could talk about it later, and my father and I took some measurements of the furniture and the carpets. There were also sheets, pillowcases, tablecloths, serviettes, and big and small towels for sale, all with Hotel Du Lac woven into them. In the kitchen, we could choose plates, cups, saucers and knives, forks and spoons, but no saucepans, as these were much too big. Armed with a long list, and a promise to return, we all walked back to the Tivoli, quite bewildered from all we had seen.

In the evening we had a big discussion and then sorted things out. The result was that our new home in the Bürgenstrasse was completely furnished with the equipment from the Du Lac, and because it was so reasonable our money went a long way.

We had a lovely set of bedroom furniture, wardrobes, chests of drawers, beds with large headboards and side cabinets, dressing table and chair, all made of mahogany. Even years later, friends admired the expensive main bedroom furniture.

The thick beautiful big bath towels, with the Du Lac name woven in, never wore out, and we had so many tea towels, that even when they got thin there seemed to be plenty more of them.

My mother had also enquired what was happening to all the net and velvet curtains, and was told that as the Du Lac had a completely new colour scheme, these, too, would be disposed off. When she offered to buy some, she was told to take what she liked for nothing.

Because all the china was also marked with the name of the hotel, my mother did not take too much, hoping soon to buy her own plates and cups and saucers. She took some of the big dishes, as they were only marked underneath.

We had enough thick wool blankets and featherbeds for all our beds, together with sheets and duvet covers, all, of course, with Du Lac embroidered or marked. From now on Family Zirkel only slept in the Five Star Hotel Du Lac!!

My mother had a hard time that month, because she was now working all day, and only had her two hour dinner break or the evenings, to prepare for the move. She borrowed the sewing machine from the laundry room in the Tivoli in the evening to make some curtains. She was sewing every free minute, because neither Christel nor I had ever done much sewing before.

My father organised the furniture part, and all the things from the Du Lac. He was even able to get some good large carpet pieces from the hotel. He said it was necessary to have them big, so that the edges, with the name Du Lac, could be cut off. My father found a *Rückwanderer* who was a carpet layer. He was an old man, not working any more, but now getting a pension from the Swiss government. He was only too pleased to help my father for a little remuneration. He also organised two friends to come and help on the day when all the furniture would arrive from the hotel.

The people in the flat in the Bürgenstrasse moved out on January 31st, and the manager of the Tivoli permitted my parents to stay another few days, until they had organised their flat.

Christel and I cleaned the new flat, my mother was still sewing, my father helped with the carpet laying. I ironed the first curtains, and my father, with his new friends, hung them up.

The day the van with all the furniture from the Du Lac arrived was a pandemonium. I had officially asked Dr Frei for a day off from college, and Christel had done the same from the hospital. The van was lent to us free by the Du Lac, and the driver and his partner wanted to return quickly, so they just brought everything up to the flat and put it down. They even had no time to assemble the bed frames, and as they wanted all their boxes back, the kitchen stuff and china was just put on to the floor. At least we were able to keep the boxes with the linen for a few days after we promised to return them, because we didn't want all those nice clean sheets put on to the floor. We all worked hard on moving day, and were glad to return to the Tivoli at night, for an evening meal and a bed.

My parents and Christel moved out. There was still a lot to do in the flat in the Bürgenstrasse, but my mother said it was liveable. I could not go and see them until the weekend, because it was quite a way to walk from the Tivoli, and having missed college time I was anxious to get on with my homework and lessons. When I did arrive at the flat, I was surprised to see how nice it looked. Both my parents smiled happily and were proud of their new home. They looked tired, including Christel. They had worked late into the night to get things straightened up.

'I am afraid we are in trouble with some of our neighbours for making too much noise late in the evening,' said my mother.

'It is because we are *Rückwanderer*,' said my father. 'Some Swiss are very kind, others resent us. We all give ourselves away with our speech, not being able to speak *Schweizer Deutsch*. We have apologised, and I have even written a letter.'

At the Tivoli, because Christel had moved out, I got another girl to share my room. She was a piano teacher, but having taken all her examinations in Germany she had to pass some more in Switzerland. She was attending a course at the Musical Academy, and as she had to practice the piano quite a bit, she often returned late from the academy, the only place where she could practice. She was a quiet girl, I hardly saw anything of her. Although we shared a room, we lived our separate lives, once we had organised the use of the bathroom.

I found the lessons at college easy, except for shorthand. Now that Christel had left, I had nobody to dictate to me and read back what I had written. I couldn't practice on my own. Dr Frei asked me one day to come into his office. He said he was extremely pleased with my progress, and then continued:

'The college fees have been paid for you up till January by a grant, and I have agreed to let you carry on for another three months free of charge. At the end of these studies you will receive a note from us to the effect that you have attended our commercial course, and what we thought of you as a student. This, of course, is not a certificate.

I feel you have done so well that it would be a pity to let you go without a proper and recognised testimony of your work here, after a final examination. I would like to extend my offer of free tuition to you for another six months, so that you can get the final certificate from our Handelsschule. In Switzerland this is a very good piece of paper to have. You deserve it, and I think you will pass the final examination with high marks, which is a credit to you and the college. If you agree, I will write to the *Kriegswirtschaftsamt*, putting forward my suggestion, and ask them to provide you with accommodation for another six months.'

I was surprised and pleased about his offer, but doubted whether I would get another grant. Still, if he wanted to try and get it for me, I would be very happy to carry on at the college. I had seen what happened to my father, and also to other *Rückwanderer* who had no recognised certificates, how difficult and nearly impossible it was for them to get a job. I agreed to Dr Frei's suggestion and thanked him very much for his most generous offer.

I should not have been so disappointed when a negative reply came, because I hadn't expected anything else, but it did hurt me. I had to give up my dream of becoming a doctor, and change to a completely different profession. I had the generous offer of free tuition but, because of lack of money for my accommodation, I could not finish the required one year study for the commercial certificate.

I felt that there was now no point in going to college any longer. I was already quite good at typing, and book-keeping was not a puzzle any more. I decided to try and get a job, and shorten my course at Dr Frei's Handelsschule by one month. Officially I should have finished at the college at the end of March, have a job for the month of April, and after receiving my first month's salary at the end of that month move in with my parents on May 1st. If I already had a job for March without telling the administration, I could work two months, whilst living free in the Tivoli, and therefore earn an extra month's money, which I could use to buy some clothes, which I badly needed.

I presented myself at an employment agency and asked for job vacancies. I informed them about my course at Dr Frei's Handelsschule, and that I could start on March 1st, if necessary.

I was given three addresses, and told to go for an interview any time between two to three p.m. to the first two offices but for the third one I would have to have an appointment late in the afternoon. The agency promised to make this for me, if I so desired.

I didn't like the look of the first place I went to. It was an office in an old house on the second floor. The hallway was not very clean, most unusual for Switzerland, it was dark, because the lights didn't work, and when I got to the door of the office I heard shouting. I stood there for a little while, listening to the loud argument behind the closed door, which I didn't understand, and then decided not to ring the bell, because I wouldn't like to work there in any case.

The second office I went to was quite nice, but the lady who interviewed me said that I would also have to answer the telephone, and as I was not speaking Swiss German yet (she hoped I would learn it soon), she felt this was not the right job for me.

I returned to the agency, and reported to them what had happened. The girl smiled a little when I said I didn't like the first place, as if she wanted to say: Neither do I. She was sorry I didn't get the job in the second office, but then rang, and made an appointment for me at the next place, called: *Buchhaltungsstelle* (book-keeping agency), where they wanted a typist. I got an appointment in the late afternoon which suited me as I was still at college and didn't want to miss too many lessons.

Mr Graber, the owner of the *Buchhaltungsstelle*, interviewed me. He was a small thin man of about forty, rather nervous, and looked overworked. His speech was very fast and, although he tried to speak the ordinary German to me, he lapsed back into the Swiss dialect again and again and at times I couldn't understand him. He was telling me that he had two businesses, one in Kriens, on the outskirts of Luzern, and this one here. He had only recently opened the Kriens office, which needed all his attention at the moment. He could only come to this office in the evenings to look through the post, and generally organise everything.

He had a lot of letters to write, which he dictated into a Dictaphone machine in the evenings, and it would be my job to type them during the day and leave them in his office for his inspection and signature. He was looking for somebody with typing skill and the capability of setting out letters after a few instructions were given.

I informed him that I was still at college, and was not yet a fast typist, but I was capable of setting out letters and working on my own. He showed me the Dictaphone, which on first sight looked very complicated, but was not difficult to operate, once it was explained. It worked like a gramophone, except that the flat record was replaced by a small thick wax cylinder, where the needle went along the grooves, which were very close together.

Mr Graber demonstrated the equipment. He took a microphone, which was connected to his machine, and spoke into it. He gave the address of a customer, and then instructions about the contents of the letter. Whilst speaking, the smooth cylinder turned, and the needle made grooves into the wax. When he had finished, he took out the cylinder, went to another room where a Dictaphone machine stood next to a desk with a typewriter, and put it into the machine. One had to have earphones to hear what was said. There was a foot control to start and stop the Dictaphone.

The needle rested in the grooves around the cylinder, playing back into the earphones the words he had previously spoken.

Mr Graber said he would leave me to write the letter as a little test, to see whether I was capable of taking on the offered job.

I felt quite relieved when he left me alone. I had been afraid that he might watch me, to see how good my typing was. When somebody watched me I usually made mistakes.

Left alone, I soon sorted things out and typed the letter. I made a few mistakes and rubbed them out. When I had finished it, it didn't look very nice, so I typed it again. I was sure that I had spent too much time on the letter, and Mr Graber would think I was not good enough, but when I gave him the letter, he said it was very good, and offered me the job with quite a good starting salary. He said I would get used to the Dictaphone, and in time become quicker. He wanted me to start straight away, but I said that I had to go to college until the end of the month so that Dr Frei could give me a reference that I had completed part of a commercial course at his establishment. I promised that I would definitely start on March 1st.

'Alright,' said Mr Graber. 'I will inform the manager of your coming. You will only be involved in typing for me, and if there is nothing from me, the manager will find you some typing. I hope you will gradually become quicker with your typing. For your information, a good typist should be able to copy one cylinder per hour.'

My mother was very pleased when she heard about my job, and said it was a good wage for a beginner. Her salary was only a little more, and she had quite a responsible job, but then Caritas was a non-profit-making organisation, who couldn't pay high salaries. My mother felt that if my wage was already so high, she would look around for something better, as we desperately needed the money.

I went to see Dr Frei and asked him for a reference, telling him that I wanted to leave at the end of the month. He was very sorry that I had not received another grant, but quite agreed that I might as well start to work, if I had been offered a job. I did not inform the manager of the Tivoli or anybody else, that instead of going to college every day, I would be going to work at the *Buchhaltungsstelle*.

Dr Frei gave me an excellent reference and said I could mention his name at any time, if a verbal reference was needed.

I started my job on March 1st at eight o'clock in the morning. Having been told by Mr Graber that a good typist would get through eight cylinders a day, I was surprised that I had only managed three on my first day. Of course I had to get used to everything, meet the other employees, and hear about the type of work that was produced there. I also lost time when I had to go and look up addresses and names, because Mr Graber often lapsed into his Swiss German.

I felt guilty for being so slow at my typing, so after a few days I told the manager that I would like to stay on in the evening to catch up with the work. He gave me the key to the office, and for a few days I worked an extra hour every evening.

I started to get headaches, and I couldn't sleep at night because as soon as I shut my eyes and relaxed I started hearing Mr Graber's voice in my head. To listen to him for eight to nine hours every day was just too much. He often made mistakes, like saying a whole sentence, and when I had just finished typing it, his voice would tell me to scrap it. The worst was when I had come to the end of a long letter, and his voice told me to scrub nearly everything. This was a waste of time and paper, as I always had to start a new letter again. After that experience I would listen through the cylinder first, before typing anything.

I had to put the completed letters with envelopes and the finished cylinders on his desk. He erased the grooves on the cylinder with a scraping machine, and was then able to use it again. The cylinders got gradually thinner and thinner until there was no wax left.

Mr Graber didn't come to the office every evening, because sometimes the work which I had done the day before was still on his desk the next day. If there was no work for me the manager made me type out lists for some of the customers.

I remember one for which I had to have quite an imagination. It concerned a customer who had a grocery shop. Every item sold in his shop was rung up on the till, and the price printed on to a roll of paper at the same time. When the roll was full, the grocer replaced it with a new roll. I was given six of these full rolls and some lists with the names of groceries and their prices. It was my job to type out what and how much was sold every day. I had to look at the price on the roll, and try and f from the list which type of grocery this was, so that I could give it a name, and type it on to my sheet of paper as being sold on that certain day. This was a very slow job, and sometimes the price just didn't seem to fit any item. The manager told me to use my imagination!!

He was satisfied if I just put the prices with the items costing nearly what it said on the price list and, if not, even put two items together to fit a figure on my roll of paper. After a time I started to know the prices of certain items, and my list grew quicker. I had no idea why the *Buchhaltungsstelle* had to do this work for the grocer or, maybe, the tax office, and the manager didn't enlighten me either, so I just carried on with my guessing game. It was certainly different from Mr Graber's voice in my ears, and I even preferred it, although it was boring.

In a way, March 1947 was quite a happy month for me. I lived free in a beautiful hotel by the lake. The spring flowers were trying to come out, and the lovely view over the lake, and the snowy mountains were a pleasure to me every day.

A shattering blow came when the manager told me that a careers adviser was coming to the Tivoli, who would help me to find a job, so that I could start work on April 1st. He asked me whether I could make sure that I was in the hotel on a certain evening. She had to interview several people. I felt a little uneasy, wondering whether my lie would come out.

The careers adviser was quite a pleasant woman, and I realised that she seriously wanted to help me. She apologised first of all that they had not been able to give me the grant for another six months.

'If we give you a grant for a further six months,' she explained, 'we will have to do the same to other *Rückwanderers*, and that is not possible, with the limited amount of money allocated for training. Dr Frei has certainly given a glowing report of your work at the college. I will now try and help you to get a good job, so that you have an excellent start to see you through a good career.'

She was surprised when I told her that I had already approached an agency, and would be going for an interview at an office the following week. She was pleased that I had thought ahead, and got on with the necessary enquiries. She wanted to know the name of the firm where I was going to have an interview, so I mentioned the one where I was ~used the job, because I was not speaking Swiss German. She didn't the firm. I also said I would like a job where I had to do a lot of ~cause I knew that in this way I would become proficient. Touch ~rtain speed was demanded in the better paid offices.

148

'This sounds well planned, and if you are sure you can manage to find a job on your own I prefer this. You learn a lot by trying for things without help, so I will not interfere. Should you be unable to get employment by April 1st, please tell the manager, who will inform me, and I will come and help you to find a job. I know two more agencies in the town who have been most helpful in the past.'

And that was that, the lady wished me good luck, and I left the interviewing room, delighted that I had got away with my little lie.

In the last week of March, I informed the manager of the Tivoli that I had found a job, and would be starting on April 1st at the *Buchhaltungsstelle*. He was very pleased, and said he would pass on the information to the relevant places.

My typing became quite good, but I never was able to type eight cylinders a day. I discovered from one of the other girls in the office that nobody had ever done it. When I typed six cylinders a day I was assured that this was excellent. Mr Graber started to come during the day from time to time and one day dictated some letters to me. I realised that my shorthand was hopeless. I had only been to college for five months, and once I left I never practised again, so I had forgotten most of it. Mr Graber soon realised what was going on and sent me away, saying he would dictate the letters on to the Dictaphone again. I told him my mother was very good at shorthand, and was also an excellent typist, but he said that this didn't help him, as she wasn't in his office.

'You can always employ her,' I said jokingly. He looked at me, but then turned silently towards his microphone, and I left to get on with my work.

At the weekend I often went to the Bürgenstrasse to see my parents and Christel, and hear the news about Astra and Hans. My brother was not a prolific letter writer, but he occasionally scribbled down a little news about what he was doing, and from it we learnt that he had quite a tough time, and lots of teasing, because he was so bad with his Swiss German. His first leave was after three months and he came home for a long weekend. He looked older, he was more sure of himself, and he spoke quite a bit of Swiss German.

'You learn to swear first,' he said. 'After that comes what to ask for. The officers are alright, the young lads are the ones who like to take the Micky out of me, but I give as much as I take. I am glad I have always been good at sport, that's a great help. We also have theory lessons, and I am usually good at those, because my German is better. We sometimes have to write an essay, and if I can help the biggest bully with some writing I have a few good days after that.'

All in all, he had settled down quite well, and found it very interesting.

The *sappers* didn't only have training sessions, but often had to help the civilian population in an emergency. Once they had to reconstruct and build a new wooden bridge over a small, fast flowing river in one of the mountain villages. The torrent of water, produced through the melting of the snow, had pulled the bridge away. This was quite a dangerous job, and some rock climbing was also necessary. The village people were very grateful and supplied the soldiers with sandwiches and drinks during their work, and the local girls came and talked to them in the evenings!

My mother had prepared a lot of food for the weekend, even baked a cake. We were all happy together; only Astra, with Monika, was missing. By the time Hans left, he had rested and eaten well, and took a food parcel with him, including the rest of the cake.

Christel, too, had now settled down at the hospital and enjoyed her work. She had finished her typing course, but said she was afraid she would forget this skill, as she had hardly any typing to do at the hospital. Like everybody else, she had her two hour lunch break, and came back to the Bürgenstrasse for a quick bite and a little rest, before returning to the hospital for the afternoon session.

My father was still trying, unsuccessfully, to get a full time job. He earned very little money, and felt guilty that it was my mother and Christel who kept the flat going. I was still in the Tivoli until the end of March.

Astra wrote pathetic letters about how unhappy she was in her work in the home. She had very little time to see and look after Monika. The little girl was in the crèche during the day when Astra was working. Because of these letters, my mother came up with a new idea, which she told us about when I came to the Bürgenstrasse one Sunday.

'I have been thinking about Astra and Monika,' said my mother. 'It seems a pity that Astra has to be parted so much from her child, because she has to work and earn money to keep herself and Monika. My idea is for us to employ Astra here. She and Monika can live with us, and cook and clean for us and we pay her. When Helga joins us, we will be three earning people. Papa is only half, but he helps as much as he can. You girls can clean your own room as you are sharing it, and I will do Papa's and my bedroom, which does not leave many cleaning jobs for Astra. Everybody pays a certain amount of money a week. We will have to work it out. It is then left to Astra to shop, organise, and manage the money, and what is left will be her wage. It should be possible to work like that. My salary is the highest, so I will give Astra some extra money, and once Papa has a better job there will be more money coming in, in any case. Astra is a qualified cook, and I know she can produce excellent meals. In this way she will be with us and have Monika with her, like every mother should have.'

The idea was quite good. Two hours for lunch was not much time, one could hardly cook a meal then, and I realised that I would not want to do any cooking in the evening after work. The question was only, would it work? Astra could suddenly refuse to cook or to clean, and we would have no power to make her do it. As long as she was employed somewhere, she would do what she was told, because she needed the money at the end of the day, but once here in the Bürgenstrasse, we would all have to keep her, even if she didn't work for us.

I mentioned my doubts. When I looked at my father I saw him smiling a little, and knew he had thought the same. My mother was sure that Astra would be so pleased to be with us, and have Monika with her all the time, that she would do anything for us. And so it was decided to put the proposition to Astra, but making the rules quite clear, and also stressing that she probably would have less money from us than she was getting at the moment.

Astra accepted everything, she didn't care as long as she could be with Monika, and with all of us. She arrived the next week with her suitcases, her big box, Monika's pram, and lots of other luggage. She certainly had already accumulated a number of things. We all turned up at the station, and didn't seem to have enough hands to carry all the luggage and parcels. The large box and one big suitcase were going to be delivered by the railway, so that was alright, but the rest had to be carried by us. On top of that Monika was crying, because she was tired.

We walked to the Bürgenstrasse, and I think the neighbours in our block of flats were quite shocked when we noisy lot arrived. We were all talking, Monika was crying, and the cases and parcels had to be bumped up the stairs to the top flat where we lived. The first thing that Astra said when we arrived was:

'But the flat is so small. I had a much bigger room in the home, as I had to sleep with Monika.'

Here we go, I thought, she has started to complain.

Still, things quietened down, Monika was soon asleep, and Astra was having something to eat. I had to leave, because I was still living in the Tivoli.

At the end of April I got my monthly salary and moved out of the Tivoli. I was very sorry to leave, it was such a beautifully situated place. (Today it is an hotel again, and very popular with the tourists). I only had one big suitcase, but it was quite heavy by now, because I, too, had collected things, particularly my books from college, which I was allowed to keep. The manager wished me good luck, and told me to come back and visit the Tivoli.

I arrived at the Bürgenstrasse absolutely exhausted from carrying my case, because I had to walk all the way. The public transport somehow didn't fit in. Christel had cleaned the bedroom, and we soon sorted my things out, as we had to share the wardrobe and other left-over spaces in the room. Christel and I always got on well, so we had no difficulties in organising ourselves. I enquired how things were going with Astra and Monika, and Christel said:

'She has only been here a few days, but I think it might be alright. Mama is helping, of course, but Astra served the dinner on time when I came home from the hospital in my dinner hour. So let's hope it carries on like that.'

I arrived on a Sunday, which was officially Astra's day off. My mother had suggested to her that she ought to go out on her own, because this was the only day when one of us, meaning herself, could look after Monika. So Astra had gone for an afternoon walk. She returned quite excited, and told us that she had discovered a place where they had Tea Dances in the afternoon.

Apparently she had heard the dance music and stood outside the café wondering whether she ought to go in or not, when she was joined by two young girls who were wondering the same. They got talking and in the end all three of them walked in and sat at a table. She had several dances, and hoped to go with one of the girls again next Sunday afternoon.

Now that I was living in the Bürgenstrasse, I didn't have to walk so far to work, which was useful in my dinner hours, as it gave me more time. I could even go and look at the shops, because the big stores, like Nordmann, didn't close at dinner time. First, of course, I had to go home and, if Astra had the dinner ready on time, we could eat straight away, and then I could go to the shops before returning to the office.

The first few days dinner was on time, and Astra had really tried hard to cook something special. Then came a day when we had to have sandwiches, because it had been raining, and Astra couldn't go out shopping with Monika. We had a cooked meal in the evening. After that came a day when Monika was naughty, and we had no dinner or prepared sandwiches. None of us had much time to argue, we had to find some food quickly, because we had to return to our respective places of work by two o'clock. In the evening there were prepared sandwiches but no cooked dinner. I have forgotten the excuse. My mother opened a tin of soup, as there was nothing else in the pantry.

From now on my mother made sure that there were a few emergency rations in the pantry, like some cooked potatoes, which could be fried over quickly, and some eggs, which could then be added to them.

Astra also started to go out to dances in the evening, so we had to clear up after the meal, and my mother even had to bath Monika and put her to bed. My father, working at the hotel Balance in the afternoon and evening, didn't know anything about this, and nobody informed him either.

The other thing that happened was that my mother changed her job. Mr Graber approached me and asked whether it was really only a joke when I said that he could employ my mother if he wanted fast shorthand and typing skills. I said that my mother would probably change her job for better pay. Mr Graber interviewed my mother, dictated a few test letters, was impressed with her skills, and employed her with a much higher salary than she got before. Caritas had omitted to give my mother a contract, and because of that she could leave straight away and join me at the *Buchhaltungsstelle*. So now we walked to work and home again together. Mama asked me to be patient with Astra, and also not to mention her failings to Papa. I paid my share of the money for my food and living, and kept quiet.

Although I had promised not to say anything to my father, this didn't prevent me from speaking out when he was not there. Papa did not eat much at home. He travelled to Zürich every morning, where he had met a Mr Müller, also a *Rückwanderer*, with whom he had started a little Import/Export business. The two of them had rented two rooms as an office, so that the business had an address and telephone number. They imported small ironmongery from Germany, and my father walked around Zürich, visiting different ironmongers, to take orders for these goods. Mr Müller was older and managed the office. There was not a lot of profit at the beginning, but it was a start. Unfortunately, my father had to come back to Luzern every day, as he didn't yet want to give up his job at the Hotel Balance, where he also had a cooked meal in the evening.

Astra did not get any better at looking after the home, but worse. Again and again we came home at dinner time and had to find our own food. I put a lot of my hard-earned money into the household account, and didn't get much in return. I knew I would be better off if I bought my own food and cooked it. I told Astra off, but she always made excuses. Even my mother got worried, and had a serious talk with Astra. After that the situation improved for a few days, and then we were back to the excuses again. On Sunday, when it was our day to cook, we always had a good dinner, and afterwards Christel and I washed up, because my mother usually cooked the meal, and Astra had a free day. We also gave the kitchen a good clean, as Astra didn't seem to find time for that either.

Suddenly I did not like this type of life any more. Getting up in the morning, going the same way to work every day, hearing Mr Graber's voice in my ears because of the Dictaphone, rushing home for a dinner which was not there, having a row with Astra, Monika screaming and crying, my mother looking more and more drawn and worried from overwork, and trying to keep the peace amongst us all. This was not something I wanted to live with for years and years to come. We had to skimp and scrape, and I could not see how we would ever get any more money.

The idea of going into the hotel trade came to me after I visited my father once or twice in the Hotel Balance. I even helped him one evening, and found it interesting.

My father was very popular with the manager and the rest of the staff, and was allowed to show me around the reception area, offices, dining room, kitchens, and one or two empty bedrooms. I felt that a job in an hotel, with people coming and going, would be much more interesting than the work in an office.

I introduced myself to an agency, and discovered that they had quite a number of jobs in small hotels outside Luzern, which included living accommodation. This was a great attraction to me.

I could not face family life in the Bürgenstrasse anymore. I felt guilty, but I knew I had to leave and lead my own life again. The only trouble was, that even if I was offered a job in an hotel, I could not start straight away, because one of the stipulations in my contract with the *Buchhaltungsstelle* was that I had to give three months notice if I wanted to leave. At the time of signing the contract, I had only thought of it the other way round, that Mr Graber had to give me three months notice, if he wanted me to leave, and that this would give me plenty of time to look for another job. I decided to go for an interview in an hotel, and then see what would happen.

The agency made arrangements for me to see Mr Riedi, the owner of the Hotel Belvédère in Hergiswil, a small village by the Vierwaldstätter See, about half an hour's train journey from Luzern. Although I had been in Luzern for quite a time, I had never left the town. Firstly, I was much too busy, and secondly, I couldn't afford to buy a rail ticket. So now I even enjoyed the train journey along the lake.

Hergiswil is a beautifully situated place, right underneath a tall mountain, and stretching along the lake shore. To reach the hotel from the station, I only had to walk down a small hill and cross the main village street, and there was the Belvédère, right by the lake. The building was old and small, with a large, newly built dining room, with big windows and a flat roof, which extended to the lake shore. House and dining room were L-shaped, and a dance floor, surrounded by tables and chairs, was built outside into the corner. There was a lovely garden by the lake, with beautiful flowers, bushes, trees and lawns, and there were steps leading into the water, for people who wanted to swim in the lake. There was also a long terrace, parallel to the lake, with more tables, chairs and umbrella stands.

It's hot here in the summer, I thought. That's why they have the umbrella stands. Later they will have sun umbrellas.

I liked the hotel, it looked pretty, clean and welcoming. When I entered the hall there was nobody about, but a small pointed sign said Office, so I followed this sign down some steps. The office door was closed, and when I looked through the large window next to it, I could see it was empty. The sliding window was like a counter, because on either side of it was a shelf. The room had probably been a cellar once, because I could see that only half the outside window was above ground. There were two desks in the office, and in the corner a small table with a typewriter and a chair. There were shelves on the wall with files and papers, and the floor had a dull patterned carpet. Next to the office was an alcove with a small billiard table in it.

I walked up the steps again into the hall, and was just going through to the other side, when I saw a man coming down the stairs. He smiled, and asked me whether I was Miss Zirkel, and had come for an interview. When I said that that was right, he introduced himself as Mr Riedi, the owner of the hotel, and told me to come with him into the garden, as the weather was so pleasant, where we could have a talk. Mr Riedi was a

155

short, well proportioned man, with the beginnings of a paunch. He was about my father's age, very friendly and charming. He knew I was a *Rückwanderer*, and tried to speak pure German to me, which I appreciated. He needed somebody in the office straight away, as he only had a young apprentice, who didn't seem to be able to cope. He could never leave him alone.

'The season is going to start now,' said Mr Riedi, 'and, although we only have twenty-five bedrooms in the house, we also put a number of our guests into private houses to sleep. All the meals are served in the hotel and we cater for up to 120 guests for lunches and suppers, and also serve meals for non-residents. I need somebody to write letters, make out the bills for the guests, take the money, and file the copies away, and several other general office duties. I myself work in the office, whenever I have time.'

I told him that I had no experience in hotel work, but that I could type. His reply was that, as long as I could do that and also could count and add up, he would soon teach me everything. He offered me quite a good wage, free living accommodation and food, but only Sunday afternoon off.

'Everybody has to work all hours of the day, during the season,' he said. 'There is no work here in the winter. We close the hotel at the beginning of October. Some of the staff then have four weeks off, and start again in a ski resort for the winter months, or find other jobs. We have a glass factory in the town, and two of my waitresses who live in Hergiswil work there in the winter. Because our hotel is only open in the summer, I always have difficulties in finding staff.'

I told him I would think over his offer, but he said he could only give me two days, and then I must let him know, as he needed somebody straight away. I tried to explain that I couldn't walk out of the present job, because I would then not get a good reference, something which was very important in Switzerland.

'That is up to you,' he said. 'I offered you the job because I think we could work well together, and I promise you a rise after a month, if I am satisfied with your work.'

Before I left, he paid me my return fare from Luzern to Hergiswil, saying that this was the usual thing to do for somebody who had laid out money to come to an interview. I was glad he did that, because the agency had told me to ask for it, but I didn't feel I could do that. I had never done it before, and I didn't like begging for anything.

When I came home, I told my mother about my interview. She said she would be sorry if I left. She liked me to go to work with her, she liked the discussions we had when we were walking along but, most of all, she relied on my financial contributions to the household. I promised I would still let her have some money every month, especially as she had started to put some money away for Hans. She had come up with the idea of sending Hans to a private school, a crammer, when he came out of the army, so that he could pass his matriculation and entrance examination to the ETH - *Eidgenössische Technische Hochschule* (Confederate Technological University). The school was rather expensive, but he could do his preparations for the university entrance examination so much quicker, and my mother was already saving every spare penny for it. She felt better when she heard that I would still give her some money.

We kept on thinking about how I could leave the *Buchhaltungsstelle* without breaking my contract, and get a reference. I felt that the best thing would be to be honest with Mr Graber.

'Mr Graber always said there was not much work in the summer,' said my mother. 'Most people suddenly come to the *Buchhaltungsstelle* at the end of the year, or in the autumn, because that's when they have to get ready for their tax. You could suggest to him that you would like to work for the summer months in Hergiswil, but you will be back again in the late autumn. If he has more work then, it will suit him. The other thing is, you, too, will have a job for the winter.'

Luck was on my side. Mr Graber, who didn't always come into the office during the day, happened to turn up early in the morning the next day. I went to see him straight away and, to my surprise, he was in agreement with my leaving the office for the summer, as long as I would return in October. He even thought it an excellent idea as at the moment he was short of work for me. He promised to give me a reference, so that I could show it to Mr Riedi. He dictated it to my mother, and I had it in my pocket already, when the two of us walked home for lunch.

CHAPTER THREE

Hergiswil - Fancy Dress Party

Once the decision was made, things moved quickly. I phoned Mr Riedi, and told him I accepted the job, and would start on June 15th, which was in two days. Knowing that I would only have Sunday afternoon off and no time for shopping, I went out and bought a summer dress, as I hardly had any clothes for the summer. I packed my few belongings, and took the early train to Hergiswil. At the hotel, Mr Riedi introduced me to the two waitresses, Maria and Marta, and to Anna, the chamber maid.

Anna showed me my room, half way up to the first floor. It was a small single room, with a bed, wardrobe, chest of drawers, and a chair in it. It had a window, looking out into a cobbled side yard, where the dustbins were standing, and washing was hanging on long lines. The room was so small, that the wardrobe door couldn't quite open, because it hit the bed, and if I pushed the bed over, it covered up the door. To pull out the drawers of the chest, one had to sit on the bottom of the bed. The floor consisted of wooden boards, but there was a small thin mat next to the bed. The chair was made of wood, and had been painted once, but most of the paint had peeled off.

I was not impressed with my bedroom, especially as I realised also that it would be very noisy. Being situated half way up to the first floor, right next to the uncarpeted staircase, I would hear everybody coming up and down the stairs. I assumed it had been a store room once, because it was much too small for a bedroom. Of course, Mr Riedi could never give a room like this to his guests, so it was used for his staff. I had been told to come into the office straight away, so I left the unpacking of my suitcase for later. There was no key in the door, which worried me, and I asked Mr Riedi for one straight away when I got into the office. He said everybody was very honest here, and I didn't need a key.

'I am not worried that somebody might take something from me,' I replied. 'I have no valuables, but I like my privacy, somebody might enter the room, even at night. I prefer to lock my room.'

Mr Riedi looked at me surprised, maybe nobody had asked him for a key before, I don't know, but he said he would try and find one. After that he showed me what he wanted me to do, and introduced me to David, the apprentice.

He said I could lock the office at 20 minutes to 12, and go and have my lunch, and then have an hour free, from 12 - 1 p.m. I would then have to start again in the office. In the morning, I would have to start at 7.30 a.m, before breakfast, because lists of the times guests were leaving and arriving had to be typed for the kitchen, chambermaid and porter first thing in the morning.

The chambermaid needed the list to know which rooms were being vacated, in order to put clean linen on to the beds. The kitchen had to be informed in this way, so that they knew how many meals they had to prepare, and the porter needed to know when guests arrived, or had to go to the station, as he was responsible for the transport of the luggage. A new list was also necessary for the office, and was hung on to the notice board on the wall. After typing these lists, I would be allowed to go and have my breakfast.

David was only seventeen years old, a clean, quiet, shy young boy, a little hesitant in his work, as he seemed to be frightened of Mr Riedi. When we two were left alone, I asked him a few things about the hotel, and the people.

'The staff are alright,' said David. 'Mrs Riedi watches that nothing is wasted. They are always short of food in the kitchen. Mr Riedi can be very bad tempered, especially after an evening of heavy drinking. He doesn't like me, and often shouts at me, which puts me off, and I do everything wrong. I haven't told him yet, but I might not stay on. I have not learnt anything here, as Mr Riedi doesn't trust me with the money side. I was supposed to be taught how to fill out bills, and enter the different amounts into the ledger. Mr Riedi does it all himself. He cannot type, and I am not very good at it either, and I think that's why he wanted you. My uncle has an hotel and has offered me an apprenticeship. He is extending, and needs more staff now.'

To get my dinner, I had to go into the kitchen, where I met Mrs Riedi, a small, nondescript woman. She looked at me without a smile, and said the chef would give me my dinner, and I could eat it in the corner of the dining room.

'The dining room is open to guests from twelve o'clock onwards, and you must have finished eating by then,' she said. 'The waitresses and the rest of the staff eat later, but my husband likes you back in the office at 1 o'clock, so that he can come into the dining room and supervise the bar.'

I found the chef, his name was Henri, and asked him for my dinner. He smiled, and was nice to me. He seemed to give me rather a lot of mashed potatoes but, when he gave me the plate, he whispered:

'Meat is always under the potatoes,' and glancing at Mrs Riedi who was on the other side of the kitchen, he winked with one eye.

Sure enough, when I was eating my dinner, I found a second piece of meat under the potatoes. The plate only showed a small piece of meat. I was fast learning what the hotel trade was like, long hours of work, little food, bad accommodation, but the staff tried to help one another.

I soon got used to the work, and quite liked the routine of the day. I learnt a number of new things, like how to settle up with the waitresses, who took cash from the guests for some of the items served in the restaurant, like drinks and cakes, and from non-residents, the money for the meals. Guests were permitted to pay at the end of their stay, and the room number was put on to the tickets. These items had to be transferred on to their bill every day, another morning job for me. Because of my lists first thing in the morning before breakfast, I knew who was leaving, and could get the bills ready for the departing guests.

Most of the guests were English and came by train, having booked with the WTA (Worker's Travel Association). They had already paid for their journey, hotel and food in England, and because of the currency regulations, were only allowed £30 spending money after that. This had to last them for trips, souvenirs, drinks, and anything extra they wanted. Some guests brought £ notes, and Mr Riedi said I could exchange these for Swiss money. He gave a very bad rate. The £ in those days was equivalent to 17 Swiss Francs, the bank gave 14 Francs, and Mr Riedi gave 13 Francs, saying to me that this was a common practice with all the hotels.

A bank employee came once a week to collect all the cash and foreign money we had, and I noticed that he paid Mr Riedi 14 Francs for one £ sterling.

We also had French and Belgian guests, often only for one or two nights, on their car journeys to their final destinations. They always had Swiss money. I was allowed to settle up with the guests, as I spoke enough English, and often had a great deal of money in my desk drawer, which worried me. I always locked it in, but I would have preferred to put it into the safe. Mr Riedi had no safe, he said he had the money collected every week, and therefore didn't need one.

Mr Riedi liked to be with his guests. He spoke excellent English, as did his wife, because they had lived in America for years, where their daughter, Myra, was born. She was about my age, and a very pretty girl. She did not mix with the staff, although she worked behind the bar. She was engaged to a teacher, and there was talk of her getting married in October, when the season in the hotel was finished. In the meantime, she was employed by her father, but was not one of us. She was the boss's daughter, and only mixed with the guests, something which I had been told, right at the beginning, not to do.

In my dinner hour, I quietly disappeared into the garden with a chair, somewhere where nobody could see me, and sat in the sun, or I walked along the road, looking into other people's gardens, or hotels, of which there were several along the lake. Mr Riedi had seen me talking to some guests one day, and pointed out to me that there was no fraternising with guests allowed in his hotel, so after that I usually slipped away quietly from the office or the hotel.

One day, Mr Riedi said he had to talk to me. He sent David off on some errand into the village, and then said:

'I think you manage the work very well, and you learn quickly. I feel David is not really needed any more. He is not much good, and often I don't know what work to give him. If he leaves, this would be extra work for you. If you agree to take on this task, I would be prepared to give you half David's salary as compensation. I myself can do some of the work, as my daughter can manage the bar on her own, when we are not too busy. You could think about it, and let me know in the afternoon what you have decided. I must also ask you to vacate your room. We have rather more guests than expected this year, and I will have to put my daughter into your room, so that we can let her bedroom also. I have made arrangements with Mrs Bürgenmeier, who has a room to let, for you to move in tonight. She lives opposite the glass factory. She knows you are coming.'

I thought about Mr Riedi's offer of taking on the extra work, and knew I could manage it. The money would also be useful, but I was sorry that David had to leave. He was not as bad as Mr Riedi made him out to be. He was shy, and I knew that if Mr Riedi would only be kinder to him, and a little understanding, David could be a very good worker. On the other hand, maybe it was as well for David to leave. He had the offer of going to work with his uncle, where he could carry on with his apprenticeship.

Late in the afternoon, I told Mr Riedi that I would also take over David's work for the extra money, and asked him to write me a new service contract, including the so-called rise in salary. He said this was not necessary, as it was an agreement between the two of us, and would save me some tax also. He would just give me the extra money. He then told me that I could leave a little earlier on that day, as I had to pack my things and move to Mrs Bürgenmeier.

Whilst I was packing my things I had a knock on the door. It was David, who came to tell me that he had been told to leave, and was going to his uncle the following morning.

I wished him good luck, and told him that I, too, had to move out of the hotel. Just before David went away, he said:

'You know, it was Mrs Riedi who employed me and signed the apprenticeship contract. She said she liked a boy in the office. Her remark was: 'Girls always flirt with everybody.' Maybe that is the reason why Mr Riedi never liked me, he probably preferred girls.'

I knew David was right. Mr Riedi often talked to his guests, preferring the younger girls or women, and if his wife noticed this, she would come and try and break it up, by asking or telling her husband something. Once or twice he had also come too close to me, and I had learnt how to avoid this. He came into the office one day, whilst I was working on my desk, stepped behind me, and put his hands on my shoulders, saying:

'What are you doing there?' Whilst saying this, he bent over, brushing his face against mine. It all happened very quickly, and the touching of my face could have been an accident, except that it happened again. The next time, he just pressed his face against mine.

'Excuse me,' I said, 'I have to get some envelopes,' and I got up, pushing my chair back, which made him step back.

After that, whenever I was sitting at the desk and he walked in, I would get up and go to the files or the typewriter, or even outside the office, to collect the money from the small billiard table. I always made sure I was not caught again with my back towards him. He knew what I had in mind, because once or twice he came in very quickly, and I only had time to twist round in my chair, but that was good enough to stop him in his tracks. The only times I felt comfortable with him was when he was sitting behind his large desk, because if he wanted to reach me then, he had to get up and walk around his desk. This gave me plenty of time to avoid him.

I was not sorry to move out of the hotel, although I had a bit of a shock when I went to Mrs Bürgenmeier. I never had a key to my bedroom so, whenever I was in the room, I wedged the chair under the door handle, and sat on the bed instead. If guests arrived after I had gone upstairs, Mr Riedi would send somebody up to fetch me, so that I could register them and allocate and show them their rooms. It was very handy to have me in the hotel, only halfway up the first flight of stairs. At night, I was often woken up by people returning late, because there was no carpet on the stairs, and the guests laughed and joked after a happy night out, stopping for breath on the half landing in front of my door. Nobody ever entered my room, but I never felt secure.

I found my new abode and met Mrs Bürgenmeier. She was an elderly lady, who lived with her son and daughter-in-law and their three children. The house was quite big, and belonged to her. The son was a foreman in the glass factory, and the daughter-in-law worked part time in the design department. She was very artistic, and had been trained to do quite delicate designs on glass. The factory manager did not want to lose her, and had offered her part time employment. I found out later that she could go to the factory at any time and do her designs. Mrs Bürgenmeier looked after the children, and often even did the cooking.

When I arrived she was just undressing the youngest grandchild to put him to bed, so I said I would wait until she was ready and could show me the room. I played with the other two boys in the meantime, who were intrigued with my poor Swiss German, which I tried out on them. They thought I spoke "funnily" and tried to copy me. By the time Mrs Bürgenmeier returned, we were all having a good laugh, and she smiled too, and told the boys to go to their mother in the garden. She then told me to follow her upstairs. We climbed up past the second floor, and into the big attic room. A corner was partitioned off with unpainted rough wood, and there was a door leading into the partition. Mrs Bürgenmeier opened this door and said:

'I told Mr Riedi that the other room on the second floor which he used to rent was let and I had this attic room, which was really only suitable for an odd night stay, as it only had a bed and a chest of drawers, but Mr Riedi said you were a *Rückwanderer*, who used to live in a tent in Germany, and as long as there was a bed you would be satisfied.'

Mrs Bürgenmeier looked a little embarrassed and uncomfortable at me, and let me enter the room. It was even smaller than my room in the hotel. It had a bed and a chest of drawers, with a wash bowl and a water jug, and there were two hooks behind the door. There was no wardrobe. A wire was draped from the corner to the centre, and on it hung a single bulb, giving a little light to the room. There was a small window in the sloping roof. Next to the bed stood one chair, and by the side of the bed was a little mat. I looked silently at Mrs Bürgenmeier and felt sorry for her. She obviously had not wanted to let this room, and had been persuaded by Mr Riedi that it was good enough for me. I also felt it was some kind of punishment on Mr Riedi's part, for not letting him come near me. I quietly said to Mrs Bürgenmeier:

'I will go and fetch my suitcase.'

I felt a little like crying, when I thought of what people imagined *Rückwanderer* were like.

'I will get my son to help you with your case,' said Mrs Bürgenmeier. 'I will also ask him to put some more hooks into the wood, so that you can hang up your clothes, as there is no wardrobe. You can lock the door at night, although nobody comes up here, not even the children.'

Both of us went downstairs, and she called her son, who helped me with my suitcase. I unpacked my washing things, and then realised I had no water. I took the water jug, and when I came to the top of the stairs, I met Mrs Bürgenmeier again and her son. She brought me some clothes hangers, and her son asked me where I wanted the hooks. I said I didn't mind, as long as they were strong enough to hold my few dresses. Mrs Bürgenmeier showed me where the toilet was and also the bathroom, where I could get some water.

'Mr Riedi said you wouldn't use the bathroom, as you can have a bath in the hotel, but you needed water, so you can get it from here.'

I didn't say much, but returned to my attic room, where young Mr Bürgenmeier had put in some more hooks for me. I unpacked my few dresses, put my other things into the drawers and then went for a walk. It was dark when I came back, but the entrance door was open. I met Mrs Bürgenmeier, and she gave me the house keys, and a key to my room. She said she had another key to my room, because she would like to sweep it occasionally, and also bring me clean sheets and towels every week. I offered to clean my own room, but she insisted it was her job to do it, and in any case, it gave her something to do. She was very kind to me, and I could feel that she liked me.

It took a long time before I went to sleep that night. Too much had happened to me that day, and I kept on thinking about it. I realised that I would have to learn to be quiet and accept things, if I wanted to get on.

The work in the hotel was not difficult, it was the long hours which I had to do which were tiring, and the quiet battle with Mr Riedi to avoid his advances.

The next day I could feel that Mr Riedi wanted me to say something about my new room, because he made one or two remarks about my moving out, also mentioned that I could use the bathroom in the hotel on the first floor, which I had used before. I never replied to anything, so in the end he said it straight out:

'Do you like your new room?'

'No,' I replied, 'but it doesn't matter, it is not important.'

He looked surprised at me, but I pretended to be busy. I had a lot to do that day as David had left, and there was the extra work. I just didn't take any notice of Mr Riedi.

In my short dinner hour I didn't know what to do. I didn't want to stay in the hotel or garden. We had more guests by now, and even my shady place in the garden, behind the trees and bushes, was occupied. So I went back to my lodgings, and asked Mrs Bürgenmeier whether I could sit in her garden for half an hour. She showed me a bench in the back garden, and said I could use it at any time, even bring a friend to sit there. I said I had no friends, so she sat with me, and told me about the glass factory, and the work that was done there.

I returned to my room very tired that evening, and found that somebody had put a lampshade over the bulb, and a mirror was hanging above the chest of drawers. I felt happy about this kindness, and knew that Mrs Bürgenmeier had organised it. I had a wash, and fetched fresh water for the morning, and then decided to go for a little walk. I walked out of Hergiswil, and along the lake, when I met Henri, the chef from the Belvédère. He, too, had felt he had to have fresh air, after the hot kitchen. We walked together, and talked. He came from the French-speaking part of Switzerland, but his German was quite good. He told me that he was engaged, and that he and his fiancée were saving to buy a small hotel, which they wanted to run together after they were married. When we came back to the glass factory, Henri said:

'That was a pleasant walk we had, we must do it again. I like walking in the evening after work. The only trouble is, that mostly I finish late, because of the evening meal.'

I showed him the bench in Mrs Bürgenmeier's garden, and told him to look for me there, whenever he was free. I also said I would mention it to my landlady, so that she didn't think he was trespassing.

The next day at dinner time I had an extra big piece of meat under my mashed potatoes, and in the afternoon Marta arrived with a cup of coffee for me, saying that Henri had mentioned to Mrs Riedi that I never got one in the afternoon. She said, if nobody brought me anything in the afternoon, I should go and get one for myself. She smiled a little and winked, because Mr Riedi was sitting at his desk. He had never offered me a free drink during the day, only my three meals, breakfast, dinner and supper. After that, he left the room, probably going to have a talk to his wife.

Myra came to see me, and asked me for the key to my old bedroom in the hotel. I said I had never been given one, although I had asked for it. She looked surprised, so I explained to her that I had always wedged the chair under the handle of the door.

'Where do you live now?' she asked me.

For a little while I looked at her, because I was astounded that she didn't know this, as I had vacated my room for her.

'In a partition of an attic in Mrs Bürgenmeier's house, opposite the glass factory,' was my reply.

She bit her lip and rushed outside. I knew there would be a family argument, but I didn't care, I had only told the truth.

I went home by train every Sunday after lunch, and returned late in the evening. If I wanted anything bought, like toothpaste or soap, my mother would do this for me during the week, as I had no time off when the shops were open in Hergiswil.

I also tried to give my mother some money every week. I had started to get tips in the hotel. Whenever people paid their bills, and I had done something for them during their stay, like looking up trains or buses, or changing money, or getting them some stamps, they would often round off their bills. The French and Belgians were the most generous. The English people had little money, and often didn't spend anything extra.

Sometimes I changed rooms for people, or organised the transport of the luggage with the porter, if guests had not brought it downstairs on time, to be taken to the station. I usually was tipped for that. I was not too proud to take it, everybody else took it, like the waitresses and the porter, and I needed that money. I also was entitled to a share-out of the 15% which was added to the bills. Mr Riedi worked these out and gave me one and a half percent. The waitresses usually got tipped when they served in the restaurant and took cash. They kept their tips, but the kitchen staff got nothing, and the chambermaids not very much, so they had a bigger share from the 15% than the waitresses. Mr Riedi also included his daughter,

Myra, who worked at the bar. Because she was Mr Riedi's daughter, people usually did not give her a tip. Altogether I earned good money. There was my salary, the extra money I got because I had taken over David's job, and there were the tips.

Mrs Bürgenmeier became more and more friendly, and one day offered me the bathroom whenever I wanted it, so that I didn't have to go and use the one in the hotel. The family often asked me to join them in my short dinner hour, or in the evening, and Mr Bürgenmeier presented me one day with a glass with Helga imprinted on it, which he had specially made for me. I was most grateful, and felt I had some friends in that house. I still have that glass, and although it is only an ordinary glass, to me it is a treasure from a time when I was friendless and had to work hard to keep on top.

At times Mr Riedi could not be found, particularly when the tradespeople came to the office and asked for him. I soon realised that he was in debt everywhere. He had built on the beautiful dining room extension, and had probably over-stretched himself. The architect came several times. At first, he accepted that Mr Riedi was not there, then he insisted that I found him, as he owed him money. The baker came, and the butcher, and the people who had let rooms to the hotel for the guests.

Half the office window was above ground. People could not see us, but we could look up, and if Mr Riedi recognised somebody to whom he owed money, he would get up quickly, and say that he could not see anybody, and that I should say he was out. I did not like to lie to people, but I had to do it. The tradespeople soon realised that I made excuses for my employer, and I think they understood.

My relationship with Mr Riedi gradually deteriorated, but because he needed me, (he would never get anybody else in the middle of the summer season), and I did the work efficiently, he kept me on.

Two things happened which made him, and me, too, very cross. The first one was one morning, quite early, and had to do with a tip I had been given. Mr Riedi would have an early swim in the lake every morning, whether the sun was shining or not, and sometimes he would come into the office, still in his wet bathing trunks, wrapped into a bathrobe, and quickly check up the bills of the guests who were leaving in the morning. On this particular day, I had to get the bill ready for a French couple who wanted to leave at 7.30 a.m. I had worked out the bill the night before, because in the morning I was always busy with the typing of the lists. The French couple came to the office to pay, but only had a large Swiss note, which I could not change so early in the morning. The clerk from the bank had collected all my money the day before. No shops or banks were open so early, so I offered to go to the station, which was a short distance up the hill.

I locked my drawer and, leaving the office door unlocked as the couple were going to wait for me, I ran to the station, where I was able to change the note. I returned, out of breath, and found Mr Riedi in the office, after his swim. He was talking to the couple. The gentleman paid his bill and gave me a very large tip, in appreciation of my running to the station, which I put into my pocket.

After the couple had left, I got on with my typing, and noticed that Mr Riedi had sat down at his desk still in his wet swim suit, and was looking at some of the bills, which I had prepared for the morning. Suddenly he said:

'Aren't you going to put the money you have just received into this box?' and he lifted up a small box, which I had noticed on his desk before. It had a label with the word *Trinkgeld* (tips) written on it.

'Why should I?' I replied.

'All tips in this office have to be put into this box, to be shared with the staff.'

'The money was given to me, in appreciation of my running to the station to get some change.'

'You did this in working time. It is part of your duty to have change when people pay their bills, and you have to share your tips.'

'The waitresses do not share their tips with anybody, why must I suddenly share my tips?'

'This box,' said Mr Riedi, pointing to the *Trinkgeld* box, 'has all the tips from the office, which are shared between you, my daughter Myra, and if David had still been here he too, would have had a share. The waitresses are separate. I have noticed that this box is always empty, and I was not sure whether you had been given a tip before or not, but now I have seen it. You had better put the money into it.'

'Is your daughter going to share her tips from the bar with me also?' I asked.

'My daughter does not get tips at the bar, or accept drinks from customers,' said Mr Riedi indignantly.

'I will share my tips with anybody, when the waitresses and the chambermaids share their tips. Until then, I will keep what is given to me in appreciation of a special service I have done for some of the guests.'

Mr Riedi was furious. He threw the box on to the desk with a bang, and shouted: "You put that money into that box or, or... '

I don't know what he wanted to say, maybe he even wanted to sack me, but then realised he wouldn't get anybody else, or maybe it was because the telephone was suddenly ringing. He stopped, stared at me, then shouted: 'Answer the phone!' and left the office.

I did not see him again until the afternoon, and then he didn't speak to me for the rest of the day. I never put any money into the box, and it was never mentioned again. Myra had a share of the 15% service charge on the bills, like everybody else.

The second thing happened on my birthday, which was on the 11th of July. Mr Riedi knew it was my birthday, because the day before he mentioned to me that he had a surprise for me for my birthday.

I was sure that the incident of the box had not been forgotten. We were on cool, sometimes slightly friendly terms. Mr Riedi had tried to come near me again when I was sitting at my desk, but he was unsuccessful. I had mentioned to him that my mother would come by train, to have lunch with me on my birthday, and have a look at the Belvédère. I asked him whether it would be alright if we had our lunch in the garden at one o'clock, or just after, so that we could be together. He thought this was a good idea, and said this would be alright, as long as all the work got done also.

On my birthday I made an early start with my lists, and had breakfast earlier than usual. I returned to the office with my thoughts already on my work, as I wanted to finish at dinner time, when a voice suddenly said:

'Surprise, surprise, happy birthday!' and Mr Riedi, who had been hiding behind the door, came forward, threw his arms around me, and kissed me all over my face.

'Leave me alone!' I hissed at him, trying to push him away. I didn't want to shout, as I was ashamed that somebody would come and see us.

'Happy birthday, happy birthday,' he said again. 'This is my surprise!' And he kept on kissing me.

I slapped his face. He stopped, got hold of my wrists, which hurt, and pulled me further inside the office.

'Let me go,' I said very firmly, 'or I will tell your wife.'

He released me straight away and spun round: 'Don't you ever say anything to my wife.'

This seemed to have been the magic word, because he just walked off after that. He must have planned this birthday surprise, because usually about this time, he would be having his swim in the lake, or would come into the office in his wet swimsuit, whilst today, he was already dressed. I did not see him again that day, and was told he had gone to Luzern on business, and I was not sorry.

My mother came and we had lunch in the garden. Henri, who knew she was coming, gave us an excellent meal, which was served by one of the waitresses. After that I showed my mother the hotel, and also took her to see Mrs Bürgenmeier, with whom she spent the afternoon, whilst I did my work. As Mr Riedi was not there, I finished a little earlier, so that I had some time with my mother. I showed her my room, and she was quite shocked.

'Our servant girls had a better room than you,' said my mother. Still, she did agree that Mrs Bürgenmeier and her family were nice, and people were more important than material things. I told my mother about Mr Riedi, and she said that she doubted whether he would touch me again, now that I had threatened that I would tell his wife.

Mrs Bürgenmeier invited us for cake and coffee, a little birthday celebration, she said, and after that I took my mother for a walk along the lake, where we met Henri. He insisted that we called in at the Alpenhof, one of the lake-side hotels, to sit in the garden and have a glass of wine. My mother looked happy and relaxed, after the little drink, and I was glad. I had not seen her like that for years. She was still a very attractive woman.

If only all the worries would disappear, she would always look like this, I thought. I knew it was the wine and the music, and being away from Luzern and the family that made her so relaxed.

My birthday, which had started with such a nasty surprise, finished up very happily. Henri and I accompanied my mother to the station, where she caught the last train to Luzern, thanking us both for a lovely day in Hergiswil.

The next day, Mr Riedi came into the office late and pretended as if nothing had happened. At 7 p.m, when I wanted to leave, he suddenly came in, and told me that I would have to stay on, as somebody had to be in the office in the evening in case there were phone calls, or one of the guests wanted something. I was surprised about this, because I always had left at 7 p.m. There was no need to supervise the phone, this could be switched through to the bar, where he or his daughter worked in the evenings, and guests seldom came to the office in the evenings. I felt that he did this on purpose, to annoy me, but I didn't say anything.

I stayed on, got all the bills ready for the next day, and then just sat there with nothing to do. There were no phone calls. When the church clock struck nine o'clock, I switched the phone through to the bar, locked the office, and went home. Mrs Bürgenmeier was surprised to see me arrive so late, she thought I had been out enjoying myself somewhere. I told her about the latest hours of work for me. She said I shouldn't do it, particularly if there was nothing to do, but I was afraid I might lose my job after all, and I needed the money quite badly.

The other thing that happened that day was that Maria, one of the waitresses came to see me to ask me for some money. She was most embarrassed. She was the one who had served me and my mother with our dinner on my birthday. She had assumed that the hotel would pay for my mother's dinner, and went to Mr Riedi to ask him to countersign the tickets. He signed for one dinner, saying that I was entitled to my food, but my mother's dinner was not his responsibility, and Maria had to get the money from me. I paid her the full price for the dinner.

'I am sorry about this,' said Maria. 'Mr Riedi should have given you a lower price, without the service charge. I asked him about it, because I didn't mind serving you, but he wouldn't have it. You must have upset him. He is usually very sweet on all his secretaries, which often upsets his wife. The girl who was here last year was thrown out by Mrs Riedi, because she found her husband kissing her in the evening in the garden. He tries it on all his secretaries, and that is why his wife wanted a boy in the office. I will mention to Mrs Riedi that you had to pay for your mother's dinner, she will know then how things are.'

Maria was nice. She lived in Hergiswil, and worked in the Belvédère every summer. She knew all the gossip in the hotel, and also what was going on in the village. She was right about Mrs Riedi, because after this incident she was quite nice to me, making a point of talking to me occasionally.

Guests came and went, except for Mr Duncan, who was the English guide, employed by the WTA. He lived in the hotel the whole summer. He was an ex-colonel, very erect and clean looking, and always extremely polite. He spoke quite good German, and would come and have a little talk to me occasionally, about the rooms for the guests or when ordering a packed lunch for a group he would take on a trip, which he did quite often. These trips, by coach, were a routine every week. He told me, in confidence, that he was quite bored with these trips, as for him they were always the same.

For the English guests, they showed the beauty of a country that had always been in peace and was so different from their homeland. There were the high mountains, with snow and ice, pastures with brown and white cows, undamaged houses with pretty flower boxes, shops full of goods, and plenty of food, which could be bought without restrictions. Sometimes I tried my little English on Mr Duncan and he laughed, corrected me, and said I ought to come to England to learn the language properly.

Mr Duncan didn't realise that he had sown a seed. I kept on thinking about England. I felt now that I had started in the hotel trade, I could and should carry on in it, trying to improve myself, and go further up the ladder. I could see how important languages were, particularly English. The war was finished, the English people would travel more and more, and gradually the restrictions on foreign currency would also be eased.

I told my mother about my thoughts, and she encouraged me to try and find out how I could get to England to learn the language. I wrote to an agency in Luzern, and was told to come and introduce myself. They had places as au pair girls in several countries, including England. This would mean signing up to live with a family with children for a year, looking after them, and also helping in the household. I wrote back, saying that I would come as soon as I could get some time off during the week, which was rather difficult, as I was in the hotel trade.

There was another hurdle to overcome if I wanted to go to England. The *Buchhaltungsstelle* expected me back for the winter, I had only been given leave of absence for the summer. My contract stipulated three months notice. My mother suggested I give notice straight away, because if I did this by July 31st, I would not have to go back on November 1st, having fulfilled the three months notice stipulation.

I gave my notice to Mr Graber, and asked for another reference. My mother told me that my letter was a bombshell. I felt sorry for her, she was the one who had to cope with the temper outburst that followed, because she was there. Officially, the employment law was not broken, and my notice had to be accepted. Even my reference, when it arrived at last, was not bad. But the nice atmosphere that had prevailed between my mother and her boss had gone and I felt guilty.

Things in the Belvédère ran smoothly otherwise. I liked my work, and my English improved through talking to people. The only thing I didn't like was the sitting about in the office in the evenings. There were seldom phone calls, and even if a call came I had to put it through to the bar, as it was usually for the Riedi family.

We always got a list of the arriving guests from England in advance. Mr Riedi would sort out where they would stay. When the guests arrived from the station they came in groups. Mr Duncan and Mr Riedi would meet them. The passports were collected and given to me, so that I could check the names with our list. They all had a drink, and a talk by Mr Duncan, and then Mr Riedi would tell them where they were going to stay. I showed the people to their rooms in the hotel. The guests in outside accommodation got a note with the name and address of their landlady, and the porter would accompany them there with their luggage, which he transported in a cart.

The allocation of rooms was only once at fault, and I discovered it by looking at the passports. It was July 7th, and about thirty people had arrived, very tired, after a twenty-four hour train journey from London. Mr Duncan gave me the passports and said he would make his speech short, because people were too tired to listen to anything much. I checked the names, and discovered that Mr Riedi had given a double room to a brother and his sister, because on our list they were put down as a married couple. I quickly found Mr Riedi and pointed out the mistake.

We had to do some rearranging, and Mr Duncan had to talk a little longer as I had to type new notes for some of the accommodations. When giving out the notes, I looked at the couple to whom we had given the double room. The young man was tall, big, and very friendly, with a warm smile. His sister looked thin and tired, rather young and innocent. She never said a word, and I could see that all she wanted was a bath and a bed. They both had a room each with Madame Bonani, a friendly French lady.

The weather that summer was beautiful, and many people swam in the lake. Although the garden was small, it never seemed to be crowded with people, because quite a number of them attended the different trips which Mr Duncan organised. One day, when I thought he should have been on a trip, he turned up at the office. I was surprised to see him and said so. He smiled, and said that he had a *Stellvertreter* (deputy).

'Do you remember the young man whom Mr Riedi put into a double room with his sister? Well, he is an excellent guide. He has been on a few trips and soon knew his way around. He said he would love to go again, but couldn't afford to go a second time, because his £30 allowance wouldn't stretch for all the trips. I told him he could go instead of me, with the new group, and as a guide, he would go free. So now I am having a day off.'

'What a wonderful idea,' I said. 'He gets what he enjoys, and you can be free for a day. Actually, I have met him. He comes to play Bar Billiards, and sometimes changes money in the office.'

The billiard table next to the office was used when the weather was not nice, or in the evenings. Ronald (I knew his christian name from his passport) seemed to like Bar Billiards. As money was needed to get the balls to come up, he often came to the office to get some change. He was always very polite and friendly, but never had a long conversation with me. He seemed to play quite often, and I wondered at times whether there was another reason, namely talking to me, but then he never said much. If Mr Riedi was in the office he wouldn't come for change, and would soon stop playing.

The groups that came from England, usually stayed two weeks. Towards the end of their stay, Mr Riedi often arranged something extra. This could be a special evening dinner, or a dance with music from records. When Ronald and his sister came, there were a number of young people in their group, and it was decided to have a Fancy Dress party and a real band to dance to a couple of days before they went back to England. The staff were not allowed to join in. Mr Riedi organised the band, and Mrs Riedi decided to have a cold supper for the guests.

It was Henri who suddenly suggested that we ought to join in. He said that if we were dressed in such a way that nobody could recognise us, we could do it. He would be finished early, because he didn't have to cook that evening. Unfortunately, the two waitresses could not join us, as they would be on duty. So there was Henri, the girl who helped in the kitchen, Alois, the porter, the two chambermaids and myself; two men and four women. We decided to be ghosts, as we could get hold of plenty of sheets. We could wrap these around us and fasten them with safety pins. The trouble was, that we also had to cover our heads. We couldn't very well cut holes into the sheets. Henri said he would think of something.

The day arrived, and it was beautiful. Hot during the day, with a warm evening and a sky full of stars. I got my work finished, and hoped to disappear early in the evening, but Mr Riedi came back into the office. Maybe he came on purpose, to make sure I stayed on. I pretended to still have some work to do. After about half an hour he left, saying that he must join his guests, as he could already hear the band playing. As soon as he had gone, I locked everything up and ran upstairs, as we had arranged to meet in Henri's bedroom.

'You are late,' said Henri. 'The party will be finished before we get there.'

He was quite cross. I tried to explain about Mr Riedi, but he wasn't interested, as he wanted me to get dressed. The others already had their sheets pinned around them, and on Henri's bed lay our headgear. Henri had bought big sheets of white cardboard. He rolled them up in such a way that one end was pointed, and the other end had a large round opening. He had cut holes for the eyes and the mouth into this cone shape. These tall pixie hats, pushed over the head, sat quite firmly. Henri had glued each one up, so that they would not unroll. I soon had a sheet wrapped around me and several hands pinned me in. Then came the hat with face mask, but because I was rather tall the point hit the ceiling when I stood up. The same thing happened to Henri, so we decided to carry our hats and put them on in the garden.

We had no idea what we would do once we were in the garden. Nobody had made any plans about that, only about our disguise. We quietly went downstairs, and Henri guided us through the dark kitchen, out of the back door, and then into the garden. We put our hats on, and just stood there, hidden by bushes and trees. I peeped through the branches, and saw people dancing on the dance floor. There were tables and chairs everywhere, and the band was playing on the lawn. People didn't seem to have dressed up much. The girls had summer dresses on, and ribbons in their hair. One or two had a big hat on, or were dressed as men, but most men hadn't bothered to disguise themselves. Some of them had put on shorts, or rolled up their trousers and their sleeves. Mr Riedi had borrowed the little white frilly apron from one of the waitresses, and had tied it around his paunch, which did look funny. At least he had made an effort. Mrs Riedi had a rose in her hair. I couldn't see Myra, who was probably serving behind the bar. Everybody would want a drink on this warm evening.

'I have got an idea,' said Alois suddenly. 'What about taking the raft and rowing out on to the lake. When we come back again, we make ghostly noises, and then we disappear again.'

'Not a bad plan,' said Henri. 'The lake is calm, and we don't have to row far. There are two oars, so we should be alright.'

We quietly made our way down to the lake, where the raft was tied up by some concrete steps. We girls were a little frightened to climb on to the raft, because there were no edges to it, and the whole thing moved and swayed each time somebody got on to it. Eventually we were all positioned, sitting close together, and Henri and Alois started to row the raft away from the steps. The lake was very dark, but looking back we could see the illuminated Belvédère garden, with the fancy lights over the dance floor, and we heard the music. We went out on to the lake, and then back towards the little landing stage, from where people used to jump when they went swimming. When we got near to the shore, we started to make loud noises of:

'Hooo - hooo- quooo - quooo,' and Henri and Alois rowed slowly.

The band stopped playing, and people started to run to the shore to have a look at the ghostly apparitions. They shouted and waved, fascinated with our little group. We hadn't realised what a sensation we would be, dressed all in white, and coming out of the black darkness of the lake. The guests thought Mr Riedi had arranged this spectacle for them, and thanked him. Photographs were taken of us. We could see the flash of the cameras.

Henri and Alois had reached the landing stage and wanted to push off again, but somebody got hold of Henri's oar and pulled us along by the side of the landing stage on to the shore. There, they helped us to get off the raft, and Henri tied it to the post. The band started to play again, so Henri said:

'We might as well find a partner and dance. - Come on girls, get on to the dance floor.'

I looked around, not knowing whom to choose, and also trying to avoid Mr Riedi. He would recognise me if I spoke, because I didn't speak Swiss German. I suddenly saw Ronald. He was sitting at a table with his sister and some other friends. For the fancy dress party, he had put his clothes on the wrong way round. His waistcoat was buttoned in the back, and so was his shirt, so that he had his tie on his back also. It looked quite funny. I approached him, and pulled him on to the dance floor.

'Come and dance with me,' I said in English.

He didn't hesitate, but came straight away, and I realised he was an excellent dancer, although he was such a big young man. The others, too, had got themselves partners. Henri was swinging a pretty girl around, and spoke French to her. I wondered whether she understood him. Alois was a hopeless dancer and, after jogging along with a lady for a bit, he suddenly disappeared. The other girls got themselves a partner each, but not for long. They, too, seemed to be shy, and decided to leave the dance floor. Only Henri and myself, two lonely ghosts, kept up the dancing.

At last, even Henri disappeared, and I felt it was time that I, too, made my way back. It was getting late, and I had to be up early.

'I will have to go back now,' I said to Ronald.

'I will take you home,' he replied, and guided me off the dance floor.

We walked through the garden, and towards the front entrance of the hotel, when I asked him his name. I had to pretend that I didn't know him, because I had never spoken to him in English before.

'What is your name,' I asked.

'Everybody calls me Bob,' he said. 'What is your name?'

I was surprised by his reply, I always had thought of him as Ronald; now he said his name was Bob.

'My name is Helga,' I replied.

'I like your name,' he said. 'Helga is most unusual, particularly for a ghost. Why don't you take your hat off? I would like to see your face.'

'Oh no, I cannot do that. I am a ghost, and must keep my face covered. But I will tell you what I will do, I am very good at telling fortunes. Give me your hand, and I will tell you what the future holds for you.'

He gave me his hand, and I pretended to study it. Then I said: 'You will never get married, but you will have four children,' and I laughed.

He looked at me shocked, but before he could say anything, I ran into the hotel and up the stairs to Henri's room. He was alone trying to get the safety pins out of his wrapped sheet. I helped him, and then he unwrapped me. His bed was full of sheets and hats, so I helped him to tidy up. We folded all the sheets, as they had to be washed, and we cut up the hats, so that they could go into the paper basket. Alois arrived with the kitchen girl, they had gone to get some orange squash from one of the cafés, and we sat on the floor having our drinks. We could still hear the band playing and I wondered whether Bob had gone back to the dance floor. I decided I liked him, and was sorry that he had to return to England in two days time.

After breakfast the next morning, whilst I was busy in the office, Bob appeared.

'Good morning,' he said. 'So I am never getting married, but I will have four children,' and he laughed.

I looked at him, surprised. 'How did you recognise me? I never took off my hat.'

'I recognised you by your watch. Although you were completely covered up, your hands were free, and I do recognise watches. I do watch repair as a hobby, and once I see a watch, I never forget it.'

'That is clever of you,' I said. 'Do you want some change for the billiard table again?'

'No thank you,' he replied. 'I wish you had told me before that you could speak English. I thought you only spoke German. Will you come and have a cup of coffee with me?'

'I am sorry, but I have to say no. Firstly I have to work, and secondly, I am not allowed to fraternise with the guests. Mr Riedi does not permit his staff to become too friendly with anybody. That was also the reason why we all had to dress like ghosts. We had to have a perfect disguise. I don't know whether he realised who we were.'

'Don't you have a lunch hour? Or an evening free? We can meet somewhere away from here. You mention a time and place, and I will be there.'

He was quite determined to see me, and I knew he was going home the next day, so I told him to meet me at twelve o'clock at Café Maurer, a small place at the other end of the village.

I was a little late, because I had a late lunch, but Bob was there. His face lit up when he saw me: 'I thought you might not come,' he said.

'I am sorry, but I had a lot of work this morning. You shouldn't have worried, because if I say something, I stick to it. I said I would come, and here I am.'

Bob had already found out quite a bit about me from Mr Duncan. He knew I was a refugee who had returned to Switzerland. We talked about the war, and I told him that the English had bombed Königsberg. He had only been in the Home Guard, because his father had produced war equipment and Bob had run the night shift in his father's factory.

I only had an hour free, but we talked and talked, and seemed to get to know one another very quickly. Bob wanted to meet me again in the evening, but I was worried, as I had already gone early the evening before.

'We can meet again at Café Maurer,' he said. 'Promise you will come. I will wait for you, but promise you will come.'

In the end I promised, and I knew I had to go, because I never broke a promise.

I was late back in the office, but luckily nobody had missed me.

I made sure I was not late for my appointment with Bob in the evening. My work was finished on time, and I felt it was really silly to sit there night after night with nothing to do. I switched the telephone through to the bar and went to my room to have a wash and change, then walked to Café Maurer.

Bob and I had a lovely evening together, finishing up with a walk along the lake. I told him I wanted to come to England to learn the language, and he said I ought to come near to where he lived, which was about 30 miles from London. I explained about the agency, and told him I would let him know once I had been for an interview. We exchanged addresses, and he said I must write to him.

'You write to me first,' I said laughingly. I didn't believe he ever would. Out of sight, out of mind. This meeting was a pleasant holiday interlude for him, but not anything that would, or could last. He struck me as a kind, considerate, very warm and innocent man, but also very very young. We were both the same age, actually I was three months older, but talking to him, I felt that it was more than three months. The war had hardly touched him, he was still living at home, and this was his first holiday abroad, away from his parents.

The next morning Bob turned up again in the office to say goodbye. He shook my hand, held it, and then stroked it. I thought he was going to kiss me, but he didn't, although we were alone.

'I will write to you,' he said. 'Please do reply, and when you come to England, we will meet. I will come and see you wherever you are.'

With that he left, as the others from his group had already gone to the station. I never really met his sister, and she hardly had seen me either.

Bob was true to his promise. A few days after he left, I had a letter from him. He said he was very sorry to have to leave Switzerland, not because of the lovely countryside, or that one could buy anything, without it being rationed (England still had food rationing and clothing coupons), but because he had to leave me behind. He reminded me to make sure that if I came to England, I must not choose a place too far away from where he lived.

I was surprised by the arrival of the letter, and the sincerity and warmth of it. I had never expected this. As I had nothing to do in the office in the evening, I put some paper into the typewriter and replied to his letter. Anybody coming into the office would think I was working. Bob and I gradually established quite a correspondence, telling one another everything that happened to us.

On the last day of July I should have had my salary and the share in the 15% service charge. Mr Riedi informed me that he was short of money, and he could not give me the extra money which he had promised me for taking on David's work until the next month. I only got my share of the service charge and my contract monthly salary. I was not worried, because I hardly needed any money, as my living was free. I had enough to give to my mother, which I did every month, to help with the household expenses.

Towards the end of August I decided not to stay in the office every evening. It was very boring, with nothing to do. I left at 7 p.m. after switching the phone through to the bar. On the last day of August Mr Riedi informed me that he had decided not to pay me the extra money for David's work, because I had neglected my duties by going home early in the evenings. He also refused to pay me the extra money for July, although I had stayed on every evening in those days. We had a quarrel, but I had nothing in writing, and I had been foolish enough to believe his promise. After that I went home every evening at 7 p.m. I felt that working eleven hours a day was long enough.

I insisted on a day off during the week, but I only got half a day. I went to see the agency about a job as an au pair girl in England. They offered me one job in London and one in Bristol. They said that they would write to the families concerned, passing on all my details, and then let me know. I also went to the official employment office and told them about the arrangement I had made with Mr Riedi, to get the money for the extra work. They said they were sorry, but could not help me, as I had no contract in writing for this money. They reassured me that there was no need for me to share a tip given to me personally, and also felt that I worked very long hours.

From time to time, Henri and I met in the evening in the Alpenhof and had a glass of wine and a dance. His fiancée came to see him one day, a lovely girl. We could not speak a lot to one another as she was French. Her German was not very good, and my French not much good either. Henri had the whole day off, but his fiancée had to leave early in the evening, as she had a long journey. Henri told me to finish early and go out with him. He didn't want to hang around the hotel for the whole evening. I closed the office at 6 p.m, with all my work done. We caught a bus to the next village and had supper there.

The next day I had a telling off from Mr Riedi, but I didn't care. I was not afraid of him any more. The more he hated me and my courage to do what I liked and thought was right, the more his wife liked me. I had now found out that he could not insist that I worked so late every evening.

In order to improve my English, I tried to speak to the English guests. Sometimes I went to sit in the garden in my dinner hour, usually in a quiet corner and, if some other people were there, I would start a conversation. In this way I met Matron Davies. She was running a children's home in Hemel Hempstead, in England. When she heard I was interested in coming to England, she offered me a job in her home. I had no idea where Hemel Hempstead was, and told her I would think about it and let her know. I intended to write to Bob, and ask him what he thought.

Bob didn't like the place in Bristol. He said it was too far for him to come and see me, and London was rather a big city, where I would be lonely. Matron Davies gave me her address. She was quite serious about the job for me. I would have no difficulties in coping with my duties, as I only had to look after the children. This involved taking and fetching them from school, and supervising them when they were in the home or in the garden. I would be a children's nurse, which was just like an au pair girl. If I decided to come, she would apply for a permit for me. A work permit was needed for any foreigner who wanted to work in England. She promised me my own room, one whole day off during the week, free food, and £2 a week as my pocket money. The money was not much, but then I had already heard from the agency that an au pair girl only got £2 a week, so this was the usual amount. A single train journey from Switzerland to London, in those days, was only £9.

Matron Davies left the Belvédère with a reminder to me to write to her. Bob wrote and was quite enthusiastic about the home in Hemel Hempstead. The place was not all that far away from his home and his work place, he even had one or two customers in Hemel Hempstead. Before I could reply to Matron Davies I received another letter from Bob. He had visited the home, and introduced himself to Matron Davies. He liked the place. It was clean and the children all looked well cared for and happy. I made up my mind to accept Matron Davies's offer and wrote to her, asking her to apply for a permit. I notified the agency that I had found a place in England and thanked them for their efforts.

My social life in Hergiswil was very dull. I only had Sunday afternoon off, and then I went home. This was not always a happy occasion. Astra was dissatisfied with being at home all the time, looking after the flat, and cooking for everybody. On Sundays when my mother looked after Monika, she went to the afternoon dances in the different hotels. She never brought anybody home, so we didn't meet her so-called friends.

Monika was very spoilt because Astra let her do what she liked. She had no control over her. My mother had the greatest difficulty in coping with the young child when I was there on Sundays and I felt sorry for her. After working hard all the week in the office, she should have been able to relax for at least one day, but instead she had to cook the Sunday lunch, and look after a naughty child.

My father's little business in Zürich was ticking over, not making much money yet, but enough to make him decide to give up the job in the Hotel Balance. He didn't like Sundays at home, because of all the quarrels, and the noise that Monika made. Occasionally he didn't come home for the weekend, saying it saved money for the train journey. He was able to sleep in his little office on a camp bed.

My mother said that the best thing would be to give Monika to foster parents, and let Astra take a job. Astra kept on talking about it. She felt she would also have more money then. On the one hand she wanted to keep Monika, and on the other she wanted her freedom. My mother advertised in the paper under a box number and had several replies. She sorted them through, and decided to visit four addresses. As she was working during the week, even Saturday morning, she only had Saturday afternoon when she could do her visiting. It took quite a time before she got round to the four families. Some of them she even visited twice. By the time a decision was made, I was already home again, as my time at the Belvédère was finished.

One evening, when I went out with Henri to the Alpenhof, we could not find an empty table. There were two men sitting alone at a table, so we asked them whether we could join them. They were very pleased to have our company. They stayed for the night in the hotel, and were travelling on by car the next morning. Of course we got into conversation, and discovered that they were two friends. One of them, Sepp, had come to Switzerland for a three months holiday. He had emigrated to America, where he opened a bakery business, and this was the first time he had come back.

'Is this your boyfriend?' he said to me, pointing to Henri.

'Oh no,' I said. 'He is the chef in the Belvédère. He is engaged to a very nice girl. I am the secretary there, and from time to time, when we are lonely, we have an evening together, like tonight.'

Sepp asked me to dance, but he was not a good dancer. He wanted to know why I didn't speak Swiss German, so I told him I was a *Rückwanderer*. He said he felt a little bit like that too, having been away for ten years. He said a few words in English occasionally, forgetting that he was not in America, so I replied to it. By the time we got off the dance floor, we were speaking English. The other two laughed, and we started to mix up all the languages, Henri with French, Sepp and I English, and his friend, Swiss German, or German. Speaking English, one didn't have to observe the more formal address of *Sie* (you) to ones partner, and the Christian names like Sepp and Helga came very easily. Speaking German again, we stumbled over it, and mutually decided to stick to the *Du* (you familiar form), and the Christian names. Altogether, we had a most enjoyable evening.

The next day - it was about eleven o'clock in the morning - I saw some legs passing the office window. I looked up, and was sure that that was Sepp, but it couldn't have been, because he only stayed one night in the

Alpenhof. About five minutes later I heard footsteps again and looked up. The same legs came back, but this time they stopped, and the figure bent down to look through the window.

'I have found you,' said Sepp. 'Come and have lunch with me, I am staying an extra day.'

'That is impossible, I am working. Mr Riedi would never permit this. My only free time is in the evening, and even that is frowned upon by Mr Riedi. I have Sunday afternoon off, which is not until tomorrow.'

'I will go and ask him. You must have a dinner hour, and you can spend that time with me. My friend has gone back by train and I am free.'

With that he walked off. I wasn't a bit surprised when he returned with Mr Riedi, this time entering the office through the door.

'I didn't know you had a cousin in America,' said Mr Riedi. 'He told me he has specially come to see you. You should have told me before that you were expecting him.'

He looked at me searchingly; I think he wasn't quite certain whether it was the truth or not. I was not sure what to reply, but Sepp had already worked it all out, and must have talked to Mr Riedi, telling him that he would take me out in my dinner hour.

'I will come and pick you up at twelve o'clock,' said Sepp, and walked off.

Mr Riedi tried to find out a little bit more about Sepp, but I only said 'yes' or 'no.' I was not giving him any information.

I never talked very much to him in any case, only discussed things to do with the office and my work. After all that had happened to me through him, he was no friend of mine any more.

I did not get back from my lunch with Sepp until nearly two o'clock, and when I came near the office I could hear raised voices. Mr Riedi and his future son-in-law were having an argument. Mr Riedi's daughter, Myra, was getting married in October, and her fiancé wanted her to have some time off to choose the furniture for their flat. He was shouting at his father-in-law that all his staff were working for him like slaves, including his daughter, and that he was glad that, when Myra was married, she wouldn't live in Hergiswil and work for him.

I wasn't very keen on entering the office, but I was late already. I felt it would probably be better to just knock on the door and go in. I did this, making the knocking quite loud. When I entered, Mr Riedi stared at me, then said:

'Go and have a walk for ten minutes, until we finish this conversation.'

I turned round, and practically ran up the stairs and into the garden. I returned after ten minutes, and met Myra's fiancé just leaving the office. He was a schoolteacher, a nice young man, and always very polite.

'I am sorry about this,' he said. 'I hope you understand, I did have to have this talk.'

I didn't reply to this, just smiled at him, understanding very well the reason for the argument. I entered the office, where a furious Mr Riedi was sitting behind the desk. He never said anything about me being late, just made a few notes, and then left the office. Myra had two days off after that, and Mr Riedi attended to the bar.

I met Sepp again in the evening. The next day was Sunday, so he stayed another night, and then took me in his car to Luzern, where we had a lovely afternoon together. He told me that the reason why he had come back to Switzerland, was to find a girl, as he wanted to get married.

'I am thirty-five years old already,' said Sepp. 'I want a home and a family. I do not like the American girls, so I thought I would find somebody in my homeland. My mother found me a girl, but I know she won't fit into the fast American life. I have quite a large business, with several shops, and need somebody with business sense.'

He stopped, looked at me and then added: 'Somebody like you.'

'I don't know you, Sepp,' I replied. 'Our time together has been too short.'

'I know,' he said, looking down and playing with his fingers.

He left early in the evening, as he had to travel to Winterthur. I went home to the Bürgenstrasse, where I told my mother about Sepp.

She was quite shocked: 'Surely you are not thinking of going to America. England is another place, but America is so far away. If you went there, you would never see your family again.'

'I am only telling you what has happened, and that I have met Sepp. I never said I was going to America. In any case, he has not asked me to do so, only told me why he has returned to Switzerland. I don't know him, or his family, or even where he lives in America.'

'Do you like him?'

'Yes. He is very nice, honest, hard working, and not bad looking. Please, Mama, don't always think I am getting married. Every time I meet somebody, you only judge the person by his profession or the business he has, and whether he will be good enough for my future. I wish I had not told you about Sepp. It is possible that I won't even meet him again.' I thought I had better add that last sentence to reassure her.

'I am sorry, my dear,' said my mother, 'but I do worry about you all. I have three daughters, and none of them has a husband. I would like you all to be happily married, and myself to be a contented grandmother.'

I did meet Sepp again, but I didn't tell my mother about it. He came with his two brothers one Sunday morning in September, and picked me up in the car. We went out for lunch, before driving to Luzern. His two brothers were Swiss farmers, who felt a little uncomfortable in the restaurant, which made me realise that they were not used to eating out. I had the feeling that I was being judged by them. My Swiss German was still very poor, and Sepp's brothers did not speak pure German very well, so we did not converse much. Sepp spoke English to me, probably trying to show his brothers that I already knew some of the language.

We parked the car in Luzern near the lake, and went for a walk along the shore. Sepp told me about his business, and how he had started. He had worked day and night to build it up, and never had much time for social activities. He had always wanted to go to America, already as a young boy, because he knew that at home, on the small farm which his father had, there would not be a future for him. There were seven children, three of them boys. His two brothers now shared the farm, and he was glad that he had left. There would have been no room for a third farmer on the land.

Sepp and I got on well, but I am afraid that I did not make much of an impression on his two brothers. We left them in the car in the end, so that we could say goodbye unobserved. Sepp held my hand. He wanted to say something, I could see that, but he never did, all he said was:

'If I write to you, will you answer me?'

'I don't know, Sepp. Is there any point in starting a correspondence?'

'I wish we had more time to know one another.'

'So do I, Sepp, so do I. Good luck with whatever you are going to do. I hope you find a nice girl.'

He suddenly dropped my hand, said goodbye and walked quickly back to the car, where his brothers were waiting.

I sat down on a bench by the lake, and thought about him and America. He was clever to have taken his trade there, where his bread rolls and cakes soon became popular. All his shops were called "Swiss Patisserie." At first he did everything by hand, but gradually he was able to afford machines, and now he had his own big baking place, from where he could supply his different shops. He was an extremely hard working man, and although he had his managers and good staff, he was even now wondering how things had gone without him, whilst he was in

Switzerland. He was looking forward to going back. He felt he had been away too long.

Sepp did write to me at the Bürgenstrasse. My mother did not give me the letter till the summer of the next year. The letter came at Christmas time. I was already in England, and my mother didn't want to disturb my peace of mind, so she said. She had no right to keep the letter. I don't know whether she knew the contents, but when I read it, I wondered whether she had opened it.

Sepp wrote that, on his return to America, he had found his business alright. He said he was sorry that people had put him off seeing or contacting me again. (He probably meant his brothers). His words were: 'You were still the best girl I met in Switzerland, and I cannot forget you.' He asked me to come to America, and offered to pay my fare. There would be no obligations. I could work in one of his shops, and gradually pay the money back. It would give us a chance to get to know one another. It was not a marriage proposal, but he was probably afraid that if he proposed, I wouldn't come at all.

The letter was seven months old when I received it. He must have thought I did not want to reply. I did not write back, but I felt sad that a good man like him had been left without an answer to a letter, where he had shown his feelings, admitted to having made a mistake, and made such a generous offer.

He must have been very fond of me, I thought.

Towards the end of September we started to have less guests, and Mr Riedi informed me that I could move back to my old room in the hotel, as Myra could have her room back again. I told him that I was quite happy with Mrs Bürgenmeier, and as I was leaving on October 8th, it would hardly be worthwhile for me to pack and unpack again. He said that if I didn't move into the hotel, he would not pay Mrs Bürgenmeier anything for the room any more. I knew why he wanted me back into the hotel. He then could just call me in the evenings when he wanted me, the same as he had done before when I lived there. I told Mrs Bürgenmeier that I had to move back into the hotel.

'Do you want to move?' she asked.

'No, but if I don't move, Mr Riedi won't pay you the rent for the room any more.'

'Don't worry about that,' said Mrs Bürgenmeier. 'He still owes me the rent for last year, and this year he has not paid anything for your room either. If you don't want to move, just stay here, and tell him so. It is not long before you leave. It is silly to get all your things together for the few days you are still employed by him.'

Mr Riedi was furious when he discovered I was not going to move. He threatened again not to pay Mrs Bürgenmeier. So I told him what she had said about the money. He just replied that that was not true, and stormed out of the office.

Myra's wedding was on October 9th, and the hotel closed on October 7th. The staff were kept on until after the wedding, except the chambermaids and myself, who left on the 8th. Henri had to prepare the big wedding dinner, but had a whole day for his preparations. He was very excited about this. He loved cooking, and said it was quite an unusual dinner for the 100 or so guests who would be coming to the wedding. He thought it was unfair of Mr Riedi to tell me to leave the day before, and wanted to talk to Mrs Riedi. I wouldn't let him do this, I didn't mind, it was just another of Mr Riedi's little revenges. I had learnt that it was wise not to let Mr Riedi see it when he hurt me.

I left the Belvédère on October 8th. Mr Riedi paid me my salary, and the share of the 15%. I never got the other promised money - half David's wages. I mentioned it to him again, but he said I had not been co-operative enough, and also had not fulfilled my contract. I did not argue with him, I was glad to leave.

I said goodbye to Mrs Riedi, who wanted to know whether I would come back next year. I was surprised by this question, and told her I had other plans, not saying what they were. I think she understood that I wouldn't work with her husband again. I wished Myra all the best, and hoped she would be very happy with her future husband. Myra was a little embarrassed when I said goodbye to her, because she realised I had been asked to leave the day before the wedding, so that I didn't have to be asked to come to the reception.

Henri gave me a present. He knew I liked marzipan, so he had made me a little marzipan loaf and put it into a cardboard box, together with little pieces of marzipan in the shape of bread rolls all around it. It looked most attractive. He had the box hidden in the scullery, and I had to make sure nobody saw me leaving with it.

I never had much contact with the other members of the staff, except for the fancy dress evening, so it didn't take long to say goodbye to them. Alois, the porter, offered to take my case up to the station, which I accepted.

Mrs Bürgenmeier and family asked me to come and see them sometimes, saying I would always be welcome. I hugged old Mrs Bürgenmeier, she had been good to me, like a mother, and I was sorry to leave her. I think I was company for her at times as otherwise she only had the grandchildren. Her daughter-in-law was always so busy with her job in the factory. I did not know it then, and neither did anybody else, that the old lady was incurably ill with cancer. Her daughter-in-law informed me a month later, that she had died peacefully and suddenly, after three days of illness, and that they had had a quiet funeral.

CHAPTER FOUR

Back in Luzern - Ball in the Schweizerhof

As soon as I got back to Luzern, I went to see the employment office, to find myself another job for a short time. I had heard from Matron Davies that she had applied for my permit, and now it was just a matter of waiting until she got it and posted it to me. I could not afford to be without a job. I needed the money to pay for my keep at home. I had saved a small amount whilst I was in the Belvédère. I decided to buy some shoes and winter clothes. The rest I put into the bank as a reserve, in case anything happened in England, and I had to come home and couldn't get a job straight away.

I quickly found employment with an architect, Mr Mattias, within walking distance of my home. Mr Mattias was hardly ever in the office. If he did turn up, it was in the evening. He would leave me some notes about letters I had to write. At the interview, we had come to an agreement. I told him I wanted some time off during the day occasionally, as I had to go and apply for my passport, health certificate and visa from the French Consul, as I was travelling through France. I also wanted to do some shopping before I went to England. Mr Mattias said as long as his draughtsman, Mr Langenbaum, who came two or three times a week was there, I could attend to my private jobs. The main thing was that the office was occupied by somebody during working hours. Mr Mattias told me:

'I have a contract for a big block of flats outside Luzern. We are short of money, and won't get any until we sell the flats. My company owes a lot of money, and people will ring up, or come to the office and ask for me, because they want their money. You have to make all sorts of excuses why I am not here. I know this might be difficult, but I think you will manage. If nobody answers the phone or the door, my creditors would think I am bankrupt, and my business might then collapse. That's the reason why somebody has to be here all the time. My secretary has left for a month's holiday, so it suits me to have somebody temporarily.'

I was a little concerned about this shortage of money, wondering whether I would get my salary. When I mentioned this to him, he looked at me for a while, then said he would pay me the month in advance.

I soon realised he was honest, because Mr Langenbaum, who had been with him for fifteen years, said he always got his money every month.

I did not have a great deal to do. A few letters had to be typed, sometimes also lists and instructions for the builders. Bills arrived, which I just entered into the book but they were not paid. In order to make myself look busy, I typed letters to Bob in England, the only correspondence I had. I even started to knit a cardigan, to keep myself occupied. Mr Mattias didn't come very often, but when he arrived he always came into my little room and said:

'I am in, but only for you.'

He then looked through the post, and gave me the bills to enter and file. The file of unpaid bills was very big. I got worried at times over all this owed money, and had to reassure myself that it really had nothing to do with me.

I got a number of phone calls, and became quite good at making excuses. One or two people came to the door, saying they had seen the light on in Mr Mattias's office, he must be there. I told them it was the draughtsman, even took them in and showed them the empty office.

We were downstairs, in a tall block of flats. Mr Langenbaum was a quiet man, and when he worked on his drawing board he was absolutely absorbed in what he was doing, and wouldn't even hear me coming in at times. I tried to understand what he was drawing, but found it difficult to imagine things. What I could understand was the big model of the flats, which were built to Mr Mattias's instructions and drawings.

The model was in the centre of the room on a large table. There were several buildings, three and four storeys high, with gardens, playground for children, and a tennis court. It all looked most attractive. Mr Langenbaum said it was a wonderful project, but got into trouble when the town pulled out of the plan and Mr Mattias had to find private backing. He had already started to build, ordered the material, and employed people, when the town council pulled out.

'He is going to be alright in the end,' said Mr Langenbaum to me, 'but he has got it hard in the meantime, and has to take quite a bit of abuse from the people to whom he owes money. He has even moved into a different flat, because people found out where he lived. I know his address, but I won't tell anybody. I can reach him in an emergency. He pays the wages to the employees and tries to pay the small firms, and those where he knows that they desperately need the money, but he holds back with the payments to the bigger firms. Even the banks won't give him any more credit.'

I started my job on October 13th, and it was a week later that I met Martin. He rang up, wanting to speak to Mr Mattias. I made the usual excuses, which he accepted. He rang again the next day.

I knew straight away who he was, because he had a rather deep and full voice, different from any other voice. I also had instructions to write down every call, and what the person wanted, so I could look up his name. When I recognised his voice I said his name straight away, which surprised him. Again I made excuses for Mr Mattias. He rang again in the afternoon, and this time he said:

'Do you know who I am?'

I said 'Yes,' and told him Mr Mattias would not be in for two days. I hoped to put him off for a bit. He rang again two days later, and this time we had quite a conversation.

'I suppose you know again who is phoning?'

'Yes, I recognise your voice.'

'Do you know that Mr Mattias owes me money?'

'I suppose so, otherwise you wouldn't have phoned again.'

'Is he going to pay me?'

'I don't know.'

'Will you tell him that I phoned, and that I want my money?'

'When I see him, I will tell him.'

'Do you like to work for somebody who owes money to people?'

'No comment.'

'That is not an answer.' - Silence.

'You are very loyal. I will phone again and again, until he pays my bills. I will even come and see him. Goodbye.'

At 5.30 p.m, I was just putting on my coat and getting ready to leave, when there was a ring at the door. Nobody had come as late as that before. When I opened the door, I saw a tall, well- dressed man in his middle thirties, who lifted his hat and said:

'May I speak to Mr Mattias?'

I recognised the voice from the phone and blurted out: 'It is you, we have spoken on the phone several times.'

He laughed and then said: 'You must have an excellent ear, to keep on remembering my voice. I thought I would come in person, to see whether Mr Mattias was in, and also because I wanted to meet you. You don't speak Swiss German, but an excellent pure German, which is most unusual in our parts here. I, too, got intrigued with your voice.'

I made him come in, so that he could see that Mr Mattias was not there, and neither was Mr Langenbaum. He was fascinated with the model of the flats, and admitted that Mr Mattias was a clever architect. He could see that I was ready to leave, so he invited me for a cup of coffee in a little café, just round the corner.

We had a pleasant hour together. He told me that he had a coal merchant's business, and a second one, making and installing office furniture, particularly the frames and shelves for the office files. It was one of his inventions. The coal business was an inheritance from his father. His name was Martin Finschnaller and every time I said Herr Finschnaller, I seemed to stumble over his name.

'Call me Martin,' he said. 'You seem to have difficulty with my name.' After that he called me Helga. This was something most unusual. People don't go into Christian names straight away on the continent, like they do in England, and by doing this so quickly, we both realised that we liked one another.

The next day when I left the office, he drew up in his car, jumped out, and said:

'I thought I had missed you. I suppose Mr Mattias is not in the office?'

'No, he went home half an hour ago.'

'So I missed him. Was he really in the office? Would you have told me if I had phoned?'

'He was there,' I lied, 'but I am not sure whether he would have liked to speak to you.'

'Never mind,' he replied. 'Come and have some coffee with me, and a nice piece of cake. I saw you looking at them yesterday. I want you to tell me something about yourself.'

We had another enjoyable hour. I told him a little about my life in Königsberg, but I was also interested in his life. All he would say was that he was divorced and had a little girl, four years old, who was living with his mother. I was surprised about this, because young children like that are usually kept by the mother. I said this to him and he replied:

'Fiona's mother didn't want her, she was only interested in parties and a gay social life.'

Martin didn't come to pick me up the next day, and I was disappointed. On the other hand, we had made no date. After that came the weekend, when he wasn't able to contact me. On Monday morning he phoned:

'May I speak to Mr Mattias?'

'I am sorry he is not here at the moment. May I take a message, Mr Finschnaller?'

I did not stumble over the name this time, and sounded quite efficient. The door of my office was open, and Mr Mattias was next door.

'I missed you,' said Martin. 'I couldn't conact you over the weekend. Will you come out for a meal with me tonight? We can go to a little place I know outside Luzern.'

'I am not sure about that, Mr Finschnaller,' I replied, thinking rapidly. Of course I would like to go, but I didn't want Mr Mattias, next door, to realise that I was familiar with one of his creditors.

'Why do you keep on calling me Mr Finschnaller? Who is in the office to overhear your conversation? Is Mr Mattias there watching you? If he is there, tell him to answer the phone.'

'Mr Langenbaum, our draughtsman, is in the office, would you like to speak to him? I doubt whether he can help you, but you can talk to him.'

'So it is he who is listening in. Anyway, I will pick you up at six o'clock outside the office. If that is alright, just say so.'

'That is quite alright Mr Finschnaller.'

'Good, at least you got my message.' And then he added quietly: 'I am looking forward to seeing you again.'

'Goodbye,' I said.

When I got off the phone, Mr Mattias came in and looked at my notes of the phone calls I had had from the week before. He saw the Finschnaller calls.

'Was that him on the phone?' he asked, and pointed to the name.

I nodded. 'He is very persistent, and you are quite good in putting him off. Mr Finschnaller supplied all my office shelving. I think I could send him a cheque on account, to keep him quiet for a while. Just type a note to go with it, and I will sign it.'

He walked back into his office, and I was glad he hadn't noticed my embarrassment about the telephone conversation. My heart was beating loudly, and I thought I would be glad to finish with all these lies and cover-ups I had to do. I was glad Martin got some money from Mr Mattias, at least this was an achievement.

At dinner time I told my mother that Martin had invited me to go out for supper.

'Put a nice dress on,' she said, 'or take it with you to change. You can leave your skirt and blouse in the office. You have got the key to the place and can do what you like.'

She even offered me her little handbag, and seemed as excited about this date as if she herself was going out. The only thing that spoilt it was her remark:

'Tell him how poor we are. We do need some coal, he might let you have some free.'

She always thought ahead, and looked out for what she could get from people when she met them, and now she tried to point this out to me also. Why could I not go out with Martin for an evening and forget everything, just relax and enjoy it. I made up my mind not to take any notice of what my mother had said. I didn't even take up the offer of the little handbag, as I didn't want to be reminded of her.

I changed into a dress in the office, and when I locked the door, I found Martin waiting outside in his car. He didn't ask about Mr Mattias, but when I gave him the letter with the cheque, he looked surprised.

'I didn't know you had such influence over him,' he said, thinking that I must have persuaded Mr Mattias to pay him something.

'I haven't,' I said. 'Mr Mattias does come in occasionally, and when he has some money, he tries to pay a little to the most long suffering creditors.'

'Thank you, that is very nice. Tonight we can celebrate.'

With that, he drove off. I had told him that I didn't know much of the district, or of Switzerland for that matter, as I had never had the time or the money, since we returned as *Rückwanderer*, to afford sightseeing. So now he drove along the lake, and stopped occasionally to let me look at the view. Eventually we came to a small village, and he stopped at a restaurant with a notice outside:

Hier kocht der Chef selbst. (Here cooks the owner himself).

'I have been here before,' said Martin. 'They serve an excellent meal, and the restaurant is quiet and informal.'

He was right. The place was small, quiet, homely, and very Swiss. There were little alcoves with tables, where one was left alone and private, so much so, that if one wanted any service, it was difficult to get the attention of the service girl.

We had an excellent meal. When I was in the Belvédère, Henri did his best to serve me with good meals, but this one was specially prepared for us, which made a difference. It certainly was true what it said on the notice outside: *Hier kocht der Chef selbst.*

Although I had made up my mind not to ask Martin for coal, I did do it in the end. I kept on seeing my mother's thin and worn face, and knew she wanted me to ask Martin, not to get something free for herself, but for all of us. Martin said he would have it delivered in the dinner hour, so that I would be at home.

'I hope I will get the coal for the wholesale price,' I said. 'That's the reason why I asked you.'

'You will get it very, very cheap,' he said and looked at me, smiling a little. I didn't know what he meant, so I didn't reply. Actually what happened was that I never got a bill for it. I did ask once or twice, jokingly, about the bill, but he said his secretary was dealing with it. Because it was never finalised, I couldn't say thank you to him either.

After that, we occasionally went out for a meal, but never on a Sunday. This was the day Martin would spend with his daughter. During the week he lived alone in a flat. He said he had sold his house after his marriage broke up. He could always stay with his mother, who lived in the big family house close to the lake.

One day he phoned and asked me to come and have lunch with his mother and his little girl the following Sunday. I was surprised about this, and accepted the invitation. He picked me up in the car from the Bürgenstrasse, and drove me to his mother's house.

Mrs Finschnaller was a very pleasant, elegant woman, with grey hair. She was tall, but slightly stooping, and needed a stick when she was walking, as she had an arthritic hip. An excellent lunch was served by the housekeeper. The little girl, Fiona, was very quiet. She didn't like her lunch and refused to eat it. Everybody tried to persuade her. I kept quiet. Fiona kept on looking at me from time to time with big eyes. Suddenly she said:

'You can feed me.'

Martin and his mother looked at me. I picked up the spoon and informed Fiona that we would play trains. The steam locomotive would puff along (meaning the spoon with food), until it reached her mouth. I was puffing away, Fiona's mouth opened, and the food disappeared. Half way through the meal she suddenly smiled. I stopped feeding her and said:

'I will play trains with you until the dinner is finished, if you promise to eat your pudding alone.'

Fiona looked at me with big eyes again, but did not reply. I put the spoon down and got on with my own meal. Mrs Finschnaller and Martin watched Fiona and me.

There was silence. I started to make a little conversation with Martin's mother, talking about the lovely house she had, how fortunate she was to live by the lake and ignored the little girl completely. Fiona suddenly said:

'You speak differently.' This was a remark because of my poor Swiss German.

'Yes, I do,' I replied. 'What about our little game? Will you promise to eat your pudding alone?'

She nodded her head and I finished the game with the steam engine, and the food was soon gone from the plate. She kept her promise and ate the pudding alone. After that, she wanted me to go into the garden, so we put on coats and went outside. We played hide-and-seek, and she showed me her favourite hiding places, whilst Martin talked with his mother. All of us had a pleasant afternoon.

When Martin and I said goodbye, Fiona hugged and kissed me. She asked me to come again for lunch, as she liked the game with the steam train. Martin said to me afterwards that the only difficulty they had with her was at lunch time. She just didn't want to eat. I suggested that she was probably lonely and needed the company of other children. Martin agreed that the arrangement he had with his mother and her housekeeper for looking after the little girl was not an ideal one, but the only one he could have for the moment.

'When she is five years old, she will be able to go to a nursery school. She won't start school until she is seven years old.'

I was surprised by this, but apparently children start to go to school later in Switzerland than in Germany or England.

Martin and I met more and more frequently, and he started to persuade me not to go to England. He knew I was only waiting for my permit. Mr Mattias's secretary did not return after her holiday. She had broken her leg and sent a doctor's certificate, so I stayed on in the office, waiting for my permit. I received my passport, my health certificate, and my French Visa, but the permit did not arrive. I wrote to Bob and asked him to check with Mrs Davies, wondering whether she had applied for it. Apparently she had made a mistake whilst filling out the application form, and a second form had to be submitted, which prolonged everything.

My mother had at last found a family to foster Monika. It was a couple who could not have children, but were very fond of them. Mrs Graf was a qualified nurse and took to Monika straight away. The arrangement was that Astra would pay a monthly subsidy for her child's keep, and help also with the buying of the clothes. Astra could have Monika for the weekend, if she so wished, or only take her out on Sunday afternoon. The arrangements could be made from weekend to weekend.

Astra got herself an office job in the government-run aircraft factory in Emmenbrücke, a suburb of Luzern. She also found some lodgings there, and as family Graf lived close by, this was an excellent arrangement.

The flat in the Bürgenstrasse suddenly seemed empty when Astra and Monika had moved out, and I could understand my mother when she said that it would be even lonelier when I, too, had left for England. Hans was now a corporal and still in the army. My father stayed in Zürich quite often to save the train fare. Soon only Christel would be left to keep my mother company in the evenings. I was often out with Martin, who wanted to see me quite a bit before I left.

By now I realised that Martin had grown very fond of me. I also got on well with Fiona and his mother, whom we visited occasionally. Martin was sixteen years older than myself, and I didn't like this big age gap. My mother said that this was unimportant.

I would not allow her to talk to me about Martin and the future. I knew what was in her mind, and I didn't want to hear it. Whenever she started to say something, I either told her to be quiet (in a nice sort of way), or I just walked away from her.

At last my permit arrived, and I told Mr Mattias that I would be leaving at the end of November. He was sorry to hear this. His secretary was still not coming back, and this meant getting another short term replacement for the office.

Martin told me not to book the train to England before the end of November. He wanted me to be his partner at a big ball in the Schweizerhof. This was an annual social occasion run by the Swiss Motor Club. I couldn't believe it when he invited me. The Schweizerhof was a Five Star hotel, the most elegant one in Luzern. I realised then that Martin was getting serious about me.

Although this invitation was something very exciting, it was also worrying. I had no evening dress, no evening shoes, and not much money. My mother and I went shopping, or at least we went to look at things. The dresses were terribly expensive. I just could not afford any of these beautiful creations. My mother could not make me anything as she had no sewing machine and also little free time.

At last we decided on a full black, long, soft skirt with a broad waistband, and a lilac coloured, long-sleeved blouse with pretty buttons.

The panels of the skirt were cut in such a way that the fullness at the bottom emphasised my small waist and minimised the hips. My mother said I could borrow her expensive diamond brooch which, pinned over the top button of the blouse, would make the whole outfit very elegant. The skirt was very full indeed, and I practised walking up and down the stairs at home, lifting the skirt to a certain height so that I would not tread on it.

It was a sensible buy. The skirt never wore out and was always useful with different blouses. I still have it today, but have had to let out the waist once or twice.

I also needed a winter coat very badly and had saved up for it. I knew I couldn't buy a coat in England. Firstly, I would earn too little money, and secondly, there were still clothing coupons in England. My mother said I must have a really warm coat, because England had a lot of fog and was cold and damp. Nordmann, the big store, had winter coats on special offer, so we went there. I didn't like any of them. I felt it was a lot of money to pay for something which looked very drab on me. The sales girl was also a *Rückwanderer* from Germany and was rather nice to us. She wanted to help. She understood that I had to be careful with my hard-earned money.

'Why don't you buy a fur coat,' she said suddenly. 'We have some on special offer for Christmas. They are quite reasonable, and they always look smart.'

'Oh no,' I said. 'I couldn't afford a fur coat!'

'They are not much more expensive than a model winter coat. Let me show you one.'

She went off and came back with the coat. The colour was natural and brown, and the style quite simple. There was no shape in the coat, as the fur was very thick. It had a small stand-up collar, and the pockets were in the side seams. She said it was a Russian fur, and she insisted that I tried it on. The front had no buttons. Because of the thickness, the coat did not overlap. The edges just met, and there were large hooks and eyes to hold the front together. To me it was beautiful. It felt warm and soft and comfortable. I was surprised about the price, it was only a little more than a winter coat. 'We only received ten coats,' said the girl, 'and five have already been sold.'

'It is beautiful,' I said. 'It is really beautiful. I will always be warm in it. But it is more money than I was prepared to spend.'

'You must take it,' said my mother suddenly. 'You will never get this opportunity again. It is a coat that you can wear anywhere. It will last forever. You have worked hard, and skimped and saved. You deserve a luxury item like this. You will regret it if you don't buy it. Think ahead, you will not need another coat for years if you have this one.'

It was a big decision to make, and would leave me with very little money. I could see what my mother meant, - she was right - and then I made up my mind.

'I will have the coat, and you don't need to pack it up either. I will wear it.' Then I added: 'It is quite cold outside.'

I did not sleep much that night, I kept on thinking about the purchases I had made, and about all the money I had spent. My own money, which I had earned by working hard. Things were looking up; I had achieved something. It was only just over a year ago that I was still in Hamburg, and before that, on the radio station. I was now the proud possessor of a lovely fur coat. I had an evening dress. I would go to a ball in the Schweizerhof, the best hotel in the town. After that came my journey into the unknown - England.

The ball was something which I will never forget. I felt like Cinderella, the poor little girl, clad in lovely clothes, and transformed and transported into a dream world.

There were lights everywhere in the hotel, chandeliers were sparkling, and the many large mirrors into which I looked when I passed them, showed me a stranger - a tall elegant woman with a smart gentleman in evening dress by her side.

That's Martin and I, I thought. We look like strangers.

The carpets were thick and soft to walk on, and I was so bewildered with all the elegance and glitter, that I forgot to lift my skirt when we came to some steps. I stumbled. Martin caught me in time, but I had to step back as I had already put one foot on to the bottom of my skirt. Martin laughed and joked:

'You must watch out. Don't look so astounded and surprised. Pretend you come here every day.'

I lifted my skirt and had another go at the steps, this time with more success. After that, it was a matter of gliding along and pretending self-confidence.

Martin introduced me to some of his friends. There were several couples, mostly in his age group. I felt very young amongst them. The women were all dressed in very expensive evening dresses. I even recognised one of the dresses, as I had seen it in the shop and knew the price. Martin had said I looked very elegant. He was glad that I had not dressed up too much. He didn't like show-off women. My mother's diamond brooch sparkled, and I wondered whether people realised that the five large diamonds in it were real and worth quite a fortune.

We had a sit-down dinner, followed by a few short speeches. I cannot remember how many courses there were for the meal. Food seemed to be coming again and again. All was served efficiently and tasted wonderful. Here I was, sitting in these elegant surroundings, eating with silver cutlery from beautiful plates. If I had told anybody that not long ago, I was so poor and hungry that I had to dig up animal fodder to have something to eat, they would not have believed me.

After the dinner there was dancing. Martin was a good dancer. We didn't like the crowds, so we moved to another room where we could still hear the music. Only a few couples were dancing there. My skirt was lovely, swinging along with me, billowing out behind me, and giving me a feeling of weightlessness. We were both enjoying the evening, and our happiness showed on our faces. From time to time we joined Martin's friends, who were sitting in a group having a drink.

'How long have you known Martin?' asked one of the women. I had to think about it, it had never occurred to me to count the weeks or days since we had met.

'I think it is about six months,' said Martin suddenly. 'We met at my architect's place, when I went for some plans.'

I knew this wasn't true, we had only known one another for two months, but I realised Martin didn't want his friends to know this. In any case, to me it seemed much longer than two months. The women tried to have some conversation with me. They were intrigued, and wanted to find out more about me. One of them said:

'Martin has never brought a girlfriend along since his divorce. You are the first one. He has never mentioned you either, although we meet nearly every month. He has kept you well hidden. He has been very hurt by his first wife. We never thought he would get over it. You know he has a little daughter?'

'Yes, I have met her. She is a sweet little girl,' I replied.

'Have you met Martin's mother?'

'Yes, I had lunch with her once or twice. That's when I met Fiona.'

'You must be somebody special to him if you have been to his mother's house and been entertained there.'

She then turned to two of the other women, and told them the news she had just heard from me. There was surprise on their faces.

'You must come to one of my evenings,' she said and, turning to Martin, who was talking to one of his men friends, she said:

'You must bring your friend next week to our evening get-together, don't forget. You missed the last one.'

'I am afraid I will not be able to come,' I said quietly. Everybody looked at me astonished. 'I am going to England next week,' I continued.

Before anybody could say anything, Martin got up, and looking at me with a smile said: 'Let's dance, I can hear the band playing a waltz.'

He took my hand, and we left his friends with their bewildered faces. We danced and we danced. There were several rooms with beautifully smooth floors, and with the doors wide open. One could just dance from one room into the next. When we were tired, we sat down on one of the many chairs by the wall to rest.

'I think I have given your friends something to think about. They were rather intrigued with me,' I said. 'Did you see their faces when I said I was going to England?' I laughed; I could visualise them sitting there and talking about me, wondering where I had come from and why I was going away.

'There is no need for them to know everything,' said Martin quietly and quite seriously. 'I have known some of them for a long time, and one or two have been very good to me when my marriage broke up. You have made me forget a lot of my unhappiness. I wish you wouldn't go to England. I am afraid I might lose you. Why don't you stay here? You can have a good job here anywhere you like. You can even come and work for me. I will sack my secretary and you can have her job.'

I could see he really meant it, but I was not altering my plans.

'No, Martin, I am not staying in Switzerland. We have discussed this before and I have told you that I am leaving. You can come and visit me in England, if you like,' I said jokingly.

I think what really worried him was that I had somebody else in England. I had told him about Bob, whom I had met in the Belvédère, and who had been to see Matron Davies in the children's home. I had mentioned that he didn't live very far from my future employer. Martin was jealous; he didn't like me having another male friend.

Even the lovely ball had to come to an end, and Martin brought me home in the early morning hours. He kissed me gently, and said he would pick me up in the afternoon, so that we could go and have some coffee somewhere. It was my last Sunday in Switzerland. I was very tired and went to bed straight away, with the music still singing in my ears.

I slept until dinner time, when Christel woke me up saying it was time to get up. I had to tell my mother and my sister all about the wonderful night that I had had.

When I was changing in my room, getting ready to go out with Martin, Christel came in and sat on my bed. She kept on looking at me, and once or twice she started to say something, but then stopped. At last she said quietly:

'Are you going to marry Martin?'

'He has not asked me,' I replied.

'You seem to be with him all the time. He has taken you to see his mother, and you like his daughter. Now he has introduced you to his friends,' said Christel.

'I know what you mean. A mistress is hidden, a decent, eligible girl is presented to the world. And now he has done this, it is a sign that he might propose. But you see, Christel, he is sixteen years older than myself, and I am not really in love with him, at least not yet. I enjoy being taken out to places which I couldn't afford. He makes me feel I am somebody, I am important to him. He is good company. We have fun together. But that is all at the moment. I don't really know him. I know he can be very stubborn, which I do not like, and I sometimes wonder what he is like when he loses his temper. There is now no time to find all this out as I am going away. I know Mama is asking the same questions as you. I won't talk to her about Martin. She has already lined him up as an eligible future son-in law. Because of this, I cannot discuss anything rationally with her. Who knows what the future will bring. At the moment I only know that I am going to England, and Martin will be left in Luzern.'

'You don't have to go to England if you marry him,' said Christel.

'I can see Mama has talked with you,' I said. Christel smiled, a little embarrassed. I was cross, so I said sharply to her:

'You can tell Mama that I have only known Martin for two months, and his big attraction at the moment is that he is quite a wealthy, good-looking man, who is spoiling me by taking me out. He has been hurt very badly by his first wife, and it will take him a long time before he can trust a woman again. I am not waiting for this. I am glad I am going away. Every boyfriend I have is straight away looked at to see whether he could be a future husband or not, and I do not like that.'

I had finished changing by now, so I put on my coat, took my handbag, and walked out. I was meeting Martin.

CHAPTER FIVE

England - The Children's Home - Bob

All preparations for my journey to England were made. I only had to buy my ticket two days before leaving. I hated the thought of all the family coming to the railway station. When I mentioned this to Martin, he said:

'Why don't you go from Basel, and I will take you there by car. Your train doesn't go until the evening, and we can have the whole day together.'

This was an excellent idea. I ordered my train ticket from Basel to London, and told my family that they would have to say goodbye to me in the Bürgenstrasse, as Martin was taking me in his car to Basel. Everybody was very surprised, but my mother was pleased. This was, in her opinion, a good sign, showing how fond Martin and I were of one another. I did not contradict her, there was no point. She had mentioned several times that she was afraid I would never come back again from England.

They were all there when I left, Mama and Papa, Christel, Hans, who was home on leave, and Astra, who had brought Monika with her. Christel cried, and so did my mother, and Papa scolded them for making things difficult for me. He made a little speech, about me going out into the world alone, and then suddenly stopped and said:

'You have always coped and shown that you can manage, even in the most difficult situations, so there is really no point in my giving you advice now. We will miss you, you have given the family a lot of support, and your strength and encouragement has helped us all.'

He hugged me hard, and I could feel and see that he, too, felt like crying, but being a man, could not allow this to happen. So he just picked up my suitcase and told Hans to take the other one downstairs. My mother cried on my shoulder and whispered:

'What will I do without you, you have always given me strength. My best wishes are with you, take care, and have a lovely Christmas. Do come back to Switzerland and to us.'

Even Astra cried a little. I don't know why, maybe because everybody else did, or maybe she, too, would miss me.

Christel said several times: 'Don't stay in England for ever, you must come back. We will miss you for Christmas.'

When I came downstairs my suitcases were already in the car, and Papa, who had not met Martin before, was talking to him. I kissed Papa and Hans quickly, waved to the others who were looking out of the window, and we were off. I didn't feel like talking, and Martin asked no questions.

We had lunch in a small village, and got to Basel in the afternoon. I registered my luggage at the station, and then Martin drove around the town, which he knew, showing me some of the buildings. I am afraid that I was not very interested in anything, but didn't tell him that. He remarked, once or twice, that I was very quiet, but I think he understood. We had an early supper, and Martin took me to the station with my hand luggage, a small bag, into which I had packed some sandwiches and a drink. I knew that the journey would be long. I would not arrive until the following evening.

When we said goodbye, Martin said:

'I do not want to lose you. If I think that somebody else is going to take you away from me, I will come and fetch you back to Switzerland.'

I think this was a reference to Bob. I had heard from him that he would come to London to pick me up. I had told Martin that I was glad about this. I had to catch another train from another station, after arriving at Victoria in London.

At the last minute, Martin gave me a present. It was packed in the shape of an oblong parcel, and he said it was something so that I would not forget him. We kissed goodbye when the guard called out that the doors of the train had to be closed. I found my reserved seat and opened the window. The train started off, and I waved and waved until Martin's figure could not be seen any more. Then I sat down and collected myself.

The day had been very strenuous, upsetting at times. I was glad to sit down and to be alone. I shut my eyes and thought about the farewell in the morning, the journey to Basel, and then the farewell from Martin. I was not sad that I had to leave everybody, on the contrary, I was excited and looked forward to the new challenge that was awaiting me.

I remembered Martin's present. I hoped it was a handbag. I only had a very cheap one, and it already looked quite worn. I had mentioned this to Martin, and said I was ashamed of my bag, but I didn't have enough money to buy a replacement.

I tore the paper off the present. Suddenly I held a picture frame in my hands and Martin smiled at me. It was a large, glass framed photograph of him, which could be stood upon a table, or hung on the wall. Somehow I felt disappointed, I had so much hoped for a handbag. The photograph was beautiful, and I think Martin hoped I would hang it up and look at it every day. Quietly, I packed it into my bag. I sat back in my corner by the window and went to sleep.

I don't remember much about the journey. I slept, on and off, all night, and during the day I walked along the corridor, as otherwise I would have become too stiff. The train stopped at Calais, and we had to walk to the boat which took us to Dover. I am not a good sailor, so I went on to the top deck to have fresh air. It was very cold, and I was glad to have my lovely fur coat. I was not sick, but I felt like it, and was glad when we had crossed the Channel, and caught the next train to London.

Being Swiss, I had to go through a different passport exit from the British people. I showed my passport and my work permit, and was told to follow a customs officer, who took me into a separate room. I was asked a number of questions and stumbled along in my poor English.

After that a woman arrived and took me into a cubicle. She told me to get undressed so that a doctor could examine me. I refused to do this. I told them I had no diseases and was perfectly healthy. The doctor arrived and argued with me. I showed them my health certificate, but refused to get undressed. In the end they gave in. I was given back my passport and permit, and was told that I could go. By now my train had left, and I had to catch the next one. At London Victoria Station I had to find my luggage. I had registered it in Basel so that I did not have to carry it when changing trains. I had no difficulties at the Customs. Nobody expected a young girl with a work permit to have precious goods, or to smuggle watches or gold, at least, not in those days.

At last I was able to leave with my two heavy suitcases in my hand. I hoped that Bob had waited for me somewhere, because I had been delayed.

I saw him standing on the station platform, big and tall, and my heart leapt. I was so grateful that he was there. I was tired, and a little frightened. I had been upset about the interview with the doctor, I still felt a little sick from the boat trip, I was cold because London was damp and foggy and dark, and it was late in the evening. All around me everybody spoke English, and although I knew a little, I could not follow the fast-spoken language.

I put my suitcases down and just looked at Bob in the crowd. He suddenly saw me, and his whole face lit up as he came towards me. He shook my hand and held it and said he was so glad to see me. He kept on talking, but I didn't understand much. It didn't matter, he was there, and now he would take charge. I was lucky to have him to organise everything. He took my cases, and he told me that we had to take a bus to another station. I just followed him.

I kept on hearing music, and could not understand this. There should not have been music on a railway station. So I decided I must be imagining it. The music did not stop, then a man said something in English, and another piece of music started again. We came outside the station and to the bus stop. There was a queue. I was surprised at the way people were queuing up, in a long line, one behind the other. In Switzerland we would stand in a group, and when the bus came, we would just get in, the strongest people getting in first. Here they were very organised. When the bus came Bob said this was not ours. The people got in one by one in the way they had queued.

I still heard the music, so eventually I asked Bob what it was. He laughed, and then explained everything. He had a small wireless with a strap across his shoulder, and that's where the music was coming from. I had never seen this before. It was something really new for those days.

We caught the bus to Marylebone station, and from there a train to Gt. Missenden. When we got out of the station it was so foggy that I could not see anything. I had never seen or experienced such thick fog. Bob said that he had a sports car, and told me to wait for him with my luggage whilst he fetched it. He had told me in London, that he would take me home to his mother's place. It was much too late to get me to Hemel Hempstead to Mrs Davies and the children's home. He was going to take me there the following morning.

The car arrived, but I could not see much of it, because even the lights seemed to disappear in the fog. Bob put my cases into the back. I then had to climb over a low side door, which either did not, or could not be opened. There seemed to be a canvas roof, but there were no windows in the car, and it was bitterly cold and wet and damp.

I don't think I like this weather, I thought.

We started off. I soon got frightened. Bob seemed to hang out of the side of the car all the time as he couldn't see much through the

MINISTRY OF LABOUR AND NATIONAL SERVICE,
Overseas Department,
Foreign Labour Division,
Russell Square House,
Russell Square,
London, W.C.1.

PERMIT

under Article 1 (3)(b) of

THE ALIENS ORDER, 1920.

Please quote the following number in any further correspondence
A.R. 21941/1947.

No. of Permit 36554   Date of issue 30 OCT 1947

Period covered by Permit **twelve** months—from the date of landing in the United Kingdom.

Employer's Name and Address.	Alien's Name, etc.	
MISS E. R. DAVIS,	Surname	Zirkel
"Chestnuts",	Other Names	Helga
46, Alexandra Road,	Date of Birth	11th July, 1924.
Hemel Hempstead,	Sex	Female Nationality Swiss.
Herts.	Employment	Children's Assistant (Resident)
I.5.		@ £2. 0s. 0d. per week.

This permit is issued to the above-named employer subject to the conditions shown below :—

CONDITIONS GOVERNING THE ISSUE OF THIS PERMIT.

(Voir dessous. Siehe Rueckseite.)

1. This permit does not constitute any obligation upon the Immigration Officer to give the above-named alien leave to land in the United Kingdom. The alien will be required to satisfy the Immigration Officer on arrival that he (or she) can comply with the provisions of the Aliens Order, 1920, which may include a medical inspection.

2. This permit must be produced to the Immigration Officer at the port of arrival in the United Kingdom. Thereafter it should be carefully preserved by the alien for production at any time to the competent authorities.

3. This permit may be used only by the alien named thereon. If an unauthorised person amends the particulars upon the permit it will thereby be rendered invalid.

4. This permit is valid only for the particular employment for which it is issued and not for employment of another kind or with another employer.

5. The alien during the period of stay in the United Kingdom is subject to the restrictions, and must conform to the requirements, of the Aliens Order, 1920.

6. This permit ceases to be valid if not produced to the Immigration Officer at the port of arrival in the United Kingdom within **two months** after the date of issue.

7. If it is desired to employ the alien beyond the terminal date of the period for which the alien has been granted leave to land by the Immigration Officer, application should be made by the employer about one month before such date to the Under-Secretary of State, Home Office, Aliens Department, ~~10, Old Bailey, London, E.C.4,~~ marking the envelope in the bottom left-hand corner " M.L. Permit." The alien's passport should not be forwarded with the application.

274-7. High Holborn,
London. W.C.1

Signed on behalf of the Minister of Labour and National Service,

b.hufeod

A.R.2A.

This permit of **four pages** should be sent intact to the alien, who will be required to produce it, together with a valid passport, to the Immigration Officer at the port of arrival in the United Kingdom.

(1/47) (19067) Wt. 47878—6547 10m 2/47 G.S.St. Gp. 344

windscreen, although he had the wipers going. We slowly made our way forward. We never met another car, and I had the feeling as if we were going along a narrow road. We certainly were going up a steep hill. I could feel this by the angle of the car. Bob did not say anything. All his concentration was needed for his driving. He was hanging out of the side most of the time, which made me feel very uneasy. The journey seemed to take hours. Suddenly we turned into a drive and I saw dim lights.

'We are home,' said Bob, and I knew that he, too, had been worried.

Indoors I met his mother and father, who had waited for us. His mother had been quite concerned because of the fog, and I am sure she was glad her son was safely home. She was very kind and understanding to me, realising that I must be cold and tired.

'Let's put the kettle on and have a cup of tea,' she said.

This was something new for me. I didn't visit friends in Switzerland, but when we visited people in Germany we usually had a cup of coffee. If it was late in the evening there would be a bottle of beer, or wine offered to us.

I have never forgotten Bob's mother's sentence about the tea, because it was her trade mark. I soon learnt that whenever somebody came to see her, or if there was a crisis, or if difficulties had to be solved, she would say:

'Let's put the kettle on, and have a cup of tea.'

The tea tasted different and warmed me up. I was too tired to have anything to eat, but I enjoyed the drink. I was shown to the guest room, and as soon as I stretched out in bed I was asleep. I had a good sleep and woke up early, refreshed, and ready for whatever the day would bring. I found the bathroom, had a wash, dressed, and went downstairs. Bob was in the kitchen making some breakfast.

'You are up early,' he said. 'My parents are still asleep. I usually go to work early. We start at 7.30 in the factory. Dad comes later, he likes to do some jobs in the greenhouse first. - What would you like to eat? We have cornflakes, or you can have toast and marmalade. I have just made a cup of tea, so you can have that first.'

I had never had cornflakes with milk and sugar before, so I tried that, and liked it. I also enjoyed the toast with marmalade, another thing that was new to me. In Switzerland, we had *Confiture* (jam with pieces of fruit) for breakfast, and *café au lait*, but I liked the sweet bitter marmalade. By the time we had finished, Bob's parents came downstairs, and were surprised that we had finished our breakfast.

Bob said he would show me the outside of the house, and then take me to Hemel Hempstead.

'I will have to have the morning off, Dad,' he said, 'so, maybe you could go to the factory a little earlier.'

'Alright,' said his father smiling, and then looking at me, he said:

'Don't keep him away from work for too long, I need him. - At least the fog has gone,' he added, 'although it is dull and cold.'

I liked Bob's father. He seemed to have a good understanding with his son. Bob took me outside, and I could see now that the house was standing in a very large garden, completely isolated. There was only one other house next door, but that was invisible because of the tall hedges. There were a number of outhouses, one of them containing a pig. There were chickens in a large run, two dogs running between our feet, and there was a big greenhouse. This was not a house but an estate, and I was impressed. Bob said they already had pigs during the war.

'We have the pig slaughtered to give us bacon and lard, and then we have another pig. The chickens give us eggs, and Dad grows grapes, tomatoes, and cucumbers in the greenhouse. There is also a big vegetable garden where we have not only vegetables, but also soft fruit and strawberries. We even used to have our own potatoes during the war. We called it "Digging for Victory," but now we don't plant potatoes any more.'

After looking around the so-called estate, I was also shown Bob's car, which I had been unable to see in the dark fog the night before. The car was a most unusual vehicle, an Alvis, yellow in colour, with large maroon mudguards, very wide running boards, and a dicky seat in the back. In the front were two very big headlamps. It had a canvas roof, and the celluloid windows could be taken out. They were cracked, and stuck together with Sellotape, not airtight, and also not a very nice sight. Because of this Bob had taken them out. They were rarely used. He was extremely proud of his car, because it was fast and sporty. The little gear lever by the steering wheel intrigued me.

My luggage went into the dicky seat and we were off to Hemel Hempstead. Bob explained that today he would take me in his car, but after that if he came to see me, he would have to come in a small van as petrol was rationed. He would have to combine his trip with a visit to a customer in Hemel Hempstead.

It was December 8th 1947 when I arrived and started in the children's home: "The Chestnuts," Alexandra Road, Hemel Hempstead. It wasn't a purpose-built home, but a large Victorian house which had been converted. Matron Davies welcomed me, and introduced me to Susan, the nurse, who was her assistant. She asked Bob to bring my luggage in and took us both to the first floor, where she showed me my bedroom. It was a pleasant small room, with the view into the large garden. I had a small table with two chairs, an armchair, a chest of drawers, a wardrobe, and of course, a bed. There was a mirror on the wall over the table, and a small carpet on the lino-covered floor. Everything was clean and fresh-looking, and I could smell the polish, which must have been put on to the shiny floor recently. I was pleasantly surprised. A picture of my room in Hergiswil flashed through my mind.

Matron Davies showed us both around the house. On the first floor were the large bedrooms, full of iron beds. She accepted children from the age of five until twelve years old. They went to school every day. Everybody had a small locker next to their bed, but their clothes were kept in another room by Matron under lock and key.

The beds looked gay, with different coloured bedspreads, and the rooms had shiny lino and pretty curtains on the windows.

Downstairs was the large entrance hall. On the left the playroom and dining room. Opposite the entrance was Matron's office, and a comfortable sitting room with armchairs and two small settees. There was the staircase in the corner and on the right, next to the entrance, one went through an arch into the staff dining room and into the kitchen and scullery, from where one could go through the back door into the garden.

There was also another door into the cellar. This was not a cellar any more, because Matron Davies had this part made into living quarters during the war, a kind of air-raid shelter. Now she lived there, and it was a very comfortable bed-sitting room, with a small kitchen and toilet.

'I can get away from the children's noise here,' she said.

Because it was dinner time, and the children were expected back from school any minute, Matron Davies suggested that Bob took me out for lunch. In the afternoon I could unpack, and she would talk to me about my duties. She told Bob about one or two little restaurants close by.

There was still food rationing in England, and I was surprised when I heard that, if one ate out in a restaurant, one did not need coupons.

'You are only allowed to have a meal for five shillings,' said Bob, whilst we were walking along the road looking for an eating place. We had left the car in the drive of the home.

'Have you got any money?' said Bob suddenly.

I was surprised by his question. Surely he wouldn't want me to pay for our dinner.

'Yes,' I said. 'I have £3, that's all I have got. I took it with me in case something happened and I needed it.'

'Could you lend me £1, I didn't bring any money. I don't need any when I go to work. We have our dinner in the factory canteen for which I do not pay. If I want petrol, I go to the pump by the railway station where the owner knows me. He writes it down, and the factory pays the bill once a month. I only have to give the petrol coupons.'

He was a little embarrassed, I could see that, and I felt rather funny having to lend him money after such a short acquaintance. I gave him £1, and he promised to post it to me as soon as he got back home. He kept his word and posted the money the same day.

We had quite a good meal for five shillings each. Bob took me back to the "Chestnuts." He left me there, saying he would come and see me on Sunday afternoon.

I unpacked, and then met Matron in her office, where she told me what I had to do. In the morning I had to supervise the children, - there were thirty-five of them, making sure that they got dressed, and also that they all came downstairs for breakfast. I had to take them to school, then return and help the two women in the house with bed making, ironing and maybe a little mending. At twelve o'clock they had to be picked up from school again and brought back for lunch. They returned for the afternoon lessons, which finished at 3.30 p.m. After that I could take them for a walk to the park, or back home to play in the garden or, if wet, in the playroom. Supper was at 5.30, and then everybody had to have a bath. It was lights out at 6.30, if possible, for the young ones, and 7.30 for the older ones.

'For the first two days Susan will do things with you,' said Matron, 'until you know the routine. After Christmas I am expecting a young couple from Ireland, and then we will not be so short staffed. I am having two women coming every day. One of them is only here for the morning, but the other one will come back in the evening. She will help you with the children, when they go to bed, and have to be bathed.'

I soon knew the routine. The children were a handful, some of them quite unruly and naughty, and often I could not find enough words to keep them in check. They were also kind, and I asked them to help me with the language, particularly when I was trying to read them a story. They enjoyed correcting my pronunciation.

One thing I had not known, and neither did Bob, that this was a Jewish home. Before each meal, I had to start off a Jewish prayer for them. Susan showed me what I had to do. She wasn't Jewish either. I had to put one hand on my head (the head had to be covered for the prayer) and the other behind my back, and then say the first two or three words of the prayer whilst closing my eyes. I only remember the first word, which sounded like "Aba." All the children carried on in a chorus. They knew their prayers and I just watched them. Some of them tried to look, but a little pat on the head soon made them close their eyes again.

In the evening, the children got undressed in the playroom, putting their clothes in neat piles on the bench, which ran all the way round the three walls of the room. The older children, who went to bed later, were allowed to play or read a little longer. They put their clothes on to the small chairs, which stood in little groups in the playroom.

Bath time, on Friday, started at 4.30 p.m, as everybody had to dress in clean clothes after that and come down to a special supper meeting with Matron. This was their religious evening, before their Sabbath, and I was never allowed in the dining room for this, as I was not Jewish. Already after dinner we got the clean clothes ready for the children. They were hung over the balustrades on the first floor landing, where everybody had a number or, for the little ones, who could not read, a picture of an animal.

To bath all the children was very strenuous. Every grown-up had back-ache after that. Susan and I would do the washing of the children, always two in the bath at the same time. Susan washed face, neck, top of the body and scrubbed arms and hands. I did the bottom part, and the scrubbing of the legs and feet. The children changed over in the bath once Susan was finished, or if I was finished. After that, both had to be dried, and on Fridays, they had to have their clean clothes on. Only the very young ones had to be dried, the older ones did it themselves. We always called four children, who were supervised by one of the helpers in the playroom. They came upstairs in their dressing gowns. It was just like a conveyer belt getting all thirty-five of them bathed. From time to time we had to have clean water, and that's when we could stretch our backs.

On Fridays, whilst the children had their supper and their prayers with Matron, we cleared up the bathroom, took all the dirty clothes and soaked them in a large bath in the scullery ready for washing the next day. There was no washing machine, and the two helpers used to spend all Saturday morning washing and hanging the clothes out, either outside, or in the attic if the weather was bad.

Matron did the cooking, mostly in the evening, and it was warmed up the next day. There were a lot of stews and minced meat, and for pudding stewed fruit and plenty of custard, as the children had to have their milk. There was a young girl of fifteen or sixteen years old, Bella, a little simple, who had been with Matron for ten years. She had no mother, and the father didn't want her. The Jewish Society had paid for her upkeep in the home for years, and after that she stayed on as a helper and was given a small amount of pocket money.

It was her job to peel the potatoes and get the vegetables ready in the morning, so that one of the helpers could put them on to boil, ready for dinner.

Bella had to be watched, and to be reminded not to forget her jobs. She often disappeared behind the kitchen door. There, she picked up the corner of her apron and wrapped it over her thumb, before putting it into her mouth. She thought that by sucking her thumb in that way it would not get so sore and nobody would notice it. She not only had to get the vegetables ready, but she also had to do all the washing-up during the day. In the morning, there was porridge for breakfast, so the plates were sticky from it, and took a long time to wash up. She didn't have to dry them, as they were stacked in a rack to drip dry. Matron cooked the porridge the night before, and often when it was warmed up in the morning, it would stick to the bottom of the saucepan, or burn. Bella used to scrape for ages before the saucepan was clean.

I hated porridge, it was a typical English breakfast, and I could not get used to it. Susan gave me a piece of toast once or twice, because we never saw Matron before eleven o'clock in the morning. Susan informed me that Matron was not a very hard-working woman. She cooked in the evening, so that she could sleep in the morning, and having a little kitchen downstairs, cooked her own meals. We never had butter, we never saw any, but Susan said we were entitled to it on our ration cards. I often just ate dry toast as I didn't like the margarine.

In the evenings, having had a cooked dinner in the middle of the day, there were sandwiches and cocoa. I often helped to prepare the sandwiches, which usually had margarine and fish or meat paste on them. From time to time there was an apple, orange or banana for everybody. The food was not very exciting, but none of the children went hungry.

There were a mixture of children from different types of homes, and there was usually a reason why they were there. The parents of one young boy had a hairdressing business, and as they were both working, they could not look after him. They came every Sunday and took him out.

Another boy only stayed a short time, because his mother had a second baby. There was a widower, who had put his little daughter into the home because he could not cope, and there were children from broken homes. Some were very poor and the Jewish Society paid for them.

Sometimes, there were two from the same family, like Hedi and Lotti. They had come on a refugee train at the beginning of the war. They fled when the Germans marched into Austria. The story was a little vague, as they were too young at the time to remember much. They got separated from their parents, and were taken by some Jewish people on to a train to Switzerland. They eventually came to England, where the Jewish Society paid for them to stay in the home. They had only recently heard that their mother was in Switzerland and their father in America. The mother had written to say that she would, or hoped, soon to come to England to see the children. She had also sent some lovely clothes. Hedi was already eleven years old, a big, broad-shouldered, plain girl, who was rather disturbed. She used to get fits, and I had to watch her. She would suddenly cross her legs, get a vacant look in her eyes, and start swaying slightly. She never fell down, but the children, when they saw this, used to be very cruel to her. They would push her, and pinch her. She never felt anything. I used to gently guide her to a chair and make her sit down. This was not easy, because she was very stiff. When she came round she could not remember anything.

Lotti was different. She was small, with dark hair and dark eyes, very vivacious, and extremely pretty. She was Matron's favourite, and spent quite a bit of time with her in her cellar flat, doing little jobs for her like dusting and tidying up. Often she just sat with Matron and looked at magazines. We did not see much of her, except that she came with me when I took the children to school as she, too, had to go to school.

School started at nine o'clock so, at twenty minutes to nine o'clock, the children had to line up in the hall in twos, the smaller ones in the front. The Infant School was close by. All children under seven were dropped off there. After that, I took the rest to the next school. At dinner time, I collected the older children first whilst the younger ones waited for me in the playground of their school. Saturday and Sunday there was no school, and unless it was raining, Matron Davies insisted that the children went for a walk. She wanted them away from the home because even in the garden the children made too much noise for her.

All children wore wellingtons, and none of the boys had long trousers, or the girls long stockings. Even women walked about with bare legs. One still needed coupons for any type of clothes, and they probably never had enough coupons to buy stockings. Sometimes it was bitterly cold, and I felt sorry for the children in their wellingtons, from which their blue, cold knees were sticking out. Still, these children were tough, hardly anybody seemed to get a cold. I used to make them walk through Hemel Hempstead towards Boxmoor, on to the meadows by the Grand Union Canal, and there we would play some running games to get warm.

For the first few days I was very tired in the evenings. I went early to bed, glad of the peace and quiet. I always took a last look into the bedrooms, and one or two of the little ones wanted a hug before going to sleep. I think that was what they missed most, the special affection which they would have got from their own mothers, but which was missing in a children's home. Gradually I got used to the noise of the children and to the work.

Bob, as promised, came on Sunday afternoon. It was damp and foggy again. I had been for a walk with the children in the morning, but it was too damp to do so in the afternoon, especially as it got dark early. To my and the children's surprise, Bob brought his big accordion. I didn't know he could play. The children were fascinated, and from that moment on he became their favourite uncle. He played anything they asked him, and if he didn't know the song, he asked the children to sing the tune and he soon picked it up and played it. He only played by ear, although he could read music. He informed me that he also played the piano and the organ. We all had a lovely afternoon, and it was easy to look after the children having such an excellent entertainer as a helper. Matron thanked Bob, and said he was welcome in the home at any time.

Matron had already told me that I could never have the weekend off, so we arranged that my free day would be Wednesday. Bob told me that he was running an Olde Tyme Dancing session every Wednesday evening, and he promised to teach me the different dances.

'I need a partner,' he said. 'People come who do not know the dances, or maybe only some of them. I have all the records, and I teach anybody who turns up.'

So on Wednesday, on my day off, I caught the bus from Hemel Hempstead to Chesham, where Bob met me. He showed me Chesham, and a little of the district, and then took me to his home, where I had tea with his parents. After that we went to Gt. Missenden, where Bob was running his Olde Tyme Dance in the factory canteen.

I was fascinated with the music and the steps for the different dances. It was pretty late by the time Bob got me back to Hemel Hempstead in his van.

Because Bob could not have every Wednesday off, we arranged that sometimes I would catch a bus on Tuesday evening and stay the night with his parents. I would then spend the day with his mother, and we would go out on Wednesday evening. Occasionally I had a day in London or looked around Hemel Hempstead. I would then take the bus to Chesham in the late afternoon, and meet Bob for his evening dancing session. Afterwards he took me back in his van.

Bob turned up at the children's home every Sunday afternoon. The next surprise he produced for the children were Mickey Mouse and cartoon films. His father had a film projector, and Bob had been able to find somebody from whom he could rent these films. The children were as good as gold all through the week, because only good children would be allowed to see the films, or listen to Uncle Bob playing the accordion or the piano in the dining room.

Christmas came, and Matron informed the staff that she would be going away for a few days over the festive season. Jewish people do not have Christmas, but as the children had holidays, and everybody talked about Christmas, with the shops and streets full of decorations, some explanation had to be given to the children. We had a small Christmas tree, with shiny balls and ribbons, but no presents for the children. Some had parcels from relatives, and some, we were told, would be going out on Christmas Day, or even going home over the holidays.

Susan was put in charge. She had long talks with Matron before she left. Once she had gone, Susan came to see me. She was quite cross.

'Matron gave me two chickens to cook for the Christmas dinner. There are probably thirty children, two helpers, you and I. The two helpers do not want their meals here, but even so, how am I going to divide two chickens amongst the lot of us? It will be potatoes and cabbage again for everybody, like we have nearly every day.'

All the grown-ups were quite upset about the poor provision for Christmas, except the children, who didn't realise what was going on. Bob promised to bring some Charlie Chaplin films on Boxing Day, because Christmas Day he had to spend at home with his sister and parents. They usually had lots of people for their Christmas dinner, and he was not allowed to miss this.

Susan's boyfriend turned up on Christmas Eve. He was in the RAF, stationed in Bovingdon, not far from Hemel Hempstead. He helped with the different jobs, and the entertainment of the children, and stayed for the whole festive season. We managed the Christmas dinner. Everybody had a little piece of chicken, and plenty of gravy. There was fruit, and there were sweets, which Matron had left behind. Bob showed the films on Boxing Day, and the children laughed and were happy. In the evening, when they were in bed, the four of us played games, and Bob was playing the piano, so that we could sing Christmas songs. It was a lovely Christmas after all, with greetings and good messages sent from all my family.

Matron came back for New Year and gave a party for her friends. This time we had plenty of food, open sandwiches with meat and sausage, and a punch with wine. Of course, Mrs Davies was able to get all this food because she had all the ration cards from the children. Susan made a few remarks, which Matron overheard. I think Susan wanted her to hear them.

There must have been at least ten couples invited (twenty people), and Susan and I were allowed to join in. We helped by handing round the food and drink, and putting on the gramophone records, so that people could dance in the hall, where we had lifted up the carpet. At twelve o'clock we wished one another a Happy New Year. Everybody was quite gay by then, and we were all very happy indeed.

We went to bed in the early morning hours, but had to get up at the usual time because it was a working day and the children had to be attended to. There was a lot of washing up to be done in the morning. Still, the two women helpers arrived and got on with it. The children had to have bread and margarine, because Matron had not cooked porridge the night before, but they didn't mind that. After that, I took them all for a long walk, because Matron had told me the night before to do this. This gave her a peaceful morning to have a sleep, and I was glad of the fresh air.

When I came back with the children, I could hear a row going on in the office, and I recognised Susan's and Matron's voices. I quickly got the children into the playroom and shut the door. After a time I heard the bang of the office door and footsteps. I opened the playroom door a little and saw Susan running up the stairs. Then I heard her bedroom door banging. Matron came into the playroom and told the children that lunch would be a little late. One of the helpers was cooking it. She then asked me to come into her office.

'Did Susan have her RAF boyfriend here over Christmas?' she said to me.

'Yes,' I replied. It was no good lying, because the children could have told her that.

'Did he stay the night?' she asked.

This was an awkward question and I tried to get out of it the best way I could:

'He was here in the evening, and he turned up again in the morning, but I don't know whether he stayed the night. I did not ask him.'

'One of my neighbours has informed me that Susan's boyfriend stayed here for several days, including the nights. I have just given her notice. I run a respectable home and cannot permit this.'

I didn't reply. I felt sorry for Susan. She was a nice nurse, I liked her, and her boyfriend had been good to us in helping with the children to give them a better Christmas. Matron should not have left us alone with all the work and the responsibility.

'I am having the Irish couple coming next week. So in the meantime we will have to manage without Susan. I will ask one of the women helpers to come back in the evening for the bathing of the children. I am afraid you will not be able to have your day off this week, because, as you can see, you are needed.'

Susan packed her bags and left in the afternoon. She came to say goodbye to the children and to me.

'I think Matron would have overlooked the fact that my boyfriend was staying here for Christmas,' said Susan, 'but I told her off for the poor provision she had made for Christmas, and that the children's food rations were used for herself and her friends. She knows this is true, but didn't like me to say it. That's the real reason why I have to go. I told her, that if she doesn't give me a good reference, I will report her. She gave me a good reference, and my money until the end of the week. There are plenty of jobs for trained nurses, I am not worried.'

She smiled, shook hands with me, and added:

'Bob is a good chap. You would do well to stick to him. I have seen the picture of your Swiss boyfriend in your bedroom (she meant Martin). He looks much older than you and too sophisticated. Bob is fun to be with, and he loves children, always a good sign. - Take care, good luck. I might write to you, I don't know. I am staying with friends near Bovingdon for a few days.'

She hugged the children, took her suitcases, I opened the door, and she left. Matron did not come to see her off.

The following week, a young couple from Ireland arrived, Mary and Michael. Their English was different, but I got used to it. Both were hard working. I liked them and we got on well. A man to do small repair jobs was needed in the home, and it was good for the boys to see somebody with tools in his hands.

After the Christmas holiday, the children went back to school, and I found an English evening class in Apsley, which I attended twice a week. There I met two German ex prisoners-of-war who had stayed on and worked on a farm, the only work place for which they could receive a work permit. Both of them came from the eastern part of Germany, like myself, but had already spent over a year in a prisoner-of-war camp in England. Here they had the chance to start again, with the possibility of getting British nationality later on. They were very interested in my journey to the west, and what had happened to Germany at the end of the war and afterwards.

Our lessons lasted one and a half hours and afterwards they often took me all the way home to the "Chestnuts," so that they could talk to me.

Bob carried on being a regular visitor on Sundays to entertain the children, and spent the evening with me.

One day I was allowed to see where he worked. Bob and his father owned a plating factory, with a department for stove enamelling. They employed about 120 people, mostly women. The reason for this was the war. Most of the men were called up, and the women had to take their places. The factory had been evacuated from Southend-on-Sea, which was declared too dangerous for war work, and they had been able to find this place in Gt. Missenden, which they rented from a farmer. There was a large barn, pre-fab outhouses for the plating and wiring, and a long building for stove enamelling. The barrelling was done in the converted stables, and the offices were in a house which backed on to the High Street and belonged to the local bank. The canteen, with the kitchen, was a solidly-built extra building next to the offices. Because of the war the factory had grown in a haphazard way, with the old buildings being made use of, and wooden huts added. Bob and his father now hoped to buy the land and build a proper factory. Bob had only been in the Home Guard, as it was necessary for him to help his father in the factory during the war, which worked day and night. He used to run the night shift, and his father was in charge during the day.

It was obvious to everybody that Bob and I had started to grow fond of one another. I felt happy with him, secure, at ease, and his warmth and understanding was a comfort to me. He was tall, big and strong, but so very young and immature. Life had already given me a few knocks by now, and I took a long time before I could trust people. Bob had never been away from home. He worked hard, but had not known any hardship through the war, like being bombed out, or starved, because there was always enough food in his home. Everything was positive for him, life was good and easy, and there was nothing he could not cope with, so he said. The things I appreciated most about him, was that he was so undemanding. He wanted nothing from me except my company.

Petrol was still rationed, but Bob turned up every Sunday in his little van, either to show the children some films, or bring his accordion to play music to them. He even mended some of their toys. He was extremely practical and could mend anything. Gradually he became a member of the Chestnuts community. It wasn't a question:

'Is Bob coming on Sunday?' but rather: 'What time is Bob coming?'

Matron liked him, so did Mary and Michael, and we sometimes had an evening all together, just the four of us, without Matron.

It was February, and England was damp and cold and foggy. The home had no central heating, and the bedrooms were bitterly cold. We had iron stoves in the hall, in the playroom, and in the dining room, and a gas fire in the staff room, which was always warm. I often dreaded going to bed because of the cold room, where even the sheets felt damp and clammy. Mary and Michael had a small gas fire in their large bedroom. There was no gas connection in my room, and Matron said it was too expensive to have an electric fire. In any case, I only slept there, I could always write letters etc. in the staff room, which was heated.

Even Bob's parents didn't have central heating, only lovely fire places. They had electric blankets on the beds, so at least one could get warm at night. All this was something typically English. Bob said people had gradually started to put in central heating but everything was behind because of the war years.

The people in England were very friendly, kind, helpful, and outgoing, as long as I stressed that I was Swiss. There was still a lot of hatred of the Germans, who had bombed England and had brought such tremendous suffering to the country, from which they had not yet recovered. Even Bob's mother hated the Germans. Some of her relatives in London had been either bombed out, or had to be evacuated, and a number of them descended on her big house and garden during the war. I had to be careful what I said, so I never talked much about my time in Germany, although the greater part of my life had been spent there.

Bob's father was different. He was born in Smolensk, in Russia. His grandfather had emigrated as an engineer and worked on the Trans-Siberian railway. He discovered that there was a tremendous amount of wood there. Because it was so cheap, it was often wasted. He built a factory by the River Dnieper, making shuttles and bobbins for the weaving factories. He didn't waste any wood, because the scraps which were left over after the machining operations were used to fire the boilers to run the generators for the electricity for the factory. Even the water power of the river was harnessed to run the machines in the factory.

At the end of the First World War, and the outbreak of the Russian Revolution, the family fled north and returned through Lithuania, and part of East Prussia, to England. Bob's father was then sixteen years old. He still spoke Russian, and a little German, because his mother used to employ a German governess. I liked Bob's father. He was always kind to me; he understood what I had been through as a refugee, and he would say a few words in German to me, to make me feel welcome in his home.

My English improved rapidly, because I never spoke anything else. The children, and even the grown ups were helpful, and there were my evening classes. It was only a general course, with no examinations at the end, but I did my homework every week, and could see the results.

Bob suddenly talked about getting engaged and married. He didn't actually propose, or even ask it directly. We seemed to have drifted into it, or at least that's how I think it happened. This, too, was contrary to my imagination. My future husband should have knelt in front of me, and asked, and pleaded with me to marry him. Reality certainly was different, and I told him:

'We hardly know one another. You have never asked me, or proposed to me. And what about your girlfriend, Sybil?'

'I have known Sybil for quite a time, she lives locally. I have never asked her to marry me, and I have not seen her lately. I always wanted to marry you. I already knew in Switzerland, that you were the girl for me.'

This really surprised me, because during his stay in the Belvédère he had made little effort to get to know me, until the end of his holiday.

Bob continued as if he had read my thoughts: 'I didn't know you spoke English. I tried several times to come near you, when I changed the money for the game at the billiard table, but you never said anything except 'yes' or 'no.' After I said goodbye to you and was sitting in the train, I felt like jumping out again and running back to you. Everybody could see that I didn't like leaving Switzerland, but they didn't know why. When I got back home, I told my parents I had met, in Switzerland, the girl I would like to marry.'

'You already told them when you got back from your holiday? But you hardly knew me then. And what about me, I might not want to marry you.'

'Don't you?,' he said, quite shocked. 'But you will, I am sure you will. You said you liked me, and that you are fond of me. You cannot say 'no.' I will just keep on coming to see you, again and again, until you say 'yes.'

'Will you come and live with me in Switzerland?'

He looked at me for a while, then said seriously: 'You know I couldn't do that. Dad and I have got a factory here, that is our work. I couldn't let him down and leave it all to him. He needs me. I like my work, it is my living.'

He sounded so sincere, and I liked the way he was talking about his father.

'I don't know whether I want to live in England. All my family are now in Switzerland. I have no friends or relatives here, and in any case, it is too cold and wet, damp and foggy, particularly in the winter.'

'We have lovely summers in England, you wait and see, and you won't be cold when we have our own home. I promise you we will have central heating, even if I have to build it myself. You can go home to Switzerland every year. We can have a holiday there every summer.'

He didn't question whether it was possible or not, he never saw obstacles, there weren't any.

'I have got a boyfriend in Switzerland, I doubt whether he will be pleased.'

'That's the same with me, I have Sybil. But friends are friends, and there is really only one girl for me whom I want to marry, and that is you. Talking about friends and relatives. I have lots of them, hundreds, you will meet them, and you will like them, you see, you will be alright.'

I didn't say 'yes' and I didn't say 'no.' I said that I would have to think about everything. I wrote to my mother, and I wrote to Martin. My mother replied to say that she didn't like the thought of me living in England but, if that was what I wanted to do, I had her blessing. She wrote:

'Already for years you have made your own decisions, and lived your own life. I know I can trust your judgement. The important basis for a marriage is love, trust, and understanding. You say that he is warm-hearted, kind, decent, but rather young. Don't worry about that. Some men never grow up, and because of that are easier to live with.'

Martin sent me a telegram: Come home at once, love Martin.

Matron was concerned about the telegram, but I said it was alright, there was nothing to worry about. In the evening she asked me to come into the sitting room next to her office, and have a cup of tea with her. She did want to know about the telegram. So I told her what it contained.

'Look, my dear,' said Matron, 'you have no mother here, nobody who can advise you, or with whom you can talk. I am a mother, I have two daughters, one of them married. I do understand and feel for you. So, if you like, you can talk to me, and I will tell you what I think.'

She was very understanding and nice, and I appreciated her concern. I told her about Martin, and about Bob, and that my mother would have liked me to stay in Switzerland.

That Martin had sent me a telegram had upset me. He had said that if he thought he might lose me, he would come to England and fetch me back. I foolishly had thought he would do that, and now all he did was send me a command to come back. I most certainly would not go back, even if I didn't marry Bob. I would stay in England for the duration of my permit until next November.

Matron said she had not met Martin, so she could not give an opinion, but she, too, was worried about the age gap.

'Think what it would be like in thirty years time. He will start to be an old man, and you will still be a young woman. It is always better to be a young man's sweetheart, than an old man's darling.'

She pointed out all the good things about Bob. His kindness to the children, his devotion to me for turning up every Sunday, and meeting me during the week, his job, and his family.

'You are staying the night with his parents every week,' she said. 'It looks as if they have accepted you. One day Bob will take over his father's factory, so there is a future for you. Many young men home from the war have difficulty in finding a job, as they have not learnt anything, except being soldiers. Are you afraid of living away from Switzerland?'

'I know all this,' I replied. 'I am very fond of Bob, but I am not sure. I don't mind leaving Switzerland, I have not been all that happy there. People in Switzerland are spoilt, they do not understand us *Rückwanderer*, because they don't know what war is like. Here in England the people had the same or, at least, similar experiences to myself. I also feel I have more freedom here as a woman. But I am a little afraid of all the newness, the language, Bob's parents, relatives and friends, all of them which I have to face alone, without any backing from my own family.'

'I suppose it would be better to wait a little,' said Matron, 'but if Bob is pushing you into an engagement, don't forget, being engaged is not being married. It is a time to know one another better, to find out whether one is suited before making the final commitment!'

We had a good talk that evening, Matron and I. She was a shrewd, experienced, understanding woman, and I often thought about what she had said in later life.

We were going to be engaged, but not before Bob had proposed to me. I felt that he should do this before I gave my reply. He was quite serious when he asked me to be his wife. He even made a little speech, saying he loved me, and he would try and make me happy.

He promised again to take me home to Switzerland every year, and then added with a smile, that he would make sure that I had central heating in our house. I suddenly knew that I would be happy with Bob. He was so sincere, and I said 'yes.'

It was the end of February and still very cold. We arranged to have a day in London, as Bob wanted to buy me an engagement ring. I was to come, as usual, on a Tuesday evening to stay with his parents, and then on Wednesday morning we would catch a train from the local station to London. Bob was going to have a day off from work.

I had asked Bob several times whether he had told his parents that we were going to be engaged, because I did not want any opposition from that side. He assured me that they knew all about it. He had told them already when he came back from Switzerland last summer, and he had repeated it since. I was therefore a little surprised, when neither his mother, nor his father, said anything in the evening when I arrived, or the next day before we went to London.

Surely they knew why we were going to London, I thought.

Bob reassured me, and said they probably wanted to wait until we officially announced our engagement.

We decided to do some sightseeing in the morning first, before buying the ring.

Towards dinner time, Bob said: 'Would you like to spend a penny?'

I looked at him surprised Why ever should I want to spend a penny? 'No, thank you,' I said.

We stopped at a little café to have a snack lunch, and Bob said: 'Would you like to powder your nose?'

Again I looked at him surprised. 'Is it shiny?,' I asked, and took out my powder case and looked at the mirror, but everything looked alright.

Bob looked embarrassed, but I didn't know why. I could see that something was troubling him, or was there something wrong with me? We finished our lunch, and decided to look into some shop windows for engagement rings. Walking along the road, Bob took a deep breath, stopped, and then said:

'I have tried to ask you something, but you don't seem to understand, so I will just have to ask you directly. Do you want to go to the toilet?'

'Yes, please,' I said. 'I have wanted to go for ages, but I didn't know what it was called.'

He then explained his funny questions from before, and we both had a good laugh. To go to the toilet did cost a penny in those days, and Bob even gave me one in case I had no change.

Bob bought me a lovely ring, with three small beautifully sparkling diamonds. The salesman put it into a velvet-lined box, after giving it another clean, and Bob put it into his pocket. Before catching the train back from Marylebone station, we had a cup of real good coffee in a little restaurant, and that's where Bob put the ring on to my finger, and just said:

'I love you.'

We were both very happy, and sat close together in the train for the return journey. We arrived at Bob's parent's house about tea-time, intending to have something to eat quickly, and then go for our Olde Tyme Dancing evening, which Bob was still running in the factory canteen.

'We will tell Mum as soon as we get in,' said Bob happily.

We entered the house through the back door, which led into the kitchen where Bob's mother was already preparing the tea.

'So you are back,' she said. 'Your father seems to be late today,' she continued, addressing Bob.

Bob took my hand and said: 'Mum, you can congratulate us, we are engaged. Look at Helga's ring, which we bought today,' and with that he lifted my hand to show it to her.

Bob's mother stared shocked at us. 'Engaged! But you hardly know one another. You can't get engaged, you are much too young,' she said, looking at Bob.

She then looked at me:

'What will your parents say when they hear you have got engaged in a foreign country, and to somebody they have not even met!'

'I have told them, they know all about it,' I replied. I don't think Bob's mother heard me. She was terribly shocked and upset. I could see that

Bob had not expected this reaction because he, too, looked upset. I did not want to hear any more, so I said:

'I think I will go upstairs and get my bag.'

Whenever I came on Tuesday evening I used to bring a small bag with my night and washing things. This morning, as we were going to London, I had left the bag upstairs, as I knew we would return.

I ran upstairs, but came slowly down with my bag, as I could hear Bob and his mother talking in the kitchen. All my happiness had gone, and I had that lump in my stomach again.

Every time I am really happy I get a *Backpfeife* (slap in the face), I thought. I have had that many times in my life, to the extent that sometimes I was afraid of being too happy, hoping in that way to avoid the *Backpfeife*.

If Bob's mother was not going to agree to our engagement, I couldn't stay on in the house, or ever enter it again. Courageously, with my heart beating fast, I walked into the kitchen and told Bob to take me back to Hemel Hempstead. I did not wait for his reply, but ran out through the back door and made my way to his van. He followed me and put his arm around me. I was crying by then.

'Please don't cry,' he whispered. 'It will be alright, you'll see.'

The window opened, and Bob's mother called out: 'You ought to wait until your father comes home. Let's talk things over.'

'I have got to go to the Olde Tyme Dancing,' Bob called back. 'People will be waiting for me.'

'Then come back here afterwards,' she said.

'Let's get away,' I said, and got into the van.

We drove off, and pulled into a little lay-by. I had stopped crying by then. I took the ring off and handed it back to Bob saying:

'I think we had better call our engagement off; it hasn't lasted long. I could never marry you against your parents' wishes. I am not prepared to come and live in a foreign country, learn a new language, give up my family and newly found homeland, and get animosity in return. You, too, would never be happy with me, if your parents haven't accepted me. Your work is involved with your father, you have to meet him every day. What do you think our life would be like? I cannot understand the reaction of your mother. You said you had told her everything, but this cannot be true.'

Bob said that he, too, could not understand his mother's reaction.

'After the dance we will go back and confront my father,' said Bob. 'You will find that he is different. I have often talked to him about you, and he likes you. Mum will come round, she probably doesn't want me to leave home. I am twenty-three years old. Dad married when he was twenty-one, and Mum was eighteen. We are not children any more. I have every right to make my own decisions. I want you to keep the ring on, we are engaged, and we will get married.'

'I will come to the dance with you, because you need a partner,' I replied, 'but after that I want you to take me back to Hemel Hempstead. I am not coming back to your house.'

I did not enjoy the dance very much and was glad when it was finished. On the way back, we had to pass Bob's parents house. He turned into the drive and stopped outside the back door.

'You cannot force me to go inside,' I said. 'If you are not taking me back by car, I will have to walk to Chesham, and take the bus from there.'

I tried to get out of the van, but he stopped me by holding my arm.

'Listen,' Bob said, 'I will go indoors and ask my father to come and fetch you, to show you that he welcomes you. Promise me you will wait here in the van.'

'Alright,' I said. 'But you must promise me to take me to Chesham to the bus if he, too, has the same opinion as your mother.'

'Yes,' said Bob. 'I will even take you to Hemel Hempstead.'

He went indoors. After a while he returned alone.

'Dad and Mum want us to come in so that they can congratulate us. These are Dad's words. I think he has had a long talk with Mum, and it looks as if everything is alright. So do come inside. Mum has made a real effort to be nice to me again, and they are waiting for us, with glasses and Mum's home-made wine, to have a drink together.'

Bob took my hand and pulled me out of the van. We walked through the back door, then through the kitchen into the living room, where Bob's parents were sitting on a settee opposite the door. There were glasses on a small table and a decanter with the home-made wine. Bob's mother looked a little flushed, as if she had already had a drink or two. As soon as we entered the room Bob's father got up and came towards us smiling, and stretching out both hands:

'Congratulations,' he said and put his arms around me. 'I am very pleased with Bob's choice, and I would like to welcome you to our family. You must forgive Mum for her outburst. She was a little shocked, but she, too, would like to welcome you.'

With that he guided me towards the settee where Bob's mother was sitting. She got up and kissed me and said: 'Congratulations.'

She then embraced Bob and said: 'I hope you both will be very happy.'

Drinks were served. - I was asked to call Bob's parents Mum and Dad. - Conversation was made. - Bob pressed my hand and smiled, - but to me it didn't feel real, it was superficial.

Maybe I am too tired to take it all in, I thought. I had had a long and exciting day. The drink made me a little light-headed too, especially as I had had no supper. I sometimes didn't understand what was said, as my English was still not good enough to follow fast conversation. People often forgot that I wasn't English. The day was supposed to have been beautiful and happy, but it had lost its sparkle and I wanted it to end. So I just said:

'I think I will have to get back.'

They all stopped talking and looked at me. Bob's father seemed to understand how I felt. He did not offer me another glass of wine, and didn't stop me when I got up. Bob said he would take me back to Hemel Hempstead.

It was very cold outside, and I shivered when we left the house, or was it just nerves? Bob said on the drive back that he was very happy that both parents had accepted me. But had they really done that? I was grateful to know that I had an ally in his father.

Everybody was very happy for me in the "Chestnuts," and said that they had seen it coming. Mary and Michael, the helpers, and even the children were excited when they heard that I would marry Bob. Matron was the only one to whom I confided what had happened when we announced our engagement to Bob's mother, but she said it would blow over. They had accepted me now.

Bob came again the next Sunday with some Charlie Chaplin films. I did not go to stay the night with his parents the next week. I had a morning in Hemel Hempstead and met Bob in Chesham for the evening, so that we could go to his Olde Tyme Dance again. It was a fortnight before I met his parents again, and both were very nice to me.

Being now officially engaged, Bob wanted me to meet his relatives in Southend-on-Sea. Matron very reluctantly let me have an occasional Saturday off. This meant that Mary had to look after the children, which was quite a job, especially as there was no school and the children had to be occupied all day.

There appeared to be a great number of aunts and uncles and cousins, when we got to Southend, and we moved from one family to another. All I remember was that every time a door opened, there seemed to be a big or a small woman, and always the same sentence:

'So this is Helga,' and then arms opened, and I was kissed and hugged. I wasn't used to all this embracing, and I hated it.

'You will have to get used to it,' said Bob. 'In England we don't shake hands with relatives, we kiss one another.'

Everybody was straight away on familiar terms. I had to call them Auntie May, Uncle Jack, Auntie Rose, Uncle Fred, etc. and I was Helga to them. I doubt whether anybody knew my family name, I was never asked for it. I was accepted by all, but found it difficult to get used to the familiarity of these strangers. People are much more reserved on the continent, and address one another very formally as Mr, Miss, and Mrs for years.

The worst thing was when I was asked to call older people by their Christian names. Aunt and uncle was not too bad, but when I met Mrs Martin, the company secretary, who was also a great friend of the family, she said to me:

'I am Elsie, how nice to meet you.'

'Surely I cannot call Mrs Martin, Elsie. She is my mother's age,' I said to Bob.

Bob said that it made no difference, she was Elsie to me, and I had to call her that, otherwise she would be offended.

CHAPTER SIX

Preparations - The Wedding

The weather became warmer, Spring was coming, and blossoms and flowers were everywhere. England was suddenly very pretty. There were daffodils and tulips in the gardens, and the meadows were full of daisies, cowslips, and dandelions. It was fun now to go for a walk with the children. Bob's mother wanted to make dandelion wine, so I took the children to the meadows by the canal and gave them paper bags, and we all picked dandelions.

Pat, Bob's sister, was at college in London. I went to see her one day, and got a tour of an English college, something I had not seen before.

Bob and I talked about getting married, and about the wedding. I told Bob that it would have to be a very small affair.

'I would like to get married in Switzerland,' I said. 'The only trouble is that my parents really have no money. They cannot even afford to go out for a meal in a restaurant. We will have to get married quietly, and my mother will cook a special meal for us at home.'

'I don't think my parents will accept that,' said Bob. 'I am the first one in the family to get married, and all my relatives would like to come to the wedding.'

'How do you want to do that? My parents cannot even afford the money for a trip to England, and a stay in an hotel. Why don't we just get married without telling anybody, and then it is a fait accompli. - Still, before we get married, we will have to find a place to live. Maybe we could rent something near your factory.'

Bob promised to enquire, and to look around for accommodation, and then we would talk again about the wedding.

Things took a different turn to anything I had planned or wanted to do. Bob's parents had discussed it, and made the wedding plans for us. They decided that it should be a big affair, with all the family gathered together. The war was finished, and this could be the first big family party.

Bob's parents were not short of food, although everything was still rationed. They had eggs from their chickens, there was the pig which gave them bacon and fat and they had sugar from the bees. A little clever dealing on the Black Market soon filled the larder. They could also employ the kitchen staff from the factory, and could get other helpers. The catering for the wedding would be no problem. - The date was fixed for July 31st, because after that Bob could be spared for two weeks from the factory for his honeymoon.

We were offered a room in Bob's parents house to live for the start, until we could get a place of our own. Bob earned £8 per week, and was used to paying his mother £2 every week for his keep. After we were married, we would have to pay £4 per week, which would cover the rent for the room, and our food.

We were allowed to do what we liked with the room. Bob designed wardrobes and cupboards, and we had them built-in by the factory carpenter. We bought a large double bed, not two single ones with a combined headboard like on the continent. I was going to be very English.

Bob's mother and I went to London to buy blankets, sheets, and an eiderdown. Everything was in very short supply, and we walked from one store to the next, only to be told that they didn't have anything. Eventually we got fixed up with the bedding, but could not find an eiderdown. Still, luck was on our side. Just as we had decided to catch the train home, late in the afternoon, one of the salesgirls at a particular store took pity on me. After I had explained that I was getting married, she took us into the back, and showed us a beautiful eiderdown. It was filled with very light down, and the outside was stitched in an elaborate design. The only trouble was the price. I thought it was terribly expensive. I had no money, but Bob had some savings, and that's what we spent on getting our room ready. The eiderdown cost £30, which was a lot of money considering Bob's earnings. I didn't want to take it, but Bob's mother said:

'Of course you have to buy it. If you cannot afford it, Bob will have to pay for it.'

She assumed that I had paid for all the other items which we had bought, and now Bob would have to pay for the eiderdown. I just couldn't explain, I felt too embarrassed, and was too proud to admit my terrible poverty. She filled out a cheque (I had paid for everything before with the cash which Bob had given me), and she said that Bob would have to pay it back to her.

In the evening, Bob's mother laughingly informed Bob about the price of the eiderdown. I would have liked to tell him myself, in a quiet moment, and could have explained things a little. He did get cross, saying it was a lot to pay for a single item. He did not mention that he had also given me the money for the other things and I felt relieved.

Invitations to the wedding were posted, and we had to make a list of items which we would like as presents. This was another new thing for me. I was taught that one did not ask for presents, and one most certainly did not mention what one wanted. But I could see the point. With such a large circle of relatives and friends, one could receive the same present three or four times. So we made a list with large and small items, thinking ahead to our future home. I would not have bought blankets and sheets for our double bed, had I known that these items could be added to the wedding list. So now when they arrived, I had spare ones!

All the family and friends were most generous with their gifts. I felt more and more embarrassed, especially after I was told that all presents had to be displayed on the wedding day, for everybody to see. My family could not afford presents.

I was going to get married in white, and as England still had coupons for clothes and material, I had suggested to my two sisters that they buy me my wedding veil in Switzerland as a wedding present, which they did. Bob's parents had some friends, Mary and Sidney, who had sold their clothes business, as they were emigrating to the Bahamas. They gave me some lovely white georgette material for my wedding dress. That saved coupons which I did not have as a foreigner, and it also saved me money.

I was very worried about the displaying of the presents. This was something I really didn't like. Everybody could criticise the choice, and the amount spent on the gifts. I was told by Bob's parents that this was always done in England, and I could not avoid it. They gave us a cheque which we used, when we eventually moved into our own home to buy a refrigerator. Another aunt from the Bahamas, who did not know what to give us, sent us a cheque. I bought my first electric sewing machine with it, and even learnt to sew.

It was impossible for my family to come to the wedding. They just could not afford it. The expense was not only for the train fare, but they would also have had to stay in an hotel. Bob would have liked to help, but his little savings went on things we needed for our room, and on our honeymoon trip. I had saved a little from my £2 per week earnings, and decided to pay my mother her train journey to England. I wanted at least one person from my family to come to my wedding. Bob's mother invited her to stay with them. She said that the two "mums" could be together. She was not at all worried that my mother spoke no English, and she spoke no German or Swiss.

My mother wrote and thanked me for my generosity (her words, not mine), and said that the thought of me getting married in a foreign country, without her being there, had already given her sleepless nights. She was only sorry that my father couldn't attend the occasion. She had no wedding present for me, but could part with some bath and hand towels which she would bring.

I told everybody that my father could not leave his business, as he had only just started it. My eldest sister could not leave her little girl, and my youngest sister, working in the hospital, could not get any time off. My brother was on the verge of taking some important examinations, and could also not attend our wedding. Everybody was very sorry, but did not press me to try and persuade my people to come. My mother would be there, and that was a consolation. In any case, we were going to Switzerland for our honeymoon.

Somehow, I felt that it wasn't my wedding. Invitations had gone out to over 100 relatives and friends of Bob's family, and only my mother would come from my side. In the end Matron Davies, and Mary and Michael from the children's home, were invited too. The final count was 120 people who had accepted the invitation, and would come to our wedding.

A distant relative of my mother-in-law's came to stay with her, to make all the dresses and wedding outfits. It was decided to have a real grand wedding, with grey top hats and tail suits, and the ladies in long dresses. I wrote and told my mother, who bought some material, borrowed a sewing machine, and made herself a long dress. By the time the dressmaker arrived, there was a change of plan. The dresses for the women were not going to be long, only Pat's, my sister-in-law's, who was going to be my bridesmaid. I quickly wrote to my mother about the new arrangements, but by then she had nearly made the dress and could not alter it, or afford a new lot of material for another one. The next thing I discovered was that all the ladies had to wear hats for the wedding. This was again something unheard of in Switzerland. I informed my mother, and she wrote back and told me she would have a long dress and a hat!

We had decided that I would leave my job in the children's home two weeks before the wedding. Unfortunately I got ill, and left earlier. It was at the beginning of July. I had my day off and stayed the night with Bob's parents. In the morning I discovered a lump on my throat. It was quite a big one, and everybody was concerned. The local doctor was called and diagnosed mumps. I looked it up in my dictionary, it was *Ziegenpeter*, which I had already had as a child. One usually only gets this once in a lifetime, so I knew the diagnosis was wrong. Still, it was felt that I had better not return to the home in case I infected some of the children. I phoned Matron and told her, and she suggested that Mary could pack my things and Bob could collect them.

The built-in wardrobes and cupboards were finished in our bedroom. When my luggage arrived, I sorted it out, and packed it away into the new units. I had a little bag with some First Aid equipment, and whilst looking through it, I found my little phial, with the cyanide which I had worn as a refugee. I had forgotten all about it, but seeing it and holding it in my hand again, brought back the memory. I started to feel cold again, and I trembled.

I must not think of it, I thought. I will never think of it again!

But I couldn't forget and started to cry. I couldn't understand why I cried. Bob found me, and wanted to know what had happened. I couldn't tell him, I didn't want to talk about it, but I had to explain about the phial. There was no need to keep it any more, so I said:

'You can have this, you can get rid of it in your factory.'

'What is it?,' he asked.

'It is cyanide,' I replied.

Bob looked shocked at me; he did not believe what I had said.

'Where did you get it from? It can't be true, surely you know cyanide is fatal. We use it in the factory in the plating shops, but we are all very conscious of its danger, and I keep an antidote in the laboratory.'

He realised that I was upset about something. He had never seen me so disturbed and persevered with his questions. In the end, I told him how my mother had got it, and that I had worn it on my flight from Königsberg. I could not tell him what that time had been like.

'I just cannot talk about that time,' I said. 'I always feel ill and cold, and I like to put it into the back of my mind. I just found the phial again, and the horror of that period came back. Please don't ask me to talk about it, or tell anybody about the phial.'

'You are very naughty to have this,' said Bob and hugged me. 'I will get rid of it. I promise not to mention it to anybody. I hope that one day you will be able to tell me all about that time.'

I did not think that I could ever talk about it, but I didn't say so. I was glad he took the cyanide; it had served its purpose. If I kept it, it would only carry on being a reminder of the time that I so desperately wanted to forget.

The swelling for mumps is usually on the sides of the neck. Mine was in the front. It was obvious that it was a swelling of the thyroid. Bob's parents suggested that I went and saw a Mr Foster, a well known homeopath, who had helped the family before. Bob took me to London, and Mr Foster said I had trouble with my thyroid glands. To cure, or reduce the swelling, I had to chop up Spanish onions, put them into a muslin cloth, and tie this around my neck, covered by a scarf. I had to do this every night.

The live-in dressmaker had arrived by now, and I had to sleep with Pat, Bob's sister. Every evening I chopped up my onions, tied them around my neck, and went to bed with my eyes streaming. Pat often went to sleep before me, so that she was asleep by the time I arrived with my smelly onions. I even smelled of them during the day, but it did the trick. The swelling went down, and I didn't have to have a wedding dress with a stand-up collar. I was always grateful to Pat for putting up with the inconvenience of the smelly onions.

My wedding dress had long sleeves, a small square neck, and a beautiful train. Bob gave me a double row of pearls as a wedding gift, which looked just right on my neck, especially as it was now back to its normal shape. For a head-dress I wanted real flowers. I didn't like the false orange blossoms favoured by most English brides. In Switzerland, brides usually have real flowers in their hair. I ordered white carnations.

I thought I would just about manage with my money by the time I had paid for the making of my wedding dress, my head-dress, and my white sandals. But then my mother-in-law informed me that I needed a going-away suit, and a hat to go with it. This time I did not have the courage to ask Bob for more money. I felt absolutely awful, and didn't know what to do. I couldn't even talk to anybody about it, as I had no friends, and my mother was a long way away.

I had left the children's home, but Matron still owed me a week's money, as I had to leave so suddenly. I gave her a ring when nobody was there to overhear me, and asked her for this money. I explained my predicament, and said I needed the money badly. Matron told me that she would let me have my wages plus two weeks holiday money, and half my train fare from Switzerland. She said that if I had stayed a year, she would have paid the whole fare, but having left early, I was only entitled to half. I was most grateful, especially as she had never mentioned this before.

My mother-in-law and I went to Aylesbury market, and I bought some thin red wool material for a suit. I knew I had a little white blouse to go with it. The dressmaker made me the suit. It was very smart, and extremely useful for years to come. For the hats we had to go to London, all three of us, Pat, Mum and I. The hats were specially made for us in a shop called Penny's, recommended by Auntie Loulie, my father-in-law's sister. We chose the design, and talked about the hats, ordered them, and then made a date for the collection of them.

Auntie Loulie and Uncle Ian were very important at our wedding. As I had no father attending the ceremony, I needed a substitute. This was again something typically English, and very new to me. In Switzerland, bride and groom plus witnesses, go to the registry office in the morning, and to the church in the afternoon, each time going together. In England, I was told, the bridegroom must not see his future wife on the day of the wedding before the ceremony in the church. He goes to church with his best man and waits for the bride in the front pew. The bride arrives with her father, who guides her up the aisle towards the altar and the bridegroom, who will wait at the altar steps. Uncle Ian was going to be my father for the day, and "give me away," as the saying goes, to the bridegroom. Auntie Loulie spoke very good German, and was going to look after my mother. Bob's old school friend, Ro, was going to be his best man at the wedding.

My mother-in-law decided that I ought to make myself my wedding night dress. She had made hers, and she said most brides in England do this, stitching it by hand. I couldn't sew, but I wanted to be co-operative. To please her I agreed. She said the night-dress should be made from pure silk material. She had read in the paper, that a firm in London was selling silk parachutes left over from the war, and one could use the material for dressmaking.

I went to see Pat at college in London and had a day with her. She knew where I could buy the parachute. I bought two, one for my mother-in-law, and one for myself. The material was a pale yellow silk, and we even had lots and lots of nylon cord, which came in useful for tying up plants in Bob's parents garden. My mother-in-law had a pattern, and we cut the night-dress out. We had to have seams where there shouldn't have been seams, because the material, by the time the parachute was unpicked, was shaped like large triangles. My mother-in-law showed me how to sew the seams by hand, and then left me to it. She enquired occasionally how I was getting on. I spent a number of frustrated hours on it, but never liked it. I got as far as the bottom hem and tried the night-dress on. Apart from the visible uneven hand stitching, there were the lines where the material had been joined together. The low, round neckline was much too big. The night-dress looked like a sack, and even if I added some lace this would not alter the shape. It was much too big for me, and I wondered whether it was the wrong pattern from the start. Maybe it was my mother-in-law's size, which was bigger than mine. I never finished it. I packed it away. When my mother-in-law enquired how I was getting on with the night-dress, I told her that I only had to do the hem. Just before the wedding I said it was finished. By then she was much too busy to ask me to produce it, so that she could have a look at it. - I wrote to my mother and asked her to buy me a night-dress, giving her the money from my little savings account, which I still had in Switzerland.

I found the parachute night-dress years later, finished it off, and put it on one evening. Bob and I had a good laugh. I passed it on to somebody who did amateur operatics, and it was used for one of the daughters in the "Pirates of Penzance."

My mother-in-law was an excellent organiser, and a good cook. She made the three-tier wedding cake, but had it iced and decorated professionally. Ballinger village hall was hired for the wedding reception, and preparations were made for a three-course hot meal in the middle of the day. Weather permitting, the afternoon would be spent in Bob's parents' garden, where tea and cakes could be served. The factory kitchen staff were responsible for the cooking and preparation of the food. For the afternoon, tea cups and saucers, the tea urn, and even chairs and tables were transported from the factory to the garden. A lot of organising had to be done, but I was not involved in it or asked.

Bob and I had to go to London to collect the hats, and to buy the wedding ring. Gold in those days was in short supply, and to get a twenty-two carat gold ring, one had to buy a second-hand one. Bob borrowed his father's car, a large black Austin 12 saloon, because it looked like rain in the morning, and his open sports car would have been a bit cold and wet.

When we got to Penny's, the hats were not quite ready, and we had to wait. It took longer than anticipated, and in the end I had to pay more for the hats than the original price quoted. I went to see Bob, who had waited in the car. He was cross about the wasted time, but made out a cheque for the amount needed.

When we eventually were ready to drive off, Bob was fuming. Everything was wrong. We were late, and now he even had to reverse, because somebody had parked close to his car in front. Trying to control his temper, he got hold of the big black knob of the gear lever between his index and middle finger and pulled really hard to change into reverse. He probably used more force than usual, or maybe the gear lever was already cracked, because the knob and the greater part of the lever broke off, and Bob's arm jerked up with the black round knob hitting his left eye.

First Aid was needed! I ran back into the shop to wet my handkerchief to bathe Bob's eye, but even so it started to swell. After that Bob had to think what to do about the gear-lever. It had broken off quite low down, leaving only 2" to 3" of the rod sticking up. He discovered that the tubular jack handle went over the top of the piece of gear-lever left, but would not remain on it, and had to be held. Bob couldn't very well drive with one hand on the steering wheel, and hold the jack handle wedged over the stub of the gear-lever, with the other hand.

'You will have to change gear,' he said to me.

'I have never driven a car in my life! I have no idea what I am supposed to do and when,' I replied quite shocked.

He soon taught me what to do. When he said: 'Ready!,' I had to push the jack handle over the gear-lever stub. He would press the clutch, I had to guide the stub into the middle which was neutral. Bob would press the accelerator, and then I had to push the handle into the gear which he named. We practised first, driving around near Penny's shop, before venturing into the London traffic. People stared at us, thinking what a bad driver Bob was, as there was quite a bit of gear crunching noises going on from time to time.

Gradually I improved, and found it was better to leave the jack handle over the gear-lever stub all the time, as there was a lot of gear changing to be done. There were traffic lights, slow and fast traffic, corners, and stoppages.

We parked the car and went to find a jeweller's shop. In those days one could still park in side streets in London. There were not so many cars on the roads because petrol was still rationed, and there was also a waiting list for the buying of new cars.

Bob knew exactly what ring he wanted for me, when at last we entered a shop. It had to be twenty-two carat gold, and it was no good the salesman showing us anything else. We didn't have much choice in the second hand market. The salesman made a rather funny face when he looked at me, and then at Bob. He moved over to another assistant whilst we discussed the rings, and the two were whispering, smiling a little, and glancing over to us. I felt a little uncomfortable, because I could see they were talking about us.

There is something wrong with us, in their opinion, I thought.

I looked at Bob, who was smiling at me reassuringly, and I noticed his swollen eye, as if somebody had hit him.

That's it! I thought. They think I have forced him to buy me a ring, so that we can get married. We have had a fight.

I whispered my discovery to Bob, and we both had a quiet little laugh.

We found a ring we both liked, and then made our way home.

Again I had to manipulate the jack handle over the gear-lever stub, but once we came out of London and on to the open road, I was able to lay down the handle for longer periods.

The swelling in Bob's eye went down, but it changed into black, blue and green. He had to put up with a lot of teasing in the factory about his black eye and being dragged to the altar. On our wedding day, the eye had recovered.

It had been arranged that my mother would arrive two or three days before the wedding, and stay on for another few days after we had left for our honeymoon. Bob wanted something special for our honeymoon, not a train journey. He booked a return flight from Northolt airport. Air travel was only just starting, and only a small airport was allocated for civil aviation. The flight, in a Vickers Viking, to Zürich, took two and a half hours in those days. To make an excuse why my mother didn't come by plane - I couldn't possibly have paid for her air fare - I said she was afraid of flying, she preferred the train.

I was looking forward to being with my mother before the wedding. There was so much to talk about, to tell, to ask, and to confide. After the wedding, Auntie Loulie was going to show my mother something of London, and Bob's parents the local district, so that she knew where I would be living in the future.

We had agreed to spend our honeymoon in my parents' flat, where my mother had got the double bedroom ready for us. She wrote to say that it looked very elegant, with the beautiful furniture we had bought from the Hotel Du Lac. By staying in the Bürgenstrasse we saved some money, which we could spend on day trips.

My mother spoke no English, so we promised to pick her up by car from Victoria station. When her train arrived it was packed with hundreds of people, and we could not find her. We waited until everybody had left the platform, hoping she would just stand there looking for us, but she was not there. We enquired about other trains, and were told that there were two more boat trains, so we waited for them.

By now, I was very worried. I imagined all sorts of things - seasickness, or a recurrence of her terrible migraine, or maybe she took a wrong train when coming off the boat. I knew she must have left, because if she hadn't she would have let us know. There was only one more train to come we were told, after she hadn't arrived on the other boat trains, and that was the milk train at four o'clock in the morning but I doubted whether she would be on that.

Bob phoned his parents to find out whether they had heard anything in the meantime. They, too, were surprised about what had happened, and advised us to come back.

I was very upset, and didn't talk very much on the return trip. I kept on thinking:

Every time I am happy, I get a *Backpfeife*.

I felt that I just could not face the wedding with over 100 strangers without a single relative on my side. By the time we reached Bob's parents' house, I was nearly in tears. Bob hugged me, tried to reassure me, said there was bound to be some news with his parents, and maybe she would arrive in the morning. He, too, was disappointed, because he had looked forward to meeting his mother-in-law.

As usual we entered the house through the back entrance, walked through the kitchen, and into the living room. Opposite on the settee, sat three smiling people in absolute silence: Bob's mother, his father and my mother!

I thought I was dreaming. This just couldn't be true. How could my mother have come all the way from London to here, without speaking one word of English, apart from not even having any money? But it was true, because she stood up and walked towards me, and I moved towards her. We embraced, and we both cried, and we both stumbled over words and questions:

'How, - when, - what happened?' etc.

My mother, having met Bob's parents, had now to be introduced to Bob, her future son-in-law. I had taught Bob a few German phrases, and he did remember them. My mother laughed and sounded happy. She had not been able to tell Bob's parents about what happened when she got off the train, so now I got the story in German, and had to translate it.

When the train arrived at Victoria station my mother got out. She was pushed along the platform with the crowd of people. She only had one suitcase, which she had kept with her all the time. She had gone through customs at Dover, so now she was able to move along unhindered. Before she realised what had happened, she was outside the station. She walked back, but didn't remember on which platform she had arrived. Not trusting people, particularly in a foreign country, she looked for somebody in a uniform. She thought people in uniform would be honest. She found a railway inspector, at least that's what he must have been by her description, and showed him the wedding invitation which we had sent her. Gt. Missenden, the place where the ceremony would be, was mentioned on it and also Bob's parents address. The inspector spoke no German, but kept on pointing to Gt. Missenden on the invitation, and said something about a bus.

A young girl passing and seeing the struggle for words between my mother and the inspector, stopped, and tried to help, as she spoke a little German. It was explained to my mother that she had to catch a bus to Marylebone station, and from there a train to Gt. Missenden. My mother had no English money, only a few Swiss Francs. There was no bank or Change place open any more. The girl said she would give my mother some coins, enough for the bus fare. My mother gave her a bar of chocolate in return. The inspector gave my mother a note to show to the bus driver, so that he would let her off at Marylebone station, and also wrote down Gt. Missenden, to where she had to catch a train. She said it was quite frightening to be on a double-decker bus. She didn't dare to go upstairs.

Everybody was very kind and helped her off the bus at the station. There she found another inspector, or railway guard, showed her note about Gt. Missenden, the wedding invitation, and her ticket from Luzern to London, thinking it included the next railway journey. The inspector carried her suitcase, and guided her to the Aylesbury train, which stopped in Gt. Missenden, and handed her over to the guard on duty. She was most grateful to him for carrying her case, and thought she ought to tip him. She looked at the few coins which she still had left after paying her bus fare. She had no idea of the value of them, so she decided to give him the largest coin, not realising that this was the lowest denomination - 1d (one penny). She said the inspector laughed, so it must have been alright. I did not then inform my mother of her mistake. I told her about it another time.

The guard on the Aylesbury train shook his head when my mother showed her ticket, and she gradually realised that he meant that she had no ticket for the Aylesbury train. She showed her Swiss Francs, and the few English coins she had, but he still shook his head. The guard must have realised that my mother would not even get a night accommodation anywhere, unless he took her to Gt. Missenden, so he put her into the guard's van with her suitcase. The train started off, and my mother travelled with the guard in his van, avoiding in this way any check up by the ticket collector. In those days, the railway still employed several people for each train.

At Gt. Missenden, the guard handed my mother and her suitcase over to the station master, smiled at her, tapped her on her shoulder, said something my mother didn't understand, blew the whistle, and the train left for Aylesbury. My mother produced the wedding invitation, the station master smiled, took her suitcase, beckoned her to follow him, and went to his office. There he made a phone call and gave her a chair to sit down.

My mother knew she was in Gt. Missenden, the notice on the station said so, and she also realised that she soon would be at the end of her journey. She thought the phone call was to notify Bob and I. She never realised that we would still be in London. So when my father-in-law arrived, she was a little frightened and upset that after all the worry she had had, and the great difficulties which she had overcome, she still had not reached me. My father-in-law, with his poor German, tried to explain things, and she did understand.

She had only arrived half an hour before us, and would I believe it, they had given her a cup of tea as a welcoming drink. Tea, something we only drink when we are ill! She could have done with a cup of coffee after all the excitement she had had.

My mother and I had been allocated a room with a double bed, and it was in the early morning hours that we eventually went to sleep, having whispered all our news to one another.

Bob heard a little more from the Gt. Missenden station master, whom he knew, about my mother's trip. The guard that my mother met on the Gt. Missenden train knew the name of Bob's parents and the factory in Gt. Missenden, and had heard that the son was getting married to a Swiss girl. He lived near Gt. Missenden, and most of the people there knew Bob's family. Bob had to pay the train fare from Marylebone station to Gt. Missenden for my mother, and once that was cleared up nobody could get into trouble by saying my mother had had a free train trip from London. My mother was most impressed with the kindness and helpfulness of the English people, and from that moment on loved England, and felt she could trust this country to make her daughter happy.

Bob's friend, Ro, who was to be his best man at the wedding, was supposed to arrive on the Friday afternoon before the wedding, so that he could be briefed for his duties the following day. The two friends had booked a room in a small hotel, The Little Abbey, to stay the night, because Bob, being the bridegroom, was not supposed to see me on the wedding morning. It came to supper time and Ro had still not arrived. I didn't think much of Bob's school friend, who couldn't even turn up on time. Eventually he arrived at eleven o'clock at night in his little car, a Morgan, completely black, as his car had broken down on the journey to us. He was only allowed to say 'hello' to everybody, and was then pushed out with Bob, so that they would get to the hotel before it closed.

Bob phoned the next morning - not seeing the bride, didn't mean it wasn't allowed to talk to her. He wanted to make quite sure that I hadn't changed my mind, and would turn up on time at the Gt. Missenden church.

My mother helped me to dress. We had practised before how to fasten the long veil on to my flowers on my head. Again, to be really English, I had decided to have the front of the veil over my face, and then have it folded back in the church after the marriage vows.

Everything was organised and went like clockwork. The flowers arrived with my flower head-dress and whilst my mother and I were getting ready upstairs, we heard people coming and going downstairs, and cars rolling in and out.

Auntie Loulie came to fetch my mother, as she was looking after her. Pat, my bridesmaid, and Uncle Ian, my substitute father, helped me into the Rolls Royce with my long dress and veil. Pat went off in the car with her parents, promising to be outside the church to help me out of the car.

Uncle Ian, very tall and erect, with his stick with a round ebony top (he had a bad leg, an injury from the war), looked extremely smart. (He became Sir Ian Campbell later). He knew what to do. He put his white gloves into his grey top hat, and rested it on his knee. With his free hand he took mine, pressed it, and said gently:

'We will wait a few minutes to let the others get ahead. You look very beautiful, and I can assure you that everything will go off alright.'

Then, after a little while, he added: 'Would you like me to make some conversation, or do you want me to be quiet?'

'I don't mind, as long as I don't have to reply.'

He smiled in agreement and pressed my hand again. Then he told the driver to start off slowly, and take the trip gently.

The white ribbons on the front of the car were fluttering in the wind, and the sun was shining. It was a beautiful day. I stared at the back of the driver. He had had a car accident a day or two before, and wore a thick white collar around his neck. I felt sorry for him.

People along the road waved, everybody loves a wedding. We got to the church, and Pat was there to help. Richard, Bob's cousin, took a film of the wedding, and there was also a photographer. The church was packed with people, they even stood outside, because the whole factory and the village had turned up. Everybody knew Bob and his parents.

Uncle Ian guided me up the aisle. I had a glance at my mother, in the front row with Auntie Loulie. I didn't recognise anybody else. And then there was Bob next to me, big, tall and reassuring. Mr Dunford, the vicar, guided us through the wedding ceremony. I had learnt my marriage vows before, but even so I made a mistake. I was supposed to say:

'. . . and thereto I give thee my troth,' but I said:

'. . . and thereto I give thee my throat.'

I doubt whether many people heard it, but Bob did. He never forgot it, teasing me sometimes over this mistake.

We signed the wedding register in the vestry, and gave the marriage certificate to Arthur Atkins, a trusted employee from the factory, who had to catch the next train to London to go to the passport office. Special arrangements had been made for this to be kept open until three o' clock, so that I could get a British Passport, as we were flying to Switzerland the next day, a Sunday. Arthur Atkins had to return to the wedding reception with my passport before we could leave for our honeymoon.

The reason for all this was because I had to change my nationality when I married. If this hadn't been the case, the vicar could have held my new passport until after the marriage. (Five years later, I got my Swiss nationality back, after a new law was passed in my home country.)

Outside the church there were plenty of photographs taken, and of course the wedding film. Rose petals and confetti were thrown over us, and the church bells were ringing for the first time since the beginning of the war.

We made our way to Ballinger Hall for the big reception. The meal, so everybody said, was excellent. I didn't eat much. I looked at my mother, from whom I had parted by taking the step to live in England, and I looked at all the strange faces in the hall, and I felt suddenly frightened and unsure.

I looked at Bob, and wondered whether his love for me was strong enough to help me feel at home one day amongst all these people and his country.

Speeches were made, bride and bridegroom were toasted, and so was the bridesmaid. My father had written a little speech in German, which Auntie Loulie translated, and Uncle Ian incorporated it into his speech. I felt happier when I heard my father's message read out loud. I was sorry he was not there, he would have been very happy and proud of me.

The weather was perfect. After the meal the whole wedding party moved off in their cars to Bob's parents' large house and garden, where we had tea and cakes, and walked about on the lawn and amongst the flower beds.

My mother, looking very elegant in her long dress and hat, was not lonely. She had Auntie Loulie, who spoke German, and cousin Nina, who had lived in Germany. They made sure that she mingled amongst the relatives, and translated for her, when needed.

My mother understood how I felt. She said:

'We will have a second celebration with our family when I come back to Switzerland. Your mother-in-law said I can take the top tier of the cake back with me, and we will use that for you and Bob to cut the cake again - a second small wedding party.'

Arthur Atkins arrived with the passport, and I went and changed into my going-away outfit. Everybody lined up the drive to see us off, throwing confetti, laughing and shouting when we came out of the house. Somebody had put our suitcases into the car. We had difficulty in getting into the car, because everybody wanted to throw confetti, or shake hands, or kiss us. Eventually the car drove off, and there was a terrible noise, as if the exhaust had dropped off and was dragging on the road. People were shouting, waving, and laughing. I turned round, and saw rows of tins tied to the back of the car, and in the centre on a long rope, an enamelled "po" bouncing along the road.

'Oh no,' I called out. I had never seen anything like it. Again something typically English, I was told by Bob.

The driver, knowing all about the English customs, was prepared. He drove us to a quiet spot in the wood, and made us get out of the car. He then produced a dustpan and brush and, whilst Bob and I cleaned ourselves up, he brushed the car out. After that we drove along quite respectably to Chalfont St. Giles, where we had booked a room at a small hotel, "Merlin's Cave," in the centre of the village. It was Bank Holiday weekend, the first Monday in August being a holiday then, and we had the greatest difficulty in finding this accommodation for one night, halfway between Gt. Missenden and Northolt airport. Our plane went early on Sunday morning.

Outside the Church

Whilst I was unpacking the night things, I discovered that somebody had stuffed confetti into our suitcases. I took everything out and cleaned it up. There was still a lot of confetti left in the cases and I decided to empty it out of the window.

I hadn't realised that our bedroom was over the front entrance. I shook the suitcase, the confetti fell out, and when I looked down (we were on the 1st floor), I saw a crowd of people who had just alighted from a coach, laughing, smiling, some of them waving, and calling out something. I quickly dived back, telling Bob what had happened.

'Where are they?,' he asked, and looked out. There were more calls, and laughing. The people from the coach entered the hotel for a dinner party, and I was too embarrassed to go down into the dining room for a meal, so we just went into the bar for a drink. In any case, neither of us was hungry.

The owner of the hotel was surprised when he heard we were only staying one night. Being Bank Holiday Weekend, he expected people to stay until Monday. He said we could not have an early breakfast, but he would leave the key in the door, so that we could let ourselves out in the morning. We settled our bill in the evening.

Archie, the owner of the car hire firm whom Bob knew, came to pick us up in his car, early in the morning, and took us to the airport.

We flew to Zürich, and continued our journey from there by train to Luzern. When we got out at the station, we were confronted by a Swiss band playing: "God Save the King." Bob just put the cases down and stared at them.

'I have specially ordered this for you,' I said and laughed.

Bob was really flabbergasted and kept on looking at the band and then at me. Quite a crowd of people surrounded the band and nobody was really taking any notice of us. Bob soon realised that it was not true what I had said and wanted to know the reason for this welcome.

We arrived in Luzern on August 1st which is Swiss National Day, and the English and Swiss National Anthem had the same tune. (Switzerland has a new Anthem now, but the old people do not like it.) The band was travelling through the town and had just stopped at the station. This unexpected welcome stayed in our memory.

My father liked Bob, although the two couldn't converse much. Christel, Astra and Hans soon stumbled along with their school English and Bob felt at ease with my family which made me happy. The bedroom - five star hotel Du Lac - looked beautiful. There were even flowers on the dressing table and space in the wardrobe for our few clothes.

I had never had the chance to see much of Switzerland before I left. Bob now took me on a number of trips which he had been on before, and I was surprised how much he knew about my homeland.

One day we went shopping because I wanted to buy him a wedding present. I took my last bit of money out of the bank, which I had put by for an emergency, and I bought him an unusual desk clock. It was a rose-gold plated four-faced clock on a small stand. The four faces were: clock with calendar, a thermometer, a barometer, a hygrometer and on the top a compass. The clock section swivelled out for winding and setting the time and date. The turret could be turned to view each face. The clock was not very big, approximately 10cm high and the turret 6cm square. Bob was thrilled with it. He loved clocks and watches and would stop in front of every shop window where there were some on show.

We collected my mother from the station and she told us about the good time she had had in England. Her return trip had been very pleasant, but she was upset about the Swiss customs officials. She had brought the top tier of the wedding cake back, so that we could have a little celebration with the rest of the family. She carried it in a box and had to open it at the border. She was charged customs duty on it. Border crossings in those days were still very strict. Switzerland exports sweets, chocolates and cakes. Anything brought into the country that is also exported warrants a duty.

We had our little celebration and Bob and I cut the cake again. I was happier then, surrounded by my own family, speaking my own language, than at the big wedding in England, where I never really could relax.

One day Bob was ill. He was sick all night and in the morning I went to the chemist to get him some medicine. When I returned I had the biggest shock. Bob was sitting up in bed with a tray in front of him. On it lay all the pieces of the beautiful desk clock.

'Oh Bob, what have you done!'

In Luzern

'I wanted to see how the clock works. In any case, it doesn't keep good time, it needs adjusting.'

'But we could take it back for that. It has a guarantee of one year, and we have only just bought it.'

At the same time I thought of my brother who always took things to pieces, and when he put them together again there were usually some screws left. His repairs only lasted a short time.

'Don't worry, I have been repairing watches and clocks since I was twelve years old.'

Bob surprised me again and again with the many gifts he had. Not only was he very musical with a lovely voice, played the accordion, the piano and the organ all by ear, but now he turned out to be a watchmaker too. He was right. The clock was put together, the time adjusted, there were no screws left and the repair job lasted.

After two weeks we flew back to England. My mother hugged and kissed me and cried:

'Be happy, my child,' she whispered. 'You have a good husband. I have the feeling we will never see one another again.'

'Of course you will,' I said. 'You will have to come and stay with us when we have our own home.'

The return flight was a little bumpy, but I had taken some tablets, so I was not sick. In England, the same thing happened to me as to my mother, at the customs.

They found Bob's desk clock in my handbag. We explained it was a wedding present, but it was no good, we had to pay duty on it. Bob and I had no money. My father-in-law had come to fetch us and we thought he might lend us the money. Bob was allowed to go and look for him, whilst I had to stay behind. He came back with his father. Dad could see how upset I was and put his arm over my shoulder, giving me a reassuring hug. He paid the duty by cheque and we were allowed to leave. It was not a very nice end to our honeymoon.

When eventually we had saved up the money to pay Dad back, he wouldn't take it, saying that he had forgotten all about it.

PART THREE

A NEW CHALLENGE

CHAPTER ONE

First Child - My Mother

My mother-in-law and I soon established a routine which worked out quite well. We were responsible for meals for the whole family on alternate days. On Saturday Bob and I went out if he wasn't working and on Sundays Mum and I did the meals together. Bob and his father had a cooked lunch in the canteen at the factory, so they only wanted a small cold meal in the evening, and we two women didn't have an elaborately cooked lunch. There was the gardener and Florrie, the domestic help, who had to have a cup of tea and a piece of toast at eleven o'clock and a cup of tea and a piece of cake for the gardener in the afternoon. I cleaned my own room and looked after my small washing, but the big washing we did together, using the washing machine.

Mum worked quite a bit in the garden, but I didn't like that and she never asked me to help. Dad had his big greenhouse where he grew tomatoes, cucumbers, grapes and lovely flowers. He often went late to work, because he liked to potter around his plants.

Mum decided it was time that I used my new sewing machine. We went out to buy a pattern and some material for a summer dress. It was very difficult for me to read the instructions in the pattern. For days I had the pattern or the instructions for the sewing machine in one hand and the dictionary in the other. I learnt a number of new words and I made the dress. It was not perfect, but I was pleased with my effort. I told my mother about it in my letters, who could hardly believe that I really had started to sew. She herself was such an expert and had tried to teach me many times.

Gradually I got bored with the everyday routine in a house which was not mine. The house was right in the country with only one neighbour whom we hardly ever saw. There was a bus service to Chesham or Gt. Missenden where the factory was, but the bus didn't go very often. Mum had a small car which she used for shopping in Gt. Missenden, visiting people or going to her meetings with the WI. All her friends seemed to drive cars. I didn't have one, in any case I couldn't drive. Bob had started to teach me in his sports car, but he could only do this on Sundays when he didn't work and by then I had already forgotten nearly everything he had taught me the week before. I was stuck in the house for the whole week. I sometimes walked to the little village of The Lee, about twenty minutes away, only to see some people and post a letter home in the village post box. I wanted my own home, but Bob disagreed.

'Why do you want to move away? You have got everything here. Things are still rationed, but Mum and Dad are well off because of the chickens and the pig, the vegetables and fruit from the garden and the sugar from the bees.'

Bob just couldn't understand that I wanted to get away from people who always watched me, so I said:

'I can never have a quarrel with you without your parents overhearing it. When we want to have a longer sleep on Sunday mornings there is a knock on the door - Come on you lazy ones, breakfast is on the table. - If we come home late in the evening your father is still up, waiting for us, as he won't go to bed until everybody is in the house and he can lock the door. So I feel guilty for being late. If I sit down somewhere and read a book your mother comes and talks to me and I can't very well say to her - Go away, leave me alone, I want to read. - If I read in our bedroom, she comes in and says - Let's go for a walk with the dogs. - I don't want to go for a walk, but I also don't want to offend her, so I go. The only time you and I are alone is at night or if we go out, because even if we sit down anywhere here in the house your parents will join us, or we all have to look at TV.'

TV was the latest attraction. Dad had bought one and everybody was fascinated with it. If visitors came whilst it was turned on, they would sit down and look at it. It was never turned off for anybody, because it was such a novelty. I only understood half of it, but it did help me with the learning of the language. The only thing was that I couldn't take in too much of it at one time. I knew I had to persuade Bob to find a place for us to live on our own, I needed my independence.

It was my father-in-law who came to my rescue. He said if Bob didn't go and look around for some other accommodation or a house, he would go with me. Bob was surprised by this statement, but he was prepared to start looking for a house. At first we thought we might rent something, but there was really nothing for rent. After the bombing of London a lot of people had moved out, and any accommodation in the country was occupied. Many people had not moved back yet, because rebuilding had not really started. We couldn't even buy a house, there were none for sale. Still, we kept on looking and Mum and I started to go to auctions to maybe buy some furniture for our future home. New furniture was difficult to get. Any items we bought could be kept in the factory until needed.

I had never been to auctions before and I was fascinated with the proceedings. The first time I didn't buy anything, but my mother-in-law did. She laughed in the end and said if we keep on going to auctions and she was the one that bought the things, we had better stop going before she spent all her money.

At the second auction I did buy something I didn't really want, but it was very useful later. What happened was this: One of the helpers at the auction would show the item for sale, the auctioneer would suggest a starting price, somebody would lift up his arm, the auctioneer then quoted a higher price, another person would lift up his arm and the bidding would go higher and higher, until only one person was prepared to pay the called out price and after the third hammer stroke the item went to the last bidder. On this day I thought suddenly, I am going to lift up my arm too, just for fun, and then let the next person take over because I didn't really want the item. The next thing for sale was an old rocking cradle with stand. It was very dusty and the wicker work in the hood was partly broken.

'Who will give me 7s 6d,' said the auctioneer. I lifted up my hand and looked around for the next person to lift up his hand, but there was nobody.

'Is anybody else interested?' said the auctioneer. - Silence - The hammer went down three times and the cradle was mine.

My mother-in-law stared at me. Oh dear, I thought, she probably thinks I am expecting a baby, and how are we all going to manage as we are living together under one roof?

I reassured her, and explained that I had only lifted my arm up for some fun. We couldn't get the cradle into Mum's car, so I had to phone Bob to bring a small van. He too was surprised about the bought item.

'You didn't tell my you were expecting,' he said, and gave me a hug.

'I am not,' I replied and explained again what had happened.

He took the cradle to the factory to store it there for the meantime. It only took the rest of the day for the whole factory to know that Mrs Bob was expecting a baby. My father-in-law was always called Mr G, his son Mr Bob, so I became Mrs Bob.

The weather got cold, autumn had passed and Christmas came. I got letters from home and a food parcel, because everything was still rationed in England. We all had plenty of butter and sausage for Christmas.

Christel wrote to say she hadn't been very well. They had a lot of work to do in the laboratory and she worked long hours. She caught a virus in her lungs and the hospital transferred her to Davos to work there, so that she could be for a time in pure mountain air. My mother visited her for Christmas. When my mother returned to Luzern she discovered a lump in her breast and had to have an operation. I was very worried, but all I could do for them was to write letters and look forward to replies.

Christel stayed on in Davos for another few months and my mother, according to her letters, got better. My parents moved to a cheaper and smaller flat as Astra, Christel and I had now left. Hans was still in the army. My mother said the flat was on the fourth floor and quite nice, but there was no lift. This was probably the reason why it was cheaper. It was nearer to her work. She did not have much convalescence after her operation as she wanted to get back to her job. She needed the money. She had started to save so that she could send my brother to a crammer to get his matriculation and entrance to a university to study engineering. My father's business in Zürich was ticking over. He didn't make much money yet.

In January, Florrie, the domestic help arrived one morning very excited and told us that she had heard about a house for sale in South Heath. It was not officially on the market yet, but she knew that the people had to move, because the owner had another job.

We went to see the people straight away, as the house was only five minutes by car from the factory and would be very convenient. I liked the place at once. It was a detached three-bedroomed house with a small front and back garden and a wooden garage. It was also on the bus route that passed "Winnats" where my parents-in-law lived. Bob had noticed the house before when driving to work. There were three built in the same style with Mansard roofs. "Southmeads" was the end one. There were plenty of other houses along the road so I shouldn't be too lonely.

It would be a struggle to pay for it. We had no savings. Bob had a rise in his salary since we got married, but even so our finances needed carefully working out. We were able to get two mortgages and an overdraft in the bank and only the necessary furniture was bought, most of it at auctions. Mum had bought a new dining room table and chairs and she gave us her old one with the chairs which was still quite good, so these were items we didn't have to buy. We had a lovely red second-hand stair carpet. We painted the worn-out patches with red carpet dye. I stained the floor boards so that we only needed small bits of carpet and I made all the curtains.

When the people left they took everything with them, even the light fittings and the strips of lino on either side of the stair carpet. I didn't realise what they had done until I washed the stairs and tore my fingers. They had just pulled the little strips of lino off every step and left the headless tacks. They also took the name plate "Southmeads" with them, which was stuck in the lawn by the front gate on a short post.

I was terribly proud when we moved in at the beginning of March. This was my own home. For the first time in my life I had a home which was mine, only shared by Bob, my husband, and not by parents or parents-in-law.

The place was still pretty empty, even the fridge and the pantry, except for 20lb of jam and a loaf of bread. Our food rations were very small and Bob, who loved bread and jam, had been able to get some extra jam. He bought a loaf on Saturday before we moved in. Mum gave me my ration cards and said she hadn't taken anything off for the previous week. On Monday morning I walked down the hill to Gt. Missenden to do my little bit of shopping. It wasn't much and looked quite pathetic in the large pantry, so I spread the jars of jam out on to the different shelves. For the fridge I had half a pound of butter, half a pound of margarine and four eggs. I had also bought some vegetables, so I cooked a great big saucepan full of vegetable soup with some bouillon cubes. This would be alright for me for several days as Bob got his lunch in the canteen. I left the meat rations for the weekend, so that I could have a small joint for Sunday, which I finished on Monday, eating it cold.

My mother-in-law, having chickens, had plenty of eggs. She sold them to people in the factory for 6d an egg, double the shop price. This was the recognised amount for extra fresh free range eggs, as one was only entitled to one or two eggs a week on the ration card. Dad brought me twelve eggs one day on his way to work. I was terribly pleased about this. When we went to "Winnats" on Sunday, Mum asked me for the money for them. I paid her, but had no more eggs after that, saying that I didn't really like them. I was too proud to admit I couldn't afford them. I didn't want her to think I couldn't manage with the money Bob earned.

I thought I was expecting a baby, so I phoned Mum and asked about a doctor. She came to see me and took me in her car to see the family doctor in Wendover. I didn't like him very much, but Mum said he was very good.

'It is probably only because you don't speak such good English yet, that you think he is brusque. He is very highly thought of in the district,' she said.

The doctor confirmed my suspicion and said the baby was due in the middle of November. He asked me to come and see him again in a few weeks time.

Bob and I were very happy with the news about the baby, but we had to be even more strict with our money. We had worked out how much we could spend every week after paying for the mortgages, the interest of the overdraft, rates, electricity and coal and coke. We had no central heating, only two radiators in the hall downstairs and the landing upstairs. This was heated by a boiler in the kitchen, which also heated the water. Bob looked after this, stoking the boiler every morning and filling it up, also filling the hods with coke in case I needed them during the day. The rooms had fire places, but if we stayed in the warm kitchen we could save on coal. We had an electric blanket on the bed, so we did not need to heat the bedroom. One of Bob's uncles had a factory making electric blankets and we had a large one as a wedding gift.

We now needed extra money for baby clothes and for my confinement. The National Health had just started, so I got the doctor and any medicine free. Because I had a three-bedroomed house I could not have the baby free in hospital. Only women living in very confined accommodation were taken into hospital in those days. I either had to have the baby at home with the district nurse coming to help or go into a private nursing home.

I had nobody to look after me, so we decided I would have to go into a nursing home. The doctor suggested The Gables in Aylesbury, where he usually attended his patients. A shared room there was quite reasonable. We thought we had plenty of time to save up, so we provisionally booked the nursing home. Bob hoped to get some extra money by selling an old little tractor which his father had given him, but first he had to repair it.

I was very frugal and looked around for the cheapest things. Bob got his petrol free through the factory, so we went out on Saturday to Aylesbury market or to Watford. I bought Clydella material in a sale and made baby gowns from it. I bought one or two nappies at the time. Sometimes I could pick up some cheap white wool and I knitted little matinee coats and hats for the baby. It would soon be winter time after the birth. Bob brought the old-fashioned cradle home and I got to work on it. I mended the hole in the wicker work and made a curtain to go over the hood. I polished the wood and covered the mattress which was still very good. Bob put a clip on to the cradle so that it wouldn't rock. I didn't want the baby to get used to it.

My mother tried to give me advice in her letters. I missed her. I had no friends; nobody to confide in and talk things over with. The doctor was not very helpful and sometimes I couldn't even understand what he said. Bob's Auntie May told me one day that I was entitled to a pint of free milk a day and vitamin tablets. The sister in the nursing home gave me a list of what to bring for the baby. All items had to be marked with sewn-on woven name labels. This was a nice little job to do, sitting in the garden and sewing.

Bob had a big army bell tent and decided we ought to go on holiday with it. He was entitled to two weeks a year off from work. He would spend one week repairing the old little tractor, and for one week we would go camping. The little yellow sports car was packed up with the large rolled-up tent and all the other things that we thought we might need, and we were off to the coast, destination Looe.

To put up the tent was absolutely hilarious. Bob had everything measured out beforehand where the different pegs and strings had to go. I had to hold the centre pole, and he gradually stretched out the tent. I used to stand for ages in the dark, holding this pole whilst he measured and pulled, and sometimes the whole contraption just collapsed on top of me. It was always my fault, of course, because somehow I didn't hold the pole right. The tent slept twelve people. This gives an idea how big it was, and how difficult it would be to attempt to put it up with only two people. On top of that I had to take care as I was expecting a baby.

Car and Tent

265

The weather was fine at first so things were not too bad. I cooked all our meals on a little stove just inside the tent and we sat and slept on lilos. We had a lot of fun and I even swam in the sea. We got to Selsey Bill. It started to rain and it got very cold. We had no ground sheet. At night our tent got nearly blown away. We had to hold down the bottom part with everything we possessed: Saucepans, stove, tins, suitcase with clothes, parts from the car like the jack and some tools, even the loaf of bread came in useful. We had a terrible night, often getting up, and I had to hold part of the tent until Bob could tighten the ropes again.

When I discovered in the morning that the clothes and all our food were wet, we decided it was time to go home. We threw everything into the car and drove off, never stopping until we reached "Southmeads." We put the tent up in the garden to dry and our neighbours told everybody that we finished our camping holiday in the garden. This holiday only cost £8 and lasted just under a week.

I learnt one thing from our camping time together. Although Bob was very young and often a little immature for his age, he was an extremely practical and inventive man. He also worked physically very hard and was very muscular and strong. The factory was his life. He often worked six days a week, always on the shop floor. He never sat in the office. Sometimes he would even go Sundays to the factory to do the testing of the solutions in the laboratory or mend one of the vans of which they had several. At the same time he built me cupboards for the kitchen and promised to build me a boiler house for a bigger boiler so that we could have central heating. Bob never stopped working. When I thought he might have nothing more to do, he would bring home a watch to mend for one of his workers. They were all his friends in any case. A kind of comradeship had developed during the war with people helping one another, and this just carried on.

Bob left school at sixteen and started work. He went to a few evening classes in London by train and got a certificate in chemistry. He told me he was often too tired to absorb much as he had already worked all day in the factory, so there was no point in carrying on. His experiences were gained through practical work rather than from books. He could mend any machinery or equipment and even in our home I never needed a repair man. He didn't realise what an extraordinarily gifted man he actually was.

Bob was never much concerned about money. He got a wage packet every Friday which he brought home and just gave to me. Sometimes he took a few coins, but there were days when he had no money in his pocket. He didn't need any as he had his food and petrol free. He didn't drink and he didn't smoke. He left it to me to work out how we could manage with his income. Sometimes he would even forget to bring his wage packet home on Friday, not realising that I needed it. So I started to walk down to Gt. Missenden late on Friday afternoon, collect the money from him, do some shopping and then get a lift back with him in the car. It was a rather steep hill to walk back, so I was always glad of the lift. If he worked late, I could at least leave the shopping in the car and walk back alone.

One Friday when I walked to Gt. Missenden I saw some beautiful grapes in the greengrocers. I could taste them in my thoughts, sweet and juicy. I knew I couldn't afford them, but I had such a craving for them that I decided to buy some. I found Bob alone in the laboratory and asked him for his wage packet. I also told him that I was going to buy some grapes. He didn't like this and said that was a luxury which I didn't really need.

I don't know what happened or what came over me. I felt suddenly that I had had enough of all the money worries and loneliness and I burst out:

'I am sick and tired of saving and scraping around, eating cabbage and vegetable soup day after day, so we can get the money together for a few baby clothes and the nursing home. I am alone all the week, you work Saturdays and often on Sundays, I have no friends and not a lot of pleasure in life, and now I want a few grapes you tell me it is a luxury.'

Bob looked most embarrassed. He lifted his hand up once or twice as if he wanted to stop me, but once I had started I couldn't stop.

'You get your agreed salary, but you work Saturdays and often on a Sunday. Any employee in the firm gets paid overtime for every hour worked extra and double pay for Sunday work. Some of your foremen earn more than you do. The excuse is always we need new machines, I can't take any more money out of the firm. You never worry about money and how I manage.' I would have carried on with my outburst, but I suddenly realised why Bob looked so embarrassed, somebody stood behind me. I turned round and faced my father-in-law who had entered the laboratory quietly. He smiled at me, and gently putting his hand on my shoulder said:

'Come with me.'

He took me to an empty office, produced a cheque book, filled out a cheque and gave it to me.

'Now here is a cheque, just for you. Go and buy baby clothes, plenty of grapes, anything you want. This is something just between us, there is no need to tell anybody about it, not even Mum. I didn't realise how difficult things were for you with the two mortgages and the bank loan. You must eat well, think of the baby. I would also like to pay for the pram. Go and choose one, never mind the cost. This will be a present from Mum and myself for the baby.'

I just couldn't believe it that anybody could be so kind to me. Dad understood how I felt. He had been a refugee himself, but he had always had his family around him, whilst I had nobody except Bob and he seemed to live for his work. I had found a second father in Dad.

Bob had a wage rise and suddenly somebody was employed to work in the laboratory so that he could have more time at home. Monday morning was washing time. I had a washing machine, but the washed clothes had to be taken out, put through an electric wringer and rinsed in the sink. Whilst working away one Monday morning, it was August 28th, I suddenly felt water running down my legs. There was no warning, I had no pain and at first I thought I had splashed some water from the sink over me. It couldn't have anything to do with the baby I thought, it is not due for another ten weeks. I finished the washing and hung it out into the garden because I was feeling alright. Suddenly it happened again and with it I had a stabbing pain. I phoned Bob who came home straight away and called the doctor. He gave me a morphine injection and told me to stay in bed.

Tuesday morning I had the first contractions. The doctor came again and said he would try and save the baby, it was much too early for it to be born. He gave me another injection and a third one in the evening. By Wednesday morning the contractions had increased and when Bob phoned the doctor he told him to take me to the Gables Nursing home, he would inform them of my arrival.

Sister Helena prepared me for the birth in the labour room which was on the first floor. It was extremely hot, even with the windows open, and I sweated a great deal. The contractions would come, become quite frequent, Nurse Helena phoned the doctor, but by the time he came they had stopped. This kept on all through Thursday, Friday, and Saturday. I didn't touch any food I felt too sick. Bob came to see me in his lunch hour and in the evenings. Sister Helena gave him some ice cream and asked him to persuade me to eat it. I didn't want it, so in the end he ate it himself. I told Bob that I was worried.

'It is not right to be in labour for such a long time. I ought to be in a proper hospital and see a specialist. Please have a word with the doctor and insist on a second opinion.'

Bob talked to the doctor, but he reassured him that everything was alright for the moment. The baby was very weak and didn't have the strength to come yet. The best plan was to wait for a natural birth. He didn't seem to be concerned about the mother, me, who had been in labour for several days. Bob believed the doctor, he was the expert. My opinion couldn't be relied on, because I was not rational any more, having been in pain for too long.

I missed my mother. She had had four children and would have come to see me and something would have been done.

By Sunday I was desperate. I was very weak, I couldn't stand the pain any longer. By now I didn't want this baby any more that had decided to come too early, and then not to come. When the doctor came in the afternoon I told him:

'If you don't do anything about this baby now, or get me a specialist, I will jump out of the window.'

With that I sat up and tried to get off the bed.

'Now, now,' said the doctor, 'don't get too upset. We will do something, I promise you. Just lie down again.'

He took Sister Helena to the side and whispered to her: 'She is hysterical, we will have to use forceps.'

The next thing I knew was the smell of ether and Sister Helena saying: 'Take deep breaths.'

Victor was born on Sunday September 4th 1949 at 7 p.m, weighing only three and three-quarter pounds.

I woke up when they lifted me into a wheelchair and bumped me down the stairs, (there was no lift) into a room which I shared with two other mothers. Soon Bob was there and I was glad it was all over. He wasn't allowed to stay long as I was very weak, having had a haemorrhage, but he promised to come the next day. He said Victor looked very tiny and Sister Helena had asked him whether he wanted the baby christened. He told her that he wanted to wait until we had a proper christening and a party with it. He was so proud of his little boy.

Poor Bob, he didn't realise that this meant, that they were afraid Victor might not live. It frightened me, but I didn't say anything. I couldn't believe that after all the pain and long labour I had gone through, little Victor would die.

With hindsight, Bob and I agreed it would have been much better for me to have been in hospital and have had a Caesarean operation. Victor would then have been in intensive care and maybe in an oxygen tent. This of course would have meant that the doctor didn't get paid, as he wasn't attending the birth.

All the mothers had their babies brought to them at feeding time, but Victor was not allowed to be moved. He had a little corner screened off in the nursery away from any draught or cold. Feeding time for him was every three hours day and night. I had plenty of milk which I had to take off because my baby was much too weak to suck the breast. During the day I went upstairs to feed him, but at night Sister Helena took over so that I could have a good rest. Victor was so weak that the milk had to be dripped into his mouth drop by drop. For this I had to use a pipette, one of those little glass tubes with a rubber sucker at the end, used to fill up fountain pens. The little boy just didn't want any food, all he wanted was to sleep. It took nearly an hour to change and feed him.

I was shocked when I saw him naked for the first time. He was not allowed to have a bath, but was gently rubbed down with a piece of cotton wool dipped in olive oil. He looked like a skinned rabbit, he hardly had any flesh. The skin hung from the bones on his arms and legs and I could count the ribs on his chest. To keep him warm strips of cotton wool were wound around his arms and legs, and then his body. Sister Helena showed me how to do this. We had a little table in Victor's corner where he was protected. Everything had to be done quickly so that the baby wouldn't lose much heat. For the first few days I watched, but then I had to take over. At first I was terrified to touch Victor's fragile thin limbs, but soon I got more confident.

The other two mothers in my room had plenty of visitors. I only had Bob in the evening. My mother-in-law and sister-in-law had gone on holiday to the seaside. This had been booked well in advance. Victor had arrived unexpectedly; his birth should not have been until November. Some of Bob's relatives sent congratulation cards and his Auntie May sent me a little romper she had knitted for baby Victor. It gave me a lovely warm feeling to realise that she cared. I always had a soft spot for her after that. Dad came one afternoon and brought me some grapes from his greenhouse. He laughed and said he knew I liked grapes. I took him upstairs so that he could see his first grandson. He agreed he was a tiny baby but said:

'You see, one day he will be a big strapping boy.'

I was told by the nursing staff that I would have to stay in the nursing home for three weeks, or at least until Victor weighed 4lb and was used to breast feeding. He gradually swallowed a little more milk from the pipette and after two weeks I started him on the breast. He didn't like it, because this meant work. Now he had to suck and swallow. Before that he only had to swallow. For the first time I heard him cry, a tiny little whimper. I wasn't upset, I felt he was now learning to be a normal baby.

After three weeks I was allowed to go home with Victor. Bob was glad. He had been lonely, but coping very well. He had even done the washing which turned out pink, as he had put my new red tablecloth into the washing machine with all the other things. He had bought some flowers and the house looked clean and welcoming. We were happy to be together again.

At first Bob, too, was afraid to touch our baby because he was so small. He watched me at bath time. I did this in the kitchen, the warmest place in the house and told him not to open the door or go out, even if the phone rang. He was surprised about the rolls of cotton wool around Victor's arms and legs, but didn't think he looked too skinny.

The next three months were a nightmare. It took an hour to change and feed Victor, which only left two hours before the next feed. This had to be done day and night. I was always tired as I never had a good long sleep. The two hours in between the feeding seemed to go so fast. There was little time for housework, cooking and washing. I had no help. Bob tried to do some shopping for me, but I had to write it down, and because I always was so tired I often forgot things. He sometimes took me in the car to Gt. Missenden with Victor in the Carrycot on the back seat, but we had to be quick so that we were back for the next feed. I lost two stone and felt at times as if I was in a dream. I had a timer and always set it for the next feed, because I would drop off to sleep at any time. Because I had plenty of milk I took it off and put it into a bottle and showed Bob how to feed Victor hoping in that way to get a longer sleep one day. I am afraid it didn't work, I don't know why, but I heard Victor cry, so I got up and fed him again.

One day we had a terrible accident in our house, probably due to my great tiredness. What happened was this:

We had no central heating and all the rooms were cold at night. My timer would wake me up to feed Victor at night. Bob was usually fast asleep and never heard the timer. His alarm clock was different, he would wake up for this. To feed Victor I went into the other bedroom and because it was so cold I had a small electric fire which I switched on as soon as I got into the room.

I always fed Victor first before I changed him and by then the room was a little warmer. The electric fire had no switch. I had to turn it on with the switch where it was plugged into the wall socket. During the day when the fire was cold I pushed it under the bed-settee which we had bought at an auction. It was our spare bed for visitors. The bed-settee didn't look very nice, it was rather worn, but the springs were good. I covered it with a beautiful blanket which went right down to the floor.

One day, although very tired, I decided it was time to vacuum the rooms upstairs. After feeding Victor I put him into his pram and outside into the fresh air. I unplugged the little electric fire as I needed the wall switch. When I finished I plugged the fire in again thinking I would then only have to pull it out from under the bed-settee at night. I forgot to turn the switch off.

I was busy downstairs when I thought I could smell smoke. I went into all the rooms and the kitchen, but there was nothing. The smell was persistent and I thought maybe it comes from upstairs.

I walked up a few steps and stopped in horror. There was thick smoke coming out under the closed door of the middle bedroom and a small stream out of the keyhole. I ran into the bathroom and got a bowl of water and opened the bedroom door a little. I quickly shut it again as the smoke was yellowish thick inside the whole room. No, I thought, I am not going inside there. If anything happens to me nobody would know, and there is Victor outside in his pram who has to be fed again soon.

I ran downstairs to the phone. I lifted up the receiver and waited for the operator, we had no dialling phone in those days. When she came on to the phone I told her I had a fire and smoke was everywhere. She said she would call the fire engines straight away. Being the local exchange she knew me, particularly as Bob and his father had the factory in Gt. Missenden. The fire station was partly run by volunteers and a number of them worked in the factory.

Then I thought I had better let Bob know and lifted up the receiver again.

'Leave it to me,' said the operator, 'I will tell them at the factory. You keep yourself and your baby safe. The fire engine won't be long.'

When I was living in Germany we had always been told once we had called the fire engines we should go into the road and guide them in so that they wouldn't lose time looking for the house. I looked at Victor, he was alright in his pram, so I went to the front gate looking for the fire engine. Whilst standing there my mother-in-law came along in her little car. She didn't stop, but opened the window and waved. She always passed my house when she went shopping in Gt. Missenden.

'I have got a fire,' I called out.

'It will keep you warm,' she called back.

At the cross road she stopped, wondering suddenly why I stood there telling her this. Then she backed until she came opposite our entrance gate, stopped, got out of the car and crossed the road. She wanted to talk to me, but I saw Bob coming at great speed and waved my arms. He shot through the gate, jumped out of the car and ran indoors. I followed him quickly and told him where the fire was. He ran upstairs saying: 'Maybe you left the electric fire on under the bedsettee. I have to turn it off.'

He got into the room, turned the fire off and opened the window. He came quickly out again, coughing and spluttering, gasping for air.

In the meantime the fire engine had arrived. They swung speedily round through the gate and in doing this pulled the bumper off mother-in-law's car. She shouldn't have left it there. The officer got his men to pull out the big hoses. Bob came out of the house shouting:

'Not the big ones, I won't have the big ones. You can do more damage with a lot of water than with a fire. Take the small hoses that's all that is needed.'

A number of firemen worked in the factory and Bob was their boss, so they did what he told them. The small hoses were used. They soon discovered that the fire had started under the bed which was very lucky. The big blanket covering it had prevented flames from shooting up. The bed was only smouldering giving off the thick yellow smoke. As the window was not big enough to push the bed through the firemen had to carry it down the stairs into the garden. Once on the lawn they pulled it apart and it was then that the flames shot into the air, partly also because of the oxygen which the fire now had. The floor boards and the wall were burnt where the bed had been and the whole room was black. The landing and stair carpet had burnt holes where bits of the burning bed had dropped off when the bed was carried out. Everything was wet and dirty.

Nobody was hurt, that was the main thing, Bob said. Father-in-law arrived when the firemen were just leaving. It hadn't taken long before everybody in the factory knew that Mr Bob's house was on fire. It was also rather a funny thing the way Bob was told about it. The operator had called the fire engine, then phoned the factory and told the secretary about the fire. Elsie went to find Bob when the siren went off announcing the fire and the voluntary firemen in the factory ran to the muster station. Elsie found Bob who looked at her and said:

'Another bloody fool has got a fire again. This is the second time this week that some of the people have to leave their work!'

Elsie, standing next to him just said: 'The one you are condemning is your wife and it is your house, so you had better go home quickly.'

With that Bob ran and got into his car.

Mum said she could do with a cup of tea. She always said this in any crisis or when there was an upset. It had started during the war and had become her trade mark. I made a pot of tea, put some cups on to the tray and put it down in the living room. I left them to it as I had to feed Victor again. Mum and Dad soon left to have something done about the car bumper, and Bob came upstairs to see me and to talk to me. He promised to come home early and help me with the clearing up.

The bedroom was in a terrible state. The smoke had penetrated into everything. I had a chest of drawers in the room where I kept all my white linen, most of it wedding presents. Everything was grey and had to be sent to the laundry as I just couldn't wash it. We also had our wardrobe in the room and all the clothes needed to be taken to the cleaners, which Bob had to do. My beautiful white wedding dress which I had hoped to make into an evening dress one day, was ruined. It never got clean again. The walls, windows and furniture were covered in a black greasy smeary film. The worst was the smell which was all over the house. It hung around for weeks. The red stair and landing carpet had to be painted again where it was singed, and we realised that soon we would have to have a new one.

We were covered by the insurance and we soon had people in to replace the burnt floor boards and part of the wall. After that the room was cleaned and painted and the smell of paint killed the smell of burning.

The district nurse called in occasionally and a health visitor, a Miss Benger, a very kind and understanding person. She said I really ought to have some help. I told her my mother was in Switzerland and I had never become very close to my neighbours. There were no young people about.

Victor started to put on weight and could gradually be eased over to a four-hour feed. By Christmas he often even slept through the night. He became a very happy and contented child with blue eyes and fair curls. Every day he was outside in the fresh air in his pram. Bob had plated the handle and all the chrome parts again and everybody admired the shiny pram when I went for a walk.

Several times we went to "Winnats" on Sunday afternoon and also spent Christmas there. Mum and Dad often had friends and we were quite a crowd for the festive season. Everybody was still talking about the war and that now London had to be rebuilt. They all knew I was Swiss, so it was assumed that I didn't know much about the war. In any case the Swiss had always been neutral, clever country! Mum came from a very big family, a number of them living in Southend-on-Sea, and I heard all about their early struggles. She was a very vivacious woman with a beautiful voice, and we often had some music. Bob was usually on the piano accompanying his mother's singing, or he would play his accordion. Dad played the balalaika and the saw. I had never heard this, and was fascinated with it. It sounded like a high woman's voice. Dad would rest his foot on a tennis ball wedged into an ashtray. He put the handle of the big saw between his knees. He made his leg on the ball vibrate, slid a violin bow along the curved back edge of the saw to make the note run along. It sounded beautiful.

I was usually busy feeding Victor in the bedroom upstairs and when I did join everybody they never asked me about my past. I soon knew all about the family and I realised that most of them were only interested in themselves and their stories. It was not until I wrote my autobiography that Bob's family knew that I had been a refugee from the east. Even Bob's mother was surprised and suddenly realised, after forty-six years, that she didn't really know me.

I sometimes talked quietly to Dad because I wanted to know about his childhood in Russia. His mother was still alive in Canada where she lived with one of his brothers. His parents and two of his brothers and one sister had emigrated to Canada before the war. His mother was a widow now and wanted to come back to England. She was eighty years old and didn't want to die in Canada. She spoke German, so I started to write to her in that language and we had quite a correspondence.

At the end of January my father wrote to say that my mother was not well. 'She works too hard,' he wrote. 'She is absolutely exhausted when she comes home from work and finds it difficult to walk up four flights of stairs to the flat. She won't see a doctor, because she doesn't want to spend the money. She is saving for Hans's education. She says she misses the contributions you made whilst you were in Switzerland.'

My mother wrote cheerful letters to me saying my father was worried about nothing. She was looking forward to coming to see me in England in the summer. Christel told me that she had finished her time in Davos, and had a few weeks convalescence. I asked her to come and stay with me and said I would pay her fare. We were not allowed to transfer money because of the shortage of foreign currency, but I was able to get a ticket for her paid in England. Bob picked Christel up at Victoria Station because I had nobody to look after Victor. The two of us talked and talked and poor Bob and the English language were disregarded. He didn't mind, as long as I was happy. Christel brought bad news about my mother. She was in hospital.

'Mamuschka thinks she has got peritonitis, but that is only partly true. She really has lung cancer. One lung has collapsed and there is not much left of the other one. The cancer which she had in her breast has gone further. I spoke with my professor who examined her and kept her in the hospital straight away. She has a lovely single room and Papa, Astra and Hans can go and see her at any time. She is quite comfortable and happy, because she has been told that there is nothing to pay. She said in that case, she might as well have a rest. She won't live long. It depends how long the lung lasts. She won't suffer, there is oxygen already in the room and she sometimes has this. I didn't want to come to you at first, but Mamuschka wanted me to go. She said you need somebody and she couldn't come yet. She is really looking forward to seeing you and Victor in the summer, but she won't live as long as that.'

Christel cried and I tried to comfort her. I was shocked by this news and told Bob about it. I would have liked to go and see my mother, but I had nobody to take care of Victor and I couldn't possibly take him with me. When I had heard from my father that my mother wasn't very well, I had started to wean Victor, giving him the bottle once or twice a day. He didn't object, he kept on putting on weight.

My mother died on March 17th. She was just fifty-one years old. Although it was expected it still was a shock. I remembered what she had said to me at the end of our honeymoon when we left. She didn't think she would see me again, and she was right. Christel and I were very upset. I wanted to go to the funeral, but what should I do with Victor? My mother-in-law said she had too many commitments to look after him. Christel and I decided that I would travel to Switzerland and attend the funeral, whilst she would stay with Mum and help to look after the baby. She moved to "Winnats" with Victor and Mum now had a baby sitter.

I was glad that I had started to wean Victor. He could now have the bottle all the time. I still had to take off some milk every day, so I took all the equipment for this with me on my trip. Bob couldn't be spared from the factory, and in the end I travelled alone by train to Luzern. I was able to help my father with all the formalities and the funeral arrangements. He was a broken man, blaming himself for not having been able to earn enough money to make life easier for my mother. The cremation was only attended by my father, Astra, Hans and I, because we had no other friends or relatives.

I sorted out all my mother's things and disposed of her few clothes. She had made a short will, not certified, but we adhered to it. She left her jewellery to different members of the family, most of it to Astra. Hans got her lovely diamond brooch which he was asked to sell so that he could use the money for his studies. After a week I returned to England.

Victor was christened before Christel returned to Switzerland. She was his godmother. For this occasion I made him a lovely gown incorporating my wedding veil. This carried on a tradition which had started in our family a long time ago. By the time Christel left she looked much better and stronger. She felt guilty for not having attended my mother's funeral. I said I was grateful to her for staying behind.

Victor was seven months old and still not sitting up. I could prop him up with cushions, but after a while he would fall over.

I was concerned about this, but the doctor said because he was such a premature baby he would be late with everything. I didn't believe him. I knew there was something wrong with our child. His legs were always very stiff and he kept on crossing them. My parents-in-law knew an osteopath in London who had helped several members of the family. Bob and I went to see him with Victor. He gave our boy a thorough examination and then told us that Victor had Little's disease.

'I could give him some massage and a little physiotherapy, but that would not alter the situation,' he said. 'It might loosen the stiffness in his legs, but not cure him. All you can do is to give him a good and loveable home.'

We had never heard of Little's disease. I wrote to Christel, hoping because she worked in a hospital she could find out more. My own knowledge of medicine was just not enough. Christel replied, it was a disease discovered by a Mr Little. This was no help. I insisted that my doctor let me take Victor to see a specialist at the hospital. He, too, was very cagey about what was wrong with Victor. But at least he acknowledged that Victor didn't behave like a normal baby, and told me to come back in two months time.

By the time Victor was one year old he weighed thirty pounds and was a happy, chubby baby with a welcoming smile for everybody. I had started to put him on a pot every one or two hours, and he was practically clean during the day. His pot was shaped like a duck and he would hold on to the head and beak of the bird so that he wouldn't fall off. At the same time I used to prop him up with cushions in a big soft chair. I could leave him alone like that for a time. When on the floor he would move his right elbow forward and pull his body towards it. He never bent his legs or attempted to crawl in the proper way. He sat in his high chair or on a little chair with a scarf tied around his waist. I knew enough about massage and exercises and from time to time I gave him this for his legs, but it made no difference.

When Victor was eighteen months old the specialist suggested that we put him into a home for handicapped children. Dr M said:

'Your child will never talk or walk and the best place for him would be a hospital where he could be looked after by trained people. I have observed Victor for months, he has hardly progressed. He is still like a six-month old baby.'

I was terribly shocked, because what Dr M was saying was that Victor was not only physically handicapped, but also mentally. This certainly was not true. I could see that he was quite intelligent. Dr M tested him every time I brought him, but I couldn't help it if Victor didn't want to build with bricks, pick up beads or put square and round pegs into their respective holes.

I told him that I would never put Victor into a home and Bob backed me up.

After that the specialist suggested irons for Victor's legs to strengthen them and physiotherapy to teach him to walk. Now I had to take Victor twice a week to the hospital for massage, exercises and the teaching of the walking pattern with the irons on his legs. The irons were very painful and made his legs sore. I knitted him socks, which were long enough to fold back over the iron once they were fastened to his legs.

I was not able to drive and to get to the hospital I needed two different buses. I had to carry Victor, who was quite heavy by now, and also his push chair. Bob arranged for a driver from the factory to take me, but that had to be when somebody had time. Often I would be taken early in the morning, but the appointment was not until noon. After I was finished I phoned Bob and if there was no driver he would come himself in his dinner hour. My life seemed to revolve around the hospital, the hours of waiting for transport and keeping a heavy child quiet on my lap. How I wished I had a car and could drive, or a friend who could take me. It wasn't all that far, but there just wasn't a direct bus.

Bob had started to teach me to drive but then he sold his sports car and we had his father's car, so I had to start to learn again. We also had no baby sitter so we had to take Victor with us. Bob's only free time was in the evening when Victor was asleep or on Sundays, the only day he could catch up with jobs in the house and cutting the grass in the garden. He had also started to build a boiler house at the back of the house for a bigger boiler so that we could have central heating. He had promised me this before we married! Mum and Dad had a great number of outside interests and had told us right from the start that they would not do any baby sitting.

I did not have a qualified driving instructor. Bob had taught his mother and sister to drive and that was very successful. There were two things which I had to learn, the mechanical part of driving and all the new words connected with it like clutch, accelerator, brake, double de-clutch etc. These were words I didn't use normally and if I didn't have a driving practice for two weeks I had forgotten the words again. We even tried to have different expressions for them like, press the banana, release the orange etc. as they were easier to pronounce and similar to German. The trouble was that I forgot which was the banana and which the orange. Bob was very patient with me and rarely got cross, but there was one incident when he really got upset.

Victor was about five months old when one Friday afternoon I walked with him to Gt. Missenden, did some shopping and then called in at the factory. Bob decided to come home early.

'What a pity I cannot drive,' I said to him. 'You could push the pram up Frith Hill and I could drive home.'

The hill was very steep with a sharp left hand bend in the middle of it. The by-pass hadn't been built by then. I had practised driving up and down the hill several times, changing gear, even stopping and starting again which was quite difficult because of the severe steepness.

'I have got an idea,' said Bob. 'We will put Victor on to the back seat. The bootflap folds down so I can sit on it backwards and hold the pram on the road. You can drive very gently up the hill. Keep the car in low gear so that you haven't to change again.'

'But I cannot do that, I haven't passed my test.'

'Never mind, nobody will see us, there is not much traffic about.'

I agreed, but decided not to start off at his working place as people might watch us. Bob drove the car out of the factory. We put Victor on the back seat and he settled himself down on the bootflap with his hands on the handle of the pram. I could see the back of him in the mirror. I was quite nervous, I didn't like the idea of this at all. I put the car into first gear and revved up the engine, but the car didn't move. My mind was in a turmoil - what is the matter, the car doesn't move - oh yes, I forgot to release the handbrake - where is the handbrake? - I found it, released it, and the car shot forward. Good, I could keep going now. I looked into the mirror.

'Oh no!' I shouted. Bob was sitting in the road. He got up and ran after the car pulling the pram behind him and at the corner a crowd of women roared with laughter. They were assembled there waiting for their children to come out of school.

Bob had fallen off because I released the handbrake so suddenly and shot forward. I stopped and waited for him to come and tell me off. I will not repeat here what he said. They were not very complimentary words, which even I with my poor English understood.

I wanted to give up and push the pram up the hill, but Bob wouldn't have this. He had to show the mothers on the corner that his clever idea with the pram worked and also that I could drive. He hoped they didn't know that I hadn't passed my test yet. We had another try and this time I started off very gently, kept the car in low gear all the way up the hill and round the sharp corner. My hands were sweating on the steering wheel and when we came to the top of the hill I stopped. I told Bob I would walk home with the pram from there as we were now on the flat.

Victor

The results of this experience were twofold: I never forgot to release the handbrake and Bob limped for a few days because of a sore behind.

To help Victor with his walking he had a walking pen, a frame with a canvas seat in the centre with two holes in it for the legs. I sat him in it with his legs through the openings, and put his hands on to the frame. Then I lifted him on to his legs and gently pushed the frame. If he fell back, he only sat in his canvas bag and didn't get hurt. He soon learnt what to do, and if there was enough space, as in the garden, he would stumble along, mostly walking on his toes. The irons were very painful, his skin was always sore and the happy child became a cry baby. I decided not to persevere.

Miss Benger, the health visitor who already had started visiting Victor after I came home from the nursing home, told me that Victor had Cerebral Palsy and was a Spastic. Now I had another name for my son's disability. She came to see me one day quite excited, and told me about a talk the health visitors had had as part of their continuous training. We had become good friends by now and she knew she could trust me, so she said:

'We are not allowed to recommend different physiotherapists to people, but Mrs Collis who gave us this talk is specialising in Cerebral Palsy. She has been to America and come back with a new method to help these handicapped children. She said the earlier she can treat them the better. She has a Cerebral Palsy unit in Queen Mary's Hospital, Carshalton under the supervision of a doctor. Go and see her with Victor, but don't tell anybody that I recommended it. If you get a letter from your doctor then you can go under the National Health and you won't have to pay for it.'

I was most grateful to Miss Benger. I thought of the sleepless nights I had had worrying about Victor for the last three years, and how I had cried when they wanted to put him into a home, and here at last was somebody who wanted to help. But I had to be careful and not expect too much; a disappointment would be terrible.

I phoned my doctor, but he point blank refused to give me a letter.

'You have got a specialist at the local hospital attending your son. There is no need to keep on going from one doctor to the next and get another opinion. You have got a diagnosis and nobody will give you a different one.'

'I know that,' I replied, 'but I want somebody to help Victor and teach him to walk properly.'

He still refused, so I phoned Queen Mary's Hospital in Carshalton and spoke to Mrs Collis' secretary. I explained about Victor and that I couldn't get a letter. She said I could come without it and gave me an appointment. Before going to Carshalton I had an appointment with Dr M at the hospital. I told him about Mrs Collis and that my doctor wouldn't give me a letter.

'I have heard about Mrs Collis,' he said. 'I am not convinced about her method, but if you want to go I will give you a letter. I will keep an open mind about any success you might have with your boy.'

As soon as we had the letter Bob and I travelled to Carshalton. Mrs Collis, together with a doctor, examined Victor and spent about an hour with him. For part of the time we had to wait outside. Victor didn't like this and cried. He had always been with me wherever we went. Mrs Collis said this was one of the things we would have to teach him, the parting of mother and child for a few hours.

Mrs Collis didn't understand what my life was like. I had no friends; all my time was spent looking after Victor, the house and the garden. On Sundays we sometimes went to "Winnats" to see Bob's parents in the afternoon, but even then I was near Victor. We never had anybody to look after him. Once a week I went to an English evening class by bus, but then Bob was at home and Victor fast asleep. I met a few German au pair girls in my class and became friendly with one or two, but I knew that they only stayed a short time in England. One of them, Gisela, became a special friend. She married a Swiss and emigrated to Australia. We have never lost contact.

Mrs Collis had quite a discussion with us and explained a number of things.

'Victor has Cerebral Palsy,' she said. 'People probably told you he is a Spastic which in this case is correct, but there are several types of Cerebral Palsy. I will give you a small book so that you can read all about it. I am convinced I can teach Victor how to walk but you have to stick to certain rules and regulations. I will only take him on my register if you promise to do exactly what I tell you. I don't waste my time on children whose parents don't co-operate.'

She spoke quite forcefully, laying the law down, either take it or leave it. She continued:

'First of all he is not allowed to walk any more until I give the word. My staff or I will show you some exercises which you, mother, have to do every day. What we will do is to try and teach Victor how to move his legs in the correct way before he puts any weight on to them, so that they do not get deformed. Part of the brain which controls his legs is either damaged or has not developed properly because he was born prematurely. We will teach the rest of the brain to take over. You are not allowed to bribe him or punish him. He has to learn to do the movements out of his own free will. He also has to have special child's furniture and be watched all the time that he keeps his legs correctly. It will be hard work and take a long time, but I promise you, he will walk. If you are prepared to do this I will take him on, if not you can carry on as before. I want you both to talk it over on your own and give me your decision as soon as you can.'

With that she told us to go back into the waiting room.

Mrs Collis was the first person who had given us hope. Bob and I felt we had nothing to lose by trying her method; it sounded reasonable. I didn't realise then how much work, disappointment, heartbreak, but also joy was in store for me for the next years. We agreed to abide by her rules. I was shown the first exercises and we were told what equipment to get.

Victor had to have a small child's chair just high enough so that his feet rested flat on the floor, and a table to go with it. Bob built these for him and made the legs gradually higher and higher as Victor grew. From now on I had to carry him again. In order to keep Victor's legs apart Bob built him a special horse. It was a small drum with four legs and a handle which he could hold. It was stove enamelled pale blue in the factory. He had to sit on it a few times a day. At first he didn't like it because it hurt the top of his legs which were now spread out, but we made it into a game, and gradually he sat on it longer.

By now he should start to learn to wash himself, but because he couldn't stand up he couldn't use the washbasin. Bob built him a low table with a large hole in it for a bowl. It was just high enough to kneel in front of it. I would fill the bowl with warm water, and empty it when he had finished. The table too could be made higher and higher when it was necessary.

Every morning, after Bob had gone to work, I had to do Victor's exercises. For this I had to undress him and lay him down on to the dining room table with a blanket and sheet underneath. I would move his leg up and down and then ask him to do it. The same with his foot, up and down, then ask him to do it. I showed him all sorts of movements and asked him to repeat them. I moved his leg up into the air and asked him to hold it. Victor just laughed, he thought this was fun, but there was no response. He couldn't talk yet and at times I wasn't sure whether he understood what I meant.

Mrs Collis told us that Victor had to be taught all the different baby stages, which also meant the proper way of crawling. Victor only pulled himself along on one elbow. I had to put him on to the floor and push his knees under his body showing him how to crawl. Day after day I worked with him. Bob did it sometimes at the weekend, but he, too, was unsuccessful. We bribed Victor, he even got the occasional smack when I felt he just didn't want to do it. These were the things which Mrs Collis had told us not to do, but at times I was frustrated.

Every month Mrs Collis wanted to see Victor in Lambeth Hospital in London, where she also had a clinic. For this Bob had to take a day off to take us there, because I couldn't go by train. Victor was much too heavy by now, and in any case I was expecting our second baby. I dreaded these visits to the hospital.

Whenever I arrived Mrs Collis was not alone. She usually had a number of physiotherapists and sometimes young doctors there who were watching. She would point out the handicap, the certain stiffness in the limbs and what she intended to do. Her method had spread and more and more people were interested in it. I had to strip Victor, lay him on to the prepared table and show what I had been doing for the last month. As there was no change Mrs Collis assumed I had not worked with Victor very much and she did not hesitate in telling me off in front of all these people.

'Well, mother, if you don't work with your child you cannot expect any results. He will never walk if he doesn't learn to move his legs.'

She always called me mother, which I hated. I was most embarrassed and sometimes felt like crying and giving up all together. I had spent hours with Victor, but he just wouldn't respond.

Bob and I felt that I might lose my baby if I kept on carrying Victor, so we got a German au pair girl to help me. This made things easier, as now I could have a rest in the afternoon whilst Gritli took Victor for a walk in his pram. Victor gradually got used to her and didn't mind it when she looked after him. I knew he would be alright when I went into the nursing home for my confinement.

CHAPTER TWO

The Family at Home - Second Child

After my mother died my brother went to a crammer when he came out of the army. After six months he was able to pass his final examinations which now allowed him to study engineering. He got a grant from our Swiss home town for his studies. Because the university in Germany was cheaper, he chose Karlsruhe for his learning. If he took care the grant would also cover his living accommodation. He was very short of money so I posted him £3 as a present. I had quite a frightening letter from the Customs and Excise Department who had confiscated the money. They told me that it was not allowed to post Sterling to a foreign country, and if it happened again I could be punished with a three months prison sentence. They assumed that I didn't know about the foreign currency regulations and would therefore not take any action this time. The £ note has a silver strip and this must have shown up when they tested the letters.

My brother needed six months practical experience for his studies, and as he wanted to learn English at the same time, Bob got him a job with one of the firms he knew. Hans came to England and worked for Murphy Radio in Welwyn Garden City. He borrowed Bob's bike and often came to us for the weekend. He was always glad if it rained on Sunday afternoon because Bob would then get a van from the factory and take him and the bike back to his lodgings. If the weather was fine my brother often developed a bad tummy, which again prevented him from cycling back. It was very useful to have a brother-in-law who could get hold of a van!

Bob got Hans a provisional driving licence and taught him to drive. When he returned to Switzerland the authorities thought this was his license, and all he had to do was to pass another test. There was no need to pay for expensive lessons any more, which he couldn't afford in any case.

Christel and my father now lived alone in the flat in Luzern. My father had started a new job, getting contracts for a firm with railway tamping machines and also selling them. The owner had been in trouble with his business and could not get any credit from the bank. My father, with the hope of getting compensation for his business in Germany one day, was able to get a loan. The two of them worked out a business deal and for the first time since the war my father was earning good money. He travelled all over Europe looking for contracts for the tamping machines or selling them. When my brother finished his studies the two of them even travelled by car as far as Denmark and Sweden. In the end my father bought a tamping machine for himself from his commission and got a contract from the Austrian Railway to repair part of their track. My father was not an engineer, but a good business and sales man. My brother was the one who had to help him with his large machine in all his holidays and was later employed by him to run it. It was a great pity that my mother had died. She could now have given up her job and had an easy life.

Astra was working in Emmenbrücke near Luzern and Monika was with her foster parents. She wrote to me occasionally and told me how Monika was progressing. Her letters were usually full of complaints about her work which was very hard, and the unkind people she had to deal with in her job. The foster parents, too, were not perfect. They spoilt her child and Monika wouldn't listen to her if she corrected her behaviour. She only saw her for a few hours at the weekend so she couldn't teach her anything. I soon realised that Astra was jealous that Monika had so completely integrated with her new aunt and uncle and was probably more fond of them than of her own mother of whom she saw so little.

Christmas was another sore point. Astra wanted to take her away from the Graf family. Neither Monika nor her aunt and uncle wanted this. They were the ones who cared for her all the year round, when she was ill, when she went to school, when she was hurt, when she was happy and then when Christmas came they should be without her. My father gave Astra some money and said:

'Go and buy the Christmas goose, take it to Mr and Mrs Graf and tell them that you all could have Christmas together.'

She did this in the end, but I don't think it was all that successful. To live or even only to be with my eldest sister was always difficult.

Astra was efficient and good at her work. She was promoted and had a good position as a civil servant with an excellent salary. She was able to move and got a beautiful small flat in Luzern by the lake.

My father moved to Zürich as he still had his other little business there. He had the urn with my mother's ashes transferred. It was put into a little grave with a memorial stone and he sometimes visited the graveyard on Sundays. He sent me a photograph and told me that it was a lovely and peaceful place with lots of flowers. The graveyard was looked after by the town. I was glad that care was taken of the grave as my father wouldn't have had the time to do it.

In September 1951 my sister-in-law, got married. Pat and Andrew bought a house close to us. They had a beautiful wedding and Bob played the organ for the ceremony. I now had somebody I knew close by. Pat was working. She was the sales representative for the Gerhardy Factory, so she didn't have much time for me, but I could call in on Saturdays when I took Victor for a walk and Bob was working, and have a chat. They had a dog and later on chickens at the bottom of the garden. Whenever they went away, Mum would look after the dog in "Winnats" and I would go and feed the chickens. Pat always insisted that I had a few fresh eggs from her every week.

Pat and Andrew did quite a bit of entertaining, and as Pat was a Cordon Bleu Cook I loved to watch her preparing meals. I learnt a lot from her. I had never cooked before I got married, didn't even know what type of cookery book to buy. I wrote to my father who sent me a big German cookery book, something like the famous Mrs Beaton one. The recipes were all for a big family and much too expensive for me to use. How could I make a meal for two people by using 1lb of butter and twelve eggs etc. Pat bought me my first sensible cookery book.

Peter was born on February 4th 1953. This time I had an easy birth. I went to the Gables Nursing Home and had the same doctor.

I would have liked to change to another one, but I didn't know anybody else and Mum said again, he was the family doctor, and was really very good. Although Peter was a big baby, he weighed 8lb, I was only three hours in labour. He was beautiful and looked so healthy. He could move all his limbs. There was no stiffness in his legs. Even so I was worried, thinking of Victor and what he was like.

I had read the little booklet that Mrs Collis had given me, where everything about Cerebral Palsy was explained. I knew there were three types, Spastic, Athetoid and Ataxic. It is often not noticed that there is something wrong with a baby when it is born. It can also be blind, deaf, dumb, of low intelligence or mentally deficient. Victor was three and a half years old and had only just started to say a few words. How intelligent was he? He had several intelligence tests at the local hospital, but he still would not pick up little items, only the large ones, and Dr M seemed to be concerned about this. I got some books from the library, but they were difficult for me to read, I needed the English/German dictionary quite often. Still, I learnt enough to help me in my thinking.

Intelligence tests are based on the normal population, assuming that all children have similar opportunities for growth, development and education and have started life with similar physical and sensory endowment. A child that cannot walk is unable to explore the surroundings and so has not the same opportunities as a normal child. How can one use a normal intelligence test on a child that cannot speak? Victor was retarded in physical and social development. I pointed this out to Dr M and he agreed. He said that was the reason why he kept on testing him over a long period. He even came to see Victor in our home as he thought that emotional disturbances or anxiety might have a disturbing effect on his mental functions.

So here was Peter, hardly any trouble, feeding normally every four hours, soon even sleeping through the night. But was he alright? Mrs Collis told me to bring him along with Victor to Lambeth Hospital and she would have a look at him.

He was only six weeks old when Bob and I took him to London. He was fast asleep in his carrycot on the back seat of the car. Mrs Collis again had a number of visitors. This time she didn't tell me off about Victor. I had not had any success with him, but one could see that he was trying to do something. Mrs Collis then asked me to undress Peter and lay him on to the hard exercise bed. Bob was holding Victor on his lap whilst I undressed the baby. Mrs Collis moved all his limbs, even his little fingers. Suddenly she got hold of one foot and leg and lifted him high up with a jerk. It was done so quickly and unexpectedly that everybody in the room was startled and held their breath. I stepped forward with outstretched hands, afraid she might drop him. Peter cried and got red in his face. He wriggled, lifted up his hanging down head, bent his back and tried to get hold of his legs with his tiny hands so that he could be in an upright position again.

'Please observe,' said Mrs Collis to the group of people, 'what this baby is doing. He doesn't like to be upside down and is trying to crawl back on his own body to the normal position. Monkeys do this if they hang on one leg from a branch. Only a normal baby will do this in the first weeks of his life. It is a long time since I have seen such a healthy baby, I only see the handicapped ones. You have nothing to worry about, mother. Enjoy this healthy child and make sure the two brothers get on well together.'

With that she hugged Peter and then gave him back to me to be dressed. This was a most unusual gesture for such an abrupt woman.

After that I felt alright. I had complete trust in Mrs Collis. Now I knew that Peter would grow up into a healthy normal child.

One day, whilst I was doing Victor's exercises he moved his foot. I had got used to no response when moving his foot up and down and asking him to repeat it. But on this day he suddenly jerked his foot up. I looked at him, I couldn't believe it.

'Victor,' I said quietly, 'you have moved your foot. Now do it again, please, let's practice it.'

'Done it,' he said, and smiled, and then did it again very slowly. He concentrated hard and that foot moved up and down. I felt like crying, but I didn't. Victor shouldn't think this was something special, this was a normal thing, everybody could move their feet. This was the beginning of the success of Mrs Collis' treatment. Victor's crawling became better. At times he was quite fast. He gradually could do what I asked him to do in his exercises and Mrs Collis grudgingly accepted that he had improved. She was never very kind to me, always felt Victor and I hadn't worked hard enough. She treated all the mothers with Cerebral Palsy children the same and many left her and her treatment because of her abrupt manner. Victor too was frightened of her and always a few days before we had to go to Lambeth Hospital he would work very hard so that she wouldn't be cross with both of us.

One day I just couldn't face Mrs Collis. I hadn't been very well. Ever since Peter had been born I had kept on bleeding from time to time. The doctor said I had my period again, but I knew this wasn't so. I was glad to have Gritli, my au pair girl to help, but I always felt tired and exhausted. Bob did Victor's exercises sometimes at the weekend, he knew what to do. So on this particular day I asked him to take Victor into the consulting room to see Mrs Collis, whilst I waited outside. When he came out of the room again he was smiling, and so was Victor. Bob said he couldn't understand why I didn't like to go in and see Mrs Collis. She had been charming to him, telling her visitors that Victor was one of her successes only because he had a mother who cared and worked hard with him.

'She praised you several times,' said Bob, 'and also Victor for working so hard.'

After that Bob and I decided that her abrupt manner was probably only put on, done on purpose to frighten the parents into working hard.

Peter was christened in April and Pat told me she was expecting a baby in September. She was going to keep on working until nearer the time of the birth. She had decided not to have the family doctor and encouraged me to find another one if I didn't like or trust my own any more. I really had no confidence in my doctor by now. I found a different one who gave me some tablets and said if the bleeding didn't stop I would have to see a specialist. It didn't come to that, because other things happened.

We had trouble with Gritli our au pair girl. She had been shoplifting in London and we had a call from the police. Bob drove straight away to London and stood bail for her, otherwise she would have had to stay the night in prison. A week later he had to take her back to court in London. The judge was quite lenient, she got a small fine which Bob paid and Gritli said she would pay it up from her wages. She seemed sorry, it was a silly thing to do. I thought it was the first and only time, but I was mistaken.

There was a mention about this incident in the local paper, so everybody knew my name and that Gritli worked for me. A woman rang me and told me that she had an au pair girl who was friendly with Gritli. The two of them had been to London several times, and she knew that Gritli had taken some expensive books from different shops. But she would have thought that after the court case Gritli would stop her spree of unlawfulness, but now she had started to cheat on the railway by not paying her fare. The woman's au pair girl had come home with Gritli on the train and Gritli had told her that she had not paid for a ticket. All she had to do when arriving at the station in Gt. Missenden was to go to the toilet and wait until everybody that came off the train had shown their ticket to the ticket collector. The man would then leave, and Gritli could leave the station without being asked to produce her ticket. I was really shocked at how brazen this girl could be. She came from a good home in Germany, her father had been a general during the last war.

Bob gave her a dressing down which she didn't like. A week later she told me her mother was very ill and she had to go home. She left four months after Peter was born, although she had a contract with me for one year.

Bob carried on teaching me to drive. Every time we went out we had to take the children with us. We knew it was important for me to be able to drive because Victor was already quite heavy and would get even heavier. It was not easy to carry him at times. In the house he crawled everywhere. He even came alone downstairs by sliding down the stairs backwards. He always wore long overalls and had to have Kiltie boots for his feet. He soon wore holes into the overall knees, so I cut up an old pair and put patches already on to the new ones. Even that didn't last long, so I bought some leather and cut patches into which I stamped small holes all the way round. These patches I would sew over the patches on to the overalls. I had to take them off when the garment went into the wash. From now on I was forever sewing on patches or taking them off, as Victor needed three to four overalls every week.

The toes of his boots soon wore out too. Not when he was indoors on the carpet, but he also crawled in the garden on the lawn. My shoemaker was very good. As soon as I bought the boots I would give them to him. He opened up the front of the boot and put a steel cap in. He also put an extra toe cap piece of leather at the front to strengthen the shoe. Victor usually lasted one week with the leather toe cap, so I had two or three pairs of shoes on the go and there was always one pair at the shoemakers.

All this was quite an expense and I remember that the child's allowance I got from the state for Peter was just enough to cover the expenses for Victor's footwear.

Soon after Gritli left I got really ill. I woke up one night in a pool of blood. Bob called my new doctor who came at once. He said I had had a haemorrhage because some of the afterbirth must have been left behind. This was probably also the reason why I had never stopped bleeding. I was shocked by this information and quietly blamed the family doctor for it. I was glad that I had had the courage to change to a different one.

I had to have injections to stop the bleeding and to avoid a possible second haemorrhage I had to stay in bed. Bob had to get some bricks and raise the bottom of the bed, and there were a number of other things he had to see to. A doctor tells you what you have to do to get better, but he is not concerned how you are going to manage this. I had two young children, my au pair girl had just left, my mother was dead and my sister-in-law who lived close by was at work all day. But as usual Bob and I managed. Bob put the playpen next to my bed with Victor in it. So now he could only crawl around the little square. He was quite content to do this as I was with him. Peter had to stay in his cot all day. The sides were high enough so he couldn't crawl out. Bob got several bottles of milk ready for him which could be warmed up on a little bottle heater. I had to forget the mixed feeding for the time being. The bottles were next to my bed. The main thing for me was not to go downstairs and not to be out of bed for too long.

At dinner time Bob came home in his lunch hour and brought me some lunch from the factory canteen. Mrs Stennings, their cook, even got a little plate ready for Victor with everything cut up. I warmed up the bottle with milk for Peter, Bob brought him to me and I could feed him in bed. After Bob left I changed Peter's nappies and put him back into his cot. Victor was clean but couldn't sit on the toilet so I had to pot him also. I didn't get out of bed too often, but I felt sorry for Peter alone in his room and for Victor having to be enclosed in his playpen all day.

Bob was very good. He did the washing in the evening, bathed the children and got the tea ready, whilst I sat up in bed sewing on leather patches for Victor's overalls or taking them off, or feeding Peter.

One day Bob met Mrs Bunce. She was a woman who lived in the council houses just the other side of the big crossroad next to us. She had four children and had a domestic job in a big house, about five minutes walk away. I had met her once or twice before when she picked up her youngest son, who was five years old, from the school bus. Bob told her that I was ill and she was shocked to hear that Victor and Peter had to be indoors all day.

'Would you like me to come and see your wife?' she said to Bob. 'I could send my eldest daughter, Anne, along to take the children for a walk in the afternoon. She is twelve years old and very good with children.'

Mrs Bunce and family became our friends. Bob never locked the back door when he went to work, because the doctor came every day to give me an injection, and so Mrs Bunce and Anne could come in. Every afternoon when Anne came back from school she would come with her sister and take Peter and Victor for a walk. One had the big pram with Peter and the other one the pushchair with Victor. Anne sometimes even changed Peter's nappies. She was a very capable girl, having had to cope with two younger brothers and a sister for years. She was glad to earn a little pocket money for baby sitting. Mrs Bunce worked every morning, but even so she would call in the afternoon to see whether I needed anything.

After a week I was allowed to get up for a little bit and gradually got back to normal. I asked Anne to come occasionally to take Victor for a walk which made it easier for me.

I passed my driving test at the beginning of July. This was wonderful, because now I didn't have to walk all the way down to Gt. Missenden for my shopping and push the pram up the hill with the two children. The only thing was that if I wanted the car I had to take Bob to work and bring the car back. I had to get up very early, Bob started at 7.30, as I had also to get the children ready in order to take them with me. I couldn't leave them at home. Victor was put on to the back seat and Peter sat in the front in a little canvas seat which was hooked over the backrest of the passenger seat. In those days there was no rule that children had to be in the back only.

Miss Benger came to see me. She was concerned and said I didn't look well at all and should have a break from Victor. It was hard work doing his exercises every day and carrying him everywhere.

'It is a pity you have nobody who could take Victor for a few days to give you a rest,' she said.

She then suggested a home in Southend where they also take handicapped children. She said she would arrange this. We took Victor there on a Saturday. I packed in plenty of overalls with leather patches and extra boots, as I didn't think anybody would take off the leather patches and sew them on again, or that they would mend the boots. When we got to the home I didn't like it. On the gate was a box begging for money for the children. The rooms were in the semi-basement and everything was rather dark. The tables had blankets as a tablecloth. It was clean, the matron kind, but the atmosphere was so depressing. Victor cried when we tried to leave. The matron got hold of him, but he screamed and tried to hang on to me. Bob pulled me away and got me outside. I kept on hearing Victor calling and crying. I was terribly upset and felt it wasn't right to leave Victor there. I knew he would never be happy in that place.

I had a terrible Sunday and by Monday I had convinced Bob that we had to go and bring Victor home. The matron had told us on Sunday when we phoned that Victor was quite happy. When we phoned on Monday she tried to reassure us again that Victor would settle down, but Bob told her we were coming to take him home. When we arrived she hadn't told Victor anything. She made us wait in her room with the door open. She fetched Victor and sat down with him outside and started to talk to him:

'Now Victor, tell me how you like the other children. You played with them yesterday and this morning, didn't you?'

Victor cried: 'I want Mummy.'

She tried again: 'But you like the children, don't you? Your mummy will come and visit you soon.'

Victor cried even more not saying anything. He didn't have a big vocabulary yet in any case, as he had only just started to talk. Hearing him like that I realised that I had been right to come and fetch him. He was so pleased to see us, his little face lit up and when I lifted him, his arms went round my neck holding on to me really tightly. He didn't let go until we got into the car, and even then he had to sit on my lap. He was still a baby through being carried all the time and there was a special bond between him and me. He had only been parted from me once before, when Peter was born, but he stayed in his own surroundings then, and Bob was at home at night. Here he had to be in a strange and dark place with strange people.

Bob had some relatives in Southend, so we went to see them at the same time and then gave Victor a treat on the children's roundabouts on the pier. Freddy, a younger cousin of Bob's came with us. We all had a ride on the little train along the pier and Freddy told Victor about the big laughing sailor which was at the end of the pier.

'You have to put some money in and then this big sailor starts to shake and rock and laughs really loud,' said Freddy.

Victor was already jumping up and down in his push-chair for excitement and kept on saying: 'The sailor, the sailor, I want the sailor.'

When we finally found the big sailor there was a small note stuck to it saying: Out of Order. Bob and Freddy looked at one another, then had a whispered conversation. They just had to do something, Victor would be too disappointed otherwise. He couldn't read the note and I pretended to look for some money until the two men had decided what to do. They had disappeared behind the big sailor and I was told to put the money in. Suddenly the big figure started to rock and there was loud roaring laughter. Freddy was shaking the figure and Bob making these loud laughing noises. Other people came along and when we left we saw somebody else trying to put some money in. It must have been a good imitation.

The home episode was a very upsetting and sad happening, but it showed us that Mrs Collis was right. Victor needed the break from me and he also required the company of other children. A more extended environment was needed for him. If my mother was alive and lived close, she would have taken Victor occasionally, which would have given him different surroundings to get used to. This was not the case, so I had to try and find a way to correct it.

First of all we gave Victor a birthday party in September, and all Mrs Bunce's children came. David, the youngest, was only one year older than Victor. We gave him a huge box of bricks as a birthday present, and I mean huge. Dr M had discovered that Victor also had a very slight spasticity in his fingers. This was one of the reasons why he never picked up small beads, only larger items. It was his suggestion to get Victor's hands and fingers working through play.

The brick box contained 276 wooden bricks. Bob had them specially cut, and our carpenter in the factory made the box to Bob's design. When it was empty, Victor could crawl into the box, it was that big. Two people had to carry it. Victor would help us to stand up the bricks like a snake, going from one room to the next. He would then push the last brick, each brick pushed the next one over in quick succession, and the whole built-up snake seemed to roll along. Victor was terribly excited when this happened, and crawled along the line of bricks as fast as he could.

For his birthday we had the box on the lawn and built a tower around Anne. When it was as high as her head, she stepped out of it, and all the bricks fell down, with all the children laughing and screaming.

Pat had a friend who was in charge of a nursery school in Terriers near High Wycombe. She talked to her, and Karen was prepared to take Victor in, although he was not able to walk. We started Victor off very gently, just a few hours for the first days. The crying soon stopped. He liked the large toys, like the engine, the roundabout, the big teddy bear, even the

slide and the sandpit, and he knew that I would be coming back to fetch him. Karen said Victor got on well with the other children, who kept on telling him to get up and walk. Victor crawled everywhere, even out of the nursery room into the playground, and the toecaps on his shoes wore out even quicker. He was always dirty, being on the floor all the time, and needed a clean overall every day. I had to buy more leather for the patches! When the weather got cold, I knitted him gloves, but left the fingers open. He wore these out quicker than I could mend or knit them.

Overall with Leather Patches

It was good that I could drive now, otherwise Victor wouldn't have been able to go to the nursery school. Every morning I was up early to take Bob to work so that I could have the car, taking the children with me. I had to leave Victor's exercises until the afternoon when I brought him back, as there was too much to do in the morning. Victor had to be in Terriers by nine o'clock, and it took me over half an hour to get there. The only one I felt sorry for was Peter. He was only a few months old, and had to be strapped into his canvas seat for ages to accompany me in the car. Often he dropped off to sleep, hanging down towards the side. He should have slept in his pram or cot.

Pat had her baby, Alister, at the end of September. She stayed with Mum for a time and, when she came back, she didn't return to work straight away. I could leave Peter in the pram in her garden several times when I took Victor to Nursery School, which was a help.

We discovered a twin pram and bought it, as it was impossible for me to go for a walk with two prams. Peter could walk when he was one year old, so when we went out, he would toddle along holding my hand or the pram handle. When he was tired, I just put him next to Victor. The two brothers got on well with one another. I never realised how conscious Victor was of the fact that he couldn't walk, until one day, when the postman rang the bell and I opened the door. Victor came crawling along and told him proudly:

'I have got a brother and he can walk.'

I had a lump in my throat. I looked at his smiling face. He wasn't jealous, just proud. You will walk, too, one day I thought, I will see to it. Bob and I had made up our minds that Victor would not miss out on anything because he couldn't walk. We didn't hide him at home. If he wanted to go somewhere, he came with us and, if it was impossible to push him in the pram, we would take turns in carrying him. People stared at us carrying a great big child. At times it was embarrassing, especially when he got older, but Victor never missed out on anything. Bob even carried him to the top of St. Paul's Cathedral so that he could sit in the Whispering Gallery.

After a year in the nursery school, Victor had to leave, because he was five years old. By now he spoke well, had got used to children, and accepted that one had to share toys. It was time he went to school to learn to read and write. He loved his story books, and also the stories which I made up for him about other boys and girls that couldn't walk. The Education Authorities advised us that he couldn't go to a normal school, so they would provide a home teacher twice a week for an hour or two. I didn't think that was enough. He would miss out on the company of other children, the talks with them and the quarrels.

There was a private school in Gt. Missenden run on Montessori lines. I went to see the headmistress, who was quite willing to take Victor. One of the teachers was very kind to him. When the other children were playing outside in break time, she would spend extra time with him so that he could improve his reading. She felt that once he could do that, he would have a new interest, another outlet.

The school was small, and the children got used to Victor. I carried him into his classroom in the morning, and sat him down at his table. Peter always accompanied me when I drove to school and, as I couldn't leave him alone in the car, he toddled next to me, holding my hand. Sometimes one of the mothers would guide him, as they could see how difficult it was for me to carry big Victor in one arm and hold Peter's hand on the other side. Peter didn't like his brother going to school. The two had become inseparable, with Peter becoming Victor's legs. He fetched and carried things for him, and even brought him his potty and emptied it by the time he was two years old.

The toilet business happened by accident. Because Victor couldn't walk, I had to lift him on to the toilet. Once I had done that, I could leave him, and he called when he had finished. It was quicker and easier to use his little ducky pot, because then I didn't have to carry him. I would do this when he only needed the pot, and Peter, too, used the same one. We even travelled with it when we went to see Mum and Dad on Sundays.

One day when I came in from the garden after hanging out the washing, I met Peter in the hall carrying the half-full ducky pot. Victor had told him to get it and then to empty it. It seemed such a natural thing to the two of them, that all I did was to follow Peter to the toilet to see whether he would spill anything. Things went perfectly, except that I had to rinse the pot out. From then on Peter did this little job with great pleasure.

It took quite a time before Victor would go to the toilet at school. It was a great worry to the teacher. Victor always said he didn't want to go, and kept it all day. We knew he was embarrassed having the new teacher taking him to the toilet.

I couldn't bring his ducky pot to school; he just had to accept that the teacher would help him. Most of the children, of course, went on their own. Eventually the teacher was successful. She just took him for a few days in the lunch hour when everybody was playing outside and none of the children could watch him, and one day he performed.

Mrs Collis still wanted to see Victor every month to keep an eye on his progress. I could drive now, but didn't like to drive in London. Mrs Collis suggested that I come and see her with Victor in Queen Mary's Hospital in Carshalton, where we had met her first. Bob showed me the way a few times and, after that, I drove alone. Peter by now didn't need his little canvas seat, and would sit in the back with Victor. He usually was bored with the journey, and would jump about, bang my shoulder or quarrel with Victor. All sorts of promises had to be made to him to keep him quiet, and I dreaded the journey at times. It was probably also too much to ask of him to be quiet and keep still for one and a half hours until we got to the hospital and then the same coming back. If the weather was nice, we would break the journey for a picnic in Bushey Park on our way. They had deer there, and one could come quite close to them. Victor fed them once or twice, but then a notice was put up forbidding the feeding of the deer.

CHAPTER THREE

Happenings in 1955 - Starting Work

The weather forecast was good for Whitsun - hot and sunny. It would be lovely to be by the seaside on a nice beach where Victor could crawl. We decided to go camping in one of the vans from the factory. Bob, as usual, worked everything out perfectly. We took Peter's cot and tied it to the side of the van. He would be able to sleep safely in it. The sides were high enough for him not to be able to climb out. The vehicle had a Luton body, with a shelf above the cab. This was Victor's bed. He slept on an eiderdown to make it soft. He couldn't fall out, because there was a board on the edge of the shelf. We had a large milk churn with fresh water, a small Calor Gas cooker, pots and pans, etc. and food. There was a camp bed and a lilo for Bob and myself. It took quite a time to get everything ready in the van.

We started off in the evening so that the children could be in bed for the journey.

Victor had a wooden spoon, and was asked to bang with it if there was an emergency, as we could hear this in the cab. After half an hour's travelling there was a banging on the cab and we stopped. Bob and I rushed to the back and climbed in. Where was the emergency?

Peter was fast asleep, and Victor looked up smiling and said:

'I wanted to know whether it would work.'

Good foresight, I thought. How could we be cross with him!

It got late, and we couldn't find a place to stop. Eventually we pulled into a large gateway leading into a field on a small country lane, and went to sleep on our lilo and camp bed.

Just after five o'clock there was a bang on the van and a voice shouted:

'Move the van, I want to get into the field to milk the cows!'

The children woke up, and Peter started crying, he was still tired. Bob got dressed quickly, went outside and looked for the farmer. There was nobody there. He had probably heard Peter crying, left, and was able to get into the field through another gate.

Two Brothers

We decided we might as well get up. The children thought it was fun to heat the water on the Calor Gas stove for washing. Bob let the backflap of the van down on the chains, using this as a table. Whilst standing partly in the road, he had his shave like that. Breakfast was hilarious, with all of us trying to sit on one blanket. We had no table or chairs, only a box with food in the van. I used the top as a table whilst cooking.

Our destination was Brean, where we found a most beautiful sandy beach. We were allowed to stay in the car park of a pub right opposite the sand. The weather was lovely and Victor crawled in and out of the water and along the beach in his swimsuit. No overalls with leather patches needed here. The two children were in their element. We dug holes, made castles and played ball with them.

Then it happened - the accident!

Bob tripped over the ball and hurt his ankle. It only took a short time to swell up. He had a lot of pain and could hardly walk.

'You will have to drive the van back,' he said.

I was shocked. I had never driven anything other than Bob's car, and I was terrified to have to manoeuvre this big vehicle. They had some First Aid equipment in the pub, and I was able to bandage the foot. In the evening it seemed a little better. I made Bob cool his foot in cold water from time to time.

Bob did drive the van back, often using only one foot, as the other one was too painful. He had to have the foot and leg in plaster for four weeks, and had to go back to the hospital several times, because part of the plaster kept on falling off. He had two crutches, but wouldn't stop going to work. It wouldn't have mattered if he had an office job and sat down, but he visited the plating shops, where water ran along the floor all the time, and people wear wellingtons.

In the end they threatened to keep him in the hospital if he didn't stop going to work. From then on he avoided the plating shops, and only went into the other places like the polishing shop. inspection, stove enamelling, laboratory, etc. The foremen had to come and report to him instead. The ankle healed up alright.

One day we took the children to the London Zoo. We were able to hire a push-chair for Victor there. It was much bigger than a child's push-chair, but smaller than a wheelchair. Even I could sit in it, a little cramped. It was light, and could be folded flat. At the end of the day, when we returned the push-chair, I saw a little notice that some of these chairs were for sale. They had a number of new ones, and wanted to dispose of the old ones, to have more space. It was an ideal push-chair for Victor, as the twin pram had become rather small for him, and Peter, being very energetic, hardly used it. We bought one, it only cost £5. Bob painted it again, and it lasted Victor for years.

My sister Christel wrote to say she would be getting married in August. She begged me to come to the wedding.

'I have no mother,' she wrote, 'and only Hans, Astra and Papa will be there. The wedding is going to be in Zürich, and the reception will be at the Storchen Hotel, one of the finest in the town. Papa said that, although he has three daughters, I am the only one who is getting married from home. So this is going to be a very elegant and expensive wedding. Please do come, I need you.'

I had always protected Christel when she was young, and looked after her. She was now marrying Mino, an Italian, and would be moving to Milan. Mino's father had been German, but became Italian after the war to save his business. Mino spoke perfect German, and Christel would have to learn Italian. I knew I had to go to the wedding, Christel had always looked on me as a second mother. Bob had his summer holiday coming up, and said that this time he would come with me.

We decided to ask Bob's mother whether she would look after the children. Victor was quite good by now looking after himself and crawling everywhere and Peter, two and half years old, didn't need any nappies. I am afraid Mum said she couldn't manage the children, it would be too much for her, especially as Peter was rather energetic. I was terribly upset. We couldn't possibly take the children with us.

Miss Benger, my health visitor, told us about a very good home for Victor in Bideford. This time we went to see it first. It was a very long way to travel, but after the bad experience in Southend, I wanted to meet the people and see for myself what the place was like. Victor was older by now, nearly seven years old and also used to being away from me during the day when he was at school. We took the children with us. The home was very nice, they had a few handicapped children, but most of them were normal. A small van took the handicapped ones to the beach every day. Victor quite liked it, particularly the thought of being on the beach.

Anne was still taking the children for a walk occasionally, and had told her mother about my predicament with the children. Mrs Bunce came to see me and we had a long talk. She offered to take Peter for the time we were away, only wanting a small payment to cover the food expenses.

'Peter can sleep with David,' she said. 'Where there are four children, a fifth one won't make much difference. They will all be at home for the summer holidays, and will enjoy having Peter. They all love him, he is such a sweet cuddly boy. The only thing is that we have no gate on our front garden and he might run into the road. So if we could use your garden, which is closed up everywhere, the children could play there safely.'

I was most grateful to Mrs Bunce. I knew Peter would be alright, he enjoyed playing with the Bunce children, and was quite obedient with Anne. It was wonderful to have a person so interested in wanting to help.

Bob and I had a glorious motor holiday in Switzerland, Austria and Italy. The wedding was very elegant. Bob had borrowed his brother-in-law's cine camera and was filming everything. Christel had asked him to be a witness at the formal ceremony on the wedding day morning. This was something new for Bob, and I am afraid it didn't go smoothly at all.

In Switzerland and Germany the marriage is performed at the registry office in the morning, only attended by the bridal couple and the witnesses, followed by the so-called wedding breakfast, with champagne and some light refreshments. In the afternoon is the church ceremony, where the bride, wearing white, and the groom arrive together by car. This is attended by all the guests. After that comes the big wedding dinner.

I was not a witness, so I didn't attend the morning session at the registry office, and Bob had to cope with the language on his own. What happened was this. The registrar read out the wedding promise and waited for Mino to say - yes, I do, but nothing happened. Christel got nervous, pushed Mino a little and said: 'Say yes.' Mino very quickly said 'yes,' but the registrar wouldn't accept this. He asked Mino whether he had understood everything, to which he replied that he spoke and understood German, but not Swiss-German, the spoken dialect in Zürich, Switzerland. With that the registrar repeated everything in pure German and Mino, now understanding this, said his yes at the appropriate moment.

Bob didn't understand anything, and when it came to the signing of the witnesses, he didn't step forward until Christel asked him in English to come and sign the paper. The registrar stopped everything and asked Bob whether he had understood the ceremony. Bob said no, his German was very poor. The registrar was Swiss, and in Switzerland everything is done properly. He picked up his book again, found the right page, and now everything was read once more in English. Bob felt sorry for Christel who, by now, was very nervous, but then at last she was married.

Christel had a beautiful dress and veil for the church ceremony. I helped to dress her, and she was so grateful that I was there. She looked terribly young walking up the aisle with Mino. I already had two children, and had settled in a foreign country. She was only starting, and I hoped she would be strong enough to cope with a new language and a new country.

During the meal in the Storchen Hotel my father told Bob not to drink too much, as he wanted him to be his driver on the way home. He had bought himself a beautiful big blue Mercedes car of which he was extremely proud. After the couple had left for their one week honeymoon, my father ordered another bottle of wine, and asked us to join him in a small comfortable lounge in the hotel. Only Bob and I, Papa, Hans and Astra were there. Papa didn't want to go home yet. He was sad to lose Christel, she had always been his favourite, and now she, too, had gone.

He talked about my mother, about our home in Königsberg, his business in Tilsit, and how we all had to fight to get a good living again. He suddenly thanked me for always helping the family.

'You always seemed to find some extra strength from somewhere to get through difficulties. Mama relied on that, although she never said so. You always helped the family, nobody ever helped you. I am glad you could come to the wedding with Bob, my second son. I like you Bob, I am proud of you. I know you will make my daughter happy. I am sorry, Helga, Mama left most of her jewellery to Astra. She probably felt that Astra needed it. I didn't sell Mama's diamond brooch to raise the money for Hans's studies. He had a grant, and I was able to pay him the rest. The brooch had five beautiful diamonds, and I have decided to share them out between you all. I gave Christel her diamond already, there is one for you, Astra. I had a ring made with a diamond for you, Hans, and will give it to you for your future wife when you get married. To the two diamonds which were left I have added a sapphire stone and had a ring made for you, Helga, in appreciation for your help at all times. I felt you deserved the extra stones for the ring.'

With that he took a small jewel case out of his pocket, opened it, took the ring out and put it on my finger. I just looked at him, and the tears ran down my face. My strict and hard father had become a soft, old and lonely man. He probably regretted that he had always punished me so severely when I was young. I could see the love for me in his face. There was so much I would have liked to say, but I didn't. All I said was: 'Thank you,' and hugged and kissed him. We understood one another. Words were not necessary.

'And now we are all going to have a drive through the town,' he said loudly, and got up. 'Come on, my son, Bob, you are going to drive us. You are the only one I trust to drive my beautiful car.'

'He hardly ever let's me drive it,' Hans whispered to me.

Papa opened the sun roof of the car and sat in the back with Astra and Hans. We drove along the lake and through the town and eventually to Papa's flat, where we all were able to shake down for the night.

My brother already worked for my father. So the next day Papa suggested to us that we take Hans back to Graz in Austria to look at his tamping machine. Bob took a film of this type of work on the railway. He found it very interesting. Anything to do with machines would draw Bob's attention. After Austria we travelled to Italy to meet Mino and Christel again, who only had a short honeymoon. Mino and his step-mother owned a house by the Lago Maggiore. We all had a few glorious days together there, swimming in the lake, visiting the different islands, and lying in the sun in the garden.

I felt healthy and relaxed when I came back to England, ready to cope again with a handicapped child and a little boy who would never keep still.

During our holiday I had wondered from time to time how the children were getting on. Peter was so young, did he miss me? Was Victor alright in the home? As soon as we got back, I walked over to Mrs Bunce to fetch Peter. I met him half-way with Anne, and expected him to rush to me. All he said was:

'Hello, Mum, I am going for a walk with Anne,' and carried on walking with her.

I was terribly disappointed. Then I scolded myself. What had I expected on my return? If Peter had rushed to me crying, I would have been convinced that he had been unhappy all the time I had been away.

Now he just accepted my return casually, which meant that he must have been and still was very happy, but I would have liked him to greet me a little more enthusiastically. Peter had had a very happy time with Family Bunce, where everybody spoilt him.

One of the helpers from the home in Bideford brought Victor as far as Salisbury on the train, so we didn't have to make that long journey to fetch him. I hardly recognised him. He seemed to have grown, and he had lost his two front milk teeth. He had been quite happy in the home, but was glad to be with us again. Bob kept on teasing him with the song: All I want for Christmas are my two front teeth.

Victor went back to the Gateway School again. Peter just wouldn't settle down at home. He was unhappy to be without his brother. Every morning when I carried Victor into the school, Peter came with me, and often he cried when we left, as he wanted to stay there. One day Miss Rowell, the headmistress, said:

'Why don't you leave him here? We have children in the nursery class who are only three years old, but if Peter is clean and can go to the toilet alone, he could stay a few hours a day. You could give it a try.'

So I left Peter behind. It was a try-out for the start, but soon became permanent, and I paid the fee for the term. Peter would not stay in his class all the time. From time to time he left and went into Victor's class, and just sat next to him. The teachers were quite tolerant, as he was so young.

Taking both children to school at nine o'clock, and leaving them there until 3.30 p.m. gave me extra time. Bob suggested that I start to work in the factory. The money would help with the school fees, and I would also learn what electro-plating and stove-enamelling was all about. I gradually worked myself through all the departments. This was not easy at times, as I was the boss's wife. The foreman in the plating inspection told Bob to move me after a time, because I became quicker with the inspection of the plated items than the other women. I didn't talk so much, that was the reason. In the wiring shop, they gave me the smallest screws to wire. Nobody liked the job. They hoped I would refuse or walk out. They didn't know me, they thought I was a spoilt Swiss girl. I soon won their respect when I didn't give up. I also had to deal with the people in the polishing shop, and make out the van lists, so that the drivers knew in which order they had to visit the customers. I wrote the dockets for the incoming work when the girl who usually did it was ill. I took over the progress chasing when the progress chaser left, until a new one was engaged, and finished up in the office doing wages and accounts. It was strenuous at times, but interesting, and I could join in with Bob and his father when they were talking about the business, because I knew what it was all about now.

We suddenly had an influx of black workers coming from the West Indies. Some of them had found work in High Wycombe, not far from us, and now more and more people arrived. They couldn't get any more work in High Wycombe, so they had to look for jobs further away. As there was a good bus service to Gt. Missenden, they even came to us to look for work. Most of them were unskilled workers who had worked on farms in the West Indies, and were just not suitable to work in a plating firm with a lot of poison about. Some of them didn't even know how to behave or apply for a job.

I was working in the progress office at the time, and they usually came into this office first, as it was nearest to the factory gate. I had a chap arriving one day with the words:

'Is boss there?'

'Can I help you?' I said.

'Want to see boss, want a job, good worker,' was the reply.

I didn't really know what to do with him, so I said I would find out whether there was a vacancy. I don't think he understood the word vacancy, but because I picked up the phone and dialled, he decided to wait. There was an empty chair and desk standing in the room, so he sat down and put his feet on the desk.

The office paged Bob, and he rang me back. I told him there was an applicant, but didn't know how to explain to him that he was not suitable. Suddenly I remembered that Bob spoke a little German, so I told him in that language to ask me questions, which he did. I only said yes or no, and he soon found out that the man was unsuitable. At the end of the conversation, I told the chap that the boss had no vacancy. He just smiled, but didn't get up. He never understood what I had said. Eventually I told him:

'Boss said - no job!' and kept on repeating it until he took his feet of the desk, looked disappointed at me, and left.

The other incident concerned Charlie. He seemed quite bright, so Bob decided to give him a chance. He employed him for a start in the plating shop to help carry things for the foreman, who could keep an eye on him.

First he took him up to the store room, so that he could be fitted with rubber gloves and wellingtons. He didn't know where to leave his shoes, so Bob showed him his locker. Bob didn't see him anymore after that until the next morning. Charlie had forgotten where his shoes were. Bob reminded him of his locker, and showed it to him again. He was very pleased to find his shoes.

'How did you get home last night,' asked Bob. 'Did you go home in your wellingtons?'

'Yes, boss,' said Charlie. 'Wellingtons not come off.'

Charlie had gone home in his wellingtons, and slept all night in them because he couldn't get them off. It turned out that they were much too small for him. He didn't know his shoe size, so just took the first pair supplied by the storeman. By now his feet were so swollen that it was impossible to get the wellingtons off, they had to be cut off. The next pair supplied to him were really big.

In the afternoon, Bob thought he must go and see how Charlie was getting on. He found him working in the plating shop.

'Boss,' said Charlie, 'water really strong here.'

Bob looked at Charlie's hands, and saw his gloves were torn. The acid solution from the plating vats had burnt Charlie's hands through the holes in the gloves. Bob told the foreman off for not watching Charlie, but he said he was much too busy to keep an eye on Charlie's hands and feet. It was then decided to give him a job loading up brackets into the van. The brackets were zinc plated, and hooked on to a rack. It was Charlie's job to collect these racks from the inspection, two racks at a time, unhook them and throw them or put them into the van. They were not packed, just laid loosely into the back of the van. We did thousands of them at the time for very little money, so there was not a lot of fuss made of them.

From the progress office where I was typing, I could see the inspection, the van drawn up in front of it and Charlie working. The foreman came outside with one rack of brackets, Charlie followed him. The foreman then unhooked one bracket and threw it into the van. As the van was empty he had to use a little force to get these brackets right to the front of the van. He talked to Charlie and probably explained things to him. Charlie went into the inspection, and after a while he came out with two racks. He stopped at the back of the van and looked from one rack to the other. He had no free hand to unhook the brackets.

He decided to lay one rack on to the back flap of the van. After that he unhooked each bracket and threw it with great force into the back of the van. One or two brackets had fallen off the second rack through laying it down. Charlie picked them up, hooked them on again and then started to unhook each bracket from the top down and threw them with great force into the van. When he brought the next two racks out, he knew he had to lay one down to get a free hand. When he picked this one up again, one or two brackets had fallen off and he couldn't reach them. Charlie knew what to do. He climbed into the van, collected the brackets and laid them towards the edge of the flap. He climbed down, picked up these brackets and threw them with great force on to the ones in the front of the van.

By now I realised that Charlie thought the unhooking of the brackets and throwing them into the van was part of the plating process. That's why he threw them so hard. The plating on them would be ruined if he carried on like that. I phoned Bob and explained things. He came and watched smiling Charlie. He was so proud of being able to manage this job at last and gave the brackets a real good throw. After that, Bob got him to sweep the yard. This was really all he was good for. We had too much poison about to let him work in any of the other shops. As we already had a yard man, Bob had to tell him to leave after one week. Elsie, the secretary, filled out his form for his money.

'Are you married?'

'No,' said Charlie.

'Any children?'

'Yes, five children.'

Elsie looked surprised at Charlie.

'Where are your children?' she said.

'At home,' said Charlie.

'You mean in the West Indies?'

'Yes, I need money for lots of children.'

Of course there was no proof, and Elsie knew from before that somehow everybody from the West Indies seemed to have children at home. They had soon found out that if they said they had children, they paid less income tax and got more money. Charlie couldn't read or write, so Elsie put down two children, just in case he did have some, but she never believed that he had five. Charlie left. We were sorry, he had been fun, and he had tried so very hard to do what he was told.

Mrs Bunce left her job and came to work for me once a week for three hours. She also had another job two mornings a week. This suited both of us. Anne became our evening baby sitter and Bob and I were now able to go out in the evenings sometimes. We were always short of money, so we avoided anything expensive. Bob's salary was low. The factory had grown during the war, but as they were not allowed to build then, they had to buy pre-fabricated huts, and make do with the old buildings which were there. The time had now come to make plans for new buildings and a treatment plant to deal with waste water from the plating processes, which would be very expensive. Even with a loan from the bank, the interest still had to be paid. So all profit from the firm went back into new machinery and buildings.

I had my lunch in the factory canteen, which was excellent. The children had a cooked meal at school, so at night there was only a small tea to be made. When I took Victor to Queen Mary's Hospital for his monthly visit, I could leave Peter at school, which was very convenient, as I was back before the school was finished.

Bob worked very hard at the factory, but still had time to make things for the children, especially for Victor. First he built some bunk beds, which were screwed against the wall so that they wouldn't rock. The bottom bunk had two big drawers for toys.

All the time we had to have new ideas to keep Victor occupied so that he wouldn't get bored. Bob built Victor a most ingenious railway layout. Victor was only one year old when Bob came home with the first Hornby 00 engine. He insisted it was for his son, but I knew it was as much for him as for Victor. From then on he carried on buying trucks, engines and the track for the railway. Everything was second-hand and, if broken, he mended it. He kept on watching the paper for adverts about anything to do with his planned train set.

He built a large table, fastened the track to it, and wired it up. There were a great many wires under the table. Unfortunately the train now took over the whole room except for the bunk beds. When Victor had finished playing with it, it took quite a time to take all the engines and trucks off and put them away, and then lean the table against the wall. We didn't want to give the other bedroom up as a playroom, it could be used for visitors to stay the night.

Bob had the clever idea to get the table on to the ceiling. I thought he was crazy. How could we get this big table on to the ceiling. And what about all the wiring underneath, this would look ugly if one looked up.

For days and weeks Bob was in thought. I kept on teasing him.

'What about this train that is going to hang on the ceiling?'

'You wait and see,' he replied. 'I am going to fix up a motor in the attic. All you will have to do in the end is to press a switch on the wall and the table will come down. When Victor has finished playing, you press the switch again and the table goes up. It won't look ugly either because the wiring will be covered up by the legs of the table.'

It all sounded a bit far fetched, but I should have known better. Bob never made statements like that if it couldn't be done. The end result was something which all his friends and relatives came to see, and with which Victor, and later Peter, played for years.

Bob's invention was constructed as follows: He panelled the legs of the table in, so that when they were folded up, they presented a smooth panel beneath the table. He then constructed a winch, powered by an ex-RAF cooling gill motor, which he installed in the attic, with counter-weights to balance the table. Four nylon parachute cords came through the ceiling and were attached to two crossbars with hooks to hook on to large eyes on the table. When the legs had been folded down and the table lowered to the floor, it was unhooked from the crossbars, which were then raised back to the ceiling.

Bob also put up a curtain on the ceiling, which rested on the edge of the table when it was raised. This prevented the dust from settling on to the track when the railway was not in use.

As the fluorescent lamp was within the curtained area, it provided a pleasant diffused light when the railway was up. A switch on the wall operated the up and down movement of the train table.

Victor had all the controls at one point, so that he didn't have to move around the table. This included uncoupling, points, track sections, etc.

Victor would sit for hours in front of the control panel moving the levers and getting the train sorted out in a certain way. Bob would sometimes give him a list stating in what order he should put the trucks. For example, he had to uncouple trucks and leave them in sidings so that they could be re-assembled in the right order, or a carriage had to be brought to another line and left there for repair. The same might have to be done with another engine. There were so many combinations, but all Victor had to do was to work out the best way, and then press switches or move levers. The only thing he could not do was to lift up a truck or an engine when they came off the track because he had moved things too fast. That's where Peter came in. He would climb under the table and come up on the other side and put the truck or engine back on to the rails. It really was a most ingenious game, which taught Victor to concentrate, and kept him happy and quiet.

For his sixth birthday we got Victor a little old gramophone which gave him hours of pleasure. We were able to get all sorts of different small records with music or stories, even German children's songs. Victor was quite musical. He could sing and keep in tune before he could speak. To be kept occupied with his gramophone was also good for his legs, feet and hands. He would sit on his little chair which had been made the right height so that his feet were flat on the floor. The gramophone was on his small table. He lifted the lid up and took out the winding handle. He put it in the hole on the side and wound the gramophone up.

He took a record out of his box, put it on to the turntable very gently, and then lowered the arm with the soundbox down carefully until the needle rested in the groove of the record. The sound came out of the trumpet-shaped horn, which was fastened to the inside of the lid. From time to time he changed the needle. All these movements were good for him, particularly the changing of the needle, which took a bit of practice at first, because of his slight spasticity in his fingers. I could leave him on his own once he had started, as I could always hear the different records, knowing he was alright. There was only one worry, and that was Peter.

Peter was a very boisterous, but kind boy. He could never concentrate long, or sit still for more than a few minutes. At times there was an excuse because of his eczema. When Victor was playing his gramophone, he sometimes burst in, wanting to tell Victor something or just be with him.

He was never very gentle and, in his excitement, could easily push the table, and the gramophone lid would drop on to the arm with the needle and break the record. This had happened once or twice and, although Peter was very sorry and kept on kissing Victor, this didn't mend the record. So, as soon as Peter burst in, Victor would hold the lid of the gramophone with one hand and, with the other hand, try and prevent Peter coming near him.

'No, no,' he would shout. 'Go away, go and sit down, you can listen from over there,' and he pointed to another place. He would then play one of Peter's favourite records for him.

Peter, too, was musical. Just before he was four years old I had taught him to sing Holy Night in German. He had a lovely, sweet and quite strong voice, and Bob and I wondered whether he would be able to sing in one of the boys choirs one day, like Magdalene College in Oxford. He would get a good, free education at the same time. We did take him to an audition there when he was eight years old, but he didn't pass. There were fifteen applicants for two places!

Peter sang his *Stille Nacht* one day at the Gateway School. They were all terribly impressed the way he stood there and sang away, not a bit shy. The Gateway School was owned by Mrs Wallbank, whose husband was the vicar of St. Bartholomew the Great church at Smithfield, London. She also ran another school there. She decided to have a Christmas Nativity in the St. Bartholomew the Great church, with the children from both schools participating. Peter was chosen to sing his *Stille Nacht*.

On the morning of this particular day was a practice in the church, and all parents had to bring their children there. St. Bartholomew the Great is a beautiful old church. When we entered it, the coolness, quietness and the holy atmosphere engulfed us, even Peter suddenly became still. Victor was in his large push-chair, and would remain in it throughout the performance. He was in the choir. The rehearsal went alright, and we all returned in the afternoon. Bob and I sat near the front. The choir sang, some of the older boys and girls read from the Bible, some of the younger ones had learnt a few lines by heart. One or two got stuck. Miss Rowell quickly prompted them. One or two of the little ones were suddenly shy and wouldn't say anything at all. The church was packed with people, it had been advertised quite well and, of course, there were all the parents and probably some grandparents too.

It was Peter's turn, and I wondered whether he would be shy. He was the youngest performer, only three years old, not four until February. He came forward and stood in front of the altar. He had to look up to the organ, which was above the entrance door opposite the altar, where Mr Wallbank, who was playing the organ, would give him a sign to start. Mr Wallbank was playing a little longer, so Peter looked around the church and discovered us. He lifted his hand and gave a quick wave. I pointed to the organ, and mouthed:

'Look up for your cue.'

Mr Wallbank gave him his cue, and Peter started to sing. He sounded and looked like an angel. He had beautiful fair curls, pink chubby cheeks, and his lovely child's voice echoed just right in the church, with its high ceiling and stone walls. The tears just ran down my face, and I could see that even Bob was shaken with the sweetness of this voice in these surroundings. I am usually quite controlled, but at that moment I was terribly touched, and I have never forgotten this incident.

When it was finished, we collected the children. One of the mothers said to me:

'Peter was just like an angel, what a beautiful sweet boy he is.'

I didn't like to tell her that I had just seen him disappearing behind the altar, and that I had to be quick in case he pulled off the altar cloth in his excitement, trying to hide from us. He certainly was no angel in real life.

I asked Peter what it felt like standing there and singing.

'I waved to you,' he said. 'When I was singing, there were funny bum, bum, bums in my ears. It stopped later. - I saw you cry. Why did you cry?'

I didn't reply, he didn't mind, he often asked questions and didn't wait for an answer. The bum, bum, bum in his ears was probably his heart beating fast. He didn't know what shyness or excitement was, but his body did.

Both children were quite happy at the Gateway School. Peter was popular, and often invited to little birthday parties. He loved playing games, and he was never fussy about food. One mother said to me one day:

'I love having Peter coming to our parties, he is no trouble at all.'

'I am so glad he behaves well,' I said. 'I always thought he was too boisterous and wild.'

'Oh, I don't mind that,' said the mother, 'but what I like best is that I never have an odd bit of food left over. I have only got to ask Peter, and he will finish it up for me.'

I wasn't exactly pleased with this reply. It looked as if Peter didn't get enough to eat at home. Both my boys were taught from the start never to waste food, and always to eat everything up. I had starved too much as a refugee; food was precious to me. I never threw anything away. Any left-overs could always go into the stockpot for soup.

Victor was never asked to come to a party, but one day he came home very excited. One of the boys he liked had asked him to come to his birthday. It was usual to give little invitation cards out for these parties, with time, place and date filled in, because one of the parents would have to bring the child by car. Victor had no invitation. I told Victor to ask the boy to let him have one, because I would have to take him, and didn't know the boy's address. I am afraid the boy kept on putting Victor off, and on the actual birthday he said to Victor:

'My Mum said you can't come to the party, there will be too many children, and somebody might push you over, and then you would get hurt.'

For the first time Victor was very seriously upset about his handicap. He cried and cried, and usually he was not a cry baby. We had tried our utmost never to let him feel that he had missed out on anything because he couldn't walk. Even Peter used to run, fetch and carry things for him. This time he was uncontrollable. Suddenly I had an idea:

'Victor, stop crying, I tell you what we are going to do. We are going to have a party for you, and you can invite whoever you want. It is going to be the best party, with lots of games and food, like sausage rolls, cakes and jelly.' That did it, Victor stopped crying, and started to think whom he could ask.

He could write, so I told him to write the names of the children down whom he wanted to invite. I didn't realise what I had let myself in for, because Victor invited the whole school, thirty-five children.

Bob was shocked when I told him that I couldn't very well back out. But, as usual, he came up with a good idea. We were going to have the party in the factory canteen on a Saturday afternoon. The place was big enough to have some games, and we would finish up showing some films, like Mickey Mouse and Charlie Chaplin. Bob's father had by now an even better projector with sound, and Bob knew where to get the films.

Victor proudly gave out all his invitations in breaktime, and told the children that there would be lots of surprises. I made sausage rolls, baked cakes, got jelly ready and little bridge rolls with fillings, and there was plenty of orange and lemon juice.

We played the team games first, and that was a lot of fun, because Victor joined in with Bob pushing him in his push-chair when it was his turn. They had to blow up balloons until they burst, eat dry biscuits and whistle after that, and there was even an egg and spoon race. We had lots of prizes, and everybody enjoyed it. We had no help, but Bob and I found the older children helped the younger ones. We mixed them up for their tea like that too, and when that was finished, they helped to carry the plates into the kitchen, and set out the chairs ready for the films.

Whilst the films were running, the children sat spellbound, and I had time to clear up everything and wash up. By the time I was finished, the first parents arrived to collect their children, but they didn't want to go, so the parents sat down at the back of the hall enjoying the film show also. When I turned on the lights at the end of the last film, I was surprised to see how full the hall was with children and all the parents that had arrived.

Everybody thought it had been a super party. At school they talked about it for weeks. After that, Victor did get one or two invitations, but he said his party was the best.

Life became quite a routine. Taking Bob to work, taking both children to school, going to work, fetching the children, Victor's exercises, preparing a meal, bathing the children, catching up with things in the house at the weekend, sewing, knitting, washing, gardening, and on Sundays going to "Winnats" for the afternoon. This was something I didn't like at times, particularly when I was busy. It was expected of us to visit Mum and Dad on Sundays, at least every other Sunday. We would also meet Pat and Andrew there, so the whole family was together. As I worked all the week, I resented the time to go to "Winnats." I would have preferred to get on with things at home. At least I always took Victor's overalls with me to sew on the leather patches. My mother-in-law remarked that she never saw me without them.

We would have tea and cake in the garden, and sometimes Dad would take out his little tractor with the cart behind it, put the children into it, and drive around the lawn. When Victor was older, he was allowed to drive the tractor, and was terribly proud of this. Whilst Peter was young, I would have to follow them around, watching that when Peter got out of the cart and ran off, he wouldn't fall or walk into the ponds. There were three large ones in the garden. We could swim in one, but after a fish once nibbled my toe, I didn't like to swim in it any more. Peter knew no fear, and I was always uneasy if he was not near me, or in the cart. Often visitors were there, and the men would play croquet, whilst the women talked and I ran after Peter. Sometimes I pushed Victor around in his pram at the same time, which was not so easy on the lawn.

One Sunday before we went home, Mum said she had plenty of vegetables in the garden and I could buy some. I did this, and continued it for a few weeks, but then thought there was really no advantage gained if I bought them from her. On the contrary, I had to always have them on Sunday, whilst if I bought them at the greengrocer, which was the same price, I could buy them when needed. I did my shopping in my dinner hour at work, as I was already in Gt. Missenden then. Mum was surprised when I told her I didn't want any more vegetables. Dad looked at me for a long time, but didn't say anything. A few days later he called in on his way to work, and laid a few tomatoes and a cucumber on to the kitchen table. These were the things he grew in his big greenhouse. He smiled, talked to the children, who were having breakfast, and then went off. He also sometimes called in after work to see the children. He often finished before Bob. Usually the children were having their tea, and he would have a small helping so that he could join them in their meal, he said.

He loved my clear soup with a few noodles or egg in it, and would always ask for this, which made the children laugh. On and off, tomatoes and cucumbers appeared on my kitchen table without charge.

More and more people bought televisions, but we couldn't afford one, we had to pay up the house. Dad decided he needed a more modern one, and gave us his old one. He did the same with his radiogram. He said, because the factory does work for E.K.Cole, he must buy something from them. In any case he would get a good discount. The radiogram was really for Bob, who loved music. He had plenty of records, but only a little portable electric gramophone. He used to take this with him when he ran the Old Tyme dances.

I knew Dad was trying to help us in a roundabout way, and I was grateful to him. He would sometimes give me some encouraging words, particularly when he saw me struggling along, carrying Victor in and out of the car. He could see that my life was not easy, only seldom could I relax.

Mrs Collis was quite pleased about Victor's progress and told me she would like to take Victor into Queen Mary's Hospital into her unit for a time.

'I want to give Victor very extensive physiotherapy,' she said. 'He can join our unit for a few months. We have a school, run by two teachers, so he won't miss out on his learning. I understand he can read already, which is good.'

I was very surprised about this. I had never expected that she would one day take Victor for such a long period into her care. She also told me to go away for a good rest.

'Take Peter,' she continued, 'and go home to Switzerland. Get your husband to come and see Victor every Sunday.'

We hoped Victor would settle down in the unit. He had had a break from us when he went into the home in Bideford, but that was a short stay. Victor didn't want to go to the hospital and, when we left him there, he cried. We were not allowed to see him for two weeks and, when we eventually saw him again on Sunday, he was very happy about this. We took him out for a picnic which I had brought, but he cried again when we left. This was repeated on the next Sunday and the next. Sister said that he soon stopped after we had left. She suggested that we come back and look through the window. She was right, there he was, happily playing with the other children, whilst he had been crying only ten minutes before. Now we took to bribery. We brought him a little present, but told him that he wouldn't get it until we left, and then only if he didn't cry. This worked, and all was peaceful.

I decided to do what Mrs Collis had suggested, and go and see my sister Christel in Italy. She spent the summer months in the big house she shared with her mother-in-law by the Lago Maggiore. Christel was pleased to hear I was coming, and wrote that my father would come also, and maybe Hans. My father wrote and said: 'Come by air and I will help you pay for the fare.'

Peter got terribly excited when he was told we would fly to Milan, in Italy, to see his aunt.

The holiday with my sister turned out different from what we expected. We flew to Milan, stayed a night in Christel's flat, and the next day Mino took us to Cerro by the Lago Maggiore. It was the month of May, flowers were out everywhere, and the weather was sunny and hot. The water in the lake was cold, so we didn't swim. I lay in the sun in my sister's beautiful garden and relaxed. We expected Papa for the weekend, but he didn't come, and there was no news from him either. The telephone was out of order, and nobody would come and mend it. Cerro, where the house was situated, was a small village in those days, and if one wanted anything special, like the repair of the telephone, one just had to wait until the engineers decided they could spare the time to come as far as Cerro.

Christel and I were very worried. We phoned Zürich several times from a friend's house, but there was no reply. Two days later we received a telegram from my brother:

'Cannot contact you by phone - express letter follows.'

The letter arrived and gave us an explanation. My father had had a heart attack and was in Heidelberg, Germany, in hospital. Papa had been travelling on the Autobahn when he suddenly had a terrible pain across his chest. He knew that this pain was serious, and that he had to find help quickly. He turned off the Autobahn to Heidelberg, and drove into the town. He saw a sign pointing towards a hospital and followed it, stopping at the front entrance. He staggered in and collapsed in the foyer. It was the best place, help was there straight away, and he was put into intensive care. The hospital staff looked through my father's things, but couldn't find any address of the next of kin. When my father eventually told them to get in touch with Hans, he couldn't be contacted, as he was travelling. A telegram was sent to the Zürich address, which my brother found. He drove to Heidelberg straight away and found my father in hospital. My father's car was still standing outside with a note that he had permission to leave it there. Hans knew that I wanted to see Papa, so he suggested that Peter and I travel to Zürich by train. He would meet us in Papa's big car, and take us to Heidelberg.

The long journey by train to Zürich was rather strenuous. Peter soon got bored. He wouldn't sit still, he was only three years old and wanted to run about. We kept on walking along the corridor. Hans picked us up from the station, and we eventually got to Heidelberg.

Peter had never met his other grandfather. He was very sorry that he was ill. We explained to him that his grandfather had to be in bed because of tummy ache. After a little while Peter took his shoes off and decided that he, too, had tummy ache, and wanted to join his grandfather in bed. Papa was terribly touched by this, and nearly cried. My father was weak and lonely, and tried to be brave. He was tired and overworked, said Hans. All he could think of was the building up of another business. He had lost everything he had ever worked for, everything he possessed, and he was getting older, time had become precious and short. It was a good thing that my brother was in the business now. Being an engineer, he was able to take over.

Peter and I stayed a few days in Heidelberg and helped Hans to look for a place where my father could recuperate once he left the hospital. We then flew back from Frankfurt, where Hans took us by car. I was sorry to leave my father, but he promised to come to England as soon as he was fit again, and the business running well under Hans' guidance.

Bob was pleased to see us back home, and so was Victor when we saw him on Sunday. He had a big surprise for us, he could ride a tricycle. His feet had to be strapped to the pedals. This was a wonderful improvement. Now Victor was mobile, we didn't have to push him everywhere in his chair.

We told him that from now on there would be no presents when we leave as a reward for not crying, but we would be buying him a tricycle as soon as he came home. He would even be allowed to come with us to choose it.

Every Sunday we travelled to Queen Mary's hospital in Carshalton, month after month. I think the car knew the way in the end. Each time we took Victor either for a picnic or somewhere else for tea, so that once a week he would get away from the hospital. His favourite place was Croydon airport, where one could have tea and cake and watch the aeroplanes.

If the weather was nice, we took him to a nearby park and picnicked on the grass. Some children in the unit hardly had any visitors. Parents were often glad to have found somebody to look after their handicapped child. This was rather sad. So, when we came, we always brought some extra fruit and sweets for those who were not as privileged as Victor.

Some children had aunts, uncles or grandparents that came to visit them, Victor always had both or one of us, with Peter. He was never alone on Sundays. Bob couldn't always come with me, because of extra work in the factory. I didn't enjoy these trips alone, because of Peter. He just could not and would not sit still. Mrs Bunce took Peter for the day a few times, and also my friend Pam and her parents, which was wonderful. To sit still and also to keep quiet for three hours whilst I was driving was just too much for Peter.

After six months, Mrs Collis phoned and asked us both to come and see her during the week, so that she could talk to us about Victor's progress. Bob took a day off, we left Peter at school, and Miss Rowell said that if we were a little late back, she would keep Peter with her in the school.

We got to Queen Mary's Hospital and had to wait quite a time. Eventually an assistant came and took us to an exercise room and told us to wait, closing the doors behind us. It was a big room, with different apparatus for physiotherapy scattered along the walls. I was looking around, wondering why we had been asked to come to this room, when the doors opposite opened and Mrs Collis slowly walked in holding Victor by his hand. I couldn't believe my eyes and a lump came into my throat. Victor was walking. Slowly, jerkily, he lifted one leg and put it down gently, gradually flattening his foot on to the floor. After that he did the same with the other leg. These were the first steps I saw Victor make.

He had tried before when he had the irons on his legs, but then he walked on his toes, holding on to his walking pen with both hands. These were real steps. He was smiling all over his face about the surprise he gave us. I started to cry, I really cried hard, and whispered:

'Oh Victor, you can walk. Now everything will be alright.'

I rushed to him and took him into my arms. He was my baby again, my little boy who had given me so much heartache.

'I have done it, I have done it,' said Victor. 'Mrs Collis told me to keep it as a surprise. I never told you that I had learnt to walk, I never did.'

Bob, too, was terribly touched, and hugged him and called him his big brave boy. Mrs Collis smiled, which she rarely did, and said:

'Victor has worked really hard. This was the reason why I took him into the unit, to see whether he was ready to put his weight on to his legs. He has still a long way to go, but he has made a good start. I would like to keep him for another month.'

After another four weeks Victor came home. When I fetched him, I was shown his new exercises, and the way he had to be helped and guided when walking. He was unable to walk on his own. I had to hold his hand and, when he did his slow short steps, he needed to be reminded to lift his legs up, and to put his feet flat on to the floor. Walking was a very, very slow process. He was never allowed to hurry. We always had to allow extra time when he walked. It was much quicker to carry him. He had become quite heavy, and I often had backache from lifting him.

Victor was now seven years old, and I felt it was time that he left the Gateway School. There were too many little children about, and not enough big boys. We had a number of Preparatory Schools in our district. Bob and I went to see them all, but none would take Victor because of his disability. The headmaster of Prestwood Lodge School was prepared to give him a try. He was a professor of mathematics, a clever but, at times, a vague and forgetful man. His wife, too, was teaching, and I think she was really running the school.

When Victor came back from Queen Mary's Hospital, we bought him the promised tricycle. He chose it himself. It was maroon, and had a box in the back where he could put in some toys or a few of his favourite belongings. He kept this tricycle for a year or two, and then Peter took it over. We had to buy Victor a larger and stronger one as he had now got too big and heavy for the other one. The time came when the saddle couldn't be raised any more, and Bob had to make an extension for it. Victor outgrew this tricycle also. He became so heavy that he always had to lean forward, otherwise his weight would lift the front wheel and throw him backwards on to the ground. He did have several accidents like that. The worst one was when he had joined the Scouts.

Bob or I would take him to the Scouts meeting with his tricycle. One day when I fetched him and Peter, who had joined the Cubs, the Scout Master said Victor had had a bad fall backwards on his trike. By doing so, he had hurt his front teeth. The top teeth had jerked behind the bottom teeth and bent these forward. I looked shocked at his mouth. There was no bleeding, but the bottom teeth, which were good teeth, were at an angle.

I got Victor home and phoned my dentist at his home, explaining the position. It was seven o'clock in the evening, but the dentist told me to bring him to the surgery straight away. Mr Keen pushed the teeth very gently back, and then just held them there for half an hour. He told Victor a few funny stories from his experiences as a dentist to keep his mind at ease, as the poor boy was quite worried about maybe losing his teeth. After that Mr Keen said the teeth might get black if the roots were hurt. Luckily this didn't happen, and Victor and I have to thank this dentist that those teeth survived.

Victor started at Prestwood Lodge School, and was allowed to bring his tricycle, which he could use to cycle around at breaktime. Every morning I took Peter to school, then went on to Prestwood Lodge, where I carried Victor indoors and sat him at his desk. After that I unloaded the tricycle and put it into the bicycle shed. At breaktime somebody would get him his tricycle, and he was off exploring the grounds of the school.

The building was an old manor house with lots of parkland. Mr Oakley, the headmaster, had a small railway in the park. Victor soon got interested, and watched Mr Oakley fiddling with the railway engine, as it was mostly in need of some repair. The headmaster took to Victor, and it was he who showed him that mathematics could be fun, and didn't need to be hard work. Victor settled down at the school, and the try-out period became a permanent stay.

From the moment Victor returned from Queen Mary's Hospital, all he wanted to do in his spare time was to look at TV. He even got Peter to do it but, at least, being so much younger, he got bored with some of the programmes which he didn't understand, and ran off, finding something else to do. Victor knew every programme by name, and at what time it was on. He said the TV in the hospital was on all the time. In the evening, the night nurses would look at it with the sound turned down but, if he crawled to the bottom of the bed, he could look at it and hear it. We had a very difficult time with Victor because we didn't want the TV on all the time. If we turned it off, there were tantrums and cross words. When I did his exercises, he wouldn't do them properly unless he was allowed to see certain programmes. The TV went wrong, and Bob had to take it in to be repaired.

He told the owner of the shop, whom he knew well, not to rush the repair job, we were in no hurry to get it back. This broke the spell, and by the time the TV came back, Victor had started to play with his gramophone and his train again, and was quite happy to look only at the programmes we chose.

Prestwood Lodge, being a boys school, concentrated quite a bit on games, in which Victor couldn't take part. He soon got bored watching the others. On Sports Day, Mr Oakley organised a race in which Victor could participate with his tricycle. He positioned the big boys at the back, the younger ones a little more forward, and Victor even more towards the front of the field. Victor won the race, and at the prize-giving he received a small can of oil for his tricycle. The headmaster must have known who would win the race!

I kept on thinking whether there was something else Victor could do instead of sport. Then Victor came up with a new idea. He had seen a series of films on TV describing the adventures of a deep sea diver. Victor announced that he would like to be a deep sea diver when he was older.

'You will have to learn to swim first,' I said.

I didn't want to tell him that with his disability he would never be able to be a diver. I felt it was better for him to find this out for himself. Now Victor wanted to learn to swim. I organised a swimming lesson at the Aylesbury outdoor swimming pool, and took Victor and Peter there after school. Peter splashed about in the little children's pool, and was quite happy. This was a very small pool which the sun had warmed up. The big pool was cold. The swimming instructor didn't enter the pool. He put a harness around Victor, and made him crawl into the water. Victor shivered, his legs became even stiffer, he couldn't move them at all. He did some arm movements, really only splashing about, and tried to be brave. After about ten minutes, and blue in the face, I lifted him out and into a bath towel. He never said a word. He knew now he couldn't go into cold water to learn to swim.

The instructor suggested that I try Stoke Mandeville Hospital, where they had a heated pool for the paraplegic patients. With Victor's handicap, he might get permission to swim there.

The next day, when the children were at school, I took some time off from work and went to Stoke Mandeville Hospital. I was lucky working in my husband's factory, I could often take time off, and bring the office work home to do in the evening. In the hospital I found the pool and met Mr Atkinson who was in charge of it. I told him about Victor, his handicap, his treatment, his school, and his dream to be a deep sea diver. Mr Atkinson smiled, then he shook his head.

'I am sorry, but I cannot let him use the pool unless he has treatment in this hospital, even if he wants to be a deep sea diver.'

I liked his humour, he was a nice man.

He continued: 'The only one who can give you permission is Professor Guttmann, who is in charge of the paraplegic department. You can try and see him. If he permits it, I am only to pleased to help Victor and teach him to swim.'

Professor Guttman was quite a famous man. It was he who had changed the lives of many paraplegics during the last war. Before that it was always taken for granted that if you had a back injury and got paralysed below the waist, you were now an invalid, either permanently bedridden or a wheelchair case who needed help all the time.

A number of soldiers had back injuries during the war, and were brought to Stoke Mandeville Hospital. Professor Guttmann told them that there was nothing wrong with the top part of their bodies, and encouraged them to develop it to such an extent that they could live independent lives again. He had different sport activities for them, like archery, basket ball and swimming. The first two could be performed from wheelchairs. Professor Guttmann organised sports competitions for handicapped people, and built it up to such an extent that it became world renowned. He was the founder of the handicapped Olympic Games. Everybody knows Sir Ludwig Guttmann's Sports Centre in Stoke Mandeville near Aylesbury, with its Olympic sized swimming pool. Sir Guttmann, as he is now called, roused the nation's conscience, and got people and industry to pay for the large Spinal Injury Department at the hospital, with all the latest equipment and sports facilities.

So this was the man I had to see now. I was quite nervous, but I kept on saying to myself that he can only say no, but I must try. I went to his office and met the secretary. I asked whether I could see Professor Guttmann.

'Have you got an appointment?' she asked, and looked at her appointment's book.

'No,' I replied, and repeated what Mr Atkinson had said about the permission I needed for Victor being able to use the heated pool.

'Have you got a letter from your doctor?' was the next question.

Again I replied: 'No,' and explained that Victor had treatment at Queen Mary's Hospital in Carshalton. She said Mr Guttmann was a very busy man, only saw patients recommended by a doctor and, flicking through the appointment's book, added:

'I cannot even give you an appointment for the next two months.'

That cannot be true, I thought, people with sudden injuries could die by then. Just then the door opened and a bespectacled grey-haired man in an elegant dark suit entered and quickly walked across the room, opening the door to the other office.

'Mr Guttmann,' called the secretary, jumping up and grabbing a folder, 'I must have some signatures from you, please.' She ran after him, and caught him in the doorway, handing him the folder.

It is now or never, I thought. I must get hold of him, I will never have another or better chance again. My heart was beating fast, my thoughts going even faster.

'Mr Guttmann,' I said, 'please may I see you for a few minutes. I promise you it will only take three minutes what I have to say. I will time myself,' and I pointed to my watch. 'I will leave your office after three minutes. I have a problem with my seven year old son who cannot walk.' I hoped to get his sympathy by saying this.

He looked startled at me, because I had spoken rather fast so that the secretary couldn't interrupt me. She looked furiously at me saying:

'I am sorry Mr Guttmann, I have explained to the lady that you are very busy ...'

'Come in,' said Professor Guttmann interrupting her, and opened the door wide.

I stepped inside the office, and he went and sat down at a large desk full of untidy papers. He motioned to the chair opposite, but I didn't sit down, I wanted to show him that it really wouldn't take more than three minutes to say what I had to say. Lifting up my arm so that I could see my watch, I started off telling him about Victor, the premature baby they wanted to put into a home, how at last I had found somebody with a treatment to get him on to his legs, and even a boys school which he was allowed to attend with his tricycle. Because he couldn't participate in sport in the afternoons, it would be wonderful if I could bring him to Stoke Mandeville to learn to swim, and give him the extra exercises like that. I mentioned that I had already seen Mr Atkinson, who was willing to take on Victor if he, Professor Guttmann, would give permission. I concluded, glancing at the watch:

'Three minutes have gone. Thank you for listening to me.'

Professor Guttmann watched me with a serious and thoughtful expression on his face until I had finished, then he suddenly smiled.

'You love your son very much, don't you? You would do anything for him, I can see that. Even pushing into my office.'

'I didn't push myself into your office, you very kindly asked me in, and I have two sons.'

Now he laughed, asked whether my second son was alright, and then replied that, if Mr Atkinson had the time and was prepared to teach Victor, he saw no reason why Victor couldn't use the pool. He called his secretary, and told her to make the necessary arrangements. He shook my hand and wished me luck with Victor, his walking and his swimming.

The secretary wasn't very pleased with me, and told me so, but I had achieved what I had come for.

Mr Atkinson said I could come twice a week in the afternoon. I arranged with Victor's school that I could pick him up when the others had games, and take him to Stoke Mandeville by car. Already after the second lesson, Victor could float on his back, and it wasn't long before he could swim. He swam on his back, with strong arm movements, kicking his legs occasionally so that they wouldn't sink down. He never made the swimming movements with his legs. He also learnt the breast stroke, but again only swimming with his arms.

Victor in Heated Pool

Victor became a good strong swimmer, and won a gold medal in one of the swimming competitions when he was older. In the school holidays I took Peter with me, as I couldn't leave him alone at home. Mr Atkinson suggested that I bring his swimsuit along, and then he could splash about in the little pool which was not very deep. So now both boys could talk about their swimming experiences.

In the winter months, the swimming for Victor was quite exhausting for me. Victor only had a certain time in which I could get him away from school, and everything had to be done quickly. I would park close to the stadium, carry him in, undress him, put on his swimsuit and slide him into the water. His walking was much too slow to let him do it. I was dressed warmly because of the cold weather, but even if I took my coat off, I still felt hot because the atmosphere in the pool changing rooms was hot and damp. To dress Victor was even more strenuous. He was sticky and damp. Even by using powder, I could never get him dry properly. He had to have his long overalls on, socks and boots which, at any time, were difficult to put on. By the time I had finished, the sweat was pouring off me. I staggered with that big heavy child to the car, to get him back to school. I was glad of the cold air outside, but that was not very healthy for me. I often had a stiff neck.

The other things that happened in 1956 were that I took a course in First Aid, run by the local Red Cross, and got my certificate, and that my sister-in-law Pat had her second baby, a girl called Hilary, just before Christmas. So we now had two children each and Bob's parents three grandsons and one adored grand-daughter.

Victor with Big Tricycle

CHAPTER FOUR

Sad Event - Wheelchair - School Changes

Hans wrote to say that although my father had recovered from his heart attack, he was not well at all. He went to recuperate in a lovely rest home, a kind of castle, where he had a beautiful room in the tower overlooking the countryside. He discharged himself after two weeks, saying that the people there were all old and ready to die. He wasn't going to wait for that.

Papa returned to his flat in Zürich, but kept on having trouble with his stomach. He couldn't keep his food down, and had to go to the toilet too often. He had taken in a lodger, a nurse who had decided to study medicine. In return for food and lodgings, she looked after him. He called her the lady doctor, and was pleased that she was there, because he even needed her sometimes at night. She was a kind woman, and seemed to become very devoted to my father. Hans was concerned about this close relationship, but had no time nor any intention of interfering.

'Please come and sort things out,' wrote Hans. 'I know Papa is ill, but he won't see a doctor. He says it is a virus, and he will get better soon. You are the older sister and I think Papa would listen to you. Astra is hopeless; she has offended the lady doctor on her last visit, and Papa has told her not to come again.'

Bob and I decided that we would all go to Switzerland for the summer holiday. I wanted Victor and Peter to see their grandfather, and I wanted to know what was the matter with him. We took the car, and Victor had his big push-chair in the boot. We flew with the car across the Channel, leaving from Lydd airport. Everything was terribly exciting for the children. Victor was allowed to stay in the car at the airport, whilst the attendant drove the car on to the plane. By the time we walked across the tarmac and arrived in the plane, he was already sitting there, pleased that he was the first one. The plane was small taking only two cars and some motorbikes, and took half an hour to cross the Channel.

We drove through Germany, and stopped in Stuttgart to see the TV tower with the turning restaurant, which was then a novelty. As we were able to stop very close to the tower, we didn't bother with Victor's push-chair, but made him walk slowly to the entrance. Bob and I usually held him one on either side, whilst Peter would skip off. People seemed to stare much more at Victor than they did in England. Because of the war, the English community had more readily accepted handicapped people than they had in Germany. The Germans, too, had their wounded from the war, and accepted them, but handicapped children were kept at home, or somewhere quiet, but not brought out into public places like the Stuttgart TV tower and restaurant.

We went up in the lift, enjoyed the view from the top, even had an ice cream in the restaurant, and came down again. Bob carried Victor whilst we were in the restaurant, but when we came out of the lift, Victor walked again, slowly and jerkily. It was most embarrassing the way people stared at us, even turned round to look at us. Victor felt it, and his walking became nervous.

'People keep on staring at us,' he said. 'I don't like it.'

'Right,' I said, 'in that case we will just stare back. What we will do is this: When the next people stare at us, I will count one, two, three, then we will stop and just stare at them until they have passed.'

We slowly walked on. Two ladies openly staring at us, approached. Their husbands followed behind.

'One, two, three,' I whispered. We stopped, and all three of us just stood there staring at them. They were most embarrassed and looked away, then turned to their husbands and complained to them about people staring at them! Victor didn't understand German, but could see their embarrassment, and thought it was fun. He wanted to do it again, but we had reached the car by then. We did it a few times after that, and it helped Victor to overcome his embarrassment.

I was always conscious of people looking at me when I walked with Victor or carried him. Sometimes there would be dead silence when I entered a public place such as a restaurant carrying Victor. It needed a lot of courage then to pretend I hadn't noticed anything. It took me years to learn to enter a place with Victor with an attitude of: I don't care what you all think. This is my son and you can stare at him and me as much as you like. I don't even see you. You don't exist.

We arrived in Zürich and found my father quite ill. I met the lady doctor, and thought her kind and concerned. She was a qualified nurse who, at the age of thirty, had decided to study medicine. She had a little money for her studies, but not enough to cover her living expenses. She was happy to care for my father. At the moment she had holidays too. The new term wouldn't be starting until October.

Papa was in bed, but got up to be with us all for a little while. When he returned to his bedroom, I went to talk to him alone. First we talked about the lady doctor.

'I like her, Papa,' I said. 'Are you going to marry her?'

'No, my child, nobody can replace your mother. She is kind, she is good, and she prays for me. She is a strict catholic, and doing good is part of her religion. If she can convert a soul, she is convinced that she will have a place in heaven. I am afraid that is not a person I could live with. Things are alright for the moment.'

Papa said he was glad I had come, and asked me, or actually Bob, for a great favour. He couldn't talk to Bob, so I would have to translate. He had made up his mind to go into hospital for an examination, as his stomach just didn't get better.

'I have only waited until you came so that I could see you all. I want to go to Freiburg in Germany into hospital. That's where the lady doctor used to work. She knows all the specialists and nurses there, and will come with me. I intended to go by train, but I am rather weak, and I don't want the lady doctor to carry all the luggage. Do you think Bob would take me by car? He could be back the same day, it is only just across the border.'

Papa never liked asking people for favours, so I was surprised by what he said. He must really feel bad, I thought, otherwise he wouldn't have asked. Of course Bob agreed, and early the next morning the three of them left on their own. There was no point in me and the children going with him, he was taken care of by the lady doctor. Before he left, he took me in his arms and held me for a long time.

'You are the best of the lot,' he whispered. 'Take care, and never lose your courage.'

Bob returned the same evening. He said they had a good trip, but he was surprised about the hospital.

'It is a Holy place, with pictures of Jesus everywhere, and the nurses are all nuns. I had a good lunch there, they even gave me a bottle of beer. Papa has a lovely room, and the lady doctor can sleep next door so that she can attend to him if he needs somebody at night. She had arranged all this beforehand. I hope your father will like this place. It is very religious, very Catholic.'

I felt uneasy about this place, but my father had chosen it. He had told me that he knew that the lady doctor was a strict Catholic. If they were kind to my father, and the doctors could cure him, then it didn't matter what the place was like.

We continued our holiday, travelling to my sister in Italy, and had a relaxing and enjoyable time with her by the Lago Maggiore. Christel had had her first baby by now, Richard, and the three children gave us quite a bit of work, but also lots of fun. The lake was warmer than the last time I was there, as it was summertime now, and we could go swimming every day.

We returned home feeling good after the holiday and life carried on as usual. The bombshell came in October. My father died suddenly. He had never left the Freiburg hospital, as the doctors didn't seem to be able to cure him of his stomach trouble.

To be able to go to the funeral, I had to find somebody to look after the children. Mrs Bunce offered to have Peter again, but what should we do with Victor?

The best place of course would be Queen Mary's hospital, I thought, where he would get all the attention needed. When approached, Mrs Collis said straight away that she would take him into the unit. Bob didn't come to the funeral; he couldn't be spared from the factory, and also, there would have been nobody to visit Victor on Sundays. The grandparents had never visited him before in Queen Mary's hospital, either.

This time I went by train. Everything had to be done quickly. The children's clothes had to be got ready, my ticket and my own packing, and the worry about some dark clothes were on my mind all the time. My friend Pam had a beautiful black coat which she lent me. I wore it for the journey, and it looked very elegant.

Hans picked me up from the station and took me to the hotel, where all the others had already arrived. There was Astra and Christel with Mino. Christel had been able to leave her little boy Richard with her sister-in-law. I arrived in the late afternoon, and the funeral had been arranged for the next day, twelve o'clock. I wanted to know straight away why it was a funeral and not a cremation. It had always been my parents' wish to be buried together. When my father moved to Zürich, he had my mother's urn transferred. I had assumed that my father's ashes would be buried next to hers. If there was no cremation, there would be no ashes.

The lady doctor told us that two days before my father died he had become a Catholic, and could therefore not be cremated. She handed us a statement which he apparently had made, saying that of his own free will he desired to enter the Catholic faith. It was signed by the attending father, the specialist and a doctor, all from the hospital where my father was. She had therefore made all the arrangements for a burial in a Catholic cemetery.

We were all shocked. It was such a surprise. My father had never mentioned this to anybody, not even my brother, who had visited him regularly. I thought of what my father had said to me about the lady doctor when I saw him last - If she can convert a soul, she is convinced that she will have a place in heaven.

Well, if this was true, she certainly got her place in heaven. It was my father's signature on the paper, but did he know what he signed? Was he converted, or did he do it to please the lady doctor? We would never know. All arrangements were made in our absence, and the funeral was the next day. Christel wanted to stop it all. She didn't believe that my father had become a Catholic, but Hans also told us that my father had left the lady doctor the same amount of money as for us children. By doing this, he had quite openly acknowledged that he appreciated her care for him, and that she was as important to him as the members of his family. The lady doctor said Papa had also given her a lovely ring, but when she showed it to us, nobody said a word. We all recognised it. My father had a ring made with a diamond from my mother's brooch, which was supposed to be for Hans's future wife. It was Hans who lost out, but he said he didn't mind. He wanted no quarrel, neither did I. My father wasn't buried yet. Christel was overruled.

We all had our doubts, but where was the proof?

My father had died very peacefully, said the lady doctor. She had left him for a little while, and when she returned he was asleep, never to wake up again. His heart just stopped. He wouldn't have lived long in any case, as he also had lung cancer.

It rained at the funeral, and everything was strange and unfamiliar to us because of the catholic service, but all was beautifully done. We four children stood by the graveside and cried. It was so sad that Papa had to be buried there. Who would ever go and visit his grave? We all lived so far away, and Freiburg was not on our route when we visited one another. My parents are together now, I thought, that's the important point. Here, we only bury the remains. We all have to get on with our lives, and Papa's last words to me were: Take care, and never lose your courage.

We all had a meal together, Astra, Hans, Christel and Mino, the lady doctor and myself, a small sad party. We decided, now that the funeral was over, there was no need to stay on in Freiburg, and we could all go to Zürich. It was necessary to go through Papa's papers and things, which we could do together before we split up again. Christel and Mino had come by car from Milan, so they took Astra with them. I went with Hans and the lady doctor, who wanted to get her belongings out of the flat now. She was going to carry on with her studies in Germany. My father, having left her some money, gave her the opportunity to study where she liked.

After two weeks I was home again, and phoned Mrs Collis to say that I would come and fetch Victor. She told me to leave him in the hospital another week and get over the shock of losing my father. I had Peter alone at home now, which was rather nice. He could have all my attention. I often felt that I gave Victor more of my time because he needed it. Peter was never jealous; he didn't notice that I had so much to do with Victor, like his exercises, watching his walking, and carrying him all the time.

I always tucked Peter in at night and told him stories, which he enjoyed, or sang to him. Being younger than Victor, he went to bed before him. In this way I tried to make up to him for the time I had spent solely with Victor during the day.

As long as the children were at school, I could manage to go to work. The difficulties arose in the school holidays. Some of the work I could bring home, but for part of it I had to be in the factory. On the days Mrs Bunce came to do some cleaning, I could leave the boys in her care for a couple of hours, enough time to fetch the work from the office and see to a few things in the factory. Even Anne could take the children out for a walk in the afternoon if the weather was good. But unfortunately Mrs Bunce moved to Prestwood to a bigger house. Now it was too far for her to come to me any more. Bob and I thought of an au pair girl. My sister and mother-in-law seemed to be quite successful with them. I had been very unfortunate with Gritli, which had put me off.

We had two very nice girls, but they only stayed six months. One of them, Marianne, played the piano a little, which was useful, as Victor by then had piano lessons at school. Both boys were musical, a gift inherited from Bob and his family.

The moment Victor started with piano lessons, we, too, had to have a piano. We had a small organ which Bob had bought for 10/- (50p) when he was twelve years old. To play it, one had to pump the two foot pedals to work the bellows.

Dad had always promised Bob that he could have the piano which stood in the factory canteen. Unfortunately we didn't have the space for it, so it was left there. It was a very big heavy instrument, as it was also a pianola, and two boxes with rolls of music went with it.

Bob built a conservatory cum playroom on to the back of the house. He had finished the boiler house, and I had got my central heating. Using the side wall of the boiler house, he designed a framework for big windows resting on a low brick wall, and taking up the space of the back of the dining and living rooms. It made a very big extra room. One stepped down from the dining room into the playroom, and through some glass French doors on to a terrace and the garden. So that the two rooms indoors were not too dark, the roof was made from corrugated clear plastic.

Along the brick wall was a long wooden bench, closed in with folding down doors, where the toys were kept. Next to it stood the big piano/pianola. We also had a large folding table and some chairs in the room, and would have nearly all our meals there in the summer months, with the windows and doors open when it was hot. I got an old carpet at an auction so that Victor didn't get hurt on the wooden floor, and the children would play there for hours. To put the toys away, they only had to fold down the doors under the seat, push them in and lift the doors up again, as they closed with a magnetic catch.

It was difficult for Victor to do the pumping action of the foot pedals to play the pianola, so Peter would do this with his hands, and Victor would pretend to play Overtures or the Moonlight Sonata. Later on, when his legs were stronger, he could do it, but we had to tie his chair to the piano, as otherwise it would gradually move backwards.

The little organ was sold to the small local Catholic church for £45, giving Bob an excellent profit.

Eventually, in 1958, we did have an au pair girl, Gisela, who stayed with us for eighteen months. She spoke no English when she arrived, but in four months she was able to hold a simple conversation. I spoke a few German words to her, and sometimes explained something in German, but otherwise she only heard English, and had to struggle along with the language. Although, by the time she left, she spoke quite good English, she never learnt to write in the language, and therefore could hardly read. I organised some evening classes for her, but she soon gave up, finding it too difficult.

By now Victor had grown out of his push-chair and, although I could always take his tricycle when we went out, he couldn't come shopping with me when it was raining, because the boot of the car had to be left open when the tricycle was in it. At other times, Peter and I would go into the shops, and Victor would wait outside, sitting on his trike. One day he had some pocket money and wanted to look at some little dinky cars which he had started to collect. My back was very bad that day. I just couldn't lift Victor and carry him into the shop. Woolworth, in Amersham, had a good selection of cars, so I went to see the manager, and explained the situation. He was very understanding, and permitted Victor to cycle round the shop. It was a big enough place, and Victor has never forgotten this.

I made enquiries, and found out that, as Victor was handicapped, he was entitled to have a free wheelchair from the NHS. I filled out an application form, and after three months the wheelchair arrived. It was quite big and heavy, weighing 40lb. I found it impossible to lift into the boot of the car. The boot flap folded down to an angle of thirty degrees, and the wheelchair had to be lifted over the top of the flap and down into the boot. Once this was done, one couldn't close the boot either. Bob could lift the wheelchair in and out. If we were together and the weather was fine, we could take the wheelchair. If it was raining, Victor had to stay in the car.

There were other wheelchairs about. I had seen them in Stoke Mandeville Hospital, where Victor went swimming. I wrote to the NHS explaining that I wanted a smaller chair. The reply was a form to fill out. Bureaucracy gone mad, I thought, when I read the paper. It was a general form covering anything supplied by the NHS for handicapped people. It started off with a great number of questions concerning artificial limbs, limb boxes and the transport of them. Right at the end were two questions of interest to me. Do you possess a wheelchair, do you need a wheelchair. This form didn't help me at all. I had a wheelchair, but wanted to change it for a lighter one. I discovered that the supply depot for limbs, tricycles and wheelchairs was near Oxford, not too far from us, and made up my mind to go there. I didn't fill the form out, but wrote a letter explaining why I returned the empty form, and said I would come in person to put my case. I also asked when it was most convenient, and could I make an appointment.

There was a very quick reply from the head of the wheelchair department. I forget his name, so let's call him Mr Smith. He informed me that if I had a wheelchair, I was very fortunate, as there was a long waiting list. He said he was a very busy man who worked, like everybody else in the department, from 9 a.m. - 5 p.m, and it was not necessary to make an appointment. His letter finished with the sentence: There is no point in you coming to see me, as we have no other wheelchairs.

'Well, that's it,' said Bob. 'We will just have to find out where they make these smaller wheelchairs, and buy one ourselves.'

'I am going to see Mr Smith,' I said. 'You find out how to get there. I want to meet this man.'

Bob usually drew me a map, otherwise I would get lost. I didn't mind driving anywhere, except London, if I had a map drawn by Bob.

I wrote to Mr Smith and informed him of the day and time of my arrival, and said that I didn't mind waiting if he was busy. When I got there, the secretary knew straight away who I was. She asked me to wait in the corridor, where three empty chairs were placed against the wall. I waited nearly an hour. From time to time people came out of different offices, chatting to one another. Some looked surprised at me, but nobody said anything. I had dressed quite elegantly, and put on a little discreet make up. I wanted to impress. I was nervous and felt uneasy. In my mind I went over possible questions, and what I would answer.

The secretary came to fetch me. We went through her room, she opened the door to Mr Smith's office and announced: 'Mrs Gerhardi to see you, Mr Smith.' I stepped inside and she shut the door behind me. Mr Smith was sitting behind his desk. He was about forty years old, with thinning mouse-coloured hair, and glasses which had slid to the bottom of his nose, so that he could look over them. He raised his eyebrows as if he wanted to say - I didn't expect somebody like you - and started talking straight away. The gist of it was the same as in his letter. There was no other wheelchair, it was a waste of his and my time to come ... etc. He hadn't offered me a seat, and he hadn't risen from his chair when I entered. He probably thought I would leave as soon as he had finished speaking. He looked tired and overworked, and I felt sorry for him. With that, I lost my nervousness and became calm. I hardly listened to him, I just let him talk. Suddenly he stopped. I think his temper had evaporated.

I looked at him with a little shy smile and said:

'Do you mind if I sit down?' With that I took a chair which was next to the door where I had come in, put it opposite the desk and sat down facing him.

'Yes, of course,' he said and rose a little from his chair and then sat down again.

'Now you have had your say, will you please give me the chance to have mine?' I didn't wait for a reply, but continued: 'Have you got children, Mr Smith?'

'Yes, three of them,' he said, and smiled fondly in recollection.

Actually, through the corner of my eye I had seen a family photograph on the desk, and realised with that, that he was fond of his family.

'Would you do anything for your children to make them happy, or don't you care about their happiness?'

'Now look here, what has this got to do with your visit. Of course I do everything to make my children happy, and so does my wife.'

'I am glad to hear this, Mr Smith, because now I know you will understand me. You see that's the reason why I am here. I will do anything to make my son Victor happy. Let me tell you a bit about him.'

I then told him in a few sentences how hard Victor worked every day on his exercises, how he was able to ride a tricycle, and was now also capable of doing a little walking. Often he had to stay at home or sit patiently in the car because I couldn't lift this heavy wheelchair. I finished by saying:

'If it is raining and I cannot take his tricycle with me, Victor has to wait in the car whilst his brother comes with me. He never cries, just sits there with a longing expression on his face, looking after us out of the window. This sad face haunts me, and I rush through my shopping so that he hasn't got to wait too long. But, if I had a small lighter wheelchair, he could come with me.'

I think Mr Smith was quite touched by my description of Victor. He got up and said:

'Come with me, I will show you something.'

He walked through the secretary's office, just saying: 'I will be back in a few minutes,' then into the corridor where I had waited before, down the stairs and nearly to the back door, where I had entered the building from the car park, and opened the door to a large room full of wheelchairs.

'Look at all these chairs,' he said. 'They all need mending. When a chair is sent back, it must be replaced with another one, and that's why we never have any chairs until the mechanic has mended them. There isn't a new or a mended chair in the place.'

Suddenly I saw it, there it was, a small wheelchair. The seat was folded, bringing the two sides and the wheels close together, making it narrow and compact. It was the type of chair that I had seen at Stoke Mandeville Hospital.

'There it is!' I called out. 'Mr Smith, that's the wheelchair I would like for Victor.'

'But that is not a wheelchair, Mrs Gerhardi,' said the man indignantly, 'that is a transport chair. You have always asked for a wheelchair.'

'I don't care what it is called, a wheelchair or a transport chair. That is the chair I want. Whose chair is this, does it belong to anybody?'

Mr Smith looked at the label hanging on it.

'It is broken, the person to whom it belonged has been given a replacement, and the chair is waiting to be repaired.'

Suddenly I had an idea.

'Mr Smith, do you think I could try and see whether I could lift this chair into the car boot? My car is just outside the back door, and at least we would be sure then that this is the right chair, whatever it is called.'

I didn't wait for his reply, but started pushing the transport chair towards the door. I couldn't open the chair up, because the wheels and sides were tied together. I walked quickly towards the back door, passing two employees, who stared at me, and at Mr Smith, who followed, a little surprised by this quick action. I unlocked the car, opened the boot, lifted the transport chair in and closed the boot.

'Mr Smith, this is absolutely marvellous. Look, I can even close the boot, and the chair is not too heavy either. What about if I keep it straight away. It is in the boot now. My husband is very handy, he can mend the chair, and I promise you that you will have the other chair back in a few days time. There is nothing wrong with that one, I have hardly used it. You will have another good wheelchair which can be passed on straight away.'

'There is a waiting list for the chairs,' said Mr Smith. 'I really should put Victor's name on it first.'

'You even save the transport costs,' I continued, pretending not to have heard what he said. 'All you have to do is to cross out the name wheelchair on Victor's form and replace it with the words transport chair. In this way you avoid the waiting list.'

Mr Smith was thinking, I could see he wanted to help and was trying to work out something in his mind. I had to be quick so that he didn't make the wrong decision for me.

'Thank you, Mr Smith,' I said. 'I will tell Victor what an understanding and kind man you are. I am most grateful to you.'

With that I took his hand, shook it, jumped into the car, started the engine, waved to him and drove off. I stopped at the next lay-by and just sat there. I felt very wound up, and needed a few minutes to relax before I was able to drive back. I drove straight to the factory to see Bob.

'How did you get on?' he said.

'Come and have a look at the car,' was my reply.

Bob came with me. I opened the boot and took out the wheelchair.

'I am afraid you will have to mend it, and I don't even know what is wrong with it.'

I then told him the whole story and he laughed. We know now that a transport chair is different to a wheelchair!

It didn't take Bob long before the transport chair was mended, and Victor was happy with the new equipment. He could even manipulate it himself by turning the wheels with his hands. Bob made sure one of the vans took the big wheelchair back to Mr Smith. I never had to sign another form, so I am assuming he did what I had suggested. I was grateful to him for his help, and wrote a 'thank you' letter.

In the spring of 1959, my parents-in-law went to Canada for three months. They didn't like to leave the big house and garden empty, so we had to take over the place. They still had the chickens and the pig, but I had nothing to do with them. This was the gardener's job. I now had free eggs and vegetables. Gisela, my au pair girl, came with us, otherwise I would not have been able to manage it. The house was rather large. It was also my job to can the tomatoes and the fruit, to pick and freeze the raspberries, strawberries and peas. My mother-in-law had a canning machine, and Bob got the tins in London. Gisela was usually off on Sundays, as she had a boyfriend by then. During the week I was working, so I had only the weekend to see to the canning and freezing. Bob often helped me. The garden in "Winnats" was beautiful, but we never had the time to sit in it. We also had our own house and garden to see to. Still, the children enjoyed "Winnats" on their tricycles.

Bob had a new car that year, a Vanguard Estate. It was big enough to stand the tricycle in it. We decided to go abroad again, first to Switzerland, then to my sister in Italy, where we could all meet by the Lago Maggiore. My brother had got married and moved to Nürnberg, where the tamping machine was working. He had a contract with the German government. Hans now wanted to dispose of the flat in Zürich, and asked me to come and help to decide what to do with everything. So this was another reason for making the trip.

Being able to take the tricycle with us was very useful. Victor could be independent once we had stopped and taken the tricycle out. In Germany he cycled around the Hohenzollern castle, even between the big guns. We called it the Sleeping Beauty castle, because it looked just like it, with its tall white pointed towers. In Switzerland we went to Luzern and took the cog railway up Pilatus. The tricycle wouldn't go into the carriages, as these were built like steps and were too narrow. The driver very kindly took the bike into his driving cubicle. Once we were on the top, Victor was in his element. He cycled everywhere, even along the narrow mountain paths. We met a gentleman, who laughingly enquired whether Victor had cycled all the way up. I sorted things out in the flat in Zürich, but there was nothing I wanted, except a little cuckoo clock. It is still in my possession, and keeps good time. It strikes just after the big, elaborately carved cuckoo clock which my father had sent to Bob before he died.

On Victor's birthday we were in Davos. To go up the mountains, we had to sit in a Gondelbahn cabin, two at a time. The tricycle had to be left in the car. Bob took Victor in his cabin, and I went with Peter. When the guard heard it was Victor's birthday, he didn't charge him for the trip. Once on the top, we didn't know what to do with Victor. He was too heavy to be carried far, and his walking was painfully slow. We saw a wheelbarrow, and I asked a man whether we could borrow it, explaining about Victor.

'I have got something much better,' he said, and disappeared. When he came back, he brought a so-called cheese carrier. It looks like a chair without arms and legs, being two pieces of wood fastened together at an angle of ninety degrees. One of the wood pieces had three adjustable straps. The man put this on to Bob's back like a rucksack, and explained that the farmers carry their cheeses like that down from the mountains. We sat Victor on to the board, with his legs hanging down, and put the third strap around his middle to hold him securely. It was a wonderful idea, and we marched off. Some of the paths were very narrow, and I got worried about the heavy weight on Bob's back. We came to a lovely meadow full of flowers, and decided to leave Victor there and climb one more small steep peak. Peter wanted to look down from the top. There was nobody there, only some cows with their bells around their necks, quite a long way off.

The three of us climbed to the top, and had a fantastic view from there, as the weather was cloudless. When we came back, the cows had come into Victor's meadow, and one of them was making her way gently towards Victor. He was terrified. Sitting so low in the grass, the animal must have seemed enormous. Victor had stretched out his hands, as if he wanted to guard himself, and kept on saying:

'Get away! get away!'

He looked so small and lost, with the herd of animals coming nearer and nearer to him. We all ran down the last part of the hill, shouting to frighten the cows away. I don't think they would have hurt Victor, but he didn't look very safe there. Bob carried Victor again on the cheese board, and we made our way back to the Gondelbahn. The children thought it had been a lovely experience.

After that we went to Italy and stayed with Christel in her house by the lake. Hans came with his wife, and Astra came with Monika. We had a real family reunion.

When we returned to England, I changed Peter's school. It was easier for me if the two boys were at the same place. I also felt that Peter needed more discipline, and Prestwood Lodge, being a boys' school, had a number of men teachers. Peter was now also able to have piano lessons.

Victor suddenly had outgrown his tricycle; Bob could not raise the saddle any more. Twice he had made a longer rod under the saddle, but now the time had come for a grown-up tricycle. We applied to the NHS and, in time, we got the trike. To get this into the back of the car, I had to take off the saddle and the front wheel. I became quite a good mechanic once I had learnt how to undo the nuts.

A letter arrived from Dr M at Amersham hospital. We hadn't seen or heard from him for years. Once Victor started at the unit in Queen Mary's Hospital, he didn't go to Amersham any more. Dr M wrote that he had started a Cerebral Palsy Clinic at the hospital, and he wondered how Victor was getting on. He asked me to bring him for a visit.

Dr M had five children, and his last child, a girl, had Cerebral Palsy. He probably started a clinic because he got personally interested. I replied to the letter, saying that I wouldn't mind bringing Victor, but only if I didn't have to wait. I remembered the hours of waiting at the hospital, and felt that as I was doing him a favour, I could ask for one in return. I got an appointment with him, and a promise that I wouldn't have to wait.

I told Victor that he had to try really hard with his walking this time, as this was the doctor who wanted him to go into a home when he was young.

When I got to the hospital and the Cerebral Palsy Unit, there were several mothers with their children waiting. I saw the nurse, and told her who I was. She had been expecting me, because she went into the next room straight away, probably to tell Dr M that I had arrived. I had only waited a little while, when a mother and her handicapped child came out of Dr M's office. The nurse called me and asked me to come in. People

346

just stared at me. I had only arrived a little while before, and was called in straight away; they had all waited for ages already. I felt guilty, but this was the arrangement.

I whispered to Victor that we would walk in, even if it should take longer. I didn't want to carry him this time. Victor tried really hard with his walking, and we entered the room. I had thought Dr M would be alone, but this was not the case. He had a number of people there. I found out that they were physiotherapists and doctors. Something like Mrs Collis used to have for her meetings with me. Dr M had risen behind his desk when I entered with Victor. He suddenly dropped back on to his chair and stuttered:

'Mrs Gerhardi, what have you done with Victor! This is not possible, I cannot believe this. The last time I saw him he couldn't even stand on his legs, he could hardly talk and I didn't think he would ever be able to move on his own.'

He came round to us and shook my hand, and turning to Victor he said:

'How are you, Victor, do you remember me?'

'Yes, I remember you. I used to come here, and you gave me toys to play with.'

Actually they were not toys, but tests to see how much he could do, and how badly he was afflicted.

Dr M then explained to the others what Victor was like in medical terms, and said that this was a wonderful surprise to realise that things could be done with these children, and one should not judge them too quickly. He also added that he took his hat off to Mrs Collis, and that he had changed his mind about her.

The people in the room then asked me and Victor questions. They wanted to see how well Victor could talk, and what I had done with him to achieve this transformation.

I told them that he could read and write, that he could ride a tricycle and even go swimming. After that I had to take off his overalls and boots, as they wanted to see how well he could move his legs, and what his feet were like. One of the lady doctors - she was elderly - said that Victor's ankles were weak, and that there was a lot of stiffness in the top of his legs. She didn't seem to approve of Mrs Collis' method, and I felt that she wanted to criticise her in a roundabout way, so I said:

'Mrs Collis is the only one who has helped Victor. Considering I was told to put him into a home when he was eighteen months old, I think he has done very well.'

'Mrs Gerhardi, thank you for bringing Victor,' said Dr M 'I am very happy to see how well Victor has developed. You both can be proud of what you have achieved. You have worked hard, Victor. Keep it up.'

I dressed Victor again. Dr M shook my hand and also Victor's, who felt very grown-up to get a handshake. Holding Victor's hand, we walked together out of the room. I, too, was proud of Victor. I felt quite elated; somebody had praised me for doing what every mother should do for her child, at least that's what I always believed.

Although I had done nursing during the war, I had no certificates, so when the Red Cross offered me lectures and demonstrations in nursing at evening classes, I joined the course and got a certificate.

In 1960 we were told that Prestwood Lodge would close. Mr and Mrs Oakley wanted to retire. The house was only rented, and nobody had come forward to take over the school. This was a terrible blow. Victor was eleven years old, and ready for secondary education. We had been to all possible schools in the district. The Education Department in Aylesbury couldn't help us either, all they could promise us was a home teacher twice a week. Then somebody told me about Stanborough School in Garston. This was a school run by the Seventh Day Adventists, but they took children from any denomination. We went to see the headmaster, who was a very kind and understanding man. He liked Victor, and said he would have to think about whether he could take him. They had a small boarding section of about fifteen boys, who were weekly boarders. If the matron was prepared to take Victor, he could start at the school.

Matron too was very kind, a motherly figure. They did decide to accept Victor.

This was the first time that Victor would have to cope on his own for a whole week. He didn't like the idea at all, and the time at Stanborough School was very difficult for him. I would take him on Monday morning with his clean clothes, books and tricycle, and fetch him again on Friday. During the week he had to struggle along to his classes, holding on to walls unless somebody helped him. The staircase was difficult, too, and the learning not easy either. Victor had always been slow, but managed because of the small classes in Prestwood Lodge. Now he had to compete with normal children. I couldn't help him, I wasn't there, and the children were not always kind to him. It was quite a religious school after all. They wanted Victor to sign a form that he would never smoke nor drink. Victor refused. He said that he might like a drink one day. We were quite proud of him, that at the age of eleven he had stood up to the teachers, telling them that he wouldn't sign the form.

We also had to find a school for Peter. Although he had started at the Gateway School in the nursery class before he was three years old, and was now seven, he still couldn't read. Victor read when he was six years old. The trouble with Peter was that he would never sit still. The Montessori method didn't suit him at all. The idea was to let children choose what they wanted to do, and never force them to do anything. So Peter would just flit from one thing to another, and never settle down to anything. At Prestwood Lodge, Mrs Oakley found it impossible to get some discipline into him. He just wouldn't work, and so didn't learn anything much.

I heard about an excellent school, Chesham Preparatory, where they prepared the children for Berkhamsted Public School, a place we hoped Peter would go to once he was eleven years old. We had put Peter's name down for this school already. I went to see the headmistress of Chesham Prep., who said she could only take Peter if he could read. She suggested a teacher for extra lessons. Luckily I found a young person who lived only a few houses from us in South Heath. Peter only needed a few lessons, and then he was well away. Once he could read, he even enjoyed books. He had a wonderful imagination, and would often make up stories. One had to watch out when he told us things, to make sure whether they were true or made up.

Peter didn't do very well in the first year at Chesham Prep. He had a young teacher just out of college, and he soon realised that he could do what he liked with her. He was the clown in the class, a disturbing influence so I was told. All he needed was a good smack and he would have behaved, but that was not permitted. The school was still run on traditional lines, with the emphasis on the three main subjects: reading, writing and arithmetic. Every week Peter brought words home, to learn how to spell them, and I made sure he did. So at school he was good at spelling. I felt that, if I could teach him, why not his teacher.

In the second year at the school, he did much better. The teacher was older, and she asked me whether she could give Peter a little smack with the ruler on his legs if he misbehaved. I gave her permission. She only did it a few times, after which he behaved. She was a good teacher, and Peter learnt well that year.

Victor, at Stanborough School, struggled along. I knew it was difficult for him. Every Monday morning when I took him on the long trip to Garston, he was very quiet in the car. He was not looking forward to going to school. When I fetched him on Friday afternoon, he was always ready, and all the way back in the car he never stopped chatting. He was happy, looking forward to going home. I realised he couldn't stay in that school; he just couldn't cope. Before I could do anything about it, the headmaster was transferred, and the new headmaster asked us to come and see him. He informed us that he couldn't keep Victor, firstly because he needed too much attention, and secondly because he, the headmaster, was worried about Victor's safety. Victor was very wobbly and unsafe on his legs and, if somebody pushed him over and he got hurt, the school could not be responsible for that.

He permitted Victor to stay until the end of term, which then would have been one year for Victor at that school.

I doubt whether Victor would have got hurt if he got pushed. He had learnt early in life to save himself if somebody pushed him. This was one of the things Mrs Collis had initiated. Victor was shown that if somebody pushed him, he had to twist quickly so that he would always fall forward on to his hands and arms. We were told to keep on giving him a push when he didn't expect it, so that eventually he would automatically twist round and fall forward, never on his back. We did this for years, and it worked. Even today it is not dangerous to give Victor a push, as he always falls forward and stops a bad fall with his arms and hands outstretched.

In October of the same year I joined the National Hospital Service Reserve of the Red Cross, and a month later I was able to help in the hospital when we had a big flu epidemic. The Red Cross phoned and explained that because of the epidemic, a great number of nurses were ill; could I possibly spare one or two days a week to help out in Amersham Hospital? I said I would do two days during the hours the children were at school.

I had no idea what my duties would be, but looked forward to them. On the appointed day I presented myself to matron in my Red Cross uniform. She took me to a ward, and told Sister that I was a new helper. Sister was pleased to see me; she said she was very short of staff. The jobs I had to do in the first week could have been performed by any domestic help, there was no nursing training needed. I had to clean the washbasins, dust the lockers and window sills, wash up the cups after the morning tea, and carry the lunch to the patients, which Sister served. The domestic help only washed the ward's floor, the rest was done by me, and I was an unpaid volunteer!

I rang up the Red Cross and informed them that if the hospital only wanted a domestic help, I was not prepared to do this. I gave up my precious time because I had been told they were in desperate need of nurses, but it didn't look like that.

When I reported to matron the following week, she must have had a call from the Red Cross, because she put me into a different ward. Now I was allowed to help with blanket baths, washing patients, changing sheets, etc. Small jobs which nurses do, but no medicine or injections. I stayed in that ward for a few weeks until the epidemic had passed, and Sister was sorry that I was leaving. She said I was a good nurse, and suggested that even at that time I could still get trained

CHAPTER FIVE

Caravan - Spastic Society - Victor's Operations

When the children were very young, we borrowed an uncle's caravan and had a holiday in Great Yarmouth. Victor could crawl everywhere because the sand was fine. Peter, in his playpen, had to be watched, because it was only a frame without a floor. He just lifted it up, or pushed it gently until he reached the water. We enjoyed this holiday, the same as the one we had in Brean, when we camped in the van.

The year when Gisela, the au pair girl was with us, we hired a caravan for four weeks. We collected it on a Sunday so that I had the time for the next four and half days to clean it and get it ready. We left on Friday afternoon for a three week trip to Wales. The holiday was a success. We always found sandy beaches for Victor to crawl about.

I remember our stay in Tenby in a very good caravan site, where we remained a few days. One day we joined a boat trip to go fishing. Everybody was given a fishing line, and all we had to do was to let it trail along whilst the boat was moving. The boys got terribly excited when the first fishes were caught. There seemed to be a great number of mackerel about and the buckets, which the fishermen supplied, were soon full. At the end of the trip, everybody was supposed to take their catch home. A number of people stayed in an hotel and were not interested in the fish. They had their trip and their fun, that's all they wanted. Victor and Peter kept on accepting presents of mackerel, and we finished up with thirty-six. I cooked some for supper, and thought I could keep enough fish in the little fridge for the next day, but what should we do with the rest? Peter then put them into a bowl and went around the campsite, selling them for 6d (2½p) each.

Late in the evening, we were just making up the beds, when there was a knock on the door and a woman enquired whether she could order some fish for the next day. We had to disappoint her, but thought it fun that Peter had been so successful with his little fish trade!

Peter (on right) with Fish

Bob and I worked it out that if we hired a caravan for two or three years, the hire money would amount to the same as buying a second-hand one. We went to look at caravans and found a cheap four-berth Sprite model, which needed a lot of work. This was just right for us. Bob towed it to the factory, where it could stay in the yard whilst we painted it. Every weekend we worked there, with the children trying to help also, particularly with the rubbing down of the outside of the caravan. They couldn't do any damage with that job.

I bought some gay-coloured material in Aylesbury market and made new curtains and covered the seats, all in the same material.

Our first holiday in it in 1961 was quite ambitious. We decided to travel to Scotland. Bob made a frame so that the tricycle could be placed in the caravan during the travelling. Whenever we stopped, and before we could go into the caravan, we had to wait until Bob had taken out the tricycle. He tied this with a chain on to the towbar, and covered it with a large piece of plastic. In those days one didn't have to go into a camping site, so we found different stops, like lay-bys, or a redundant old road, where a new one had been built. One of the best stops was an old airfield in Scotland, where even some huts were still standing. The tarmac runway was a lovely racing track for Victor on his tricycle. From time to time we had to go into a campsite so that the children could have a bath.

We had only reached Pontefract when we had our first puncture on the caravan. The spare from the car fitted, and Bob changed the wheel. We bought a retread, as that was cheaper than a new tyre. In Scotland the other tyre burst, and we had to have another new one. On the way back, the retread punctured or burst, I can't remember what happened and, as we were not far from Pontefract, Bob called in at the garage where we had bought the tyre and complained. We bought a new tyre, paying only the difference between the retread and the new one. The caravan has two wheels, but we had to have three tyres on that trip.

It wasn't much of a holiday for me. Scotland was wet and cold. We did have some sunshine, but never more than half a day. We just couldn't get all our clothes dry. When we stopped for lunch, or in the evening and it rained, Bob got very wet by the time he had fixed the tricycle with the chain and covered it. I had to go into the caravan first to take off the washing line and the wet clothes. After that we would carry Victor in quickly. Peter, too, climbed into the caravan. Bob and the boys played games whilst I did the cooking. I had a pressure cooker, and would often prepare food in the evening for the next day's lunch. We then only needed a small evening meal.

Still, we got to John O Groats, the furthest point, and the children decided that to look out at sea was no different than being at the seaside in Cornwall or Devon. They enjoyed the castles we visited, and liked the mountains.

After this holiday Bob improved the caravan a little. He built in a pump, so that I didn't have to lift big cans of water, we had a decent toilet and a small carpet on the lino floor.

For several summer holidays we used this caravan and explored the English countryside from John O Groats to Lands End, travelling to Cornwall and Devon again, and also to Wales.

We found a small caravan site on a farm in West Mersea, near Colchester. At Easter time we would leave the caravan there, and could then go by car just for the weekend, and also spend part of the summer holidays on the sandy beach there. It was a safe place, with no main road, and both boys could have their tricycles there during the long holidays. I would stay with them for a few weeks with the car, and Bob would come by train for the weekend to Colchester, from where I would fetch him.

In 1965 we all bought a second-hand speedboat, a Fletcher 120. The boys paid £50 each from their pocket money, and we parents covered the rest. It was made from glass fibre, had a 40 hp Mercury outboard motor, and could do 35 knots. Once the caravan was established on the campsite,

Bob towed the boat behind the car. We took it with us every time we went to West Mersea. The caravan was safe on the site, but we were not sure about the boat. In the winter, Bob hung the boat up in the garage over my little Mini car, which I had by then. This was another of his clever inventions. He pulled the boat up on cables which went over some pulleys, using the power of his car. The cables were hooked on to the towbar of the car, which was driven gently forward until the cables could be hooked onto a strong hook on the back wall of the garage. The car could then be rolled back and the cables taken off the towbar.

The boat was another interest for Victor. Something to make up for the fact that he couldn't walk. He soon learnt how to manipulate and steer it. He couldn't start the engine, as this needed a good bit of strength, and he was also much too unsteady on his feet. This was always Bob's job. Bob and Victor explored some of the waterways in the area. They got good charts, worked out the times of the tides, and then travelled up the River Colne to Colchester, or along the river Blackwater to Maldon. Once or twice they branched off into unknown creeks, and got stuck on sandbanks because of low tide. Bob just climbed out of the boat, lifted up the motor and turned the boat round, pushing it back into the deeper water. Before coming back to the caravan, the boat had to be washed to get the salt water off. Bob was very particular about this. So he always called in at a garage. The boys helped to empty the boat, as they sometimes took a picnic, and always had swimming vests, and then Bob would hose down the boat and wash out the engine.

Peter was not too keen on the slow boat trips, but suddenly decided he would like to do water skiing. We had seen this in the Strood, the stretch of water between Mersey Island and the mainland, where there was a large smooth water area. Before buying Peter some skis, which were quite expensive, we decided to let him have a lesson first, to see whether he would take to this sport. Bob, Peter and I went to a skiing school and booked up a lesson for Peter. Whilst discussing price, skis etc. the instructor said to Bob:

'Why don't you also have a go? If Peter falls off, we will have to bring him back to the shore, and whilst he gets ready for the next trip, you could have a go. You have to pay by the hour, so you might as well make use of the time.' Bob agreed to this.

For the first lesson that Bob and Peter had, they didn't go into the water. They were shown how to hold the handle attached to the towing rope, how to put on the skis, what position to have in the water and what to do when they fell off. The lesson after that was in the Strood, where we had watched the skiers before. A road like a bridge went across it, and people usually stood there watching the boats and the skiers. Bob had a cine camera, and suggested that Victor and I drive to the road and take a film of father and son having their first lesson.

The water was not very deep on the shore, and Peter and Bob stood in it for the start. Peter was the first one to go. He put on his skis, got hold of the handle of the towing cable, and the boat pulled away gently until the rope was tight. Peter sat in the water with bent knees and half the skis sticking into the air. The instructor shouted something, the engine roared, the boat moved away and Peter stood up. For a few seconds it looked as if he was going to be alright, but then he fell forward with a great splash and let go of the towrope. He had a swimming vest on and bounced up and down. The boat returned, and the instructor just pulled him back to the shore, as he hadn't gone far. He was told to put his skis on again for another turn.

Now Bob had a try. The same procedure - once the rope was tight, the engine roared and the boat pulled away. Bob was in a hunched position, knees bent, skis against the water, outstretched arms holding the handle. He came up slightly, but his bottom was still in the water. He looked really funny with his red swimsuit, and his yellow swimming vest having moved up, touching his ears.

'Come on, Dad,' shouted Victor, whilst I was trying to film this happening, but was at the same time shaking with laughter.

'Come on, Dad,' shouted Victor again, and I shouted with him.

Bob is a very tall, heavy man; he just didn't seem to get his bottom out of the water. He couldn't stretch his legs. The boat went faster and further and further away. Victor shouted, and the people around us got very excited. They all wanted him to get his bottom out of the water.

'Come on, Dad!' It had become a chorus, with everybody joining in the shouting.

It was no good. Bob never made it. He suddenly let go, and all we could see was his yellow swimming vest, which bounced up and down in the water. The boat made a half circle to collect him. We could see how they tried to lift him into the boat, but he was much too heavy, and it looked as if the boat would turn over. In the end they took his skis, and just pulled him with the rope to the shore. Bob decided he had had enough. His bottom was sore, his hands hurt and he was cold. I have a wonderful film of his water-skiing.

After that, Peter had another go. This time he soon stood up in the water, wobbled a bit, but then went a long way, with his skis cutting through the water fast. The boat made a large turn and came back. Peter was very proud that he had done so well, he let go with one hand and waved, not realising that this would shift his balance - splash - he was down in the water again. He had a few more tries, always quite successful, and we knew he would be alright.

We bought him some water skis, but didn't buy Peter a wet suit. They were very expensive, and he hadn't finished growing yet, so would need a new one every year. This was of course a drawback. The water was often cold. Peter was wet during his skiing. The boat had to go fast, and the cold air upset his tummy. He was ill several times after his water skiing.

To prevent this, he had to have a hot drink as soon as he had finished. When Peter went water skiing, we each had a job. Bob got the boat into the water and started the engine. Victor manoeuvred and steered the boat, and I waited by the shore with a flask of hot tea. From time to time I also took some film of the three men with the boat.

One summer we decided not to go anywhere, but spend the holiday in West Mersea, doing trips by car and boat. Victor also had his big tricycle there, and the boys would go off on their own. Peter walked, helped to push Victor, if the road was uphill, and stood on the bar on the back of the trike when they went downhill. Victor was quite responsible. This arrangement went very well for a time, until the day they met a policeman, who told Peter he wasn't allowed to stand on the tricycle. After that, Peter didn't want to go with Victor any more.

In the evenings, we often played games or cards and listened to the radio. It was the time when the different pirate radio stations had started. People wanted different music, and new stations opened up, which was not allowed by law. So we suddenly had ships out at sea broadcasting music all day. As long as they kept in international waters, they couldn't be stopped. Advertising fees paid for the equipment, the crew and the so-called DJs (Disc Jockeys). The boys' favourite station was RADIO CAROLINE. They adored the different DJs, and listened to the music, the jokes and the talk of these young men all day, and in the evening when we played games.

Victor suddenly had the idea to visit the ship 'Mi Amigo,' RADIO CAROLINE.

'We have got our boat,' he said. 'It isn't all that far out to sea. They say you can see the ship from the shore in good weather.'

Bob fetched the map, and we all studied the possibility.

'We could tow the boat to Frinton-on-Sea, and start from there,' said Bob. 'That's not so far to go. We will need a can of extra fuel, as I doubt whether we will make the journey on one tank full. It is better to be on the safe side in any case.'

I didn't like the idea at all. The boat was very small. It was one thing going along small rivers and doing water skiing in the Strood, where the water was calm, but going out into the rough sea with the boat was quite dangerous. I am afraid I was overruled. The three of them went, leaving me behind.

I was told to listen to RADIO CAROLINE, and they promised that when they got there, they would ask the DJ to put a message through to me, so that I knew that they had arrived.

I was surprised at Bob taking on this adventurous trip. He was usually very cautious. All three had swimming vests on, there was the spare tank with fuel, Bob had his toolbox, they had warm clothes, a First Aid Kit, and they had maps and a compass. If anything went wrong with the engine, Bob was clever enough to put it right. But all three were inexperienced sailors, and Victor and Peter were children, one of them handicapped.

I listened to the radio all day. I didn't like the music, but I didn't want to turn it off. When I had to go to the toilet block, I asked our neighbours to listen to it. Unfortunately they forgot, and so I didn't know whether a message had come through whilst I was away, because none came at any other time. By late afternoon I was very worried. The three had started off really early in the morning, as they had to travel quite a way by road first. They reckoned to be back in the afternoon. If anything had happened to them out at sea, nobody would have known, I was the only one who would miss them. I had no car and no telephone. I could walk to the farm and phone the coast guards, telling them about their trip, and that they hadn't returned. But what about if they hadn't started from Frinton-on-Sea, but from somewhere else? The coastguards would search for them in the wrong part of the sea. On the other hand, they might have already returned, and gone to have a meal before coming back to the caravan. I gradually got myself into quite a state, and decided that if they didn't turn up by seven o'clock, I would go and phone the police.

Three wet, cold, excited sailors returned before I started to walk to the farm for help. I was so pleased to see them that I forgot to tell them off for not sending me a message. I hugged and kissed them, got them dry clothes and a hot cup of tea, and then listened to their stories, which all three wanted to tell me at the same time.

Their boat trip did start off from Frinton-on-Sea. They had made enquiries, and people in the harbour knew that they had gone, because the trailer was left behind. It was quite rough when they got out to sea, and Peter was soon sea sick. None of them wanted to return, because they could see the ships in the far distance.

It took about an hour to get to them, and they circled all three ships: BRITAIN RADIO and SWINGING RADIO ENGLAND on one ship, RADIO LONDON, and RADIO CAROLINE. The people on the ships were quite intrigued by the little boat, and shouted to them and waved. The DJ on RADIO CAROLINE promised to send me a message. This could have come through when I went to the toilet block. Bob had taken his cine camera and, when I saw the pictures later, I could see how rough the sea had been. Peter was sick again on the trip back, but the boat was safe, and the engine never stopped. When they got on land, they found a garage and washed the boat and engine down, and then Peter saw a Wimpy Bar and wanted something to eat. He felt better, and having emptied his stomach several times he was now hungry. All this delayed their return. They were sure that I had had the message from the DJ, and never imagined that I was worried.

The pirate ships were in trouble for years until a law was passed forbidding them to broadcast. There were even demonstrations in London and other places in support of the broadcasting. Bob, Victor and Peter took part in a peaceful demonstration march in London, with Bob pushing Victor in his wheelchair along the road. They had anoraks in case it rained, and I had made them sandwiches, as it would take all day. As it happened, it was very hot, so they never wore their coats, but they ate all the sandwiches. It was an expensive outing, because they lost the empty bag and Victor's anorak.

After the realisation that Victor couldn't stay on at Stanborough School, I was desperate. Nobody could or would help me with Victor's education. I couldn't even discuss it with anybody. Bob didn't know much about schools, only the one he had attended, and that was in Southend. I hadn't grown up in England to be familiar with the education offered for young children. I really didn't like the idea of a home teacher twice a week. Victor was twelve years old, he should have the company of other children, not only his mother at home.

When Victor was six years old, we had joined a small Cerebral Palsy group in High Wycombe, and went to their meetings. They had a film called: "Born that Way," which was introduced by Wilfred Pickles, the entertainer. He, too, had a Cerebral Palsy son, and did quite a bit of fund raising for the Spastic Society. The High Wycombe group asked Bob and myself to help them raise some money, as they hoped to open up a small school for the Cerebral Palsy children in the district. Bob had the projector from his father, and we travelled around to different societies, like the Women's Institutes or Mother's Groups, in the evenings, showing the film.

I usually gave a talk about Cerebral Palsy, and I think people gradually understood more about these handicapped children. Bob and I raised quite a bit of money in this way. Eventually the group had enough money to start a school.

The local Education Authorities said they would give them a grant if they had ten children to start at the beginning of term. They were going to employ a teacher and two or three helpers. Most of the children were quite badly handicapped, and I didn't think one teacher would be enough. The group eventually had nine children, and they asked me to register Victor there also, to make up the ten children so that they would receive the grant.

Victor was then at the Gateway School, and could already read and write by now. He was doing well, so I refused. I knew what would happen. Because he was so much more advanced than the other children, - none of them could read or write, although some were already eight or nine years old - he would probably be given a book to read, and be left alone, whilst the teacher concentrated on the other ones. The little group didn't get the grant, and in the end didn't even start. The parents blamed Bob and me because we didn't send Victor there.

I went to see one of the mothers in Hyde Heath, a charming woman. Her daughter was fourteen years old and could just about read a few words. She had a home teacher twice a week, and a physiotherapist. I asked her:

'Do you help your daughter with her reading?'

'No, I couldn't do that. She has her teacher, and is actually doing very well. I am sorry the school hasn't started, it would have helped me. My daughter could have gone every day, and this would have given me more free time. All my friends have the day free because their children are at school. I always have to be at home because of my daughter. You are lucky that your son can go to a private school.'

'What about her exercises. Do you do them with her every day?'

'Oh no,' she replied. 'I pay for one physiotherapy session a week, and I get a grant for the other one. I couldn't do any walking practice or exercises with my daughter. That is much too difficult for me. We are having this arrangement already for years. She is much better, and can walk a little now.'

I had met her daughter. She was a beautiful girl, but I think she was also mentally backward. I was surprised about the mother's attitude. For me it was the most natural thing in the world to do everything possible for my handicapped son. I didn't rely on other people if I could do it myself, and I think, because of that, Victor got on.

The Cerebral Palsy Group in High Wycombe gave us the cold shoulder after this incident. We didn't get any more news from them about the meetings or any Christmas parties for the children. We returned the film and stopped the fund-raising for them. I kept a collection box for the Spastic Society in my home, where people sometimes put money in, and I sold old newspapers to Bob's factory which they needed for packing. I always emptied the box for Christmas, and passed on a cheque.

Years had passed since we belonged to the High Wycombe Cerebral Palsy Group, but I remembered this mother who always spoke to me. Because I was so desperate to find a school for Victor, I rang her up one day to have a chat. Maybe she had heard about a school, and I thought I could enquire about her daughter at the same time. She was very pleased to hear from me, and told me that her daughter was in sheltered accommodation, coming home for the weekend occasionally. The little walking efforts she had made had come to nothing, and she finished up in a wheelchair. The mother couldn't cope with her any more, and the Spastic Society had put her into one of their homes.

'Unfortunately my daughter is much too old to go to school now,' she said. 'This is really a pity, because the Spastic Society have started this wonderful school in Tonbridge. It is a Grammar School, the only one in the country, and she might have been able to go there.'

My heart was beating fast, and my hands holding the telephone started to sweat. I got all excited, because this sounded just the right school for Victor. I asked her some more questions, and found out that the school was called Thomas Delarue School, and was near Tonbridge in Kent. Mr Delarue had donated the big manor house and park to the Spastic Society. It wasn't easy to get into the school, as the children had to be quite intelligent. Classes were small, so they took only five or six children every year, the same number as were leaving.

I didn't write, I didn't fill out an application, I just went to London to Park Crescent, the headquarters of the Spastic Society.

I met a secretary, the usual person in the "ante - room." I told her about Victor, his successes at school, his swimming, his walking and his piano playing, as by now he had passed several examinations in this. She listened patiently, and then told me I could fill out a form, and she would put Victor on the waiting list.

'But that is no good,' I said. 'Victor has no school to go to in September. He is twelve years old, a highly intelligent boy, what is he going to do in the meantime?'

'I am sorry, that's all I can do,' she said. 'You will have to see your local Education Authority about Victor. They are responsible for giving him an education until the age of sixteen, and if handicapped until the age of eighteen. In any case, it is not easy to get into the Thomas Delarue School. We have a strict assessment for it every year. There is one coming up in two weeks time, so your son won't be able to be assessed until next year, depending on the waiting list.'

'Can't Victor come to the next assessment?' I asked.

'Oh no,' she said. 'We have already chosen the applicants for this, and it is full up. There are only six places for the school this time.'

I started to tremble inside. I had seen an opportunity for Victor, and now it was slipping away. I had to do something. It was essential that he be permitted to come to the next assessment. I started to talk again, describing Victor's good points, begging to let him come to the assessment, and gradually talked myself into a crying fit. I cried and cried, and the poor secretary rushed off to get some help. I had three women and a man around me in the end, offering me cups of tea, trying to calm me down.

'I only want you to assess him' I said. 'That doesn't mean he will be accepted at the school. Why won't you let me bring him to the assessment? You will be surprised when you see him. He really is very clever.'

'All parents think their children are the best, that's only natural,' said one of the women.

'Have you got children?' I asked, still sobbing a little.

'Yes,' she said.

'Don't you think they are the best in the world?'

'Yes,' she said, and laughed suddenly.

The group of people left me with the untouched cup of tea. I knew I couldn't drink it. They all had a whispered conversation whilst I dried my face and blew my nose.

The secretary I had spoken to first came back to me, whilst the others left.

'We have decided to let your son come to the assessment,' she said smiling. 'I will fill out the form for you. This doesn't mean he will get a place at the school, but he will have a chance like all the others, that's all.'

I could only say 'Thank you.' I felt drained and exhausted from all the crying.

Two weeks later Bob, Victor and I turned up at Park Crescent for the assessment, with Victor's school and music certificates. Victor had been primed by me what to expect. I knew he would get several intelligence tests. Dr M and even the school in Carshalton had given him plenty. There are only a certain number of tests, and I thought Victor must have got through them all by now. I told him that if he recognised one not to mention this, but just to take his time before answering.

'Always think first,' I said to him. 'Even if you know the answer straight away.'

It took all day to get through the tests. There must have been twenty children. Some in wheelchairs, some very deformed, with crossed legs, a few of them crawling, but only one or two walking. I looked at them all and thought what one woman in the Spastic Society Office had said to me. All parents think their children are the best. I certainly thought so; Victor was the best in my opinion.

The three of us had to see the doctor, who assessed Victor's spasticity. He wanted to know the medical background. Victor saw the psychiatrist on his own and came out smiling.

'You were right,' he whispered. 'I had the picture with the flag and the sun where the shadow goes the wrong way. Then I had to fold the paper again and again and tell him how many squares there were each time. I didn't answer anything too quickly,' and he laughed, pleased with himself.

Nobody could tell me that Victor wasn't bright. He also saw the headmaster of the school on his own. Bob and I were interviewed by somebody from the Spastic Society without Victor. The questions were: What hopes did we have for our son? Would we encourage Further Education after sixteen or eighteen years of age? Were we prepared to help him if he goes to university? The idea behind these questions was, if the Spastic Society gave him a good education, would we encourage and help him to get on or, once he was finished, let him drift into sheltered accommodation. The schooling in Thomas Delarue School would then have been a waste of time and money.

At lunchtime we were supplied with sandwiches and a drink, and at three o'clock all assessors had a meeting to decide who would be able to start at the school in September. Victor was one of the lucky ones. I just couldn't believe it when they told us that Victor was accepted. We saw the headmaster, Mr Davies, a Welshman, who was very impressed with Victor's piano certificates. He promised to see to it that Victor had piano lessons at school also. Bob and I were very happy that our son now could go to the Thomas Delarue School, but Victor was apprehensive. He kept on thinking about Stanborough School, and how difficult it had been. We then made an agreement with him. If, after two terms, he didn't like the school, or was unhappy, we would take him home, and he could have a home teacher.

This school was different; it was geared for handicapped children's education and for their needs. Five boys had a house mother to look after them. If they couldn't dress or bath themselves, it was her job to help. The classes were small, depending on the subjects taught, often only five or six children in the class. There was physiotherapy, there was sport in wheelchairs, and there was a heated pool. Later on there was horse riding, but Victor didn't like that.

I am glad to say that Victor never looked back. After two terms, there was no talk of him leaving. He had made friends for the first time in his life, because the others were handicapped too. They all helped one another because they understood, and there were also girls in the school. He had to look after himself and became independent. We would go and visit him on the occasional Sunday and take him out for the day. He was pleased to see us and Peter, and never minded going back to school. Once or twice during the term he was allowed to come home for the weekend. I would fetch him on Friday afternoon by car, and we took him back on Sundays. This was much better than the Sunday visits. Tonbridge in Kent was quite a long journey for us by car.

The independence Victor learnt in his new school also showed itself in other ways. He had joined the Scouts movement quite young. I always took him to the meetings by car. He was never interested in the summer camping holidays, but suddenly he wanted to go. The Scoutmaster worked in Bob's factory. The two of them had a talk, and it was arranged that Victor would join the trip to the summer camp. Bob supplied a van and a driver from the factory. All equipment, all Scouts plus Victor and his big tricycle were packed into the back, and they were off. The van returned empty, and after a week collected them all again. The Scoutmaster told us that it had been very successful. Victor was able to join in most of the time.

His comrades helped him to erect the tent, and even to get him in and out of his sleeping bag for the night. Whenever the boys walked somewhere, Victor cycled. When the boys played in the wood, where the tricycle couldn't be used, Victor helped to cook the dinner. He said he had had a marvellous time, and came back with dirty clothes, and needing a bath. The thirteen year old boy was growing up.

Once Victor entered the Thomas Delarue School, he left Mrs Collis' treatment. The school had their own doctor and physiotherapists. People didn't watch Victor's walking any more. He was given a stick, and told to get on. He discovered that he could move faster if he didn't take care of his legs and feet, so he just stumbled along with his stick. I got very worried about Victor's legs. I could see how they gradually got worse. His feet twisted towards the outside, until he was nearly walking on the inside of his ankle bones. There were no arches left. He also started to bend forward when walking, and had difficulty in straightening himself up. Mrs Collis' advice was disregarded. I was glad that she couldn't see him walking. In the short time Victor was at home, I couldn't correct what was damaged through his life at school. Eventually I made an appointment with the doctor at the school. Bob and I went to see him. He had different ideas to Mrs Collis, but they, too, were good, and they were feasible.

'If you keep on reminding Victor how he should walk, watch him all the time, never leave him alone,' said the doctor, 'you will find he will never become independent. All his life he will wait for a voice to tell him what to do, not only how to walk, but also when he has to make decisions. I am sure you don't want that. You will have to let go. You have achieved a great deal getting him to walk, that's more than most young people with his disability can do. I agree he is starting to get deformed, and will probably have to have some operations to correct this. This will have to wait until he is fourteen years old. His feet will have stopped growing by then.'

This was something we had never expected. I could see what the doctor meant, and realised that Victor now had to get on and grow up, but I was sorry to hear that he would have to have several operations. He was still a child; I didn't want him to suffer.

I rang Queen Mary's Hospital in Carshalton. I wanted to talk to Mrs Collis, get her opinion about Victor. I spoke to Bertha, the head physiotherapist, who told me that Mrs Collis had given up the unit.

'Mrs Collis had a stroke,' she said. 'After that she decided to give up everything. I go and see her from time to time, and report to her about the progress of the children, but she isn't all that interested any more.'

Mrs Collis had been very fond of Victor, so I said: 'Do you think she might like to see Victor? I could take him to her on one of his free Sundays, or in the holidays.'

'No, don't do that,' said Bertha. 'She won't see any of the children. She is paralysed down one side. Her husband has to carry her and dress her. She has always told the children, where there is a will there is a way, and if you want to walk and work hard you can walk. She doesn't want anybody to see her in a wheelchair. She has cut herself off from the outside world. Even I can only see her occasionally for a short time.'

I felt terribly sad. Here was a woman who had helped so many children, given hope to parents, worked long hours to build up a successful unit, with physiotherapists and a school, and now she was stricken with a similar disability, but with one that couldn't be cured. Life was cruel, she didn't deserve this.

We needed a bigger house. The boys wanted a room each by now, with all their possessions. We also had two vehicles in the drive, as Bob often brought a small van home so that I didn't have to take him to work every day in order to have the car.

Bob had very little time, so it was up to me to find a bigger house. I cannot remember how many I visited. Some of them I only saw from the outside and knew that I wouldn't like them. The agencies kept on sending me more and more papers. A great number of houses were too far away from the factory. This was an important point, the house had to be close to Bob's work. He only looked at two houses, one near High Wycombe, which neither of us liked, and the other one in Wendover. I had fallen in love with "Long Meadow" the moment I saw the house. Years before, we had driven along this lane, and I had said to Bob then:

'I would like to live here. It is quiet and peaceful, near the railway station, and not far from the shops.'

All the houses were situated on one side of the lane. Opposite was a large field, with a footpath leading to Wendover Station. "Long Meadow" had quite a good-sized front garden, with a beautiful round bed full of roses. The house had a built-in garage, and another wooden one standing next to it. There was a large back garden, slightly sloping, and at the bottom fields again. All together there was an acre of land. The garden was quite neglected, and everything inside the house was painted in dark colours. We knew it would need a lot of work, but Bob was prepared to do it, if we could get the price down. We even discovered woodworm, but knew that that could be treated.

We made an offer, it was accepted, and we bought the house with a bridging loan, as we hadn't sold our old house yet. The people moved out, and Bob started to work on the house. He rewired everything, and he helped to put in central heating, with the boiler in the built-in garage. This was going to be his workshop. The plan was to have a new double garage built, with a playroom above for the children to play with the train and maybe table tennis, and a billiard table later on.

1962/63 was a bad winter. Bob worked every evening on the house, often not coming back until one o'clock. He would always phone if he was going to be late, and I had a hot drink ready for him when he returned. It was very cold, and he had no heating in the house. One night when it was snowing heavily, he didn't phone and he didn't come home. I got worried, wondering whether he had got stuck. He arrived at three o'clock in the morning. He had left the house, and coming down the lane he saw a snowdrift across it. He revved up the engine of the car hoping to shoot through it, but he got stuck. He got out and started to shift the snow from the front of the car. He then moved the car forward and again shifted the snow from the front. As fast as he moved the snow from the front, the space at the back filled up with the drifting snow. He couldn't even return to the house to phone me. Eventually he came to the main road, which was cleared by the council. Our new house stood in a private road, we had to do our own snow clearing!

Peter, although quite young, went to school alone by bus from our present house. The bus stop was just outside our gate. In Chesham he had to get out and catch the school bus. There were two more children from near us taking the same bus, a boy and a girl. Trudi was older, and would make sure that all three crossed the road safely in Chesham. In the afternoon, either Trudi's mother or I would pick up the children from school. We took it in turns, except when I had to take Peter to his piano lessons. He did quite well with his music. He got his first piano certificate in 1961 and the second one in 1963. We stopped his singing lessons when he wasn't accepted at Magdalene College as a choir boy.

We sold our house at Christmas, and moved into Long Meadow in the spring of 1963. Peter always remembered that day. He went to school in the morning by bus from South Heath, and came to the new house in Wendover in the afternoon by train. He only had another term in Chesham Prep. so there was no point in changing his school.

Mrs A, his headmistress, had been rather concerned about Peter, and told us to get some advice about his future education. We took Peter to Oxford to see a specialist, but told him it was because of his eczema, which kept on recurring. The final outcome of the different tests he had in Oxford was that we were strongly recommended to send him to boarding school, especially as Victor, too, was attending one.

Bob and I talked things over and felt that, as long as I was working, we could afford a boarding school for Peter. Victor's school fees were paid partly by the local authorities and partly by the Spastic Society. The doctor had recommended one or two schools in Oxford but, as we had already provisionally put Peter's name down for Berkhamsted School, we entered him for the entrance examination, which he passed. Peter started at the school in September 1963, when he was ten and a half years old. Because of his beautiful voice, he soon joined the choir. On his exeat Sundays we would attend the church service, so that we could listen to him singing in the choir, and afterwards take him out for lunch, or bring him home for a few hours. Peter never liked boarding school. He had to sit still, conform, concentrate and prove himself in fights with other boys and bullies, all things he didn't like, but it kept him out of mischief, supervised and safe.

In order to save money, I decided to decorate Victor's bedroom myself. First of all I had to get the old wallpaper off, which had been over-painted several times. This was pretty hard work, as I had to use a scraper. After a day's work, the top of my right arm and shoulder started to hurt. This was nothing new. For years I kept on getting the same pain, and I had always put it down to a draught in the car. Bob liked the window open when it was too hot, but I made him shut it again, as I was convinced the draught would give me pain in my right arm.

The children were coming home for Easter, and I wanted the room painted by then, so I carried on in spite of the pain. On the third day my arm suddenly dropped down. I had to use my left hand to lift it up again. I certainly needed medical attention. We had not registered with a new doctor after our move, so we decided to do this at the same time.

There were three doctors in the Wendover practice, and we chose Dr R, the youngest and latest arrival. Bob and I went to his evening surgery and asked him whether he would accept us as his patients. He said yes, and after the formalities were concluded, I said I wanted to see him straight away about my right arm, which I still could not move unaided. He was very concerned, and felt I needed X-rays straight away. It was Friday evening, the weekend was in front of us, there would be no X-rays in the hospital until Monday.

It turned out that Dr R had trained and worked in the RAF hospital in Halton, just up the road. He still had friends there, and good connections. After two phone calls everything was arranged, and I had an X-ray the next morning. After that things went very quickly. The X-ray showed that I had some calcified deposits. I could see the little lumps myself. I needed an operation to remove them. The deposits had moved on to a nerve, which prevented me from moving my arm. At some time in the past I must have torn a muscle in the top of my arm, which was not allowed to heal with rest. Gradually calcium deposited itself there, forming the lumps. I could now also understand the pain I got from time to time when I thought it was from the draught. I mostly carried Victor on my right arm. Suddenly everything fell into place.

I had the operation in Halton, and was allowed to go home after a few days with my arm in a sling, as the stitches had to stay in for ten days. Bob couldn't fetch me and there was no spare driver that day in the factory, so he asked his mother, who arrived at the hospital with a bunch of beautiful flowers. Bob had wanted to give me a surprise, and had fixed up some shelves in the lounge and a cupboard by the window. For this he had to saw wood and use his electric drill. When I entered the room, I saw the surprise straight away, but also the dust and the dirt. I went into the kitchen and noticed the washing machine full of washing. My thoughts went to food, as the boys were coming home for Easter the next day. There wasn't much in the pantry or the fridge. Still, I could move my left arm, so I would have to get on with things.

My mother-in-law had followed me into the house, and enquired where she could find a vase for the flowers. I gave her one, and she put flowers and vase in the centre of the dusty table.

'You ought to go and have a rest,' she said. 'You look very tired.'

'Yes, I will,' I replied.

I heard her car reversing in the drive when I started the washing machine and, whilst she was driving along the lane by the front garden, I had the vacuum cleaner out and had started pushing it with my left arm. I was able to move my right hand, but couldn't hang out the washing, so it was left in the machine until Bob came home.

Victor came home before Peter, and we went out for the day. I could drive as long as I kept my right arm in my lap and held the steering wheel like that with my right hand. The left arm and hand did the driving. Near Oxford we saw a small plane coming down somewhere, and Victor wanted me to find the airport. We did find it, and it turned out that the plane did pleasure flights. Victor wanted to go on it, but it was expensive for one. It was much cheaper for three people to share. I didn't want to go because of the stitches in my shoulder. We waited to see whether another couple would turn up, but nobody came. The pilot approached us and gave us a special price for two people. He wanted to give Victor the pleasure of being up in the air. Some people would be especially kind to Victor because of his handicap, and when I looked into his silently pleading eyes, I just couldn't refuse.

The pilot brought the plane closer to the buildings so that Victor didn't have to walk so far. Two staff members helped us into the plane and strapped us in. Victor sat next to the pilot, and I sat in the back, being absolutely petrified, because the plane was very small indeed. We were off and soon up in the air for our ten minute flight over Oxford. The sun was shining, there were no clouds, and Oxford, with its old buildings, towers and spires, looked beautiful.

'Would you like to feel the plane?' said the pilot to Victor, pointing to the half wheel in front of him.

The plane had dual controls and every time the pilot moved the half wheel, Victor's moved too. I could see how excited Victor was when he put his hands on it. We dropped down, after that we came up again, then moved to the side, seemed to wobble and I started to feel sick. I could hear the pilot laugh, and so did Victor, and the two of them talked to one another. I was in a haze, feeling terrible, and my only hope was that the ten minutes would be over soon. We landed, bumped along the grass until we reached the buildings, and the two men helped us out again. I think they had more trouble with me than with Victor, who kept on talking to the pilot. All I could think of was that I mustn't be sick. I don't know how I drove back home. Victor never stopped talking, he was so excited. Neither of us have ever forgotten this trip when I still had the stitches in my shoulder.

We had a double garage built, high enough to put the caravan in if needed. The playroom above was reached by an outside wooden staircase at the back. Victor was able to get up and down these stairs alright, except in winter, when we had to make sure there was no snow or ice on the stairs. The playroom was the children's haven. They had the railway there, a Scalextric racing track, later on a three-quarter size billiard diner table, with a board on top for table tennis. They could entertain their friends there without supervision. For parties, the billiard table could be lowered and made into a dining table, seating twenty people easily. We had an intercom to the room so that we could talk to one another.

The old wooden garage was erected again at the bottom of the garden, where we kept the garden tools. Bob resurrected the orchard at the bottom of the garden by gradually pushing the mower further and further, and disposing of the ant-hills which had developed over the years of neglect. The middle part of the lawn was flattened, grass sown again, and it became our croquet lawn, with a summerhouse at the side. It took Bob over three hours at the weekend to cut the lawns, but it gradually became a lovely place. I attended to the front garden with the rose bed, and the top part of the back garden with flower beds at the side, although I hated gardening.

There was a space at the side of the house for the caravan which, in later years, became our overflow spare bedroom. Bob had a wire coming out of the downstairs toilet into the caravan to provide it with electricity. We even had a young Swedish boy living in there for six months. He had come to learn English, and worked in the plating factory, as his father, too, had the same business in Sweden, which he was supposed to take over one day.

Even Victor made use of the caravan when he was at college. He could spread out his books and papers and leave them there when he went to bed at night; nobody disturbed his work.

Victor was quite badly deformed by 1963, and it was obvious that he needed operations to correct this. The doctor at his school recommended to go and see Mr Sharrard in Sheffield. By now Victor was old enough to discuss things. He didn't want any operations, but agreed to see several specialists and listen to their opinions. We went to see a Harley Street orthopaedic specialist, who was more interested in Bob's uncle, William Gerhardi, the writer, than in Victor. At least he agreed that Victor needed operations on his feet, and possibly on his hips. He, too, recommended Mr Sharrard, but added that there was also a good surgeon at Guy's Hospital in London. We paid him his high fee, and felt that the visit had been a waste of time and money. Victor hadn't changed his mind.

The next thing I did was to phone Bertha, the head physiotherapist in Queen Mary's Hospital, Carshalton. She promised to find out who was the best specialist for the type of operations Victor needed. She arranged that Victor and I could see another surgeon in the hospital there. He was a well-known man, who sometimes performed operations in Queen Mary's Hospital.

I will never forget meeting Sir Mc because he was such an elegant and charming man. Victor and I had arrived early at the hospital, and waited in the secretary's office, looking out of the window. Suddenly a Rolls Royce arrived. The chauffeur stopped the car at the entrance to the building where we waited. He opened the door and out stepped a small plump man in an immaculate dark suit with a yellow carnation in his buttonhole. He seemed to bounce like a ball up the steps to the open entrance door. I wonder who that is, I thought. He looks as if he is going to an important meeting, or a wedding.

A little later we were called in to see Sir Mc, and when I met him, I realised it was the little ball from the Rolls Royce. He had studied Victor's files, and was well informed. He was charming, very polite, and treated Victor like a grown-up person.

I explained to him that Victor was against the operation, and because of that I had promised him to have several specialists opinions.

Sir Mc suddenly asked me to sit on the table. Then he knelt in front of me and removed my shoe. He took my foot in his hand, and showed Victor what a normal foot looks like. Twisting it in different directions, he explained what the operations on Victor's feet could, would and should achieve.

Tendons would be stretched, bones reshaped, and the ankle fixed, allowing the foot only to be moved up and down, not sideways. Walking would still not be perfect, but the feet would have a natural position. After all these explanations, Sir Mc slipped my shoe on again, got up from his kneeling position, sat down and added:

'Victor will probably also need a hip operation. He bends forward too much when he is walking. A more upright position should be possible. And now Mrs Gerhardi, I would like to have a word with Victor alone.'

He got up and, walking towards the door, which he opened, he asked me to wait outside. Sir Mc and Victor seemed to have a long talk, but maybe I only thought this, as I was nervous and apprehensive. When at last they entered the room again, both of them were smiling, and gave the impression that they understood one another.

'I think Victor will agree to have the operation,' said Sir Mc.

I looked at Victor, who nodded his head. Then he thought of something.

'I would like you to operate on my feet,' he said. I could see that he had complete confidence in Sir Mc.

'I am sorry, Victor, but I cannot do that,' he replied. 'I do a number of different operations, but not the shaping of a foot. The best man in the country is Mr Sharrard in Sheffield. He is a busy man, but go and see him, and if he sets your feet he will probably also perform the operations on your hips.'

He then turned to me and continued: 'Make a private appointment with Mr Sharrard. He will then give you more time, and explain everything to Victor. Your son wants to understand what is to be done to his limbs. Knowledge and understanding will help him to face up to the operations.'

He shook hands, wished Victor good luck, and left. We saw him being driven off in his beautiful car. The physiotherapist informed us that he had already performed two operations that morning, and was off to London to a meeting. I thought that was probably the reason why he was so elegantly dressed, but Bertha informed me that he always dressed like that. I was grateful to him for having found the time to see Victor, and wrote to him later telling him about Victor's progress.

Bob took a day off, and the three of us went to see Mr Sharrard in Sheffield. He, too, explained everything to us, even made some drawings for Victor, as he wanted him to understand what he was going to do to his hips. We had assumed that the operation would be on the hip bone, but it turned out that Mr Sharrard intended to take out a triangular wedge of bone from the femur, and the scar from the incision would be at the top of the leg. He showed Victor in the drawing that he would finish up with a metal plate and a large screw, which would remain in the femur bone for life. Victor was absolutely fascinated with it all, and his objections to the operations disappeared.

Mr Sharrard asked us whether we wanted these operations privately as we had made a private appointment, but Bob and I had to tell him that we were not insured for this, and couldn't possibly afford to pay for it out of our own pocket.

'That's alright,' said Mr Sharrard, 'I will perform the operations under the National Health. My secretary will let you know as soon as possible when there is a vacancy. I don't want to leave it too long, as Victor is now at the right age. We have a small hospital just outside Sheffield in the Rivelin Valley, called King Edward VII Hospital. It has beautiful gardens, and the wards and rooms are small. Victor will be happy there. He will have to stay in hospital for four or five months, but a teacher will visit him so that he doesn't fall behind with his education. It would help if you could bring a letter from his school, advising the hospital teacher what should be covered in the next few months.'

After seeing Mr Sharrard, we visited a cousin of Bob's who lived in a small farmhouse in Thrybergh near Rotherham. Raymond and a friend ran a car business, buying and selling second-hand cars and hiring them out. The friend was married and had his own house, but Raymond, a bachelor, lived in the farmhouse. It was handy for him to work on the cars which stood in the yard, and he had an excellent workshop in the stables. The house didn't have much furniture, there was no comfort and it was cold. Raymond said, that if we wanted to save ourselves the hotel fees when we visited Victor, especially as this would be for months, we could sleep on a mattress on the floor in one of the rooms. He would put an electric fire into the room, and if we phoned him before we came, he would put it on. We were most grateful because we realised what an expense staying in a hotel would be. I was used to sleeping on the floor when I was a refugee, so I didn't mind doing it again, and Bob had been in the Homeguard during the war, so this was nothing new to him. Victor liked Raymond, who promised to visit him in hospital.

It was February 1964 when Bob and I took Victor to King Edward VII Hospital. During the admittance registration, the Sister suddenly asked us to sign a form.

'It is only a formality,' she said.

'What formality?' asked Bob.

Sister then explained that by signing the form we would permit another surgeon to perform the operation on Victor's feet in the unlikely event of Mr Sharrard not being able to do it. Bob refused to sign the form.

We had come to Sheffield, a long way for us, because we wanted Mr Sherrard to perform this special operation, and if Mr Sharrard was not able to do it, we would wait. We could have gone to Guy's Hospital in London, which was much nearer. Sister didn't like our attitude, but we were glad later on that we had resisted her demand that we sign the form.

We stayed the night with Raymond, sleeping on the mattress, and keeping the little fire going nearly all night, as it was bitterly cold. They didn't want us to see Victor the next morning, as they had to get him ready for the operation, but told us to phone at dinner time, when it would be all over and we could probably see him in the afternoon.

When Bob phoned at dinner time, he was told that the operation had not taken place. Mr Sharrard had been called away to do some emergency operations in the Sheffield Infirmary because of a car accident. We had not signed the form permitting somebody else to take over. I can only say that I was very pleased about this, but felt sorry for Victor that he would have to go through all the preliminaries again.

No date could be given for when Victor would have the operation, but they would keep him in the hospital until they could find a slot. The operation might have to be done in the Infirmary in Sheffield. We were told to go home, and they would inform us by phone.

Three days later the call came through in the morning to say the operation would be in the afternoon. Bob couldn't go to Sheffield, so I went alone by train, and Raymond collected me and took me to the Infirmary where the operation was going to be performed. I had also asked Raymond to book a room in a small hotel close by, as I would have no car in Sheffield.

I arrived soon after Victor had had the operation and was wheeled back to the ward. He was still very drowsy, but pleased to see me. His bed was in the corner by the entrance of a very large men's ward. There were thirty beds in the room. Sister said there was no room anywhere else for Victor, as this was an operation which had to be slotted in. He would be transferred in a few days time to King Edward Vll Hospital. In the meantime, being close to the entrance, they could keep an eye on him. He was only fourteen years old, still half a child.

Gradually Victor woke up and complained about pain. This was understandable. His feet had been cut about, set into a new shape and put into plaster. Sister said I could stay with him as long as I liked. Victor wanted no food, and was sick several times. He kept on whimpering about the pain, even after a pain-killing injection. By nine o'clock in the evening he said he thought his feet were going to burst. I just didn't think I could leave him, as he kept on holding my hand. By ten o'clock, the Night Sister said I would have to leave. She was going to give Victor a sleeping pill, and he would soon be fast asleep. I left, and phoned Bob and Raymond to keep them informed.

The hotel where I stayed was very good, the bed comfortable, but I couldn't sleep, worrying about Victor. I was up early, and got to the Infirmary before nine o'clock. Nobody stopped me, so I just entered the ward. The curtains were drawn around Victor's bed, and I could hear him crying before I opened them. He was in a terrible state.

'My feet are terribly hot, they hurt, and I think the plaster is going to burst,' he said.

Victor was never a cry-baby and I knew there was something wrong. He tried to be brave, but the pain was too much for him. I reassured him, and told him I would try and see Mr Sharrard. I went to find Sister. She was a different one from the day before, and was surprised to see a visitor so early, but I told her that I had permission to come at any time because Victor was much too young to be in a men's ward. I said I wanted to see Mr Sharrard, as I was very concerned about Victor and the pain he had in his feet. She, too, didn't think it was normal after an operation to have these symptoms.

'I have already passed on my concern, and Mr Sharrard will be here this morning.'

When she heard that I hadn't had any breakfast nor any supper, she told me to go to the canteen and have something to eat.

I went back to Victor and told him that Mr Sharrard would come soon. I sat next to the bed and held his hand. Gradually he dropped off to sleep. I left the corner quietly, and told Sister I would take her advice and have some breakfast.

Half an hour later I was back, and was surprised to find Victor's bed empty. I got frightened and went to Sister's office.

'It's alright,' said Sister. 'Mr Sharrard came and had Victor moved. They are going to make some tests. Mr Sharrard thinks he might have had a haemorrhage inside the plaster. You can wait here in my office until we hear what will happen next.'

Sister was very kind, and looked after me as if I was one of her patients. It was true that Victor had haemorrhaged, and they had to take the plasters off again and put on new ones. He came back to the ward at dinner time, and I sat with him until he woke up. This time he only had a little pain, and even wanted something to eat.

The next day he was feeling better. One or two of the men who could get up had started to come and talk to him, and by the afternoon I knew that he would be alright and I could return home the following day.

Victor stayed a week in the Infirmary and was then transferred to King Edward VII Hospital. We drove to see him every weekend. Sometimes we left on Friday night and visited him Saturday and Sunday. At other times we left Saturday morning and got our visits in on Saturday afternoon and Sunday morning. At first we slept on the mattress in Raymond's house, but then we brought the caravan to Sheffield and put it in the corner of the farm yard amongst the cars. Raymond used to warm it up with a small electric fire before we came.

We always had fish and chips from the same take-away place near Leicester on Friday night. We even became quite elegant and brought our own plates and knives and forks with us, so that we didn't have to eat with fingers out of the paper. Because it was cold outside, the car windows steamed up from the hot meal and people couldn't look in. The journey often took us over three hours, because it was the time when the motorway was being built. We had many diversions or had to stop at traffic lights at the different road working places.

Peter was at boarding school in Berkhamsted so we were able to get away. He came with us in the Easter holiday. Bob's cousin, Raymond, was very good. He visited Victor every Tuesday as this was the official evening for visits. If he couldn't go he sent his girlfriend, who later became his wife. Occasionally we took Raymond out for a meal. He knew some lovely little pubs that served excellent steak. We couldn't afford to go out all the time, so it was as well that we had the caravan where I was able to do some cooking or make sandwiches.

After two months the plaster on Victor's feet came off and we were allowed to take him out for the day. I had prepared a picnic, the weather had started to get a little warmer, and as the hospital supplied us with a wheelchair we thought we could find a sheltered spot in the sun in the Rivelin Valley. Raymond also turned up that day for a visit, which was unusual. He was always busy going to motorcycle or car hill-climbing races on Sundays.

'Take Victor somewhere quiet,' said Sister. 'He shouldn't have too much excitement. He has been very ill and is used to the quiet hospital life.'

This was true. Victor was in a large room with three beds. Occasionally he had another young man joining him for a short spell, but mostly he was alone. He had a wheelchair and was able to wheel himself into the other rooms by now, so that he wasn't too lonely. Everybody knew him. Other patients came and left, but he was always there. A teacher came twice a week and he had quite a bit of school work to do on his own.

When we got to the car park with Victor and his wheelchair, we discovered why Raymond had turned up on this particular Sunday. He had arranged with Victor that he would take him to a car hill-climbing race. He knew all the adjudicators and helpers, always got in free and also could bring his car into the compound and put it in one of the prime positions. Victor was terribly excited and promised not to tell Sister where he had been. So we all went and had an adventurous day, bringing him back very tired. We promised to take him out again the following week, but Mr Sharrard put a stop to it. Victor's feet had healed well and it was time for the next operation, the one for his hips, taking a wedge out of his femur bones.

This time I stayed with a young couple, friends of Raymond's. I had no car, but Helen took and fetched me from the hospital. Victor had the operation in King Edward VII Hospital. Afterwards he had to lie flat in his bed, unable to move. The nurses turned him gently on to his tummy every two hours.

Victor was in a different room now, and his companion was a young man who had broken his back. He was in a kind of cradle contraption which could be turned automatically to change his position from resting on his tummy to resting on his back. He wasn't even allowed to raise his head. At least the two young boys could talk to one another. The young man had plenty of visitors, as he was from Sheffield.

I stayed with Victor until the weekend when Bob came, and we both went home by car on Sunday. The only thing that Victor was afraid of was that somebody could touch him.

'Don't touch me,' he said, if anybody came near him. Even so, the nurses had to give him injections in his bottom, which looked like a pin cushion by the time he had thirty. The pain wasn't too bad this time. The scars on the top of his legs were about eight inches long and looked like railway lines with sleepers going across.

Victor was soon able to sit up in bed. He had lessons again, and we brought him games and things to make. He suddenly took a liking to Origami, the old Japanese art of making shapes from paper, and there were several books on the market. I still remember his face after he built the dodecahedron. He was so surprised and pleased that he had worked it out, and kept on counting the twelve faces. He loved to say the word, and every nurse entering his room had to be told about it.

After four weeks, he was well enough to be put into a wheelchair with his legs up, and we were allowed to push him around in the beautiful hospital gardens which were like a park. By now he had been four months in hospital, and the weather was warm. Again I brought picnics which we all could have together in the open air. We couldn't take him out yet because he had to have his legs stretched out in front of him.

We were glad that Raymond or his girlfriend went to see Victor every Tuesday. He could have been lonely otherwise. We visited him at the weekends and he looked forward to this. I mentioned to Bob's parents that they, as grandparents, ought to go and visit Victor. They each had a car, and could easily have gone one day during the week or at the weekend. This would also have given us a break. It wasn't easy for us to give up every weekend. We were both working all the week, and there were plenty of things to do at the weekend. We had no time for any social life. I did all my washing and ironing in the evenings, including Victor's little bits, as they were not done in the hospital. If Peter had an exeat on a

Sunday, we would go to Sheffield on Friday night and return Saturday night in order to be able to take Peter out for the day.

Eventually we just took the grandparents with us and made the journey in one day. All I remember about that trip was that my mother-in-law complained about the smell of petrol in the back. Bob had to confess to his parents that we always took two cans of petrol with us from the factory, for which we didn't have to pay, as otherwise we couldn't have afforded these trips to Sheffield every weekend. The firm paid for Bob's car, the maintenance of it and the petrol. This was a perk which all the directors enjoyed, including my mother-in-law and Bob's sister Pat, who worked in the factory, being in charge of the Sales Department. Pat and family also visited Victor in the Easter Holidays. This was the only time Victor had some visitors from the rest of the family.

Victor had started to be interested in cars, radio and electronic equipment. His grandmother had the CHILDRENS NEWSPAPER, AUTOCAR and the magazine PRACTICAL ELECTRONICS sent to him at school, and this continued whilst he was in hospital.

Victor's school was in an old building, and the Spastic Society decided to erect a purpose built school in the same grounds. The move into these new buildings happened before the official opening. Whilst Victor was in Sheffield, we heard that the Duke of Edinburgh would be opening the new school. This was something which Victor wanted to attend. Mr Sharrard permitted Victor to come home for a few days so that I could take him to Tonbridge. I collected Victor by car from the hospital, brought him home for one night, and took him to his school the next day. I was not allowed to stay, as no parents were permitted to attend the big ceremony. Victor was in his wheelchair, with slippers on his feet. He could not wear shoes yet. A special place had been erected and prepared for the landing of the Duke of Edinburgh's helicopter. Victor was full of excitement, and never stopped talking about the ceremony on our way back home. The next day I drove him back to Sheffield. He has never forgotten that big special day.

I knew that Victor wouldn't be able to walk straight away, once everything had healed up, but he could go back to school in his wheelchair. There were plenty of wheelchair pupils in the Thomas Delarue School. We reckoned that Victor would be back at his school in June. With Peter also at boarding school, Bob and I decided to take a holiday alone. We intended to drive to my brother in Germany, and then to my sister in Italy. I was a bit concerned about the driving. Bob had done such a great deal with all the travelling to Sheffield, but he said he didn't mind. It was good to get away from everything and everybody. We certainly needed a break by now.

Mr Herzog was in charge of King Edward Vll Hospital, and one Saturday, when we visited Victor, he asked us to come and see him in his office. He told us that Mr Sharrard was pleased with Victor's progress, but there was still one more operation that Victor should have. He couldn't straighten one leg, because he had kept it bent for years. This could be corrected by cutting the tendon slightly behind the knee and then stretching it. This would mean a longer stay in hospital. We told Mr Herzog about our plan to go and see my family, as we had thought Victor would be back at school.

'It is not a big operation,' said Mr Herzog. 'I will perform it myself. Do go away; you have had a tough time and need a break. When you come back you will feel better and strong enough to get on with the next challenge, to get Victor on to his legs and walking again. If you give me an address, I will write to tell you how the operation has gone, and how Victor is progressing. Surely you have some other relatives that can come and visit Victor. You will only be away for three weeks.'

We talked to Victor, and gave him a camera and a lightmeter as a reward for being so brave all the time he was in hospital. He had changed; he had grown up, the boy had become a man. He understood that we, too, had suffered, and had to give up a lot to be with him in his need. He didn't mind if we went away, because when we came back he would come home for good. I was surprised by his understanding, and realised that he must have worked things out for himself whilst lying for hours alone in a hospital bed. Raymond promised to visit him more often.

We had a good holiday. Mr Herzog wrote a long letter to us, keeping his promise. Victor told us later that he came to see him several times, making sure he was not too lonely. Before the operation, he gave him quite a fright, and Victor never knew whether it was a joke or a genuine mistake. On the morning of the operation he came to see Victor, and said to him:

'It is on the right leg where we have to stretch the tendon, isn't it?'

'No,' said Victor, shocked, 'it is the left leg.'

He was terribly afraid that the wrong leg would be operated on. When he gradually woke up after the operation, he immediately felt his knees, to make sure the left leg was bandaged. He also had learnt another thing by now, how to cope with the feeling of nausea. This time he asked for a bowl of soup straight away, ate it all, then was violently sick, and felt alright after that.

When we came back from our trip, I spent three days in Sheffield, being shown what exercises I had to do with Victor, so that his legs would get stronger and he would walk again. After that I brought him home for the summer holiday.

Victor had been in hospital for six months. He left home as a boy and returned a young man.

CHAPTER SIX

Studying Again - Another Operation

Just after Victor had gone into hospital, Bob's cousin Nina and her husband visited us. They had moved to Chesham, not too far from us, and we met occasionally. In the course of the conversation, Nina mentioned that she was going to study again. She had decided to become a teacher.

'I am starting in September at Wall Hall College, in Aldenham, near Watford,' she said. 'They are short of Infant teachers, and there is a special two year course which I am going to attend.'

'How did you know about it?' I asked. 'What did you have to do? Tell me everything from the beginning.'

'A friend of mine started last year on a three year course,' said Nina. 'That's the usual time for this type of training. You have to have at least two A-levels to be accepted at the college. My friend has joined a class of young students, all girls just coming out of school, but she said it is fun. Because they are so desperate for teachers, they have now started a two year course for mature students. The curriculum is the same as for the three year course, but it is felt that people who have had children already have more experience, and will also take their studies more seriously, so they should be managing in two years. I applied to the college last September, and they sent me the forms. You always have to apply a year in advance. I had an interview with the principal a month ago, and have just heard that I have been accepted. I even get a grant, because I worked before, although that was a long time ago.'

'How are you going to manage?' I asked. 'You have got three children.'

'I will only be away when they are at school,' replied Nina. 'The girls are old enough to look after themselves. They are fourteen and twelve, and old enough to keep an eye on Hugh until I come home. I feel it is the only job I could have, because I will always be at home in the school holidays.'

'What a wonderful idea,' I said. 'I wouldn't mind doing it myself. I never finished my studies when I was young. I always felt I would like to achieve something in my life; finish some kind of training, with a certificate at the end. Working in Bob's factory is alright, but the holidays are always difficult. One even gets a grant. I wouldn't miss out on the money when I stop working. We do need this, as Peter is now going to boarding school.'

'Oh, Helga,' said Nina, 'that would be wonderful if you could come also. We could study together. I don't think you could start in September, as the applications should have been in already last year, but if you apply now, you could start next year. There is also the possibility that somebody drops out, and they have a vacancy. It would be absolutely wonderful to do this together.'

Bob had listened to us talking, and interrupted by saying:

'Helga has no certificates. She also didn't go to school in England. Her English is alright, but how is she going to prove what type of education she has had?'

'That's true,' I replied. 'The only thing I have got is my identity card from the Königsberger University, showing that I studied medicine. That should be good enough. You cannot go to university unless you have A-levels.'

It was decided that I would apply to Wall Hall College. Bob kept on doubting that I would be accepted, but I proved him wrong. I filled out the forms, and two weeks later I had an interview with Miss Dickinson, the principal of the college.

I had expected Miss Dickinson to give me some kind of examination in view of the fact that I had no certificates, but meeting the principal was very informal. Wall Hall is a beautiful old manor house situated in a lovely park. Miss Dickinson entertained me in her sitting room. The secretary took me to the room and introduced me. Miss Dickinson invited me to sit down in an easy chair, and asked me whether I would like a cup of tea. A tray with all the tea things was on the table, and I could see that she expected me to say 'yes.' She served the tea, offered me a biscuit, which I declined, smiled, and talked about Wall Hall and its surroundings. She said she was looking forward to the Spring, when the park always looked at its best. She wanted me to feel at ease. After that we just had a conversation. She asked me questions about my past. She told me that she had had two other students who had been educated in Germany, and she had found that they had had a much better grounding in a number of subjects, particularly in mathematics. I wasn't quite sure what that had to do with teaching infant children. Their mathematics, up to the age of seven, was not very complicated. She was impressed with what I had learnt at school, especially that I had attended Latin classes, but that was necessary for me as a future medical student.

She wanted to know what life was like under Hitler, and was sorry that I had become a refugee. She, too, remembered the war very well.

She was pleased to hear that Victor and Peter were at boarding school, which would give me time to concentrate on my studies.

'The course is not easy,' she said. 'To cover in two years what others cover in three needs extra time for homework. You also have quite a journey to come every day. If you are accepted, you can apply for a grant, which you should use to get help in running your home, so that you have free time for your work.'

Miss Dickinson made me feel relaxed, and I enjoyed talking to her. Even the concern about not having any certificates was brushed aside. It was just like I said to Bob. Having studied medicine for a time was a good advertisement. I never realised that I had been an hour with the principal, when she suddenly said:

'We still have two places for the course starting in September. We will let you know our decision, but because you are not English by birth, you will have to have the approval of the Cambridge Institute of Education, who are also responsible for the assessment and examination of the students at our college. The director of the Institute will probably write to you. I have enjoyed meeting you, and hope you get a favourable reply to your application.'

With that we shook hands and I left. She had hinted that she liked me, and I felt sure I would be accepted.

The letter came a week later, telling me that I had a place at Wall Hall subject to a satisfactory medical report and the approval of the Cambridge Institute of Education. This meant that I had to go to Cambridge. I was given a date and time to meet the director of the Institute.

The tea was missing in this interview, and it was in an office. I remember entering a large uncarpeted room with a big old-fashioned fireplace to the left, and a seating corner to the right, with a small table with an ashtray on it. A man was sitting behind a heavy-looking desk opposite the door. The desk top was covered with papers, and there were two telephones. I couldn't quite see the man's features, as the bay window behind him blinded me. It was a beautiful sunny day. There was an empty hard chair opposite the desk.

This is unfair, I thought. He is hiding his face in the shadow, whilst mine will be exposed to the bright light from the window. I felt this had been done on purpose. Why not the seating corner, that would have been more comfortable.

I assumed that the man was Mr F, the director of the Institute of Education, but there was no introduction. He looked at me silently, holding ruler in his hands as if he was going to break it in half. I slowly moved forward because I assumed the empty chair was for me. He just watched me crossing the room. There was a faint echo from my steps, because of the wooden floor. I stopped next to the chair.

'Mr F?' I asked. 'I am Mrs Gerhardi.'

'Yes,' he said. 'I know, please sit down.'

I took the chair and put it by the side of the desk.

'The sun is blinding me,' I said apologetically, and sat down.

He didn't like this, because I saw how he gripped the ruler and bent it, but it did not break.

'I understand from Miss Dickinson that you would like to attend the two years teacher's course at Wall Hall, but have no certificates, only a registration card from the university of ... '

He picked up a letter from the pile of papers in front of him and glanced at it. He was looking for the word Königsberg, but either couldn't find it, or couldn't pronounce it, so he just added

' ... some kind of German university. Now tell me something about your life in Germany.'

'Where would you like me to start?'

'I don't mind, please yourself.'

'In that case I'd better start at the beginning. I was born next to the Lithuanian border in a small town called ...'

I just carried on describing how we moved to Königsberg, what happened when Hitler came to power ... I stopped, looking questioningly at him.

'Tell me some more,' he said.

I talked about my school, how by chance I met Hitler. Here he interrupted me with the words:

'Fascinating, tell me some more.'

He got up and positioned himself in front of the fireplace, gripping the shelf with one hand, whilst the other rested in his pocket. I could see now that he was a thin, tall man, with an athletic figure. He was really interested in my story, and I just carried on. Every time I stopped, he just said:

'Tell me some more.'

He was a man of few words. I seemed to give him my whole life storey. I didn't like to tell him everything, so I jumped a few years, and told him when I got married, that I had two children, and that one of them was a spastic and had just undergone several operations.

'Tell me some more.'

By now I could have screamed at him - what more do you want me to tell you!

'I think that's more or less all,' I said, refusing to give him any more details about my life.

'Fascinating,' he said again. 'Absolutely fascinating. You ought to write a book.'

People had said that to me before. In those days I was not ready yet for this big task, especially as I didn't like to think about the time when I was a refugee. That was something I always pushed into the back of my mind.

I sat there, looking at him. I had finished talking, and it was up to him to end the interview.

'I will write to you,' said Mr F. 'You may go now.'

I got up and walked towards the door with my steps again echoing through the room. Mr F watched me from the fireplace.

I stopped by the door, looked at him and waited, wondering whether he would come and open the door for me. He hadn't been very gentlemanly-like from the moment I had entered his office. It irritated me. I had never been treated like that. He suddenly seemed to realise what I expected of him, and stepped forward. He opened the door and said goodbye. I felt his eyes on my back whilst I was walking along the corridor on my way to the car park. I didn't turn round, so I might have been mistaken.

I didn't know what the interview was all about. Mr F had never asked me questions. I must assume that he only wanted to know how good my English was. Teachers should not speak a faulty English, or have a strong accent.

After I told Bob and the boys about Mr F, the sentence "tell me some more" became a joke in our family.

A short formal note arrived from Cambridge, confirming that I could start in September 1964 at Wall Hall, and would be joining a course designed to teach children up to thirteen years of age.

I was terribly proud to be able to study again. This time, if I got through the two years, I should be rewarded with a teacher's certificate, which would be quite an achievement at the age of forty.

Nina was very happy when she heard that we could both start at the same time.

'Miss Dickinson must have liked you,' she said. 'They had a great number of applications, and they only take twenty for the class, all mature students.'

She couldn't comment on Mr F as she didn't have to go to Cambridge. She laughed when I told her the story about my interview.

Victor and Peter went back to boarding school in September, and I started my studies as a teacher. Everybody in our class was married and had children. The moment we entered College, our families were forgotten, and we were young girls again, chatting, laughing, joking and uninhibited in our behaviour. We helped one another, we were comrades, and new friendships were formed. Some of the tutors were younger than us, but that didn't seem to matter. We were all keen to learn again after having stagnated for years. We had only lived for our families, doing the housework, cooking, washing, ironing, looking after the children. We were thirsty for knowledge, and didn't mind any amount of homework. For me, the best thing was that I had to read books again, and got advice which ones to choose.

I got some help for the garden, and I also organised somebody to do the housework. I still carried on with the washing and cooking and looking after the boys in the holidays.

The work for the college was tremendous, as the curriculum was very varied. The main subject was education, and a whole day a week was given to it. We started with the natural endowment and development of children from birth onwards - their needs and behavioural tendencies, intelligence, individual differences among children, learning and play, motivation, remembering, forgetting, imagination, reasoning, solving problems, and even had some lessons and discussions about the special needs of handicapped and gifted children. We talked about methods of teaching, and organisation within the class and the school. We had three periods of teaching practice at different schools, the final one of six weeks at the end of the second year.

We visited schools, observed lessons, helped at nursery schools and had trips to museums in London. We had to write reports and give our opinion after every visit. We were very well educated in a great number of subjects. The only thing we were never taught was how to teach. I talked to the teachers I met at the different schools, and they said the only way to learn that was by experience and watching other teachers.

We also had physical education which, for us "old ones," was very hard. Our tutor was a young woman, and seemed to enjoy putting us through the most awkward exercises and dances. Hardly any of us had done anything since we left school, and our limbs were not supple enough. We all finished up with aches and pains. Nina got so bad at times that she had the greatest difficulty getting in and out of the car. I wasn't too bad because, having to carry Victor for a number of years, and now again after his operations, I was used to backache, and was probably also more muscular than my fellow students. The idea was that we should experience first what we were going to teach to the children. The Cambridge Institute of Education, who set the curriculum, had forgotten that women of forty are not as mobile as children or young girls just leaving school. Nobody liked physical education and changing into leotards, which showed up our mature figures!

Everybody had to write a dissertation of 10,000 words on any subject covering education. After the first year, an outline and rough draft had to be handed in to Miss H, our education tutor, for inspection and discussion. The whole dissertation had to be typed and given in towards the end of the second year. It was part of the final assessment. The title of my dissertation was: Spasticity and its Effects on Children's Education. There were two reasons why I chose this title. Firstly I felt I knew a great deal about it by now, because of Victor, and secondly it gave me the chance to study this subject further, and discuss it with my tutor.

One girl in the Chesham library was very helpful to me. She looked up a number of books about handicapped children, cerebral palsy and education of slow learning children, and then ordered these books for me. All I had to do was to go to the library and pick them up. This saved time, which I could utilise to read the books. I went to Queen Mary's Hospital in Carshalton and observed the teaching methods in the Cerebral Palsy Unit, and I did the same at Victor's school. I included several child studies in my dissertation, and also photographs of children using special equipment.

The first draft of my work had 20,000 words, but Miss H did not allow me to cut it. She was very impressed with my study of the subject, and sent the final dissertation to Cambridge, where it was kept for over a year. I had to write several letters before it was returned to me. Miss H always said I should publish it, as it would be of great interest not only to parents with cerebral palsy children, but also for teachers, nurses and health visitors. That was probably also the reason why it was kept so long in Cambridge.

We had to make our own equipment for our teaching practices. This was prepared in Art and Craft lessons at college, and at home. I was very lucky, because this was something which Bob could help me with. I made beautiful cards with sums for mathematics. For reading and writing practice, I designed cards with sentences and certain missing nouns, which were replaced by pictures. The children had to copy the sentences, and replace the pictures with the written nouns. Bob spray-lacquered the cards in the factory. Dirty children's hands couldn't mark the cards now. To explain feet and inches, Bob cut me wooden rods in those sizes, even half a foot, and sprayed them with different coloured glossy paint. He did the same for the wooden shapes, like circle, triangle, square, rectangle, etc. which the children could use. They were able to feel them and draw around them. I bought a small scale with brass weights which were marked in pounds and ounces. When I went to my teaching practice, I had a great big bag full of equipment, which I also used later when I was teaching full time.

The first teaching practice I had was in a small Infant School near Abbots Langley. It lasted two weeks, and was supposed to be an introduction to teaching.

I was to observe the teacher, to see how she handled the class, then take over a few lessons and, after a fortnight, be able to teach for a whole day. The first day was alright, as I only did what the class teacher advised me to do. The school was very small. There were only two infant classes, one taken by the headmistress, and one by Miss P The two ladies were great friends, and had run this school for years. They had made their own rules and their own time table, were very efficient, and co-operated with one another.

When I arrived on the second day, I was told by the headmistress that Miss P was ill and I would have to take over the class without any help or supervision. I was stunned and shocked, and entered the class of forty-two children with a pretended confidence. I was glad that I had prepared my own teaching material. It always helps to introduce something new to children, particularly if it is colourful. They would soon break up for Easter, so my theme for the two weeks was "Easter time" or, as I explained to the children, we would split up the word and call it "Easter" and "Time."

We drew, made and counted Easter eggs and rabbits, and constructed a large "Frieze" on the wall. For "Time," we drew clocks, using the different sized, round coloured wooden blocks which Bob had made. I hung up a cuckoo clock which I brought from home, and everybody stopped working when the little cuckoo came out and counted the hours.

It was a successful fortnight, and I got an excellent mark from the college examiner who came and watched me towards the end of the second week. By then I was quite confident, and knew the children. Miss P never returned whilst I was there.

My second teaching practice was more difficult. This was in Nash Mills. The children came from a working class background and were tougher, at times quite unruly. Often both parents worked, and the children were left too long alone and unsupervised. I had a number of so-called "Latchkey" children. These were children who had the house key on a string around their neck, or it was hidden in the garden because the parents would not be home when school closed.

I had fifty-two children in the class, and there was hardly any teaching material. I spent half the night and all the weekend preparing new teaching material. My practice lasted four weeks, and the class teacher disappeared into the staff room every day, to give me free rein.

'I won't be in your way,' she said, 'and I won't interfere. Just get on with things. Most of them don't want to learn in any case, and don't get any encouragement from home. Be careful with your teaching material; some of the boys are very rough, and break everything. If you cannot manage, come and get me from the staff room.'

She gave me the names of the rough ones, and also the ones who could not read yet, although they were seven years old, and then she left me.

The class teacher was right. There were too many children in the class, and the greater part of the day was taken up with trying to keep them quiet, and to make them sit still. I had to have eyes in the front and in the back of my head. At college we were taught to encourage children with praise, never shout at them, avoid punishment, always be kind to them, even when it was necessary to reprimand them. I was soon convinced that none of the tutors had ever had to teach an unruly class of fifty-two children.

When I entered the class on my second day, the children were shouting, screaming, climbing over desks, running around, fighting, and didn't take any notice of me. Quietly I put my bags on the desk and just stood there watching them. One or two suddenly saw me and whispered that the teacher was there. A few started to sit down after that, then a few more. I just stood there waiting and looking at them. Gradually they all sat down except for one. He loitered around by the window. He put his hands in his pockets and pretended to be interested in something outside. I knew he was one of the worst troublemakers.

'Sit down, Ken,' I said quietly. He turned slowly and started to make a step in the opposite direction to his chair.

'Sit down, Ken,' I bellowed, and pointed to his chair.

For a few seconds there was a frightened look on his face, and then he quickly sat down. One or two of his friends giggled openly when they saw that he had obeyed. I looked at my watch, and then announced:

'We have lost nearly five minutes of our lesson because of your running around and screaming. To make up for the lost time, you will all go out five minutes later when it comes to playtime.'

I made sure I stood near the door when the bell rang, and occupied them all five minutes longer. I also told them that this would happen every day. By the end of the week everybody rushed to their seats as soon as I entered the room, and kept quiet.

Ken always seemed to have sweets and chocolates, and I also discovered that he had money in his pockets. At first he would hardly talk to me. He was annoyed that I had made him sit down on the first day. Gradually he became more friendly, especially when I produced the scale with the brass weights, and showed him how to weigh chestnuts, dried beans and peas, and then count them. He told me that he had plenty of money, and knew how to get more. His father looked at TV every Saturday to watch the football. Ken just misbehaved and was noisy, or tried to talk to his father, which prevented him from concentrating on the game, so he gave his son some money to get rid of him. If it wasn't enough, Ken would come back after a time and try the same trick again, and then got some more money. The boy was very good with figures, but he had difficulties in reading, and didn't like it.

Nash Mills was quite a big school and had a headmaster. He informed me one day that he would come in the afternoon to see me take a mathematics lesson. The afternoon in an infant class was usually reserved for art and craft, but I was told to re-arrange the lessons for that day. So that Ken would behave, I gave him the scales to work on. The lesson went quite well. The headmaster was surprised about the equipment I had made and brought along. He told me to come and see him after the school was finished. He had the key to a store room full of equipment, which he showed me.

'You could have some cardboard or paint from here, and could also have asked for some books or counting equipment. We are well supplied at the school. The teachers have to sign for everything they take out at the beginning of term, and return it at the end. Anything that is missing they have to replace. Of course, you are only here for four weeks, so it wasn't worth while letting you have anything.'

I just looked at him and thought how stupid this explanation was.

I didn't want any equipment for myself, it was supplied for the benefit of the children. He should have let every class have some, and if it broke replace it. I knew that every year schools got an allowance for equipment. No wonder the store room was full of it. The teachers probably didn't ask for it, as they didn't want to replace it out of their own pockets if it got broken or disappeared. So the children were deprived.

The headmaster gave me a good report at the end of my teaching practice. He said if he had a vacancy after my two year training, he wouldn't hesitate to offer me a job. I thanked him, but said I preferred a place nearer to my home.

My third teaching practice, at Goldfield Infant School in Tring, was closer to my home. The headmistress was young and charming and the school quite new with good equipment. Although there were over forty children in the class most of them wanted to learn and participated in the lessons. Two or three of the boys had to be watched as they were a disturbing influence in this top infant class of six to seven year old children. I brought my cuckoo clock again and all my teaching equipment and the six weeks passed quickly. Several college examiners came and watched me teaching and so did Miss B the headmistress. I only had one disturbing incident.

There was one rough boy in the class. Most of the girls didn't like him. He misbehaved on and off, and at times I felt like hitting him. He was bad at reading and could hardly count. He was seven years old and would have to leave the school by the end of the term to go to the next school. If he couldn't read by then he would probably never catch up after that. I spent extra time with him in the afternoon whilst the others were drawing or painting or making things. Often he wouldn't concentrate, only think what he could do to annoy me or show off to the other children.

One break time when I opened the door for the children to go out to play he waited for everybody to go out, then followed them and urinated just outside the door in full view of everybody. The girls screamed and ran away in case they got wet. I lost my temper and hit him. I got hold of him and wanted to take him to the headmistress, but he pulled away and shouted:

'You hit me, you hit me, you wait until I tell my dad!' and he ran off.

I went to see Miss B and told her what had happened. She looked at me concerned and said:

'You shouldn't have done that, although I understand why you did it. The boy's father is a big, strong, uncouth man. He is unemployed and will probably come to the school. You will see him coming from your classroom. Don't talk to him, leave this to me. I will deal with him. Never hit a child again, never mind how much they provoke you.'

Sure enough, we had only just started our lessons again when I saw a big, broad-shouldered man walking quickly across the playground to the back entrance of the school. It must have been at least half an hour later that he walked back slowly. Miss B never told me what she had said to him. The boy was a little quieter for a couple of days, but then he became the usual trouble-maker again. The subject was never mentioned between him and me.

The class teacher was going to leave at the end of term and Miss B offered me her job for September. She had seen me teaching and she also knew that we would get on with one another. She wanted me to take over the same age class. It was reassuring to see what confidence she had in me. I hadn't even taken the final examination yet.

We all seemed to study day and night towards the end of our last term in Wall Hall. There was a lot of work to be handed in, and I developed a corn on my finger from all the writing I had to do. The day arrived when everything was done except the oral examination. We were told to come to college for two days when the examiners would be there. Not everybody had an oral question time, there were far too many students to be tested. Only a handful would be picked out, but everybody had to turn up.

I wanted to do some revising on the last weekend before the oral examination, and Bob and I decided that I could do this in West Mersea at our caravan site, whilst relaxing at the same time. Bob picked me up from college late Friday afternoon.

For the last year I seemed to have had more back pain than ever before. The reason could have been the physical training we had to do at college and also the fact that I had to carry Victor again since he came out of hospital. He was not a child any more, and quite heavy. His walking progressed, but there were times when he had to be lifted or carried.

Our weekend at West Mersea turned out to be a disaster. When I tried to get up on Saturday morning, I literally collapsed. I just fainted and crumpled to the floor. The pain in the lower region of my back was horrendous. Bob wanted to get a doctor, but I wanted to get home. I was afraid that I might have to go into hospital and preferred the advice of my own doctor. Bob helped to dress me, which was not easy lying down. He then brought our estate car close to the caravan door and somehow got me into the car. He had put the car seat down and taken one of the mattresses from the caravan out, so that I could lie down.

The journey home was not too bad as I had taken some pain killers. When we arrived at our house Bob stopped close to the front door and stood me on to the door mat in our hall. I couldn't walk, so he just pulled the mat along to the stairs and I practically crawled up and into bed. The doctor was called and diagnosed a slipped disc. I had never realised that that could be so painful. I had to have a board under my mattress, no pillow and lie flat for a week in bed. It was even painful to lift my head up.

This meant, of course, that I couldn't attend the oral examination at Wall Hall. I phoned our course tutor, Miss H, but she assured me that I had nothing to worry about. She couldn't give me the results of my work, but by reassuring me I knew that I had passed. She phoned me at the end of the week very excited to confirm that I had passed in the teaching examination and was the only one who had a distinction in dress design, costume and needlework.

'Congratulations,' she said. 'You have done very well indeed. Now get better quickly so that you can attend the college "Farewell Party."'

The week in bed seemed to drag on. I had nothing to do; I couldn't even hold a book in my hands to read, it was too painful. The boys were at boarding school, I had no visitors and nobody to look after me. Bob came home at lunchtime and brought me some dinner, which I could hardly eat. The cook in the canteen was well-meaning and sent me large portions along. It is not easy to eat lying flat on ones back. I made Bob squash some potatoes and vegetables into the gravy and then feed me with it. In this way I could swallow some nourishment. He asked the cook to make me some jelly, another thing I could easily swallow. He left me a flask of tea, but sometimes it was too painful for me to pour the tea into the invalid cup with a spout, the only way I could drink it, so I just waited until Bob came back. Those were the days when I wished my mother was alive or I lived near my sister Christel.

Once I was up again I saw a specialist who prescribed a corset with strong thick metal bars back and front. Every time I sat down the bars in the front pushed under my ribs. Even after returning twice to the hospital for alterations, padding it every morning with cotton wool, I still got sore and when my skin was raw, I refused to wear it again.

Miss B offered me the job at Goldfield Infant School in Tring as promised. I had an interview with the Hertfordshire County Council who approved of me, and I started my first teaching job in September 1966. I soon settled down to the routine of teaching and enjoyed it. The only trouble was my back. In an infant class all tables and chairs are low. Sometimes, after bending over to a child for a time, explaining and showing things, I couldn't straighten up again. I would then walk slowly from one table to the next in the bent position, still talking to the children so that they wouldn't notice what had happened, and make my way to my desk where I could slide on to my chair.

I went to London to see Mr Langley, the osteopath who had told me that Victor had Little's disease. He examined me and told me I had a worn disc, probably because of carrying Victor for years. The disc is the gristle between two vertebrae. When this slips out to the side it presses on the sciatic nerve which can produce tremendous pain.

'I know you have the pain in your back,' said Mr Langley, 'and it extends from there to the right thigh and down to the calf of the leg. But because your disc is worn, I can move it and manipulate it also over to the left side where you then will experience the same type of pain.'

To prove it, he did just that, and I had the pain on the other side. Lying in bed a few days makes the gristle slip back into its usual place. He told me I must not lift anything any more, avoid bending down, rather kneel and treat my back like glass. Wearing a corset wouldn't cure it, it would only weaken the muscles in the back.

After the operations in Sheffield Victor returned to school in a wheelchair. Gradually he got on to his feet again and eventually walked with a stick. He was interested in Technical Drawing, Mathematics, Science, Electronics, Metal and Woodwork and had lessons in all these subjects. He passed his O-levels in Technical Drawing and Mathematics in 1966. The school also sponsored Victor and his friend Richard so that they could build a small computer. They were allowed to join the boys from the local Public School for special classes on computer-building once a week. I thought that the school bus took them there and back every week because of their handicap, but Victor told me later that they had to catch the normal bus to complete the course.

Whenever Victor came home for holidays or the occasional weekend, he was always full of new ideas of what to build next. His bedroom was cluttered with screws, wires, crystal sets, microphones, condensers and valves, and the little boy who was so dependent on his mother for years turned to his father who was more up to date in science and electronics.

Victor could not participate in a lot of sport, but he could swim, and at school they had wheelchair dancing. He also belonged to the basket ball team. It was fascinating to see the teams playing this game and to observe

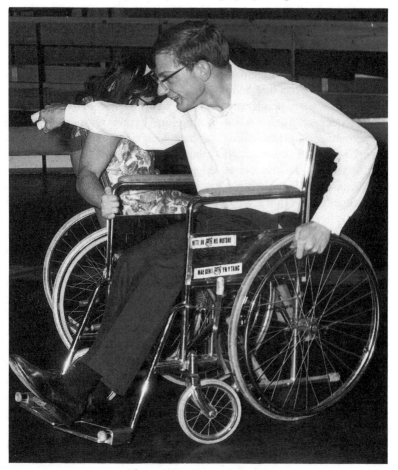

Victor Wheelchair Dancing

how skilful these young people were with their wheelchairs. The only other exercise Victor could do was cycling on his big tricycle. He got the Bronze Medal in the Duke of Edinburgh Award Scheme for cycling 100 miles to Canterbury and back.

Gradually Victor became very independent. I used to fetch him by car for the occasional weekend at home during the term, but then he decided it was time to come home on his own. The train journey from Tonbridge to London was easy, but after that he had to go by underground to Marylebone station to catch the train to Wendover. He had to learn how to manage the escalators with his unstable walk, having a stick in one hand and a small suitcase in the other.

'I just drop the suitcase on to a step of the escalator,' said Victor, 'and hope it will shoot off at the bottom or at the top. People sometimes help me or pick up the suitcase. Actually I prefer it if they carry the suitcase rather than help me. I know what I am doing, and I am alright once I can grip the moving handrail and stand on a step.'

His suitcase was tough, dirty, dented, strong and never broke.

One weekend when I was expecting him, I had a phone call from his house mother on Friday telling me that Victor wouldn't come home as he wasn't very well. I thought he might have a cold or the flu, and was surprised when she said it was his leg.

'Victor is walking with two crutches,' she said. 'He has terrible pains from time to time in the top of one of his legs. If it doesn't improve you will have to take him back to Sheffield so that he could have a check-up with Mr Sharrard. We felt it would be better for him to stay at school for the weekend. In any case it is impossible for him to take the train to come home.'

I suggested to come and fetch him by car on Saturday morning, but she said there were several other boys who hadn't gone home for the weekend so he would have company.

We had just finished our supper when we had a phone call from the stationmaster in Wendover:

'Your son is here in a wheelchair and would like you to pick him up by car,' he said.

Bob and I dashed to the station. There was Victor sitting in a wheelchair, holding two crutches and his little dented suitcase, smiling all over his face.

'I have made it,' he said. 'I wasn't going to stay in the school for the weekend, I told them so. I left a note for Miss Peach, my house mother, so that she won't worry.'

He told us that he had phoned for a taxi and met it at the gate so that nobody in the school could see him entering a car. He got into the train in Tonbridge with the guard's help. In London he again got a taxi and the driver was very kind, bringing the car on to the station nearly to the platform, and helping him into the train. The stationmaster at Wendover knew him and helped him out of the train and then phoned us.

It was quite an achievement and Bob and I were proud of him. I knew then, that whatever happened to him in life he would be able to cope, find a way out and succeed.

One day the headmaster's secretary phoned with a message that the headmaster wanted to see us as soon as possible. She wouldn't tell me what it was all about. At least she assured me that he was alright. So what had he done that was so important that we had to come to the school? We were very worried and concerned when we were shown into the headmaster's study. We had only met the new head of the school once before. He was different to old Mr Davies, younger, full of new ideas, and one could see how proud he was to be in charge of such a beautiful new school. He came straight to the point.

'Victor is refusing to be confirmed,' he said. 'We are coming to the end of the confirmation classes which Victor has regularly attended, but now he is refusing to take part in the actual confirmation.'

'Is that the reason why you have asked us to come and see you?' I enquired. I just couldn't believe it, that he had made us come all the way to Tonbridge because Victor didn't want to be confirmed. This was something which could have been discussed on the phone or by letter. Bob had to take a day off and it was a very long journey, too.

'We are all very upset here at the school about this sudden about turn, and felt sure you would want to come and talk to him, so that he changes his mind.'

'You are mistaken, it is not an about turn. Victor had his doubts before he started with the classes,' I said. 'He didn't want to take confirmation classes but we persuaded him to go along. He said he would do it if we promised not to force him to be confirmed if he decided against it at the end. We gave him this promise and he attended the classes. He is a sensible boy, old enough to know what he is doing. If he has decided not to be confirmed we will back him in this decision as promised.'

The headmaster just stared at us. He tried to show us how wrong we were not even to try to make Victor change his mind. Bob told him quite firmly a promise is a promise, even if the boy is still at school.

'In any case,' added Bob, 'Victor can be confirmed in later years, actually any time he wants to. I wasn't confirmed until I was forty years old and then it was my own decision. I promised then to attend church regularly and I do. Victor probably doesn't want to do that. He doesn't want to promise something which he knows he won't keep.'

After meeting the headmaster we saw Victor and took him out for tea. It was just as Bob had said. Victor didn't want to promise things which he already knew he wouldn't keep. He was sorry that we had to come all the way to Tonbridge because of this. Nobody had told him that we were coming, and nobody had wanted an explanation from him either, when he informed them that he wasn't going to be confirmed.

The pain in Victor's leg got worse. It would suddenly attack him without warning and he would fall to the ground. We went to see Mr Sharrard who discovered through X-rays that a small screw which was holding the plate in the top of Victor's leg, had become loose.

'The bones have healed very well,' said Mr Sharrard. 'The plate can be taken out.'

We made arrangements that Victor would have Christmas at home, but come to Sheffield for the operation straight after that.

I always remember what happened after this operation. Bob, Peter and I arrived in the afternoon. It was New Year's Eve and Victor had had the operation before dinner.

They hadn't wheeled him back to the ward because they said there were some complications. We found Victor in a room next to the operating theatre behind some screens with two nurses talking to him. They explained to us that Victor could not return to the ward unless he passed water. One of them said:

'We have given him an injection, talked to him, let the tap run like you do for young children, and even lifted him out of bed and on to the cold floor, hoping that the shock would make him urinate.'

'Maybe you have done too much,' I said. 'Would you like me to try? I have known Victor a long time.'

They promised to leave me alone with Victor, and Bob took Peter to the canteen for a drink. Victor told me how hard they had tried, but he just couldn't do it. He always had difficulty when other people were watching or wanted him to perform. To relax him I made a joke and we both laughed.

He was wide awake after the operation and didn't feel sick. We just talked like we always did. At seventeen years of age Victor was a young man. Because of his disability and the difficulties with which he had to cope, we had become friends for years, rather than being mother and son. I think at times he even forgot that I was a woman. After ten minutes he had filled up three bottles and the so-called complications were overcome. He was wheeled back to the ward. We stayed with him until he went to sleep.

It was late when we drove back on the motorway. We stopped at a rest place called "The Captain's Table" where we had a meal and at twelve o'clock saw the New Year in with coffee. I had my own little wish for the coming years - please let this be the last operation that Victor has to have. The future proved that my prayer was answered.

Victor was only twelve or thirteen years old when he started to learn to drive. He would sit with Bob who did all the manipulations with his feet, and Victor would steer the car. Of course this had to be on private ground. So whenever we went away in the caravan and parked for the night on old airfields, sports grounds or other empty places, he would have a drive. At the age of sixteen Bob let him use the foot controls. We thought he might have to have an adapted car, but Victor didn't want this. He managed the controls alright with his feet and legs. As soon as he was seventeen Bob had to put an L-plate on my car and take Victor for lessons everytime he was home. In my second year at Wall Hall Bob had bought me a red Mini. This was just right for Victor to practice on. He also had official lessons to make quite sure he was taught with up-to-date methods.

Suddenly he didn't want to go back to school by train, because if I took him, he could drive all the way to Tonbridge with me being the passenger. The surprising thing was that he could drive straight away after his last operation. We collected him from Sheffield, bringing my mini, and when we got to Leicester he said he would like to drive a little. He drove all the way home! Soon after that he passed his driving test, and I lost my car as soon as he got home from school. He was a good driver and Bob and I felt we could trust him to take the car whenever he wanted to.

In 1967 Bob's father wanted to retire, and the factory was sold. For the first time in our married life we had some extra money. Bob got a five-year contract from the new firm to stay on as a director and a good salary.

My back kept on giving me trouble. I went to see another specialist who recommended a different corset. Again with metal bars front and back, but this time much longer, going up until under my breasts. Sitting in it was most uncomfortable, but at least the bars didn't push under my ribs. I only wore it when I was really bad. I lived a lot on pain-killing drugs. The specialist also told me that I had to give up teaching small children as I shouldn't bend down all the time. Miss B, the head mistress, and the Hertfordshire County Council were sorry to lose me, but my health was important.

CHAPTER SEVEN

Peter - Victor - A Wedding - Another Job

Having talked a great deal about Victor I might have given the impression that my other son, Peter, was neglected. This was not the case. Peter was a very affectionate and loving child and just as important in our family as Victor was. The two boys got on well together. Peter would always fetch and carry things for his brother and help him whenever he could. He never resented it that he had to run around doing little jobs. Victor was the brain, Peter his willing servant. I trusted them already quite young to go out on their own on their tricycles. Later on Victor had his big tricycle and Peter his bicycle. Peter was faster in cycling, but he would always wait for Victor and push him up a hill if necessary. The playroom above the garage was the place where they could play undisturbed. They spent hours there with their toys, the train and their Scalextric racing cars, which they never had to put away.

We discovered that Peter was not an academic and realised that he would never go to university. He didn't seem to be interested in anything except sport. He joined the Young Farmers and became their tennis champion for Buckinghamshire. He always liked food and would sometimes watch me in the kitchen, even suggesting different items to use to make the food tastier. One day he informed me that he was going to be a chef. We took up this idea, because he didn't seem to be very practical either and didn't excel in wood or metal work at school. There was no point in paying high fees at a public school if he wanted to go to college one day, so we changed him to Rodbourne College in Gayhurst near Newport Pagnell because they, too, had a boys' choir. Peter still had his lovely voice until the age of fifteen. I am glad we made several recordings of his singing. One of them we specially recorded in the church in Gt. Missenden, with Bob playing the organ for accompaniment. Victor did the recording, and I supervised everything! We were all involved that afternoon. Peter never liked to be a boarder, so eventually we let him go to the local school, John Colet, in Wendover.

Peter Choir Boy

We had a difficult time with him after that. Being used to the restrictions of a boarding school and suddenly finding that he could go off on his own at any time, he took advantage of this. He met different types of boys and there were girls too! He was like a young foal let loose. He joined the troublemakers rather than the ones who wanted to learn. We needed a lot of patience and had to get him out of scrapes several times. We couldn't lock him up. He looked old enough to go to the pub and why shouldn't he join some of his school friends there?

Peter got the Certificate of Secondary Education and passed the entrance examination for the general catering course in Aylesbury College. Here he had even more freedom and could miss classes without our knowledge. Peter as a teenager certainly was a handful.

One day he came back early from college and informed me that he had been sent home because the teacher thought he had jaundice. I looked at him. He was pale, a little yellow in his face and he said he felt sick. I told him to go to bed, have a good sleep and stop smoking.

He grinned sheepishly and enquired: 'How did you know?'

'I was young once too, and in any case you reek of cigarette smoke.'

I was worried about him smoking, because Peter suffered from bouts of asthma and hay fever and also got eczema from time to time on his wrists. The pollen affected him in Spring time. Sometimes when he walked up the lane to our house, he would practically collapse when he got in, gasping for breath. He always carried a small inhaler with him. I am glad to say that the smoking period didn't last long. Our doctor gave him a lecture and a fright, and after that he stopped.

Towards the end of the first year of Peter's catering course Miss B. the head of the department asked me to come and see her. We knew one another slightly because I had attended evening classes in Dressmaking. She informed me that she didn't think that Peter would pass the examinations and would therefore not be able to carry on for the second year. This was a shock to us. To have a City and Guilds of London Certificate in catering after a two-year course would have been the foundation for any job in the hotel or restaurant trade as chef, waiter or on the bottom step as manager.

I made an appointment to see Mr S the teacher in charge of Peter's class.

'There is nothing wrong with Peter's abilities,' he said. 'He is quite capable to be a good chef. He is clean, hard-working when he is with me in the kitchen, but he is a disturbing influence in other lessons. Particularly the lady teachers have the greatest difficulty managing him. I have pulled his ears a few times and now he has knuckled down with me.'

Mr S knew I was a teacher and wanted to help me. I had told him what Miss B had said about the second year.

'If Peter passes the examinations nobody can stop him from coming back after the summer holiday to attend the rest of the course. Pull his ears like I did and get him to revise and work hard. I will make sure he is up to scratch with his practical work in the kitchen and the restaurant,' he said.

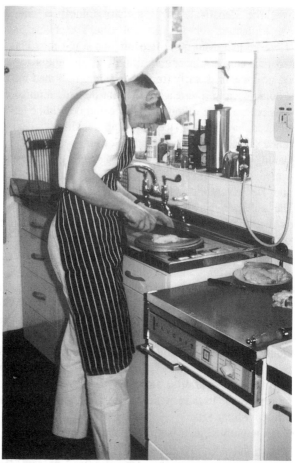

Peter as Chef

Mr S had given me good advice. I wrote to the City and Guilds of London Institute and got copies of the examination papers for the last six years. Peter was too big for me to pull his ears, but I made him sit down and learn. I was quite open with him, told him about the interviews I had had with Miss B, and Mr S, and encouraged him to give them all a big surprise by passing his examinations. I learnt with him and we would fire questions at one another at any time. At the weekend he put on his chef's uniform and cooked and served us a meal to have a practice. He was even successful in making mayonnaise by hand, dripping the oil gently into the egg yolk without letting it curdle. This was something I had never been able to do!

He had two examinations. In the first one he had to answer questions only and in the second one he had to write a long essay. He had to take the heading for this from a choice of three. For the practical examination he had to cook and serve a three-course meal in a specific time. A week before, he was allowed to work this out on paper and order the ingredients.

Looking through all the old examination papers I realised that an essay on hygiene might come up. There had also been hardly any questions about this subject in his first paper. So we concentrated on hygiene. Peter really knew everything by the time he went to college for his second examination. He came home smiling, the essay had a great deal to do with hygiene and he felt great. Even the practical test was successful and Mr S told Peter he had done well.

Peter passed his City and Guilds of London Institute examination with a credit and Miss B was shocked. She had hoped to get rid of a difficult student, but had no excuse now to stop him from taking his second year. The only trouble was that Peter didn't want to go back now. He felt that there had been several other teachers who had looked forward to his disappearance, and they would make it difficult for him.

Peter had the choice of one year full-time training at college or two year training as an apprentice in a kitchen with a day-release course at a college. He preferred to work in a kitchen and was lucky to get a place at Harrods in London and a place at Westminster College for a day-release catering course.

Every morning he took the first train to London at 6.20. He never missed it. Sometimes he went out in the evening in London with friends, and I never knew when he would come home. He had learnt to drive and passed his test, so from time to time I would leave my mini for him at the station, particularly when it was raining. Bob would drive me back. There was a footpath opposite our house, across a big field, leading to the railway station, but on wet days one had to go round the field along the road, a much longer way.

As an apprentice Peter had to go through the different stages of cooking. He had a spell in the pastry, soups, fish, gravy and hors d'oeuvre section and then became the "chef de plonge." This sounds very big, but only means washing up. The kitchen at Harrods is on the top floor with a glass roof. At times it was terribly hot and Peter got small asthma attacks, which he tried to hide. The detergent in the water and even some of the food inflamed his hands and the eczema returned. Harrods were very particular about cleanliness and hygiene. When his hands were bad, he was sent home. He wasn't allowed to touch food. This happened several times and we got worried. How would Peter cope in this environment for the rest of his working life?

Harrods training officer had a long talk with Peter about his future. She phoned me up and suggested a meeting. Bob and I had a most interesting day, meeting the training officer, the kitchen staff and being shown around the kitchen with an excellent free meal at the end. We talked with the head chef who told us that with Peter's health problem he would not be able to cope in a kitchen environment. The training officer had in the meantime found out that Peter was interested in meat, and as he wanted to stick with food, she suggested training in butchery for him. She arranged for us to meet the head of the butchery department who was willing to take Peter on as an apprentice. We all hoped that from the health point of view Peter would be able to cope. The atmosphere would be cooler, and his hands would only touch meat, not strong detergent. He also liked the idea of selling as he would have contact with customers. Peter always gave a good impression when he talked, he was very polite and it was in his nature to help other people. The few years at boarding school had given him an excellent English vocabulary and a good manner.

It was all settled on that day. Peter was apprenticed in the butchery department and went one day a week to Smithfield College. The greater part of his wages was for his railway ticket which he bought every month. It seemed to go up all the time. Getting up so early every day and being on his feet all the time made him very tired and he often went to sleep on his journey home. From time to time I had a phone call to come and fetch him by car, because he didn't wake up in Wendover and had travelled through to Aylesbury, the last station on the route. After a year when the railway ticket had gone up again he decided this was too much. There was no point in carrying on like that, he could easily find a job nearer home, which he did. He worked for a family butcher in Gt. Missenden where the factory was.

I had realised that Peter learnt much better if somebody worked with him, in a one to one teacher-student relationship. So when it came to the revising for college I studied his notes and books and then asked him questions. I learnt a lot about meat and how to cut it. At the end of his two-year course at Smithfield college he passed his examinations with a credit and got his Institute of Meat Certificate. A year later he was proposed as a member of the Institute which he proudly accepted. He became more and more confident in his trade, and is an excellent butcher now.

Now began a very difficult time for me and, looking back on to that period I realise that I only managed it because I had a kind and understanding husband and one or two friends, who helped me occasionally. The pain in my back hardly ever left me for the next two years, and carrying on from day to day often became a struggle.

With the extra money we had from selling the factory we bought a new modern caravan, an Eccles Sapphire. The following year we all went with it to Spain. We took the boat from Southampton to Bilbao to save time. Victor always wanted to go to Lourdes. He wasn't convinced that he would be cured there, but he said he would like to give it a try. We were very impressed with this Holy place. Victor drank plenty of water and we took several bottles with us when we left.

To get to the Costa Brava we crossed the Pyrennees which was quite a dangerous trip with the caravan. Bob hadn't realised how steep some of the mountain roads were. There seemed to be an unending number of bends and soon the car was boiling. He informed us that he couldn't stop, as the caravan was too heavy. He would never be able to start again. Bob opened up the heating valves to let the hot air out. We had all the windows open and we were sweating. Bob blew the car horn to warn the traffic that he couldn't possibly stop. Before every bend we could see the road above and with the horn blowing and us waving, most cars understood and let us go by. I was very frightened, so Victor and Peter said:

'Don't look at the road, but look out at the side.'

This was even worse, because all I could see there was a steep drop. We got to the top, where there was even some snow, and called in at a petrol station.

'You are boiling!' said the attendant and pointed to the steam rising from the front of the car.

'He is really telling us some news, isn't he boys!' called out Bob and laughed, relieved that we had made it to the top. Now it would be easy to go down the other side.

We stopped for a night in Andorra la Vella, the little tax haven where the price of a bottle of champagne was only the equivalent of 50p. Victor decided to forget about the Lourdes water, he preferred to drink the bubbly liquid. We met another English driver who wanted to know which road we had come up. He was rather concerned about the steep road although he had no caravan, only a tent. Bob told him what had happened, and he was quite shocked. He decided to take the easier road, even if it was much further round.

We got to the Costa Brava and had a lovely holiday on the beach and in the water. Swimming was good for my back, and Victor was able to participate as the water was warm. He could swim every day. Peter had a blow-up boat, and spent nearly the whole time in the water with it. We had a day in Gerona and went to a bullfight, which Bob filmed. Peter felt very sorry for the bull. He could see "the tears in his eyes."

For our return trip we had planned a route through France. I had my back trouble on and off, but as we never drove too long during the day I managed with pain-killers. The journey through France was longer and in the end I just couldn't sit in the car any more. I tried to stretch out in the caravan whilst travelling, although this wasn't allowed by law, but this made me car-sick. The caravan swayed and it was a very eerie feeling, as one couldn't hear a car engine. The silence was oppressing. We had allowed ourselves extra time and had to use this as I couldn't travel more than half a day. I was glad when we were home again.

Victor had come to the end of his schooling and it was time to decide what he should do next. Unfortunately or fortunately he was good at a number of subjects: Technical Drawing, Mathematics, Electronics, Physics and Wood and Metal work. Victor didn't know in which subject to specialise. The careers adviser at school couldn't show him a way either. We also knew it would be difficult for him to find a job because of his handicap. Only one thing was certain; he had to live at home and find a job or some training near our home to be able to get there under his own steam. To do this, we gave him my car. He had passed his test in it and loved the little vehicle. Soon the dashboard was full of different instruments like a rev counter, an oil pressure gauge, an ammeter, etc., all of which he built in himself.

We made an appointment with the local careers adviser but he, too, couldn't help us with Victor. I remember what he said to Bob.

'Mr Gerhardi, you own a factory, surely you could find a job amongst your acquaintances for your son.'

It was the old story again - it is not what you know, but whom you know. So Bob tried a few people. Victor had some interviews, but they all felt that because of his handicap, he would not be able to cope. They didn't even want to give him a try.

In the end he was successful in getting an apprenticeship at Possum Controls Ltd in electronics. The firm situated in Stoke Mandeville, made equipment for handicapped people. Victor also signed up at the College of Further Education in Aylesbury as a day release student and got his ONC (Ordinary National Certificate) in Electrical Engineering.

Victor had always enjoyed Technical Drawing and once he got his ONC he felt he could step up to a better job. He applied and was accepted at Angus Fire Armour as Intermediate Draughtsman and Technical co-ordinator. Two years later he changed to PPD Engineering Ltd and had the job as Electrical Draughtsman. He was on his way up. He had shown everybody that he could hold down a job and compete with ordinary young people.

Victor on Drawing Board

Being able to drive and having his own car was the making of Victor. He could now go anywhere on his own and became confident and self assured. He kept in touch with his school friends who used to come and stay with him. He was particularly close to Richard who had gone to university to study mathematics and computer science. In later years Richard and Victor founded their own computer company.

Although I was not teaching any more, I was kept busy in the house. Victor and Peter, living at home now, had to be looked after, and there was the housework, gardening and shopping. I had suddenly become a housewife. My interest in sewing had continued. I was particularly encouraged to carry on with it after the excellent mark in my examination at Wall Hall College. I joined dressmaking classes at Aylesbury College and later tailoring classes at Oxford College of Further Education.

In March 1969 my father-in-law died. He had only enjoyed his retirement for two years. He always worked, never rested. He had one or two warning signs, but took no notice of them. Nobody stopped him and he just collapsed with a heart attack and was dead a few hours later. This was a terrible shock for me. He was the one in the family who had always stood up for me. I knew I had an ally in him. Many times he would just press my shoulder when he saw me carrying Victor, or wink with one eye when I told Peter that he had to behave. We seemed to have had a quiet understanding. When I was working in the factory I told him one day that he always looked so worried and miserable. After that he would give me a great big exaggerated smile every time he saw me. My parents had died so young and he was like a second father to me. Bob too was absolutely shattered. He and his father had been very close.

My brother was getting married at Whitsun and wanted Bob and myself to come to the wedding. His first marriage had ended in divorce, with his wife taking the two boys. There was nobody else involved; things just didn't seem to work out. I think Hans married Sonja too quickly after my father's death, he needed somebody and she was there. Hans was rather young when my mother died and after Papa's death he was a little lost.

I was worried about the long journey by car to the south of Germany. Hans lived in Nürnberg and the wedding was going to be in Hersbruck. My back gave me a lot of trouble. I was alright when I walked, I could also stand for quite a time, but sitting was not a good position for me. I always had a small cushion which I could push into the hollow of my back. If I had nothing and was away from home I would push my handbag into my back. The moment I felt the disc coming out, I would go and lie down. After a few hours rest on my hard bed I was a little better. Sometimes I had two or three days in bed, and if I had a really bad attack, it could be a whole week resting.

Bob had a new Vauxhall Estate car. He suggested that we fold the seats flat and I could lay down there on a sleeping bag.

'You will travel as if you are in an ambulance,' he said laughingly.

Peter had his Whitsun holiday so we took him with us, as Victor wanted to go away with some friends. We flew across the channel from

Southend to Ostend, stayed a night near Aachen and called in at some friends in Reutlingen. I travelled very well in the back, getting up whenever we stopped. In Reutlingen Bob discovered that his right foot and leg were black. He had no pain.

'It's dirt,' said Peter and laughed.

'I did knock my leg on the bumper of the car before we left,' said Bob.

It looked very much like bruising. We visited the local doctor. He said Bob needed blood tests and an examination at a hospital. When he heard that we were going to a wedding near Nürnberg, he advised us to go to Erlangen the university hospital which was very good.

My brother was quite shocked when he saw Bob's leg, so was Inge, his future wife and her family. They all agreed, Erlangen was the best place. It was late afternoon when we arrived in Hersbruck, so we decided to leave it until the next day. My brother had booked us into a beautiful little Bavarian hotel, situated next to a wood. We intended to stay for another week after the wedding as my sister Christel and her husband were going to do the same. Astra, too, was expected and it was going to be a family party where the four of us came together again.

Peter, Bob and I had a walk in the wood that evening and then sat down on a bench at the edge of the forest. We had a beautiful view over a meadow full of spring flowers. It was quiet and peaceful, with the evening sun just starting to disappear. A deer moved slowly and cautiously out of the wood not far from us. It sniffed the air anticipating danger. We all kept perfectly still. What a beautiful place this is, I thought. I was looking forward to staying here after the wedding.

The next morning we drove to Erlangen and Hans came with us. The Outpatients section of the hospital was full of people. I explained to the receptionist, in German, about Bob's leg and the wedding the next day. She was quite sympathetic, but said we would have to wait and take our turn to see Dr M. She glanced at the crowd of people who were already there. We sat down in the large entrance hall and waited. A few names were called, people disappeared, others arrived and soon half an hour was gone. I could see we would be here for hours.

Two doctors in white coats rushed through the hall. The receptionist called:

'Dr M, I have some papers for you to sign.'

He just waved to her and made for the stairs on the other side of the hall. I jumped up, ran after him and caught him on the stairs.

'Dr M, please, maybe you could help me. I am Mrs Gerhardi. My husband and I are on holiday from England. My brother is getting married tomorrow. My husband has hurt his leg, it is very black, and he needs medical advice. We have already waited for an hour and our time is rather precious. This is an emergency. I understand you are the person we are supposed to see.'

I smiled charmingly, but he only looked at me with a frown. He gestured towards the hall:

'All these people are waiting and you just will have to take your turn.' With that he quickly walked up the stairs and disappeared.

Five minutes later our name was called and we were shown into a room where we met Dr M. I knew we had jumped the queue because people were still waiting who had been in the entrance hall before us. Dr M examined Bob's leg and foot and I translated. He confirmed that it was bruised and, although the skin was not broken it had become septic inside and needed to be cut open. He suggested a stay in hospital for two or three days.

'But my brother is getting married tomorrow and we have specially come over from England for that.'

'Your husband needs an anaesthetic. For this we have to examine his heart, lungs and general health and that will take half a day alone. Of course he can always have a local one and we can do it here and now, but it will be painful.' he said. The last sentence sounded like a joke as if he didn't think that Bob would permit this.

I translated everything and Dr M asked: 'What did your husband say?'

'My husband said he had better take his jacket off, he is getting quite hot with the thought of having it cut now.'

Dr M was surprised, pressed Bob's shoulder and said: 'OK.'

Things went very quickly after that. Another doctor arrived, nurses rushed around, and I was sent to wait outside.

I don't know how long I waited before I was called in again. When I saw Bob he looked a little pale, but said he was alright. He had a bandage and splints on his leg.

'Your husband is a brave man,' said Dr M' Now keep the leg up and damp by pouring cold water on to the bandage. Come and see me the day after the wedding. Ask the receptionist for some crutches.'

Before leaving the room he turned round: 'I am sure he could do with a stiff brandy. There is a good *Kneipe* (pub) opposite the main entrance.'

'He is right,' said Bob. 'I could do with a brandy. Both doctors were very good.'

Bob put his shirt on again, but when I tried to help him to put on his trousers I realised that they would not go over the bandages. Nobody had thought about that.

'I will have to open up the inside seam of the trouser leg,' I said. 'But what about tomorrow? You brought a good suit for the wedding, I can't very well open up the seam in those trousers too. You will just have to go in your old suit.'

I opened the seam and was able to get the trousers on. After that we got some crutches. Hans, who had driven into Nürnberg in the meantime, had returned and was quite surprised when he saw Bob and heard his story. We went to the *Kneipe*, and all of us had a brandy. The back of the car was this time occupied by Bob and not by me!

There was another complication. We had brought Travellers Cheques to get German money, but foolishly had them only signed by one person and that was Bob. Hans said we would not be able to park near any bank so that Bob could go and get some money. In any case, Bob was not feeling very well. Then Hans had an idea.

'We will go to the airport, it is not all that far. They have a bank there and one of the assistants might even come to the car to witness Bob's signature.'

We were lucky with the parking. Hans stayed in the car with Bob, ready to move off if he had to, whilst I went to find a bank or change place. The clerk was very helpful, he did come outside to the car and Bob signed several cheques.

We spent the rest of the day with Hans and got back to our hotel late in the evening. I had to take over the driving which was not easy for me as I wasn't used to driving on the right hand side of the road. When we got into the hotel we realised that we were on the second floor and there was no lift.

'Never mind,' Bob said. 'I will sit on the stairs and move up backwards in that sitting position. They have a very nice carpet, it looks new, all shiny and clean.'

With that he gave me his crutches and sat down. He had only gone two or three steps when he stopped.

'Oh no,' he said. 'The carpet is wringing wet, and so are my trousers now.'

I touched the carpet. Sure enough it was wet. After that he tried to hop on his left leg, but he was a heavy man and it would have been impossible for him to get to the second floor like that. So he finished up sitting again on the stairs. Luckily the stairs were only wet until the first floor.

We discovered the next day, that the staircarpet was a new type, which was watered every evening with a watering can, and then vacuumed the next morning. They promised us a room downstairs as soon as one was empty, but in the meantime would not water the carpet in the evening until we were upstairs.

For the wedding I got Bob early into the church with his crutches. It was me who had to take the photographs and use Bob's cine camera whilst Peter held my bag and helped me. In every photograph we stationed Bob with his crutches in the back row and nobody would have known that he had a bad leg. At the reception he sat next to a good friend of the family who spoke English. He had his leg up and we kept putting water on to the bandages to keep it cool. My Italian brother-in-law stuck a rose into the foot bandage as a joke which looked really funny.

The couple went off on their honeymoon and I took Bob to Erlangen hospital the next day. Dr M saw us straight away. The receptionist must have been told to inform him of our arrival. Dr M didn't like the look of Bob's leg and said to me:

'You have two choices. Either he is admitted here to the hospital or you drive like hell back to England.'

Bob didn't want to stay, so it meant I had to drive him back. There was no charge for the treatment as it would have taken too long to sort out. Dr M wanted me to be off. He wished us good luck. We wrote to him later from England, thanking him and included a present.

We packed up, settled the hotel bill, but decided not to start until very early in the morning. Christel and her husband were disappointed. We all had looked forward to our few days together in this lovely place. We offered Peter the chance to stay on with them, but he felt he ought to come back with us in case I needed somebody. Unfortunately he couldn't drive yet; he was only sixteen years old.

We started off early the next morning. There were plenty of lay-bys on the German Autobahn and we stopped every two hours for me to lie down on one of the hard tables. My back was giving me quite a bit of trouble. I lived on codeine tablets, brandy and dry bread, as I was feeling sick most of the time. We got to our night stop near Aachen which we had booked on our outward journey, hoping we could get it again, although we were a week earlier. It was full up as the Nato exercises were in progress. The owner was very sympathetic and helpful when he saw Bob with his bandaged leg. He had a single room left, which he gave to Peter and he put us up in his own spare bedroom in his house. It is surprising how kind strangers can be.

Again we found understanding and helpful people at Ostend airport. The planes went every half an hour and there was a space later in the evening. They accommodated us straight away. One car was just pushed forward every half an hour and had to wait.

Bob felt guilty about his leg and that I had to drive with my bad back instead of lying down. He sat on the back seat with his leg up. He hardly had any pain, but by now the leg was smelling.

In Southend I got into trouble with my driving. I had got used to Bob's new car and to driving on the right, but now I had to drive on the left-hand side of the road. Once I was in the left traffic this was not difficult, I just followed the cars, but then we came to a roundabout. I went round, but couldn't get off. I kept on going round and round not daring to move right or left. In the end Bob had to guide me and tell me when to turn.

We got home late in the evening, tired and worried about Bob's leg. I phoned our doctor who was not on duty. His partner advised me to phone in the morning, because there was nothing he could do except get Bob into hospital. There he would only see a young inexperienced houseman, who would leave things until the morning in any case.

I phoned the next morning and our doctor came straight away. He never looked at Bob's leg. The smell told him enough. He asked where the phone was and told me to pack a bag as Bob would probably have to stay in hospital. He phoned the RAF hospital in Halton and talked to one or two people there and then told me where to take Bob. It was wonderful that Dr R still had this connection. Bob was seen by Air Vice Marshall Morley who hoped that Bob would not get gangrene. He ordered a course of penicillin straight away and raised the leg on cushions. Bob had to stay five weeks in hospital because Air Vice Marshall Morley was afraid that if he came home he would not keep his leg up. We will always be grateful to him because he saved Bob's leg.

One day when I came back from shopping I couldn't get out of the car. Every time I tried to move I had terrible pain down the side of my leg and back. I felt giddy and was afraid that I would faint. I sat like that for two hours until Bob got home from work and practically lifted me out of the car. From time to time I would just collapse on to the floor and lay there until Bob or Peter came home and helped me to get up. If I couldn't get up in the morning I had to stay in bed until I was better, often two or three days. I knew that I couldn't go on like this, because I had to look after my three men and the house, life had to go on. Sometimes Bob would help me into the big corset and stand me up. After that I would do some cleaning and cook a few meals which I could freeze, and then go back to bed again.

Bob fixed up a TV in the corner of the bedroom, just under the ceiling. I could only have one station as I was not able to get up. I switched it on and off from the main switch next to my bed. There was no remote control in those days.

If I was in bed Victor and Peter would get the meal ready, also for Bob, when there was food in the deep freeze. Sometimes there were arguments about the washing up, particularly when they all wanted to go out afterwards. I could hear this upstairs and it worried me. If this happened I would just struggle out of bed and into my corset and get downstairs to take over. This made it worse, because after that I would have to stay in bed even longer.

My friend Queenie did some shopping for me a few times, but it was Myra who really saved me once from despair. I had been in bed a few days with little food and codeine pain killers every four hours day and night, when I suddenly had cramp all over my body. My hands, arms, feet and legs curled up stiffly and painfully. Bob called the doctor who diagnosed dehydration. With nobody in the house I had not been able to have a drink during the day as I couldn't get up. Bob usually left me a flask of tea, but sometimes I couldn't pour it out. I had to wait for the boys or Bob to come home. That's what happened this time. Bob had to give me a few spoonsful of warm milk every half an hour and gradually the cramp disappeared.

The telephone was always at my bedside for an emergency call and the front door was on the catch for the doctor to walk in at any time. In desperation I phoned Myra, a family friend. She had nursed two husbands and knew what being ill was like. She arrived towards dinner time and brought little tins of baby food which she warmed up. Gently she fed me and I felt better. She made some jelly and prepared a salad tea for the boys in the evening. She came every day until I was out of bed again. Her idea with the baby food was excellent. It was so easy to administer and to swallow, that I kept some in the pantry after that so that Bob could give it to me at any time.

This big attack of back pain made me realise that I could not carry on living like that. It was not fair on my two boys and Bob to have an invalid in the house. I also didn't like to have to be dependent on other people. All my life I had managed to cope with everything. Surely there must be something that could be done, apart from wearing a corset.

Through recommendation I went to see Mr Campbell Connolly at the Orthopaedic Hospital in London. He was a neurological surgeon who only operated as a last resort. Mr Campbell Connolly got me on a course of exercises, hoping to strengthen the muscles in my back. Suddenly I got better. I felt happy and had hopes of being completely healthy again one day.

The dream was shattered after two months. I was back in bed for a week. After that I carried on with the exercises, encouraged by Mr Campbell Connolly, but the painless state was short lived. I got stuck in the car again one day, not being able to move, and had to wait for Bob to come home to lift me out. He phoned the specialist who now felt that the only way out would be an operation. Luckily we had subscribed to a private medical insurance for years and I could therefore go into hospital straight away.

I was only one week in the Italian Hospital in London and all I have now is a small scar on my back. The surgeon took part of the disc away which kept on coming out, but left enough to cushion the two vertebrae. Now I had to do new exercises for my back. Gradually I recovered. Suddenly things were reversed, whilst before I was for days in bed to get better, now I preferred not to go to bed as this was often painful. Lying down, I would get stiff and many times I had to roll out of bed on to the floor first. But there was a great improvement and after six months I felt that the operation had been a success.

This all was twenty-five years ago. I still get back ache occasionally. I always use a cushion in the hollow of my back, especially for travelling, but I have never had to stay in bed again and rest. I still do my exercises, never lift anything heavy and I am always conscious of the fact that I have to take care of my spine.

Victor came of age in 1970. He had two parties for his 21st birthday, one for the relatives and one so that he could invite all his friends. We decided to have the young people's party in our home and make it a weekend celebration. Victor invited fifteen friends. The boys slept in the playroom in sleeping bags and the girls in the house. One or two arrived by car, the others by train and had to be fetched by car from the station. We were glad of Bob's big car because of the wheelchairs. Gerry came all the way from Scotland! Victor had friends to stay before but never in such numbers.

The weather was beautiful and it was a very successful weekend. Our big billiard diner table was excellent to serve the meal on. Bob, Peter and

I never sat down, but just served Victor's guests. In the morning we put out bowls of water on the terrace for their wash, and after that they all sat down in the garden for their breakfast of eggs and bacon. I cooked three dozen eggs and Peter ran in and out with the plates whilst Bob made the toast and served the coffee. It was very hot by lunchtime, so the meal was served in the shade under the cherry tree. I cooked Hungarian goulasch in advance and served this up with mashed potatoes and carrots and they drank gallons of coke and orange squash. The dessert was plenty of ice cream. In the end they collected some money and one of the boys went out in his car and bought me a large box of chocolates as a thank you present. Everybody said they had never been to a better party.

Late on Sunday afternoon the young people had to leave for the station and Bob, Victor and I took our cars (three cars full!) to transport them. Peter had to walk as there was no room for him, but he got a ride back. The guard helped all of them into the train plus their wheelchairs, crutches, sticks and bags and promised to see to them at Marylebone station so that they got a taxi or further transport. We all had a most enjoyable and busy time.

The party with the relations was in a small hotel where we had a sit-down meal. Usually there is dancing afterwards, but as Victor couldn't do this he organised a film show. For years Bob had taken cine films of the family. Victor took these movies and cut out anything relating to him. In other words he made a film of his life, from the little boy who couldn't walk, to riding a tricycle and then driving a car. Victor added music and I spoke on it giving short explanations from time to time.

It was and still is an excellent portrait of Victor's life showing the tremendous progress he had made and how he conquered his handicap.

Friends and relatives wanted to give him a birthday present, so Victor opened up a so-called car account where they could put money in for his future car. Everybody thought it was an excellent idea. We promised to give him the difference so that he could buy a new Fiat 127 which he very much wanted. Once he had bought the car he became quite adventurous. Now his ambition was to go abroad. He asked me to come with him so that I could help him with the language. We decided to visit my brother in Nürnberg with Victor doing all the driving. I was allowed to help with the German language and read the map.

The trip was another step towards the end of my worry about Victor. The little baby who was supposed to go into a home because he would never talk or walk, was driving round Europe manipulating his own car and managing very well.

In 1970 I passed the City and Guilds of London Institute Certificate in Dress. The following year I took courses in dress, tailoring and furnishing at Oxford College of Further Education. Being in possession of a teacher's certificate I knew I could also teach at a College of Further Education if I qualified myself in some subjects taught there. I particularly wanted to teach tailoring. My back was getting better all the time, but I felt it would be advisable not to get back to teaching small children because of the low furniture and the bending that had to be done.

Bob had a friend at the Rotary Club who was a Savile Row tailor and had a shop and work place in Amersham. He suggested that I took courses at the Tailor and Cutter Academy in London and come and work for him as a part-time apprentice. This was an excellent idea and I certainly learnt the trade, not only from the courses, but particularly from working for Nancarrow & Temple. I had to do everything, whether it was hand or machine sewing. Most of it was bespoke gentlemen's tailoring and Mr Temple would permit me sometimes, with the permission of the customer, to attend a suit fitting.

I got a Diploma of Merit of the First Class from the Tailor & Cutter Academy and Institute of British Tailoring in Cutting Ladies Tailor-made Garments, and also a Diploma of the First Class with Honours for Tailoring Ladies & Gentlemens Garments' from the same Institute. In 1971 I won the tailoring prize at Oxford College and was presented with it by the mayor of Oxford at the Fashion Show in the Town Hall.

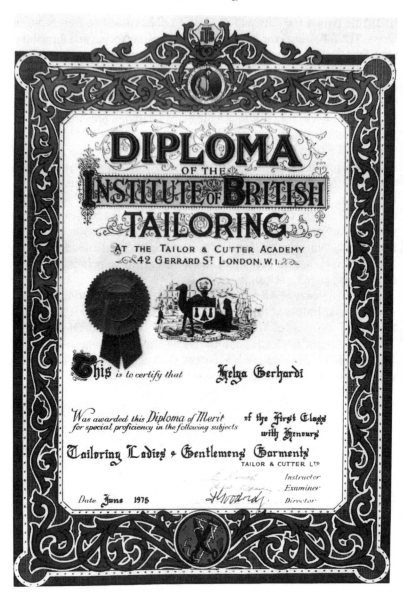

The tailoring course in Oxford was not as advanced as the one in the Tailor & Cutter Academy in London, but I attended it to get the City and Guilds of London Certificate. In December 1972 our tutor left and the head of the department approached me suggesting I take over the class in January.

'Having attended the courses in London at the British Institute of Tailoring and being apprenticed with a Savile Row tailor, I feel you are much more qualified and experienced than just having the City and Guilds of London Certificate,' she said.

She promised to give me a completely free hand to do what I liked as long as I prepared some of the students for the City and Guilds examinations.

It was not easy at first when I returned in January to Oxford College, not as a student, but as a teacher. Gradually I got the confidence and co-operation from all the students. Over the years I built up the tailoring section, having introduced Gentlemen's Bespoke Tailoring for the first time. Younger students and older ones made suits or trousers or fancy waistcoats for husbands or boy friends. The men were allowed to come to the college for a fitting if they promised to show the finished garment at the big fashion show in the Town Hall.

It was quite a sensation when for the first time in the college fashion show men walked on to the cat walk. Peter and Bob became one of my first models. I always remember the first time Peter came. I had made him a suit and also an evening suit with a beautiful pale blue, shiny, satin lining. One of the tutors had a list with the description of the garment the person wore. Over the microphone she would announce the christian name of the model, then a few words of explanation and who had made it. The students lined up in the back and when their name was announced would step on to a catwalk, slowly walk along towards the other side of the big hall, turn a few times on the large platform and then return. Everything was timed and I had to see to it that we kept to it, making sure that the students didn't run or were too slow.

Most of the students were nervous, some practically refused at the last minute to go on to the catwalk. Peter too got cold feet and didn't want to go.

'Go on,' I whispered. 'You'll see, they will all clap, particularly if you show them the beautiful lining of the jacket.'

With that I pushed him on to the catwalk and he was in the bright light. He made a few steps and sure enough people started to clap. This was a good-looking young man in an evening suit, so different from all the ladies garments they had seen. Peter opened up his jacket showing the lining.

'Ah! - Oh!' exclaimed the audience.

They cheered and they clapped. By now Peter had reached the platform. He was enjoying the admiration. He turned and turned, and then decided to take the jacket off completely and show all the inside.

Peter on Catwalk

This was a sensation, the audience got to their feet and shouted:

'Bravo, bravo! More, more!'

I made signs to Peter to come back, time was precious, but he enjoyed himself too much. He took up double time which I later had to correct with the other students. From that evening on he always offered to be a model. Bob too went on to the catwalk showing a three-piece suit. He had instructions to take off his jacket because his waistcoat had a paisley back lining. He became my instructor for years. I could leave it to him to teach the new models, husbands and boy friends, how to walk and turn whilst I got on with the other students.

Eventually I had three tailoring and two dress-making classes. Many times I had to turn students away because the classes were full up. A few students came for years, some took the two-year course and finished up with the City and Guilds examination and others came

Bob, Helga, and Peter at Fashion Show

until they had made a suit or two and then felt they could manage at home. I even had a male student once. He made himself two suits and a jacket.

I was proud of my students, nobody ever failed the examination, they all passed with a credit or distinction.

In the Spring of 1973 we felt it was time for Victor to leave home. By now he was twenty-four years old and had a good job earning enough money to live on. He ran his own car, travelled all over England visiting friends and going on holiday with them. We were not sure whether he would be able to cope on his own. If anything happened to Bob and myself Victor should have learnt to manage on his own. He walked very unsteadily with his stick. Could he do his own shopping, cooking, cleaning, washing, all the chores so necessary to life?

We got him a flat, furnished it and found somebody to clean it every week. Victor didn't want to move. It was rather comfortable at home, and cheap! I am glad to say he soon discovered it was quite nice to be away from the supervision of his parents, and he could always come home to Mum for a good meal on Sunday or have his buttons sewn on. I carried on doing his washing to save him the money and the time for the launderette, but he had to bring the clothes to me. Once or twice I had an emergency phone call when he was ill, but he coped very well and often had friends from school to stay.

In the same year we had our 25th wedding anniversary. As Peter was going to be twenty-one years old seven months later, we organised a combined party, three months late for us and four months early for Peter.

It was a really big affair. We were over 100 people on the Saturday evening and about forty stayed the night and had lunch with us the next day. I had organised the catering with the old staff from the factory canteen and it was most successful.

This time I also had my own family in England. They all had been notified well in advance. Neither of my sisters wanted to fly, so they came by train and boat. Christel brought her daughter with her from Milan, but her husband flew from Sicily where he was on business. Astra took the train from Luzern. Hans and his wife flew from Nürnberg. All arrived at different times and some not on the same day, but we managed to collect them all. It was the first and only time that we four were together in England, and it made me very, very happy that I had been in the position to invite them all. I knew my parents would have been proud to see us together.

A New Challenge

Bob had hired a minibus and after the Sunday lunch we travelled to London with my relatives to show them some of the sights like Buckingham Palace, Big Ben, Westminster Abbey, St Paul's Cathedral, etc. Being Sunday it was not too bad travelling around. Bob would stop to let us all get out and return after a certain time. In this way we didn't have to look for a parking place and could also be brought close to the tourist attraction.

We did a similar trip the next day, but this time we looked at the shops like Harrods, Selfridges, Dickins and Jones, etc. and even had time to do some shopping in Marks and Spencers. For lunch we bought sandwiches, drove to Hyde Park and sat in the minibus eating, drinking, laughing and talking. It was a lot of fun. I felt sorry for Bob because we mostly spoke German, but he didn't mind being our chauffeur and not understanding much. He was happy to see me happy with my own relatives, which was such a rare occasion.

The next day we had to be quick and travel from the airport to Victoria station to get them all on to the plane or train for their journey home, except for Astra. She went home a day later. Bob had to take her to Victoria station as I had to teach in Oxford that day.

The years have gone by. Bob and I are retired. Victor and Peter are married. England is my home now, I am happy here, and we are looking forward to our 50th wedding anniversary.

ABBREVIATIONS

BDM   Bund Deutscher Mädchen (Band of German Girls)

HJ   Hitler Jugend (Hitler Youth)

NCO   Non-Commissioned Officer

SA   Socialistische Arbeiterpartei (Socialistic Worker's Party) Later they were called Sturm Abteilung (storm troops) which were paramilitaries and wore brown shirts.

SS   Schutzstaffel (military formation of the Nazi party) This was the elite black uniformed corps which was Hitler's principal instrument of control. The Waffen SS wore grey uniforms, had the same role as the SS, but as an army command.

HELGA

The true story of a young woman's flight as a refugee and how she re-united her war-scattered family

This book breaks the silence about the horrors faced by people from the Eastern states of Germany at the end of the Second World War. It is the story of a Swiss family trying to live an ordinary life in Hitler's Germany.

The story is told by Helga, the daughter, who was born near the Lithuanian border. It tells how, as a young girl she met Hitler and how she supported her mother when the SS repeatedly searched their home. As a medical student, she cared for some of the thousands of wounded soldiers returning from the Russian battlefields in cattle trucks.

Alone, she joined the refugee treks in the severe winter of 1944/45, fleeing over land and frozen lakes, chased and shot at by the Russian army. With no food, no shelter, or warmth, Helga's courage helped her to survive the nightmare of those terrible, cold winter months which brought death to so many.

This is a rare slice of autobiography. Helga's multifarious experiences offer an unusual perspective on the Second World War.
The Spectator

Helga's early life, including her encounter with the "Führer" himself, is recaptured with charm and humour. It is an intriguing social history of how Hitler's regime gradually gripped rural Germany.
Bucks Free Press

Published by Virona Publishing at £6.99

ISBN 0-9521933-0-2